Teaching and Assessing Low-Achieving Students with Disabilities

The University of New Mexico
At Gallup

Zollinger Library

Teaching and Assessing Low-Achieving Students with Disabilities

A Guide to Alternate Assessments Based on Modified Achievement Standards

edited by

Marianne Perie, Ph.D.
National Center for the
 Improvement of Educational Assessment, Inc.
Dover, New Hampshire

·P A U L·H·
BROOKES
PUBLISHING Co ®

Baltimore • London • Sydney

Paul H. Brookes Publishing Co.
Post Office Box 10624
Baltimore, Maryland 21285-0624
USA

www.brookespublishing.com

Typeset by Broad Books, Baltimore, Maryland.
Manufactured in the United States of America by
Versa Press, Inc., East Peoria, Illinois.

An earlier version of this publication was developed under Cooperative Agreement
S283B050019 with the U.S. Department of Education. This work was supplemented fur-
ther with funding from the National Center for the Improvement of Educational
Assessment, Inc. However, the contents do not necessarily represent the policy of the
Department of Education, and the reader should not assume endorsement by the
Federal Government. Likewise, the contents do not represent the viewpoints of all
members of the National Center for the Improvement of Educational Assessment, Inc.

Library of Congress Cataloging-in-Publication Data

Teaching and assessing low-achieving students with disabilities : a guide to alternate
assessments based on modified achievement standards / edited by Marianne Perie.
    p.   cm.
Includes bibliographical references and index.
ISBN-13: 978-1-59857-117-2 (pbk.)
ISBN-10: 1-59857-117-6
    1. Remedial teaching—United States. 2. Slow learning children—Education—
United States. 3. Learning disabled children—Education—United States. 4. Effective
teaching— United States. I. Perie, Marianne. II. Title.

LB1029.R4T43   2010
371.9'043–dc22   2010015245

British Library Cataloguing in Publication data are available from the British Library.

Contents

About the Editor

Marianne Perie, Ph.D., Senior Associate, National Center for the Improvement of Educational Assessment, Inc., Post Office Box 351, Dover, New Hampshire 03821

Dr. Perie received her doctoral degree in educational research, measurement, and evaluation from the University of Virginia. Prior to joining the National Center for the Improvement of Educational Assessment, Inc., she worked on district, state, and international assessments as well as on the National Assessment of Educational Progress as an employee of first the American Institutes for Research and then the Educational Testing Service. Her primary interests are standard setting, reporting, accountability, and validity studies. Dr. Perie has conducted standard-setting studies in more than 16 states, districts, and foreign countries. She taught a course in standard-setting as part of the federally funded Graduate Certificate Program and coauthored a revision of the 1982 publication *Passing Scores,* published in 2008 by Educational Testing Service as *Cutscores: A Manual for Setting Standards of Performance on Educational and Occupational Tests.* Dr. Perie is currently working with several states on exploring a validity argument on alternate assessments for students with significant cognitive disabilities and enhancing the technical documentation of the assessments.

Contributors

Jamal Abedi, Ph.D.
Professor
School of Education
University of California
One Shields Avenue
Davis, California 95616

Christopher S. Domaleski, Ph.D.
Senior Associate
National Center for the
    Improvement of Educational
    Assessment, Inc.
Post Office Box 351
Dover, New Hampshire 03821

Stephen B. Dunbar, Ph.D.
Professor and Director
Iowa Testing Programs
334A Lindquist Center
University of Iowa
Iowa City, Iowa 52242

Meagan Karvonen, Ph.D.
Associate Professor of
    Educational Research
Western Carolina University
Department ELF
250 Killian Building
Cullowhee, North Carolina 28723

Scott F. Marion, Ph.D.
Associate Director
National Center for the
    Improvement of Educational
    Assessment, Inc.
Post Office Box 351
Dover, New Hampshire 03821

James W. Pellegrino, Ph.D.
Liberal Arts & Sciences
    Distinguished Professor
Distinguished Professor of
    Education
Co-Director, Learning Sciences
    Research Institute
M/C 057
University of Illinois at Chicago
1007 West Harrison Street
Chicago, Illinois 60607

David K. Pugalee, Ph.D.
Director
Center for Mathematics, Science,
    and Technology Education
University of North Carolina at
    Charlotte
9201 University City Boulevard
Charlotte, North Carolina 28223

Rachel F. Quenemoen, M.S.
Senior Research Fellow
National Center on Educational
    Outcomes
207 Pattee Hall
150 Pillsbury Drive S.E.
Minneapolis, Minnesota 55455

Robert J. Rickelman, Ph.D.
Professor
Department of Reading and
    Elementary Education
University of North Carolina at
    Charlotte
Charlotte, North Carolina 28223

Catherine Welch, Ph.D.
Professor
University of Iowa
320 Lindquist Center
Iowa City, Iowa 52242

Foreword

In March 2002, two deputy commissioners from the New York State Education Department (NYSED) co-wrote a memo titled *Supplemental Guidelines for Participation of Students with Disabilities in State Assessments: Locally Selected Assessments.* This was New York State's attempt to find an appropriate assessment system for students who did not qualify for New York State's alternate assessment for students with severe disabilities but who, due to their unique disability needs, were unable to meet grade/age-level expectations for the regular assessment program. I was the Director of Instruction for the City School District of Albany at the time that memo was released issuing instructions to school systems regarding the students who are now commonly referred to as *the 2% population.* That memo was my start on the journey that has culminated in this book, but there is still one more memo that needs mentioning.

Based on this early memo describing who these students might be, we embarked on a research project in Albany to identify these students, determine what they could do, and identify instructional programming that would appropriately validate their performance. This was my introduction into the world of large-scale assessment for special populations. We never finished the work because shortly after the release of the memo, two things happened that changed my life: 1) I left the school district to take a position with the NYSED, overseeing the design and development of its testing programs; and 2) New York State had to change its approaches for assessing this population of students, based on the U.S. Department of Education's findings from the George W. Bush–era Title I (2003) peer review.

Designing and administering comparable grade-level tests for students with disabilities who are significantly behind their peers is a sizeable challenge. There was, and still is, controversy as to the identity of these students and the types of programs that are best suited to their needs while ensuring that they have the opportunity to learn without the constraints of low expectations. There are also issues tied to the

types of credentials they should earn and what those credentials prepare them for in terms of postsecondary education and the work force.
The problems pertaining to this assessment were even more pro-
nounced, as states are required to submit all of their Title I assessments
to the federal government for a formal peer review. These reviews are
rigorous and high risk. A state can invest substantially in the design,
development, and implementation of an assessment, only to have the
federal government reject the assessment's use for Title I purposes.
This is exactly what happened to a number of states that embarked
upon this work. After the U.S. Department of Education rejected the
first submissions, Janet Filbin published a paper detailing the findings
of peer review. That document formed the basis for what would eventually become this book.

In late June 2008, staff from the New York Comprehensive Center
(NYCC) sent a memo to the NYSED, telling us that the U.S.
Department of Education was going to release grant monies to states
for research that would have a direct impact on test development and
design. My colleagues at the NYCC were persistent and urged us to
apply for a grant. Department staff met and agreed that a grant in this
area would be best used if we applied it to researching the 2% testing
problem. We had received Filbin's paper from the U.S. Department of
Education, detailing the reasons that states were rejected in the first
round of peer review, but what we did not have were answers to questions in key areas that were causing problems with the development
and administration of this assessment.

We discussed the ramifications of taking that document, analyzing
it, and enlisting measurement experts from around the country to
address each major section. We knew that we could generate a superb
white paper that would help us take the next steps, but we also thought
that this type of research could culminate in a book that would address
a number of topics which would help all state departments of education. We chose our researchers and suggested to the NYCC that we
wanted to work with the National Center for the Improvement of
Educational Assessment, Inc. (Center for Assessment) on the project.
Two memos, separated by 6 years, bring me to the volume you have in
your hands today.

The research community and aspiring measurement experts need
to see the importance of working collaboratively with the testing divisions of state education departments. These divisions are required to
design and implement assessment programs that state and federal
policies dictate. Due to limited capacity, costs, and time, it is difficult
for states to do the type of research that is in this volume. This grant
enabled New York State to bring together national experts in multiple

areas of expertise to work on a complicated assessment problem. Without the grant from the federal government, it would have been nearly impossible for us to assemble such a diverse and well-regarded panel of experts. This volume is an example of what can happen when the federal government provides the support to a state department of education that enables these departments to work with groups of experts on research issues tied to assessment that will ultimately benefit all students.

Designing and implementing a large-scale assessment is a multimillion-dollar endeavor, and those costs are even higher when designing highly specialized assessments like an alternate assessment based on modified achievement standards (AA-MAS). In many states, policy makers were still not convinced that the federal government had the policy right, and the assessment was controversial. The design issues for the AA-MAS were well known. The Title I Elementary and Secondary Education Act (ESEA) put forth a series of prescriptions that seemed almost impossible to meet. Although a handful of states attempted to design the assessment, many sat on the sidelines. At the same time, the longer a state waits to design the right assessment, the longer administrators and teachers are deprived of the information they need to design instructional programs for students in order to aid the learning process.

It was clear that, at the national level, there was and is dissension as to the appropriate categorization and approaches for students who qualify for an AA-MAS. Federal policy makers were concerned that state policies would inadvertently limit students' learning potential by assuming that they are not capable of learning and achieving at rates comparable to their grade-level peers. This view was balanced by those who believed that it is important to make sure that students have their needs met, that they are not put into situations where they cannot succeed, and that their failure is not due to lack of ability but to inability to meet expectations due to their disabilities. No state wants to invest in designing an assessment to meet policy goals if the goals are not feasible and the assessment not possible. This is the challenge that awaits all states as they grapple with the design and implementation of alternate assessments.

There is a series of vexing questions that emerge when trying to design this particular assessment, and these questions formed the core of what we wanted the research in this volume to address: How do we correctly identify these students; how do we ensure that we have developed the right learning experiences for them; how do we capture the expected learning on their individualized education programs; how do we ensure that the assessment yields information that can be used to inform curriculum and instruction; how do we design and implement an assessment that meets students' needs and is based on "grade-level" content standards; how do we ensure comparability with the general testing program; how do we determine what the appropriate credential for them is; and how is this worked into the state's accountability system?

Asking these questions led to the three-part design of this volume: Identifying and Understanding the Population and Their Curriculum, Test Design: Understanding Content and Achievement Standards and Incorporating Appropriate Item Modifications, and Technical Considerations and Practical Applications. Test builders cannot design tests if the target audiences for the instruments are not clearly defined, and learners cannot have a fair chance at demonstrating their knowledge if they have not had appropriate instruction to ensure that they are adequately prepared.

It is easy to read the insightful chapters in this book and focus on this one specific group of students, but the critical reader will see that, although the focus is tight, the approach and the insights in this volume apply to the design of any testing system for any group of students. If studied closely, this work has the ability to make strong contributions in this area. It provides a template for all of the decisions and areas of interest that ultimately combine when designing a testing program to certify student achievement. Based on the expertise and interest of a particular reader, a volume like this can be read in many ways—cover to cover from start to finish or in part, based on a particular interest. After watching the work that occurred to produce this book, I can attest that one is best served by reading it in its entirety. Not only will graduate students and professional researchers better understand the issues surrounding this particular group of students, but they will also see the current processes and needs that are required to design and validate any testing program in this era of standards-based education reform.

It is clear that this volume is the product of the work of many people, all dedicated to ensuring that our students get the best education possible, and that policy makers and test developers are working together from a solid, research-based perspective. I thank my colleagues from NYSED, Dr. Rebecca Cort, Deputy Commissioner, Office for Vocational and Educational Services for Individuals with Disabilities, and Candace Shyer, Bureau Chief for Test Development, for their insights and assistance with everything from determining the topic of the research and working with our authors to reviewing the chapters. I also thank the exceptional authors who worked hard to ensure that their chapters would help all states, not just New York

State, and the reviewers who participated in conference calls and meet-ings to debate and inform the work. I thank the staff at the NYCC for their assistance in generating the application to win the grant and for helping to coordinate the work.

Finally, I want to personally thank and credit Marianne Perie from the Center for Assessment, who worked to coordinate this project; she was superb. I know from the e-mail chains and many calls that Marianne worked long hours with everyone to ensure that deadlines were met, and her editing of the entire volume was indispensable. It should also be noted that she did all this while writing her own chap-ter on the issues pertaining to standard setting and developing per-formance-level descriptors. Her tireless efforts, good cheer, and keen intellect took a raw idea and transformed it into the excellent work that is in your hands. Working with her was one of the most enjoyable things that I have ever done.

David Abrams
Albany, New York

REFERENCES

Elementary and Secondary Education Act of 1965, PL 89-10, 20 U.S.C. §§ 241 *et seq.*

Title I—Improving the Academic Achievement of the Disadvantaged: Final Rule, 68 Fed. Reg. 68,697–68,708 (Dec. 9, 2003) (to be codified at 34 C.F.R. pt. 200).

Acknowledgments

The book came about following a white paper commissioned by the New York Comprehensive Center (NYCC) in collaboration with the New York State Education Department (NYSED). That white paper was funded by a cooperative agreement with the U.S. Department of Education, with Fran Walter as the project officer. Although the contents of this book do not necessarily reflect the viewpoints of all associated with those groups, it is important to acknowledge individuals who supported this work. During the project, authors received support from Larry Hirsch of NYCC as the project director. In addition to David Abrams, who wrote the Foreword to this book and provided immeasurable support and good direction, two other staff members of NYSED deserve recognition. Rebecca Cort offered a great deal of background information about the types of questions state policy makers in special education had about instructing and assessing low-performing students with disabilities, and Candace Shyer supplied specific information about state policies in New York, allowing authors to provide concrete examples in their work.

Both during the project and after the project concluded, the National Center for the Improvement of Educational Assessment, Inc., funded further development of the work of the chapters authored by staff members as well as the work required to turn the white paper into a publishable book. We would like to thank the executive director, Brian Gong, in particular for his support.

Throughout this process, the authors have benefited from reviews of other experts in the field. They gave a lot of their time reviewing multiple drafts and participating in team discussions of each section of the book. The authors would like to acknowledge and thank Howard Everson, Claudia Flowers, Brian Gong, Suzanne Lane, Katherine Ryan, Gerald Tindal, and Phoebe Winter. Their comments on the individual chapters were insightful and valuable, and more important, they helped shape the chapters and the organization of the book from the beginning with their ideas and suggestions.

Introduction

The purpose of this book is to describe the primary challenges in developing an alternate assessment based on modified achievement standards (AA-MAS) based both on an earlier paper describing states' challenges with the AA-MAS (Filbin, 2008) and the authors' own experiences. It provides a research-based analysis of the design and development issues and focuses on the theory behind each issue. In addition, this book explores the existing research and best practices in identifying and assessing these students. The authors approached their chapters with an intention to help states think through the issues, make appropriate decisions regarding the allocation of resources, and ultimately improve opportunities for students with disabilities. Although the initial intent was to help state policy makers think through issues of understanding, instructing, and assessing students with disabilities, particularly those who are currently not performing well on general assessments, this book is also intended for university use, hopefully to spur additional research into areas in which we need more in-depth understanding.

Upon the completion of early drafts of these chapters, the authors and reviewers recognized the utility of the information beyond the application to fulfill the federal regulations regarding an alternate assessment for purposes of accountability. Much of the discussion in this book relates to instruction and assessment of all low achievers and specifically of low achievers with disabilities. Therefore, even if the regulations were to be rescinded, the authors believe the information provided in this book will continue to be applicable as the field works to improve our knowledge and understanding of how low-achieving students with disabilities—and perhaps those without disabilities who are also struggling with grade-level achievement standards—learn, organize information, and communicate their understanding.

BACKGROUND ON FEDERAL
REGULATIONS GUIDING THE AA-MAS

The 2001 reauthorization of the Elementary and Secondary Education Act of 1965 (ESEA; PL 89-10), known as the No Child Left Behind (NCLB) Act of 2001 (PL 107-110), required that all states assess all students in reading[1] and mathematics in Grades 3 through 8 plus one grade in high school. In addition, they were required to assess all students in science at least once in elementary, middle, and high school. A minimum of three performance levels had to be developed for each test—one defining proficiency, one above that, and one below that—with the goal of all students reaching proficiency by 2014. Up to 1% of students with the most significant cognitive disabilities could be categorized as proficient using an alternate assessment based on alternate achievement standards (AA-AAS). States also had the option of developing an alternate assessment based on grade-level achievement standards (AA-GLAS) for those students who were capable of performing at grade level but who needed a format other than the traditional multiple-choice test to demonstrate their knowledge and skills.

Some state and local leaders argued that there were still some students with disabilities who were not being well served by the assessment program because they were ineligible to take the AA-AAS and unable to retrieve all of the content and skills assessed on either grade-level assessment. Before NCLB, many states used out-of-level testing to assess certain students with disabilities. For example, a student who was in Grade 8 based on his or her age, but was instructed significantly below the eighth-grade level, might be administered a Grade 6 test. NCLB ended that practice and enforced the Individuals with Disabilities Education Act (IDEA) principle that students should have access to the general curriculum by holding schools accountable for teaching students grade-level content.

In April 2007, as part of its governance of NCLB, the U.S. Department of Education (2007a) released new regulations that allowed for the use of an AA-MAS. These regulations supplemented the NCLB legislation regarding the development of grade-level assessments and AA-AAS. States could use this new assessment for students with disabilities to count up to 2% of students as proficient for purposes of adequate yearly progress (AYP).

The AA-MAS was intended to fall between an AA-AAS and a general grade-level assessment to provide a more appropriate measure of these students' performance against academic content standards for the

---

[1]The law requires an assessment in reading, although some states include reading in a broader English Language Arts assessment and use that to meet NCLB requirements.

grade in which they are enrolled. The regulations state that "there is a small group of students whose disability has precluded them from achieving grade-level proficiency and whose progress is such that they will not reach grade-level proficiency in the same time frame as other students" (34 C.F.R. §200). However, this statement has raised countless questions as state policy makers try to determine who this small group is within that larger group of students who are not eligible for the AA-AAS but who are not performing well on the grade-level assessment.

An emphasis of the regulations and the nonregulatory guidance (U.S. Department of Education, 2007b) was that this assessment must be challenging for these students. The assessments are required to cover the same breadth and depth as the other grade-level assessments. They could not be linked to content from a lower grade level or exclude content standards that were assessed by the grade-level general assessment. Modified achievement standards were described as being challenging for eligible students although defining a less rigorous expectation of mastery of grade-level academic content standards. States also were not permitted to apply their new modified achievement standards to that same general assessment; a new assessment must be developed. Students assessed using the AA-MAS must have access to grade-level content and be working toward achieving grade-level goals. However, it is important to note that the regulations do not require states to develop this assessment and provide flexibility for states to develop an AA-MAS only for a particular grade or subject.

Eligible students include students with a disability in any of the 13 disability categories defined in IDEA and who have an individualized education program (IEP). To determine eligibility, the guidance stipulates that

- There must be objective evidence demonstrating that the student's disability has precluded the student from achieving grade-level proficiency

- The student's progress to date in response to appropriate instruction, including special education services designed to meet the individual needs of the student, is such that even if significant growth occurs, the IEP team is reasonably certain the student will not reach grade-level proficiency within the year covered by the IEP

- The student's IEP must include goals that are based on the academic content standards for the grade in which the student is enrolled

States must establish participation guidelines for IEP teams to use to match the student to the appropriate test, typically the grade-level assessment with or without accommodations, an AA-GLAS, an AA-MAS, or an AA-AAS. The guidelines must include criteria based on evidence that demonstrate the student meets the three eligibility requirements previously outlined. Students should not be locked into taking an AA-MAS every year but must have the opportunity to move from the AA-MAS to a general or alternate grade-level assessment from one year to the next. Also, a student might take the AA-MAS in one subject but the general assessment in another. All of these decisions would be made each year by the student's IEP team.

In Spring 2008, six states submitted their "modified" assessments for peer review to determine whether they could be used for purposes of AYP. In June 2008, the U.S. Department of Education released a report written by Filbin (2008) that describes the issues raised during the peer review of the six state AA-MASs. None of the states received approval for their AA-MAS, but lessons learned from the review of their designs provided much information for all states. As of the writing of this Introduction, one state (Texas) had received federal approval to use its AA-MAS in its accountability system, and several other states had begun the process of peer review. With only one state receiving federal approval, the authors of this book looked beyond current practice and focused on theory of cognition and test design, examined best practice in other areas of instruction and assessment, and applied research findings from existing studies to develop recommendations on understanding, instructing, and assessing students with disabilities.

SETTING THE STAGE FOR THE REMAINING CHAPTERS

A driving question for many states is whether the development of this assessment will yield useful information to guide instruction and be cost effective. More specifically, in times of budget cutbacks, how can the limited funding available best be allocated to support the learning of these students? The first issue in answering this question is determining who "these students" are. Subsumed within that question is the possibility of expanding the subject of this book beyond the current federal regulations, focusing on students who may not be receiving grade-level content. In addition, it is important to consider the challenges of using the data to guide instruction—as desired by many policy makers and educators—when the primary focus of many of these assessments is simply to provide an additional measure for purposes of accountability. Although additional description regarding the students and the uses of the assessment is provided more fully in the following chapters, it is important to provide a context and lay out the assumptions that the chapters in this book follow regarding fidelity to the federal regulations and guidance.

Authors were encouraged to adhere to the law laid out in the most recent IDEA and ESEA reauthorizations and to stay true to the federal principles. However, if there were aspects of the April 2007 regulations permitting the development of the AA-MAS that authors found too constrictive, they were encouraged to address areas for change. The process of reauthorizing ESEA was under way during the publication of this volume, and the authors recognized that the regulations surrounding the AA-MAS may change. Moreover, there is some disagreement on the assumptions behind this 2% population, but this book is written from the assumption that all students can learn (and should be taught) grade-level content standards with appropriate instruction and support. However, the degree to which all students achieve the grade-level content standards may vary. Of course, even these assumptions lead to more questions about whether students will be taught the exact same content or whether it will be modified as well as the time frame in which they will be expected to learn the content. These more specific issues are addressed in the first section, but the authors started from these basic principles of learning grade-level content. Finally, in the chapters that focus on subject-specific material, the authors focused on the content areas of reading and mathematics, as those have received the most attention under the current version of ESEA.

ORGANIZATION OF THE BOOK

The authors started by reviewing the article written by Filbin (2008), which outlined areas that were challenging for states. These included

1. Identifying students eligible to take the AA-MAS

2. Providing guidelines for writing standards-based IEPs and then monitoring the implementation of those guidelines

3. Designing an assessment based on grade-level content standards that is of an appropriate difficulty and depth of knowledge for this population

4. Determining the relationship between the AA-MAS, the general assessment, and the AA-AAS

5. Writing appropriate modified achievement-level descriptors

Although these five issues were the starting point, the authors and reviewers who helped guide the development of this book identified additional issues related to understanding student cognition, applying lessons learned about low achievers to students eligible for the AA-MAS, modifying instruction appropriately, determining issues related to the comparability of the AA-MAS to the general assessment, evaluating the validity of inferences made from the test scores, and incorporating the results into an existing accountability system. Ultimately, this book was organized into three sections that focus on different aspects of designing and developing the AA-MAS, with three chapters in each section.

Section I: Identifying and Understanding the Population and Their Curriculum

The first issue raised by Filbin (2008) and identified by states involves determining who should take this assessment. During an early discussion, authors and reviewers recognized that the issues of identifying the students were wrapped up in the National Research Council's assessment triangle of assessment, instruction, and cognition (Pellegrino, Chudowsky, & Glaser, 2001). Thus, it was decided that this first section should discuss the issues of identifying the students and understanding their cognitive abilities, including the interaction among instruction, cognition, and assessment. This section could be titled "Who Are the Students, Vis à Vis the Curriculum?" It includes three chapters: Chapter 1 focuses on identifying students appropriate for this assessment, provides a policy context and summarizes research related to the teaching and learning of students with disabilities, and lays out a framework for state policy makers in considering how to identify students who might benefit most from an AA-MAS. Chapter 2 takes this argument one step further by examining various instructional strategies for teaching students with disabilities, with a focus on the issue of writing standards-based IEPs. This focus on instruction is complemented by the discussion of cognition in Chapter 3, which describes the importance of understanding student learning characteristics and cognitive processes in assessment and theorizes on sources of differences among students' cognition that have implications for learning, instruction, and assessment. In essence, this section lays the framework for determining how students gain and demonstrate knowledge, which is essential for determining appropriate test design.

Section II: Test Design: Understanding Content and Achievement Standards and Incorporating Appropriate Item Modifications

This next section starts the discussion on test development. The main question with which the authors wrestled was how to make the assessment more accessible for students with a wide range of disabilities while maintaining the reliability and validity of the results. A deep understanding of the content and test design was necessary, as well as an understanding of what is meant by modified achievement standards. Chapter 4 begins this section with a discussion of the content domains of reading and mathematics, including topics of aligning curriculum, instruction, and assessment and developing content standards. This chapter begins the discussion of modifying content, which is then carried forward into Chapter 5. Chapter 5 begins with a discussion of best practices in test design and applies the ideas discussed in the previous chapters to the challenge of developing items and test forms in reading and mathematics that better match the learning characteristics of the population identified for the AA-MAS, focusing on reducing the difficulty while maintaining the reliability of the assessment. Chapter 6 picks up the issue of determining how the modified achievement standards fit between the grade-level achievement standards and the alternate achievement standards, describes issues of defining *modified* proficiency, and provides practical advice for writing achievement-level descriptors and setting cut scores, discussing the theory behind each.

Section III: Technical Considerations and Practical Applications

The third section addresses three issues related to the technical quality and use of the assessments: examining the validity of these assessments, determining the comparability of these assessments to the general assessment, and understanding how these assessments will be operationalized and used in a state accountability system. Chapter 7 explores issues of comparability of the AA-MAS with the general assessments and grade-level achievement standards, focusing on different types of comparability and discussing the required degree of comparability for each desired inference. Chapter 8 focuses on creating a validity argument for an AA-MAS, starting with a guiding philosophy, moving through a theory of action, and then describing types of validity evidence that can be gathered throughout the test development process and beyond and how to use this evidence to evaluate the assumptions in the validity argument. Finally, Chapter 9 provides practical advice and a theoretical discussion of using these assessments in state accountability systems, focusing on how the AA-MAS fits into existing accountability systems and giving specifics on practical topics.

At the end of this book is a glossary of terms that encompasses vocabulary used in both the assessment and disabilities worlds.

REFERENCES

Elementary and Secondary Education Act of 1965, PL 89-10, 20 U.S.C. §§ 241 et seq.

Filbin, J. (2008). *Lessons from the initial peer review of alternate assessments based on modified achievement standards.* Washington, DC: U.S. Department of Education, Office of Elementary and Secondary Education Student Achievement and School Accountability Program.

No Child Left Behind Act of 2001, PL 107-110, 115 Stat 1425, 20 U.S.C. §§ 6301 *et seq.*

Pellegrino, J.W., Chudowsky, N.J., & Glaser, R. (Eds.). (2001). *Knowing what students know: The science and design of educational assessment.* Washington, DC: National Academy of Sciences.

U.S. Department of Education. (2007a). Final Rule 34 C.F.R. Parts 200 and 300: Title I—Improving the academic achievement of the disadvantaged. 72 *Fed. Reg.* 67, Washington, DC: Office of Elementary and Secondary Education. Retrieved July 12, 2008, from http://www2.ed.gov/legislation/FedRegister/finrule/2003-4/120903a.html

U.S. Department of Education. (2007b). *Modified achievement standards: Non-regulatory guidance.* Washington, DC: Office of Elementary and Secondary Education. Retrieved August 27, 2008, from http://www.ed.gov/policy/speced/guid/nclb/twopercent.doc

I

Identifying and Understanding the Population and Their Curriculum

The first challenge we face in considering the development of an alternate assessment based on modified achievement standards is to determine who the students are who are in need of a new assessment. The focus is on students with disabilities who are not achieving proficiency in grade-level standards and who do not appear to be making significant progress toward achieving that proficiency. Beyond that, however, it is important to explore various aspects of these students, including the nature of their disability, how it affects their cognition, and why it might hinder learning. We would also be remiss not to explore the issues of curriculum and instruction to see whether opportunity to learn is having a larger impact on performance than the nature of the disability.

These three chapters tie together these ideas to describe the population in terms of who they are, necessary elements of their instruction, and how they gain knowledge. More specifically, each chapter delves into different theories involving the fluidity of this population. Chapter 1, by Rachel F. Quenemoen, focuses on the notion of the least dangerous assumption by considering exclusionary criteria. It provides a history of regulations regarding students with disabilities and discusses applications of the current regulations to the school environment.

In Chapter 2, Meagan Karvonen concentrates on procedural integrity by providing an overview of standards-based individualized education programs and describing how to promote improved opportunities to learn the standards-based curriculum with specialized instruction, services, and supports based on individual student learning characteristics.

In Chapter 3, James W. Pellegrino informs our understanding of explanatory constructs by discussing the broader concept of student cognition. He describes possible sources of differences among low-achieving students that have implications for learning, instruction, and assessment.

Understanding who the students are and what and how they are taught and identifying any barriers to learning is a first step toward understanding how best to assess what they know and can do. This section provides the backbone for the later sections on test development and technical issues.

1

Assessing Students with Disabilities Using Modified Achievement Standards

Rachel F. Quenemoen

States and district assessment systems include options to assess students with disabilities in varying ways, generally under the rationale that some students need different ways of showing what they know to improve the validity of the interpretations. When these varying approaches include setting of different achievement standards from what is set on the general assessment, then caution must be taken to protect students from negative consequence. The history, development, and issues surrounding implementation of alternate assessments based on modified achievement standards (AA-MAS) illustrate how these cautions can be considered.

This chapter starts with a historical perspective of the regulatory language creating AA-MAS and informs readers of the initial rationale for creating AA-MAS and the concerns of advocacy groups. The preliminary requirements for identifying students who may be eligible for participation in AA-MAS are also discussed. Research findings about low-performing students are introduced to provide the readers with an understanding that low-performing students are students with and without disabilities. These findings also illustrate that identifying students who will benefit from participating in AA-MAS, or other assessment options, requires much more than knowing the students' previous large-scale test performance or the students' disability category. Although student characteristics are important, they are only part of the consideration for determining test eligibility. A discussion of teacher perceptions of student characteristics and opportunity-to-learn (OTL) issues is followed by potential best-practice interventions and instructional practices (e.g., response to intervention [RTI], progress monitoring) to provide readers with information regarding strategies that may benefit all students. It is followed by an examination of policy assumptions about instructional and curricular strategies used with students and how they relate to assessment choices. Ultimately, states and districts make policy decisions that will define students who may participate in AA-MAS or any other option in an assessment system. These policy decisions are framed within a discussion of social justice, guiding philosophy, and coherence of the overall instruction, curriculum, and assessment systems. The chapter ends with a set of questions for states and districts to answer as they consider their options and potentially develop and implement an assessment option that permits different achievement standards from the general assessment.

The chapter is written in the context of the imperatives of a system accountability model because the AA-MAS was conceptualized initially as an option within such a model. That is, this chapter assumes that an assessment option under consideration is a key component of a policy that is designed to improve student achievement and narrow achievement gaps that have affected certain groups of students differentially over time. The underlying policy assumes that poor performance by students on the state assessment will result in consequences for schools and districts that will motivate educators to provide better services to students, services that will enable them to learn and achieve proficiency. The path to these improvements is through improved instruction and curriculum, although that implication seems to be missing in many discussions about assessments used for system accountability. Because of this essential but sometimes neglected component of system accountability, examples of standards-based instruction and curriculum strategies and interventions are included in this chapter (as well as in Chapter 2) to augment this volume's focus on the assessment component of the policy imperative. Possible validity-related questions regarding the relationship of high-quality standards-based instruction and curriculum to achievement of students with disabilities on standards-based assessments are posed in the concluding section, and examples of studies that have uncovered these relationships are cited (e.g., Barr, Telfer, & DiMuzio, 2009; Cortiella & Burnette, 2007; Donahue Institute, 2004).

HISTORY OF ASSESSMENT OPTIONS RELATED TO AA-MAS

In the development of any new assessment option, it is important to provide an opportunity for close scrutiny of the intended policy outcomes and the possibilities for unintended and negative outcomes. Thus, in order to understand which students may meet the requirements for participation in an AA-MAS, we must begin with a review of the policy discussion that framed the initial regulation. There was immediate and intense debate surrounding the announcement of the proposed regulation, primarily focused on the research that the U.S. Department of Education cited as the rationale.

In April 2005, addressing a group of chief state school officers and other officials, Secretary of Education Margaret Spellings announced new flexibility in assessing students with disabilities under the No Child Left Behind (NCLB) Act of 2001 (PL 107-110). Secretary Spellings called it a "workable, sensible approach that was based on scientific research," permitting states to develop and use modified assessments for students with "persistent academic disabilities." These students were defined as those "who need more time and instruction to make substantial progress toward grade-level achievement" (U.S. Department of Education, 2005b). The research base cited was summarized and sent to all chief state school officers. These materials began with a reference to the earlier (2003) NCLB regulation permitting alternate achievement standards for students with significant cognitive disabilities, defined first in a notice of proposed rules in 2002 and finalized in 2003.

The 0.5% cap originally included in the August 2002 proposed regulation ("the 1% regulation") was based on data outlining the prevalence rates of students with the most significant cognitive disabilities. It was tied to a definition of such students that 1) excluded students with mild mental retardation and other students who were 2 or fewer standard deviations (SD) below the mean, and 2) included students with intellectual functioning and adaptive behavior 3 or more SD below the mean. When this rule was finalized, the U.S. Department of Education expanded the cap to 1.0% to allow states and districts more flexibility in its implementation and removed the definition from the regulation. However, research conducted and reviewed by Reid Lyon at the National Institute for Child Health and Human Development and Jack Fletcher at the University of Texas suggested that the 1.0% cap is, in fact, too low, if the U.S. Department of Education (2005a) follows the definition provided in the December 2003 regulation's preamble (a student in 1 of 13 disability categories who cannot reach grade-level standards, even with the best instruction possible).

The U.S. Department of Education (2005a) provided a summary of research that supported this increase in students who could participate in alternate assessments against less challenging achievement standards. In the research summary, Lyon and Fletcher found that "the best-designed instructional interventions achieved a range of success from a low of 50% to a high of 90% of participating students reaching grade-level reading standards." They concluded that the "totality of this research suggests that there are about 1.8% to 2.5% of children who are not able to reach grade-level standards, even with the best instruction" (U.S. Department of Education, 2005a).

Advocates for students with disabilities responded to the proposed new flexibility with concern. Central to their concern was the fear that students who participate in an assessment based on a lower standard will also receive instruction in a lower curriculum. The implication was that the option of modified achievement standards would limit struggling students' access to academic instruction and needed research-based interventions to accelerate learning and, over time, preclude their attainment of a standard diploma. One advocacy group, the National Council for Learning Disabilities (NCLD), critiqued the research base summarized by Lyon and Fletcher for USDE, noting that, although the research on effective reading interventions cited was important for remediation and for new methods for identification of learning disabilities, these reading intervention studies did not support the federal policy changes proposed in the new regulation (Wendorf, 2005). More recently, NCLD concluded

> The studies that were originally used by the U.S. Department of Education in 2005 to justify the 20 percent number were flawed. In fact, in one of the major studies cited to justify the new policy, only 11 percent of the students were special education students and the additional studies cited did not include any special education students (Kaloi, 2007).

A number of the requirements in the final regulation reflect compromises that resulted from this vigorous debate (e.g., students must have standards-based goals in their individualized education program [IEP]; students are not precluded from earning a standard high school diploma), but the controversy related to use of modified achievement standards—and implications of use for student achievement—remains.

Given the controversy, state policy makers have to grapple with whether they believe this is a distinct group, separate from both the group of students defined in the "1%" regulation as having significant cognitive disabilities and from other students with disabilities. State policy makers, educators, and advocates had far less difficulty in coming to consensus on the appropriateness of alternate assessments based on alternate achievement standards (AA-AAS) as a pathway to higher expectations and achievement. In many ways, the students referenced in the 1% regulation were, by and large, unarguably a distinct group, albeit a heterogeneous group of students with unique characteristics, many with complex disabilities. However, in implementation, some students may be inappropriately included in AA-AAS instead of a more challenging assessment. Historically low expectations affect decision making, as do past performance patterns of students who have not been taught the content to be assessed. Students who are inappropriately included in an AA-AAS may be harmed by assumptions that they cannot learn the full range of grade-level academic content when the result is that they will never be taught that content, leading to a self-fulfilling prophecy.

As quoted from the U.S. Department of Education (2005a) 2% materials, the earlier 1% figure was established as a compromise; the estimate of how many students may have the most severe intellectual and multiple disabilities initially (0.5%) was supported by data in states that report moderate and severe mental retardation separately from students with mental retardation and from Centers for Disease Control and Prevention data on incidence of correlated disability diagnoses. Thus the 1% cap on inclusion of scores from AA-AAS as proficient for adequate yearly progress calculations incorporates some flexibility already, but to balance the flexibility, the cap was intended to prevent inappropriate inclusion of too many students in a different achievement expectation. The controversies of AA-AAS tend to be about the nature of the content being taught and assessed and the technical issues related to test design, but not whether different achievement standard(s) could be an appropriately high expectation for students with significant cognitive disabilities.

In contrast, there is limited consensus regarding students referenced in the 2% regulation. Some policy makers reference students who are "just above" the students who participate in AA-AAS, with an achievement expectation far below the grade-level expectation, perhaps adding to the students already included in AA-AAS through the flexibility of the compromise 1% cap. Others suggest that these students are those who "just miss" the proficiency determination on the general assessment, and the modified achievement standard should be "just below" the grade-level achievement standard. Yet another interpretation is that students with disabilities perform on a continuum with no defined borders; thus additional achievement standards may be necessary in order to count more students as proficient against multiple standards on a sliding scale set. The regulatory language and research base referenced in the regulation are not clear about the target population for AA-MAS.

Ultimately, state-defined modified achievement standards, or any other options different from those expected for students without disabilities, should be policy statements reflecting an appropriately high expectation for some state-defined group of students, an expectation that should improve their achievement and outcomes in order to be consistent with the letter and the spirit of federal and state requirements. It is essential that state policy makers articulate who the target students are and how they build competence in the academic domains tested before deciding whether and how to develop an assessment based on modified achievement standards. Then, decisions about the design of the assessment itself can adhere to the policy imperatives, instead of the assessment choices inadvertently shaping the policy outcomes.

WHO ARE THE STUDENTS?
THE COMPLEXITY OF REGULATORY REQUIREMENTS

The regulation specifies two primary requirements for participation in an AA-MAS. The student must be identified as having a disability that precludes attainment of grade-level achievement standards (GLAS) within the current year, and the student must have an IEP that references grade-level content.

Limitations of Assignment to Disability
Categories in Predicting Attainment of Standards

As cited in the research summary underlying the regulation, students with disabilities are defined as having a primary disability label in 13 categories. The learning characteristics of students assigned to these categories vary greatly both among and within the categories. See Figure 1.1 for the distribution of students with disabilities by primary disability category.

On the basis of the 2007 Individuals with Disabilities Education Act (IDEA) Part B Child Count data in the United States and outlying areas (Data Accountability Center, 2007), 43.6% of students received special education services for specific learning disabilities (see Figure 1.1). The next largest disability group is speech or language impairments, totaling 19.2%, followed by the category of students with other health impairments at 10.5%, mental retardation at 8.3%, and emotional disturbance at 7.3%. Students with autism make up 4.3% of students served in special education, and students with multiple disabilities make up 2.2% of these students. Smaller categories of students in special education include students with developmental delay at 1.5% (category for ages 3–9 only), hearing impairments at 1.2%, and orthopedic impairments at 1.0%. Students with visual impairments and

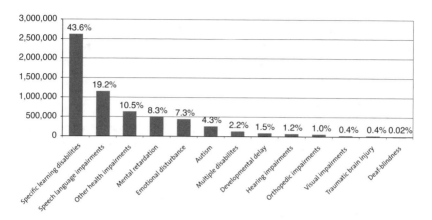

Figure 1.1. Distribution of primary disability categories. (*Note:* Percentages in this figure are based on a total number of 6,007,832 students receiving special education services [Data Accountability Center, 2007] counted under primary disability only. *Developmental delay* is applicable only to children ages 3–9.)

traumatic brain injury each make up 0.4% of students served by special education, and the remaining 0.02% of students make up the deaf-blindness category.

The criteria used to determine student eligibility for special education and related services under IDEA are defined by each state (within certain federal parameters), and thus the criteria vary from state to state. Although a few categories include criteria that are relatively objective (e.g., vision, hearing, physical characteristics), all categories include more subjective judgment as well. Some categories (e.g., specific learning disabilities, mental retardation) have widely varying criteria that are subject to interpretation in multiple ways. It is common within and across states to have the criteria yield students who have very different learning characteristics sharing the same label and students who are very similar to one another having different categorical labels.

The National Association of School Psychologists (NASP, 2002, 2009) position statements on categorical labels have evolved over time, reflecting concerns about labels and their implications for instruction. In the earlier position statements, they expressed concern that students with labels in the mild disability categories of specific learning disability, mental retardation, emotional disturbance, and speech/language impairments showed significant overlap in skills and received instruction that is highly similar to those who are considered to be slow learners but who have not been labeled. In 2002, the position of NASP also noted that these students tended to be placed in programs based on labels regardless of instructional needs. By 2009, NASP endorsed a multitiered model of evidence based instruction and intervention because it requires that all students receive research-based instruction and consideration of student characteristics such as race, culture, and other characteristics, as well as educational need. NASP (2009) summarizes the shift thusly in the online version of their position paper:

> NASP believes that all children learn best in inclusive environments that provide high quality instruction to all students, and that access to appropriate academic support services should not require that students be assigned to categorical special education groups. NASP also has advocated for alternatives to categorical labeling that typically reflect traditional approaches to service delivery. (p. 4)

These complexities related to disability categorical labels and criteria for determining eligibility for special education services affect some groups of students more than others. For example, English language learners (ELLs) are disproportionately identified as also having disabilities, and in many states, ELLs with disabilities are the lowest-performing group overall. The challenges of determining whether a student is eligible for special education services in the context of limited English proficiency (or culture, ethnic, or socioeconomic status) provide an additional reason to use caution in assuming that special education categorical labels are useful for purposes of identifying students for assessment options (see Abedi, 2006, 2007; Artiles & Ortiz, 2002; and Minnema, Thurlow, Anderson, & Stone, 2005, for more information on these learners).

Still, some general comparisons can be made about the nature of the disability categories. For example, the relationship of categorical label to students' ability to learn was described by disabilities expert Martha Thurlow, director of the National Center on Educational Outcomes, as follows:

> Seventy-five percent of students in special education have learning disabilities, speech/language impairments, and emotional/behavioral disabilities. These students, along with those who have physical, visual, hearing impairments, and other health impairments (another 4–5 percent), are all students *without intellectual* impairments. When given appropriate accommodations, services, supports, and specialized instruction, these students (totaling about 80 percent of students with disabilities) can learn the grade-level content in the general education curriculum by going around the effects of their disabilities, and thus achieve proficiency on the grade-level content standards. In addition, research suggests that many of the *small* percentage of students with disabilities *who have intellectual impairments* (less than 2 percent of the total population of all students, which is *less than 20 percent of all students with disabilities*), can *also* achieve proficiency when they receive high quality

instruction in the grade-level content, appropriate services and supports, and appropriate accommodations. (Thurlow, 2007, p. 40)

The reality that many students with disabilities currently do not achieve at proficiency raises questions of whether or not they are all receiving the required high-quality instruction in the grade-level content, appropriate services and supports, and appropriate accommodations.

Beyond that type of general observation across disability categories, it is difficult to define how the specific categorical labels differentiate how students learn and demonstrate their learning, or how, as required in the regulation, this disability prevents them from attainment of grade-level achievement within the current year.

IEPs and Access to the General Curriculum

The second primary requirement for states to meet in designing participation criteria for the AA-MAS (in addition to being identified as eligible to receive special education services under IDEA) is the requirement that the student must have an IEP that references grade-level content. In some ways, this requirement is redundant of the foundational requirements of being eligible to receive special education services. That is, having access to the curriculum in order to meet the educational standards of the public agency is how special education is defined in IDEA: "Specially designed instruction, at no cost to parents, to meet the unique needs of a child with a disability, including instruction conducted in the classroom, in the home, in hospitals and institutions, and in other settings . . ." [20 U.S.C. §1401 (29)]. Specially designed instruction is defined as follows:

> Adapting, as appropriate to the child's needs, the content, methodology, or delivery of instruction to address the unique needs of the child that result from the child's disability; to ensure access of the child to the general education curriculum, so that the child can meet the educational standards within the jurisdiction of the public agency that apply to all children. [34 CFR §300.39 (b)(3)]

These definitions are not new to IDEA 2004. In 1999, disability rights attorney Paul Weckstein (1999) wrote the following:

> An IEP that sets lower goals and does not focus on these standards [that is, the educational standards of the public agency] is usually illegal. Nor is it generally legal to assign a student with disabilities to a low-track regular program that does not teach to these standards. These rights are protected by the federal IDEA and Section 504 of the Rehabilitation Act of 1973. (p. 314)

These rights were reinforced through NCLB in 2001 and the reauthorization of IDEA in 2004, according to Karger and Boundy (2008):

> These two statutes [NCLB 2001 and IDEA 2004] together have lifted
> expectations for learning and have underscored the legally enforceable
> rights of students with disabilities to be effectively taught by highly qual-
> ified teachers, to be provided an opportunity to learn to the same high
> standards as their peers without disabilities, and to be included in all
> state and district-wide assessments . . . [T]hese students must be provid-
> ed meaningful opportunities to learn the knowledge and skills necessary
> to attain proficiency on their respective state standards; full and fair
> opportunities to demonstrate their level of mastery of state standards
> through participation in appropriate assessments used to improve their
> instruction and learning; and equal opportunities to be counted in the
> publicly reported data system that is used to hold schools, districts, and
> states accountable for the academic performance of all students. (p. 11)

Even though IDEA has required that all students who receive special
education services should be provided the services, supports, and specialized instruction so that they achieve proficiency on the state standards, many students with disabilities have not been receiving that
instruction. In 1984, special education researcher Anne Donnellan
wrote that "the criterion of least dangerous assumption holds that in
the absence of conclusive data, educational decisions ought to be based
on assumptions which, if incorrect, will have the least dangerous effect
on the likelihood that students will be able to function independently
as adults" (p. 142). She concluded that, barring proof to the contrary,
educators need to assume that poor performance is due to instructional
deficits instead of student deficits. The regulation requires that IEP
teams examine objective evidence demonstrating that a student's disability has precluded the student from achieving proficiency, and the
guidance suggests that "Such evidence may include the student's performance on State assessments or other assessments that can validly
document academic achievement" (U.S. Department of Education,
2007, p. 17). IEP teams will have to determine that such evidence is
sufficient to ensure that instructional deficits are not the cause of low
performance, as opposed to the student's disability. Using data from
large-scale assessments of content that the student has not been taught
seems to result in circular logic for this purpose. That is, documenting
student academic achievement on content that has not been taught
by an assessment of that content tells us nothing about whether or
how the student's disability precluded their achievement and only
tells us what the student knows and can do before instruction. Later in
this chapter and in the next chapter, discussions are provided of methods for documenting the effectiveness of instructional and curricular

strategies that could be used to ensure that instructional deficits are not the cause of low performance.

The specification in the regulation that students who participate in an AA-MAS must have standards-based IEPs was meant to assuage the concerns raised by advocates that a less challenging achievement standard would result in further inappropriate instruction in a lower-level track. Whether or not the stipulation was in the regulation, states have an obligation to make sure that all students with disabilities are receiving the services, supports, and specialized instruction necessary for them to make progress in—and achieve proficiency in—the curriculum based on the state standards defined for all students. Unless there is assurance that this has occurred, the least dangerous assumption is that poor performance relates to poor opportunities to learn. (See Chapter 2 for more information on how the IEP process can be used to improve opportunities to learn.)

OPERATIONALIZING THE REGULATORY LANGUAGE: IDENTIFYING WHO MAY BE ELIGIBLE

Translating regulatory language into practice is always daunting. Since the AA-MAS regulation was finalized, states have struggled to identify the students who are low-performing and might be eligible for this assessment. Fortunately, these policy imperatives often are followed by a flurry of research aimed at understanding regulatory options in the context of educational logic. Additionally, a few researchers have attempted to understand what opportunities to learn the low-performing students have had. Given the initial controversies about the research base, the limited utility of categorical labels, the necessity of ensuring access to the general curriculum, and the lack of agreement in the field of who these students are, these studies have been challenging. There are debates regarding whether states should identify the students based on a percentage (i.e., the 2% of students with disabilities with the lowest scores) or whether studies should be based on the characteristics of the population and their instruction in the content defined in the regulation (i.e., those taught the curriculum but not likely to be proficient that year). Most studies have taken the former approach, mining state assessment data for students who perform at the lowest end, although data from OTL investigations are increasingly challenging the assumptions that all low-performing students have indeed been taught the standards-based curriculum.

Studies of Low-Performing Students

States have tried to operationalize who the eligible students are in varying ways (Fincher, 2007; HB 05-1246 Study Committee, 2005;

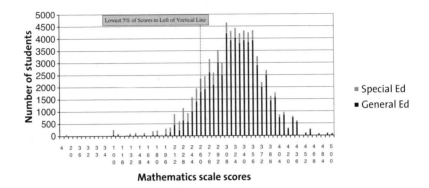

Figure 1.2.   Grade 4 mathematics scale scores by special education status. (From Marion, S., Gong, B., & Simpson, M.A. [2006, February 6]. *Mining achievement data to guide policies and practices on assessment options* [Slide 5]. Teleconference on Making Good Decisions on NCLB Flexibility Options. Minneapolis, MN: National Center on Educational Outcomes. Retrieved April 4, 2009, from http://education.umn.edu/nceo/Teleconferences/tele11/default.html; reprinted by permission.)

Marion, Gong, & Simpson, 2006; New England Compact, 2007). One of the first investigations looking at how students with disabilities currently perform on large-scale assessments under NCLB was done by researchers at the National Center for the Improvement of Educational Assessment. As indicated in Figure 1.2, the scores of students with disabilities occur at all scale scores in the distribution, and the scores of students without disabilities also occur at all scale scores in the distribution (Marion, Gong et al., 2006).

This study foreshadowed results of studies in multiple states: the lowest-performing students on state assessments under NCLB are not all students with disabilities. For example, Perie (2009) summarized data-mining approaches in two states, Georgia and South Carolina. Georgia mined data from 3 years of the state test, identifying persistently low performers in grades 5 and 8 as students with 3 years of data scoring in the lowest of three achievement levels. South Carolina looked at grades 4 and 7, identifying students with 2 years of data scoring in the lowest of four levels. In Georgia, the percentage of persistently low-performing students who have documented disabilities ranged from 40% to 55%; in South Carolina, the percentages of students with disabilities among the lowest performers ranged from 39% to 49% (Perie, 2009). These data will vary across states on the basis of the nature of states' proficiency standards and depending on the number of years for which data are available. That is, 2 years of data may show different patterns than 4 years of data. The studies vary in methodology and findings, and many of the research reports are included in the accompanying resources list. Chapter 9 addresses ways states can learn from these efforts to design their own data-mining study.

Student Characteristics and Opportunity-to-Learn Investigations

Several states have attempted to understand more about the educational characteristics of these low-performing students. Perie (2009) summarized results of teacher surveys and focus groups in several states that captured teacher perceptions about the nature of these students' learning. These findings of teacher perceptions indicate the following:

> That the core academic curriculum is significantly modified or specifically designed for the student; the student is making fairly consistent progress but not at expected (or targeted) level; there is a gap between actual performance and targeted level of performance which is evident over a period of time (at least 2 consecutive years); the gap continues to widen or remains the same; despite the provision of "good" interventions, the student is not progressing at the rate expected for grade level; accommodations alone do not allow the student to fully demonstrate knowledge; and all appropriate accommodations have been exhausted. (Slide 18)

Georgia has conducted a curriculum implementation survey of teachers that asked whether low-performing students were receiving instruction in the grade-level curriculum and to what depth and degree. Teachers self-reported their instructional practices and curriculum choices; the investigators suggest that teacher interviews and direct classroom observations would be preferable but are not feasible with resources available. Although the results of the study are not yet published, their initial findings suggest that at fifth and eighth grade in mathematics and at eighth grade in reading, general education teachers have higher expectations (deeper levels of understanding) for students than do special education teachers, but fifth grade reading responses showed higher expectations among special education teachers (M. Fincher, personal communication, April 16, 2009). Qualitative data are being used to help illuminate these differences, but results are not yet available.

The New England Compact study of the gap included interviews with teachers and substantial direct quotations from teachers. Compare and contrast the following teacher observations of similar students (Parker & Saxon, 2007):

Teacher 1: They tend to be slow learners. They tend to be "shady 80s," that is what I call them. Seventy to 75 makes you mentally retarded or learning impaired. If you are in the 90s, then you are okay. These are shady 80s. They show up every day for school, and they sit down and crank out their little homework. They don't have a clue what the homework means, but they have it done. They always have a notebook. They always have a sharpened pencil . . . These guys are good students in the classroom. They have their notebook and their pencil. Clueless. They have no mechanism to practice it . . . They never move from that very pretend area of teaching. They do it fairly well. These kids are going to get 70s. These kids will get it right, but they don't have a clue how they got it right. It never becomes theirs. (p. 7)

Teacher 2: My teaching practice just in the past year has changed dramatically. My thrust now is to really concentrate on eighth grade GLEs [grade-level expectations], even though most kids I have in my resource room are third grade level for math, maybe fourth grade . . . I found math strategies presented on the third, fourth grade level . . . they were exposed to strategy on their level, so then we worked through problems up to the eighth grade level. So that's a new direction for me, because I'm not sure I've always had the expectation that they could do eighth grade math. So my expectation has changed, and my teaching practice as a result of that has changed. (p. 8)

Clearly, as evidenced by the first teacher, not all educators are implementing the least dangerous assumption related to their expectations for these students. In some cases, refocusing attention on the needs of struggling learners changes teacher behavior (Teacher 2), but that is not always the case (Teacher 1).

At the request of the Colorado State Legislature, a Colorado study group reviewed their reading and math data (grades 3–10) and found that not all of the students performing in the lowest one third on the state tests were students receiving special education; accommodations were not consistently provided to all eligible students; and they saw "substantial longitudinal growth" toward grade-level achievement for the majority of the students over time. When the study group initiated actual observations of instructional opportunities, they found that students (with and without disabilities) who were making the greatest gains toward grade-level achievement were those attending schools that provided "intensive, targeted, research-based instruction" (HB 05-1246 Study Committee, 2005). The next section elaborates on possible strategies to improve OTL and to identify students who may benefit from participation in AA-MAS.

STRATEGIES TO IMPROVE OPPORTUNITIES TO LEARN AND IDENTIFY STUDENTS WHO MAY BENEFIT FROM AA-MAS

There are studies focused on what is occurring in schools where students with disabilities are performing well (e.g., Barr et al., 2009; Cortiella & Burnette, 2007; Donahue Institute, 2004). These studies consistently identify common characteristics among schools where students with disabilities achieve at high levels. As summarized in one study, the schools have 1) a pervasive emphasis on the curriculum and alignment with the standards; 2) effective systems to support curriculum alignment; 3) an emphasis on inclusion and access to the curriculum; 4) a culture and practices that support high standards and student achievement; 5) a well-disciplined academic and social environment; 6) continuous use of student data to inform decision making; 7) unified practices supported by targeted professional development; 8) access to resources to support key initiatives; 9) effective staff recruitment, retention, and deployment; 10) flexible leaders and staff that work effectively in a dynamic environment; and 11) effective leadership (Donahue Institute, 2004).

A recommendation from the Colorado study of students in the gap was that the state should implement sound "data-driven recommendations that focus on student learning and on valid measurement of that learning" (HB 05-1246 Study Committee, 2005, p. 21). The implementation of RTI strategies in many states is meant to ensure that research-based early-literacy screening and early-intervention processes are used to help identify struggling learners as soon as possible. According to the National Center on Response to Intervention (n.d.)

> Response to intervention integrates assessment and intervention within a multi-level prevention system to maximize student achievement and to reduce behavior problems. With RtI, schools identify students at risk for poor learning outcomes, monitor student progress, provide evidence-based interventions and adjust the intensity and nature of those interventions depending on a student's responsiveness, and identify students with learning disabilities.

In addition, RTI can help identify students with learning disabilities sooner so they can achieve more. This approach is not limited to students with disabilities and can assist states like Colorado that have a commitment to improve instruction and outcomes for all students identified as low-performing, with and without disabilities. As such, RTI holds promise for states that choose to emphasize intervention on instruction and curriculum as opposed to relying solely on large-scale assessments to improve achievement and outcomes.

There is strong research and best practices documentation for RTI in reading, especially in the primary grades. The Institute of Education Sciences published a practice guide based on currently available evidence, explicating five recommendations for implementing RTI to identify students in need of intervention. It further described how to carry out each recommendation and identified potential roadblocks to implementation (Gersten et al., 2008). The authors noted that, although multitiered efforts like RTI can prevent learners from falling behind through early implementation of interventions, "some aspects of RtI, however (such as tier 1 instruction), are still poorly defined, and there is little evidence that some practices of targeted instruction will be effective" (p. 8). Still, they suggested that a coordinated multitiered program can prevent beginning readers from becoming struggling readers in the later grades and possibly prevent referrals to special education. They provided an exhaustive reference list to support their recommendations and categorized the recommendations based on the strength of the evidence in the research base (Gersten et al., 2008).

Fuchs and Fuchs (2006) also provided helpful guidance to states and districts considering use of RTI related to reading. They documented differences among educators about the appropriate use of RTI, noting "The first group views RtI mostly in terms of providing prevention and advocates for more tiers. The second group regards RtI mostly as identification and classification procedures and argues for fewer tiers" (p. 94). In addition, they suggested that practitioners and researchers vary in their preference for application of RTI, with practitioners viewing RTI as a problem-solving approach while researchers favor the use of standard treatment protocols. They identified numerous unanswered questions and unresolved issues, including the challenge of false-positive identification for special education services in use with a problem-solving approach and false-negative identification in use with a standard treatment-protocol approach (Fuchs & Fuchs, 2006). They questioned which error is worse, but did not answer the question. Ultimately, that becomes a critical policy decision to be made at the local and state levels in implementation and something that must be monitored closely.

Fletcher (2008) summarized issues for consideration that may serve to inform states' efforts to grapple with defining students who meet the regulatory requirements for participation in an AA-MAS. He noted that RTI is not appropriate solely as a special education initiative or method to meet criteria for identification of learning disabilities; it ultimately is a regular education initiative for all students. Once students are identified as meeting criteria for special education services on the basis of not responding well to interventions, that does not give us the information needed to understand why they are not responding or how to teach or assess them, as Fletcher suggested. Echoes of advocates' concerns about the strength of the research base under the regulation seem to be borne out in his conclusion that "more research is needed on the characteristics of students who do not respond well to intervention since we have not really had the opportunity to study this subgroup from cognitive, interventional, and neurobiological perspectives" (p. 9). The regular education basis for RTI also has potential benefit for states that feel an obligation to intervene on behalf of all low-performing students who do not have disabilities. RTI processes have the potential to improve outcomes for all struggling students, not just those with disabilities.

Other progress-monitoring approaches also may contribute to improved achievement for all students. Curriculum-based measurement (CBM) is of particular interest, given the strong research base for many CBM methods. Recently, Fuchs, Seethaler, Fuchs, and Hamlett (2008) proposed CBMs as meeting the requirements for determining eligibility under the 2% regulation:

> That is, CBM progress monitoring can be used to provide the necessary database on (a) whether grade-level proficiency is expected, (b) whether appropriate instruction has been provided, and (c) whether progress in response to that instruction is appropriate. Moreover, as it satisfies the three-pronged requirement for evidence related to identifying the 2% population, CBM progress monitoring simultaneously provides the added advantage of helping schools enhance special education outcomes (p. 160)

Given that CBMs often are used within an RTI framework to monitor progress after an intervention, these authors suggest that efficiencies of scale will emerge that produce data to determine eligibility for an AA-MAS.

Placing these approaches within the context of standards set for the grade level, as required in current standards-based systems, is essential. Deno, Fuchs, Marston, and Shin (2001) discussed the implications of a normative approach to setting achievement expectations that assume that the current typically observed growth rates for students with disabilities are reasonable and predict future growth. These assumptions lead to the conclusion that students with learning disabilities will learn at a slower rate than peers without disabilities. The researchers speculated that this kind of reasoning reflects the "well-accepted fact that special education, as typically practiced in this country, fails to regularly incorporate demonstrably effective methods" (Deno et al., 2001, p. 515). If this is true, then systemic interventions on the system of special education in this country to correct these deficits should be a priority in every state, as opposed to accepting lower rates of student learning.

These progress monitoring approaches hold much promise for improved outcomes and higher expectations. Still, critical contextual challenges must be addressed. These challenges affect the implementation of effective progress monitoring for students with disabilities. They include historical limited access to challenging standards-based curriculum, instruction, and assessment; concerns about the target of measurement, that is, whether only basic skills or a full range of rich and challenging grade-level content should be measured; and limited practitioner understanding about use of data for effective provision of instructional strategies, interventions, and supports in a standards-based system (Quenemoen, Thurlow, Moen, Thompson, & Morse, 2003). In most schools, the path to assurance of the least dangerous assumption requires guideposts of continuing staff development, support, and oversight.

Even with the identification (and improvement) of OTLs through instructional quality and curriculum access, the validity of assessments hinges on whether all students who have learned the grade-level content can show what they know on the assessments. The National Accessible Reading Assessment Projects are conducting a program of research and development designed to make large-scale assessments of reading proficiency more accessible for students who have disabilities that affect reading. They suggest that creating "accessible reading assessments based on accepted definitions of reading and proficiencies of reading requires knowledge of the issues specific to each disability and how they affect reading and the assessment of reading" (2006). They have prepared a series of articles by categorical label to serve as discussion guides for partners working on test development, summarized in Thurlow et al. (2009). This may serve as a resource to state stakeholders and consultants as they grapple with how to first teach and then assess students with varying characteristics. Still, there are limits to what discussions based on categorical labels will yield, given the well-documented subjectivity of state-defined eligibility criteria used to determine categorical labels and the heterogeneity of students within each category.

REGULATORY OPTIONS, POLICY
PREROGATIVES, AND IMPLICATIONS

State policy makers have a great deal of flexibility in decisions about whether and how to implement AA-MAS, as they do for any other assessment option. They also have a responsibility to articulate thoughtfully the philosophy and beliefs that these decisions reflect. This thoughtful decision making yields two important tests of whether the choices made are sustainable. The first test is whether students who have historically been underserved and ill-prepared for adult life will see improved outcomes. The second is whether the technical defensibility of an assessment rests in validity arguments that begin in these decisions and play out in each step of assessment design. This second test is discussed throughout this volume in multiple chapters; the first test begins with the choices on who participates in AA-MAS and the effect of that participation on their access to high-quality standards-based instruction and curriculum and, ultimately, their academic achievement.

Key Political and Social Justice Issues

The test of whether students will see improved outcomes must be considered as the initial decisions are made. Public articulation and discussion of these decisions can ensure that historically low expectations and opportunities to learn are not reinforced. In the spirit and the letter of federal requirements that are the context for the option, implementation of AA-MAS should expressly raise expectations and result in higher achievement for students who participate in the option. In a standards-based accountability-driven reform model, any option that encourages or rewards less challenging standards for any student who could achieve at grade level (assuming they have access to the curriculum and are instructed effectively) undermines the entire system of school reform. For most students, with and without disabilities, we cannot predict with any accuracy whether they will achieve at grade level when instructed effectively. Thus the least dangerous assumption requires that all students receive that instruction. Careful monitoring of consequences of the system is essential to ensure the intended positive consequences are occurring and unintended negative consequences are not.

Data mining of current student performance such as that described in Chapter 9 can shape the dialogue among stakeholders. Key questions to consider include the following: What evidence exists to suggest that students with disabilities who are low-performing differ from minority students or poor students who are low-performing? What evidence exists to support the policy assumption that some of these students cannot achieve at grade level even if their OTL is appropriate? What do direct observations of student instructional and curricular opportunities tell us, and how does that compare and contrast with teacher perceptions? What evidence exists to support the notion that OTL is appropriate for all students in the subgroup? States need to articulate the belief systems that underlie their policy decisions and justify these beliefs on the basis of data. There is a fundamental tension within the regulatory options. If the consequences of participating in an assessment option are positive, how can we deny the same opportunities to other students with similar achievement profiles other than disability status? If the consequences are negative, how can we justify the use of the options for students with disabilities?

Varying State Assumptions, Philosophies and Beliefs, and Their Implications

As states articulate their philosophy and beliefs related to students who may participate in an assessment, they are constructing the foundation of their assessment choices. Examples of underlying philosophies and beliefs, which yield very different definitions of eligible students, assessment options, and eventual student achievement, are presented next. These are very different positions; most states participating in public discussions can categorize their philosophy as more or less similar to one of these three options, at least one of which does not seem to match the AA-MAS regulatory requirements. Each of these philosophical positions has infinite variations, many of them controversial, but the dominant profile of each is presented here for general consideration. This process of analyzing possible philosophical positions and their implications is helpful as any alternative approaches to assessment for students with disabilities are considered. The AA-MAS requirements are used here as an example.

Guiding Philosophy 1

Description

Student performance based on past test results and instructional opportunities predict appropriate expectations for future performance. There is a group of students with disabilities who are being instructed in a modified curriculum, one linked to the general curriculum as required by IDEA, but different from that of their enrolled-grade peers. Thus the state needs to provide a modified assessment to match the curriculum. Given that many of these students will never catch up to their enrolled-grade peers, this will result in very different long-term outcomes. Thus policy choices focus on modifying the assessments to match a modified curriculum. The target population for inclusion in these modified assessments includes students who may be participating in a modified curriculum.

Implications

The assumption that there is a group of students with disabilities who participate in a modified curriculum different from that of their peers without disabilities or development of an assessment option that does not result in a standard diploma would raise peer review and advocacy concerns under the requirements of the 2% regulation. Instead, this assumption better fits a very small group of students who may now participate in AA-AAS but for whom the current alternate achievement standards are not an appropriately high expectation. In other words, these are students who currently may be topping out on the AA-AAS or performing at the very lowest levels of the general assessment. There generally are very few students in most states who fit into this group, once OTL barriers are taken into account. An assessment built under this assumption would better match the requirements for a new, more challenging AA-AAS than the requirements of an AA-MAS. The 1% regulation permits states to set more than one alternate achievement standard. Some states do not have a full 1% of students participating in the AA-AAS, whereas other states recognize that, although they have 1% or higher participation, the AA-AAS does not reflect a sufficiently high expectation for some students who participate. Given the assumptions of separate track curriculum, assessment, and outcomes assumed in this first philosophy, development of a second AA-AAS with higher performance expectations than those of the existing AA-AAS may be warranted.

Guiding Philosophy 2

Description

Student achievement needs to be considered in the context of systematic OTLs (services, supports, specialized instruction, etc.) the general curriculum on the basis of grade-level content and achievement standards. For students who do not as yet have these opportunities, intervention on their OTLs is the first priority in order to accelerate their learning. Given that it will take some time for these students to regain any lost ground from previous limited OTL, short-term AA-MAS options are an appropriate interim measure to hold schools accountable for students' learning. These AA-MAS should cover substantially the same content as the general assessment, but may have more content coverage at the lower end of the grade-level content expectations. Still, the state policy is based on an assumption that eventually, with strong interventions and evidence-based practices in student services, supports, and specialized instruction, these students will achieve the same outcomes as peers without disabilities.

Implications

This philosophy seems to match the language of the 2% regulation, although it is still challenging to conceptualize how to use AA-MAS as interim accountability measures with the expectation that students will catch up over time. (See Chapter 9 for examples of how this may affect design of the assessment system.) Those students who are identified through state data-mining efforts as making gains each year but who are still below proficiency over several test administrations may be the target population under this theory. RTI and progress-monitoring tools should be in place to obtain better data to understand their needs and to plan improved services supports and specialized instruction to ensure that they do, indeed, catch up over time. A state working under this philosophy may consider requiring data from multiple sources (e.g., RTI, progress monitoring, interim assessments, and so forth) to document a decision about a student's participation in AA-MAS each year and also require documentation of the evidence-based practices that have been implemented for the student on the basis of these data. This evidence of opportunities could be included in requirements under the accountability system in addition to the assessment data themselves. They may also decide to implement an AA-MAS only at selected grades and instead promote and support through training and other resources district/school efforts at other grades to prevent students from falling behind. States and districts may need to design intensive training and coaching efforts to ensure teachers have the skills necessary to effectively teach these students. Alternatively, a state may require that students exit from the AA-MAS in a set number of years, or sunset the AA-MAS completely, depending on what data reveal about whether the combined practice of increased OTL and selected use of AA-MAS support improved achievement for individuals and for the subgroup over the longer term.

Guiding Philosophy 3

Description

Student characteristics (related to disability, ethnicity, poverty, and other demographic categories) have been associated with a history of low expectations and limited OTL. Until we intervene to change learning opportunities, we cannot use past performance to predict which students could achieve to proficiency. This is true for students with disabilities and for those without disabilities. Designing a new assessment option now jeopardizes an opportunity for reform to ensure all students are taught well. The state policy must ensure students are being taught first, then see who is left achieving at low levels once all are taught well before building any assessment options that may risk perpetuating lowered expectations and outcomes.

Implications

This approach assumes that the state will provide leadership and resources to intervene on historical lack of OTL for all the students described as the low performers in state data sets discussed earlier in this chapter. Certainly systematic interventions like RTI and progress monitoring, new interim or formative assessment options, and continued efforts in states to implement programs such as positive behavior supports contribute to this effort. These efforts are difficult to take to scale, but are laudable and necessary. They are not, however, sufficient to ensure that all students who historically have had limited OTL and continued low expectations for their performance achieve at higher levels. States that voice this philosophy will look for ways to intervene on attitudes and beliefs of educators and the public who still find it appropriate to expect less of students simply because they have a disability label or are poor or of minority status. They will support these educators with increased training and coaching on evidence-based methods to effectively instruct all students, with and without disabilities, in the challenging standards-based curriculum.

This philosophy results in a choice not to develop an AA-MAS at this time. However, the state systematically is addressing a key component of the accountability system, that of leveraging improvements in standards-based instruction and curricular access for all students, especially those students who have historically been underserved, including those with disabilities. As such, this philosophy highlights the choices states have to make on how to most effectively use limited resources to ensure the best possible outcomes. The costs associated with these decisions include opportunity costs of those choices not made.

Another Philosophical Stance Outside the Parameters of the Current Accountability System

There is another philosophy underlying assessment choices in states that is not included in the preceding discussion because it does not assume that participation in these assessments should lead to systematic improvement in instruction and curriculum for low-performing students and, ultimately, to improved student achievement, as is assumed in the current accountability model. That set of beliefs is focused around the need to provide what is often described as "relief" to districts and schools from the consequences of system accountability for students with disabilities. If this philosophy dominates state discussions, then much of the guidance in this volume will be overdesigned for state purposes in developing such an assessment. A more straightforward and less expensive method to support this option is to exempt up to 2% of students from the assessment and accountability, but then the state leaders would be responsible for supporting the implications of that decision, both under federal compliance requirements and from advocacy groups interested in protecting the rights of students with disabilities.

Relationship of AA-MAS to the State Options on Accommodations and Alternate Assessments Based on GLAS

Regardless of the underlying philosophy, states will have to define how the AA-MAS contributes to an overall system of assessment for accountability purposes. That is, there should be a coherent educational logic or relationship between the AA-MAS and other alternate assessments (based on AAS or GLAS), as well as with the general assessment. Universal design, accommodations policies, decision-making guidelines, training, and monitoring should support the validity of the assessment system so that all students are included in ways that support use of assessment results in a standards-based accountability system.

Use of accommodations on a standards-based assessment assumes that careful consideration is given to whether the grade-level content and achievement standards being measured remain constant despite the use of the accommodation. The collective knowledge base on the effects of accommodations on the content being measured is growing, but there are considerable complexities in the case of the most challenging content and student combinations. This can result in students who have learned the skills and knowledge assessed on the test scoring below proficiency. Some students with disabilities may have barriers to showing what they know on the state general assessment, even with accommodations. These barriers may be related to several different disability characteristics (e.g., processing, sensory, physical, or emotional barriers). In order to ensure the validity of inferences of the assessment system for these students, states may need to consider an alternate assessment based on GLAS (AA-GLAS).

Perie (2009) posed key questions that states will have to answer related to the relationship among the state assessment options:

> Do we expect to see smooth transitions from one assessment to the next? How do the performance expectations relate? Is Proficient on the AA-MAS similar in nature to Proficient on the general assessment? Is it closer to Basic? Or is it somewhere in between? Is there an expectation that the AA-MAS may provide a stepping stone for students to reach Proficient

on the general assessment? Or, is the expectation that students taking the AA-MAS are a unique population that will always need the modifications provided? Is a student who scores Advanced on the AA-MAS prepared to take the general assessment or an AA-GLAS or are they simply exceeding the criterion on their own assessment? (pp. 25–26)

Standards-based assessment systems should include strategies that permit all students to show what they know and can do on the academic content standards defined for peers without disabilities of the same age and grade level, despite the barriers of disability. However, any change in academic achievement standards for a group of students should be reviewed to ensure that these options raise the bar of academic expectations and thus increase system accountability for the outcomes of students who may participate in the option. The foundation for decisions about assessment options must rest and be defended on the basis of a publicly articulated set of beliefs about teaching, learning, and eventual outcomes for all students.

QUESTIONS FOR STATES AS THEY CHOOSE, BUILD, AND DEFEND THE VALIDITY OF THEIR APPROACH

States must build an argument to defend the validity of their approach to assessment options that begins with articulated definitions of who the students are who will benefit from the option and why. The types of questions states must answer in their validity argument need to be framed while they are making the decision to develop an option, during its development, and in their continuous improvement and consequential validity studies as they implement. Related to identification of the students, these include questions about the students who may participate; the instruction, support, and resources provided to these students at the local level and the quality of IEP decisions made about their participation; and how the assessment option is appropriate for its articulated purposes and uses—including those of improving achievement for students who participate.

Later chapters in this volume (especially Chapters 8 and 9) focus on the validity argument and on practical implications of state choices. It is important to include questions about how a state can validate that the appropriate students are identified and participate in an AA-MAS. This chapter is written under the assumption that implementation of AA-MAS should expressly raise expectations and result in higher achievement for students who participate in the option. That is a testable assumption and should be considered as a state makes choices and implements an AA-MAS. Questions about the appropriateness of

AA-MAS for improving student outcomes include the following (adapted from Marion, 2007):

- How does this assessment provide a more accurate measure of the knowledge and skills of the participants compared with the general assessment?
- How does development of an AA-MAS yield better inferences about the students than other assessment approaches, such as improved general assessment design, appropriate accommodations, or development of AA-GLAS?
- What are the potential costs and benefits of competing uses of resources, including targeted staff development on instructional and curricular interventions for teachers of struggling learners instead of assessment development and implementation?
- How will the inclusion of the AA-MAS as part of the state's assessment system lead to better instructional and curricular opportunities for these participating students?
- Other questions identified by policymakers and stakeholders

Marion (2007) identified potential sources of data for many of these questions in the form of a workbook for AA-MAS development and documentation. Design of validity studies should begin while planning for any assessment option, and tools such as this volume and earlier work done by Marion and others can guide those designs.

In conclusion, in order to make decisions about whether and how to design any assessment option for students with disabilities, states need to articulate a guiding philosophy that defines which students will benefit from participating in the assessment and how they will benefit. States then can design the assessment on the basis of the specific learning characteristics and OTL of students who may participate. The AA-MAS is a model for how these steps can be applied to any assessment option under consideration.

REFERENCES

Abedi, J. (2006). Psychometric issues in the ELL assessment and special education eligibility. *Teacher's College Record, 108*(11), 2282–2303.

Abedi, J. (2007). English language learners with disabilities. In C. Cahlan-Laitusis & L. Cook (Eds.), *Accommodating students with disabilities on state assessments: What works?* (pp. 23–35). Arlington, VA: Council for Exceptional Children.

Artiles, A.J., & Ortiz, A. (Eds.). (2002). *English language learners with special needs: Identification, placement, and instruction.* Washington, DC: Center for Applied Linguistics.

Barr, S., Telfer, D., & DiMuzio, M. (2009, February). *The Ohio Improvement Process (OIP) as a strategy for creating a viable SSOS for all Ohio districts and schools.* Ohio Department of Education presentation to U.S. Department of Education Intradepartmental Work Group, Columbus, OH.

Cortiella, C., & Burnette, J. (2007). *Challenging change: How schools and districts are improving the performance of special education students.* New York: National Council for Learning Disabilities.

Data Accountability Center. (2007). IDEA Part B Child Count: *Students ages 6 through 21 served under IDEA, Part B, by disability category and state: Fall 2007* (Tables 1–3). Retrieved September 30, 2008, from www.IDEAdata.org

Deno, S., Fuchs, L., Marston, D., & Shin, J. (2001). Using curriculum-based measurement to establish growth standards for students with disabilities. *School Psychology Review, 30*(4), 466–472.

Donahue Institute. (2004, October). *A study of MCAS achievement and promising practices in urban special education: Report of field research findings (Case studies and cross-case analysis of promising practices in selected urban public school districts in Massachusetts).* Hadley, MA: University of Massachusetts, Donahue Institute, Research and Evaluation Group. Retrieved March 23, 2006, from http://www.donahue.umassp.edu/docs/field_rsrch_findings

Donnellan, A. (1984). The criterion of the least dangerous assumption. *Behavior Disorders, 9,* 141–150.

Fincher, M. (2007, June). Investigating the academic achievement of persistently low performing students. In *Assessing (and teaching) students at risk for failure: A partnership for success.* Session conducted at the Council of Chief State School Officers Large Scale Assessment Conference, Nashville, TN. Retrieved August 15, 2007, from http://www.ccsso.org/content/PDFs/12%2DMelissa%20Fincher%20Paul%20Ban%20Pam%20Rogers%20Rachel%20Quenemoen.pdf

Fletcher, J.M. (2008). *Identifying learning disabilities in the context of response to intervention: A hybrid model.* Retrieved March 4, 2009, from the RTI Action Network Web site: http://www.rtinetwork.org/index2.php?option=com_content&task=view&id=331&pop=1&page=0&Itemid=45

Fuchs, D., & Fuchs, L.S. (2006, January–March). Introduction to Response to Intervention: What, why, and how valid is it? *Reading Research Quarterly, 41,* 93–99.

Fuchs, L., Seethaler P.M., Fuchs, D., & Hamlett, C. L. (2008). Using curriculum-based measurement to identify the 2% population. *Journal of Disability Policy Studies, 19*(3), 151–161.

Gersten, R., Compton, D., Connor, C.M., Dimino, J., Santoro, L., Linan-Thompson, S., et al. (2008). *Assisting students struggling with reading: Response to Intervention and multi-tier intervention for reading in the primary grades. A practice guide.* (NCEE 2009-4045). Washington, DC: National Center for Education Evaluation and Regional Assistance, Institute of Education Sciences, U.S. Department of Education. Retrieved April 2, 2009, from http://ies.ed.gov/ncee/wwc/pdf/practiceguides/rti_reading_pg_021809.pdf

HB 05-1246 Study Committee. (2005, December 31). *Assessing "students in the gap" in Colorado.* Retrieved May 7, 2006, from http://education.umn.edu/nceo/Teleconferences/tele11/ColoradoStudy.pdf

Individuals with Disabilities Education Improvement Act (IDEA) of 2004, PL 108-446, 20 U.S.C. §§ 1400 *et seq.*

Kaloi, L. (2007). *A misunderstood policy with the potential to harm millions of kids.* Retrieved March 8, 2009, from http://www.ncld.org/twopercentrule

Karger, J., & Boundy, K. (2008, Fall). Including students with dyslexia in the state accountability system: The basic legal framework. *Perspectives on Language and Literacy International Dyslexia Association, 34*(4), 11–15.

Marion, S. (2007). *A technical design and documentation workbook for assessments based on modified achievement standards.* Minneapolis, MN: National Center on Educational Outcomes. Retrieved April 4, 2009, from http://cehd.umn.edu/nceo/Teleconferences/AAMASteleconferences/AAMASworkbook.pdf

Marion, S., Gong, B., & Simpson, M.A. (2006, February 6). *Mining achievement data to guide policies and practices on assessment options.* Teleconference on Making Good Decisions on NCLB Flexibility Options. Minneapolis, MN: National Center on Educational Outcomes. Retrieved April 4, 2009, from http://education.umn.edu/nceo/Teleconferences/tele11/default.html

Minnema, J., Thurlow, M., Anderson, M., & Stone, K. (2005). *English language learners with disabilities and large-scale assessments: What the literature can tell us* (ELLs with Disabilities Report 6). Minneapolis, MN: University of Minnesota, National Center on Educational Outcomes.

National Association of School Psychologists (NASP). (2002). *Position statement: Rights without labels.* Original statement adopted by NASP Delegate Assembly in 1986. Revision adopted by NASP Delegate Assembly, July 14, 2002. Retrieved March 10, 2009, from http://www.nasponline.org/about_nasp/pospaper_rwl.aspx

National Association of School Psychologists. (2009). *Appropriate academic supports to meet the needs of all students* [Position statement]. Bethesda, MD: Author.

National Center on Educational Outcomes. (2008, March 10). *Previous studies that examine who the students are who may qualify to participate in an AA-MAS.* White paper for Expert Panel Meeting Multi-State GSEG Consortium Toward a Defensible AA-MAS. Minneapolis, MN: Author.

National Center on Response to Intervention. (n.d.). *What is RTI?* Retrieved March 9, 2009, from http://www.rti4success.org/

New England Compact. (2007). *Reaching students in the gaps; A study of assessment gaps, students, and alternatives.* Newton MA: CAST, The Education Alliance, EDC, INTASC, Measured Progress.

No Child Left Behind Act of 2001, PL 107-110, 115 Stat. 1425, 20 U.S.C. §§ 6301 et seq.

Parker, C.E., & Saxon, S. (2007). *Teacher views of students in the gaps.* New England Compact Enhanced Assessment Grant. Retrieved March 9, 2009, from http://www.necompact.org/Teacher_views_of_students.pdf

Perie, M. (2009, February). *Understanding the AA-MAS: How does it fit into a state assessment and accountability system?* Presentation to CCSSO SCASS meeting, Orlando, FL. Available at http://www.nciea.org/publications/Cross SCASS_MAP09.pdf

Quenemoen, R., Thurlow, M., Moen, R., Thompson, S., & Morse, A.B. (2003). *Progress monitoring in an inclusive standards-based assessment and accountability system* (Synthesis Report 53). Minneapolis, MN: University of Minnesota, National Center on Educational Outcomes.

Thurlow, M. (2007). The challenge of special populations to accountability for all. In D. Clark (Ed.), *No Child Left Behind: A five year review* (Congressional Program, Vol. 22, No. 1) (pp. 39–44). Washington, DC: The Aspen Institute.

Thurlow, M.L., Moen, R.E. Liu, K.K., Scullin, S., Hausmann, K.E., & Shyyan, V. (2009). *Disabilities and reading: Understanding the effects of disabilities and their relationship to reading instruction and assessment.* Minneapolis, MN: University of Minnesota Partnership for Accessible Reading Assessment.

U.S. Department of Education. (2005a). *Raising achievement: Alternate assessments for students with disabilities.* Retrieved March 8, 2009, from http://www.ed.gov/print/policy/elsec/guid/raising/alt-assess-long.html

U.S. Department of Education. (2005b). Secretary Spellings announces more workable, "common sense" approach to implement *No Child Left Behind Law* [Press release]. Retrieved March 8, 2010, from http://www2.ed.gov/news/pressreleases/2005/04/04072005.html

U.S. Department of Education. (2007). *Modified academic achievement standards: Non-regulatory guidance.* Washington, DC: Author.

Weckstein, P. (1999). School reform and enforceable rights to quality education. In J. Heubert (Ed.), *Law and school reform: Six strategies for promoting educational equity* (pp. 306–389). New Haven, CT: Yale University Press.

Wendorf, J. (2005). Open letter to Secretary of Education Margaret Spellings, March 27, 2005. Retrieved March 8, 2009, from http://www.ncld.org/twopercentrule

2

Developing Standards-Based Individualized Education Programs that Promote Effective Instruction

Meagan Karvonen

States have the option to create alternate assessments based on modified achievement standards (AA-MAS) for students with disabilities who perform persistently and significantly below grade level. This population is heterogeneous within states and may also be defined differently across states (Perie, 2009; see also Chapter 1). Regardless of their characteristics and needs, this population of students requires extensive supports and effective instruction in order to meet high expectations and transition back into eligibility for grade-level assessment.

The importance of effective instruction for this target population of students was recognized in the final regulations on the AA-MAS (U.S. Department of Education, 2007a, 34 C.F.R. § 200.1[f][iii]). There are three alternate assessment options under the No Child Left Behind (NCLB) of 2001 (PL 107-110): 1) those based on grade-level achievement standards (AA-GLAS), 2) those based on alternate achievement standards (AA-AAS), and 3) AA-MAS. Although access to instruction based on grade-level academic content standards is recognized for all students under the Individuals with Disabilities Education Act (IDEA) amendments of 1997, the regulations for AA-MAS represent the first explicit assumption under NCLB that instruction has afforded the student maximum opportunity to learn (OTL) what is assessed. OTL requires a curriculum that is well-aligned to state standards and assessment so students can show what they know and can do. For the population of AA-MAS–eligible students, a well-aligned curriculum is a critical foundation. Because these students have not been successful with previous classroom instruction, they also need this curriculum to be designed and delivered using the best, evidence-based instructional practices available.

The nonregulatory guidance on AA-MAS (U.S. Department of Education, 2007b) reinforces the responsibility of the local education agency (LEA) to design a highly effective curriculum and instruction and requires a standards-based individualized education program (IEP):

> The primary reason for requiring IEP goals based on grade-level academic content standards is to ensure that students who participate in an assessment based on modified academic achievement standards receive instruction in grade-level content so that they can make progress towards meeting grade-level proficiency. (p. 28)

In other words, the IEP is a way of driving the student's academic curriculum toward the goal of transitioning back into grade-level assessments. Although states have some latitude in how they interpret this goal (i.e., expecting the student to have an ongoing need for a separate form of assessment because of the student's disability, or assuming eventual eligibility for the traditional grade-level assessment despite the disability), the IEP provides a mechanism to guide local educators' progress toward that goal. The IEP also provides the evidence for how the instructional program will incorporate supports to address the student's characteristics stemming from the disability.

Although states may differ in how they plan to approach AA-MAS or educate their students who may be eligible for this assessment, there are federal requirements related to the contents of IEPs that are universal across states. The IEP cannot completely capture the entire academic curriculum for a student eligible to take AA-MAS. However, planning and writing the IEP can help educators think systematically about how to design high-quality instruction for this population. Effective instructional design requires teachers to know all three vertices in the assessment triangle (Pellegrino, Chudowsky, & Glaser, 2001). With an understanding of how students who take AA-MAS learn academic content (cognition) and how knowledge is demonstrated through classroom and large-scale assessment (observation), teachers bear responsibility for using assessment data to inform instruction and IEP planning (interpretation).

The purpose of this chapter is to describe how a standards-based IEP can support a well-designed educational program that ensures access to grade-level curriculum using effective instructional practices. After a description of the IEP as a document, some principles are offered for effective instruction for this population of students. Next is a description of how the IEP can promote good instruction, followed by suggestions for how states can provide guidance to IEP teams that are responsible for creating standards-based IEPs for this population of students. Requirements for state-level monitoring of IEP systems are also reviewed. The chapter ends with a section on validity evidence related to curriculum and instruction, as well as general conclusions. Although most of this chapter is written with the intent to promote ideal and potential best practices, there are still some areas in which current, realistic practices have been challenged to reach the optimal, "best practice." The conclusion of this chapter acknowledges some of these challenges. Along with the other two chapters in this section, which discuss possible characteristics of the target population, including how they learn, this chapter sets the stage for the remaining chapters on designing and implementing an AA-MAS.

AN OVERVIEW OF THE INDIVIDUALIZED EDUCATION PROGRAM

The IEP is written at least annually for each student with a documented disability. Although there are several required components, the general idea is to consider the student's present levels of performance and documented needs and strengths in order to create a comprehensive plan for the student's priorities that year. Those priorities do include academics, but also reflect other supports that are essential to provide the student with meaningful instruction given the features of his or her disability that make access more challenging. By specifying these supports, students can more fully participate and be successful in the pursuit of their educational goals. The IEP is written and its contents agreed upon by a team that includes one or more special education teachers, a general education teacher, other educational professionals (e.g., speech/language therapists, counselors), the student's parents or guardians, and, in some cases, the student as well.

IEPs have been part of special education services since 1975. However, they have not always played a central role in describing the academic curriculum. Karger (2004) reviewed the historical literature on IEPs and noted a variety of problems, including a disconnect between IEPs and the curriculum, poor congruence across sections within the IEP (e.g., between documented needs and annual goals), and special educator perceptions that the IEP was irrelevant to instruction. In the early years, IEPs documented special education services that ran parallel to general education (Ahearn, 2006). In the 1990s, IEP teams began determining that students would spend more time in general education settings, often for nonacademic activities (e.g., music classes, lunchtime in the cafeteria). This trend toward inclusion in general education settings gave students with disabilities more access to the school building, but did not give full access to the academic curriculum that was taught to students without disabilities. What special educators now refer to as "access to the general curriculum" was mandated in the purpose of special education as written in IDEA 1997:

> To address the unique needs of the child that result from the child's disability; and to ensure access of the child to the general curriculum, so that he or she can meet the educational standards within the jurisdiction of the public agency that apply to all children [34 C.F.R. § 300.26(b)(3)]

With the enactment of IDEA 1997, IEPs were required to address the student's present levels of performance, include annual goals and short-term objectives to help the student progress in the general curriculum, and document program modifications and supports the student would need in order to progress in the general curriculum. Thus IEP teams were first required to address general curriculum access just over a decade ago.

The next reauthorization of IDEA came after NCLB, in 2004. Under IDEA 2004, IEPs must now contain the following elements:

- A statement of the child's present levels of academic achievement and functional performance
- A statement of measurable annual goals, including academic and functional goals designed to (a) meet the child's needs that result from the child's disability to enable the child to be involved in and make progress in the general education curriculum; and (b) meet each of the child's other educational needs that result from the child's disability
- A statement of the special education and related services and supplementary aids and services, based on peer-reviewed research to the extent practicable, to be provided to the child, or on behalf of the child
- A statement of any individual appropriate accommodations that are necessary to measure the academic achievement and functional performance of the child on State and districtwide assessments consistent with section 612(a)(16) of the Act, and if the IEP Team determines that the child must take an alternate assessment instead of a particular regular State or districtwide assessment of student achievement, a

statement of why the child cannot participate in the general assessment and why the particular alternate assessment selected is appropriate for the child (34 C.F.R. §§ 300.320–300.324)

In designing the IEP, teams must consider the student's strengths, parents' concerns, results of the most recent evaluation, and "academic, developmental, and functional needs" of the child [34 C.F.R. § 300.324(a)(1)(i–iv)]. In addition, teams must decide whether certain special factors must be considered in planning the educational program for the student:

1. In the case of a child whose behavior impedes the child's learning or that of others, consider the use of positive behavioral interventions and supports, and other strategies, to address that behavior.

2. In the case of a child with limited English proficiency, consider the language needs of the child as those needs relate to the child's IEP.

3. In the case of a child who is blind or visually impaired, provide for instruction in Braille and the use of Braille unless the IEP Team determines, after an evaluation of the child's reading and writing skills, needs, and appropriate reading and writing media (including an evaluation of the child's future needs for instruction in Braille or the use of Braille), that instruction in Braille or the use of Braille is not appropriate for the child.

4. Consider the communication needs of the child, and in the case of a child who is deaf or hard of hearing, consider the child's language and communication needs, opportunities for direct communications with peers and professional personnel in the child's language and communication mode, academic level, and full range of needs, including opportunities for direct instruction in the child's language and communication mode.

5. Consider whether the child needs assistive technology devices and services. (34 C.F.R. § 300.324[a][2])

There is language throughout IDEA 2004 [see § 300.321(a)(1–7), § 300.321(b)(1–3)] that clearly emphasizes the academic curriculum and the link between assessment and instruction. The importance of academics is even recognized in guidance that general educators should be members of the IEP team. Relative to academic instruction, the IEP is now to reflect how the student will access the general curriculum and what the academic priorities are. New guidance on AA-MAS also calls for monitoring progress toward academic goals.

WHAT DOES IT MEAN FOR
AN IEP TO BE STANDARDS-BASED?

In interviews with representatives from 18 states, Ahearn (2006) found some confusion over the term *standards-based* as it applied to IEPs. Part of that confusion came from the different types of standards (i.e., content and achievement). IDEA 2004 requires "(i) A statement of measurable annual goals, including academic and functional goals designed to—(A) Meet the child's needs that result from the child's disability to enable the child to be involved in and make progress in the general education curriculum" [34 C.F.R. § 300.320(a)(2)(i)]. IEPs that meet the IDEA requirements include a broad range of information to explain how the student will access the general curriculum.

The two key elements specific to students who take AA-MAS are that there must be annual goals based on grade-level academic content standards and that there must be mechanisms in place to measure progress toward achieving those goals. The final AA-MAS regulations require that students' IEPs must:

1. "(A) include goals that are *based on the academic content standards for the grade in which the student is enrolled . . .* " That is, although students may have their performance evaluated against modified achievement standards, they must be taught academic content based on grade-level content standards.

2. ". . . and (B) be designed to *monitor the student's progress in achieving the standards-based goals*" [U.S. Department of Education, 2007a, 200.1, (f)(2)(ii)(A-B), emphasis added]

Although access to a curriculum based on state content standards has been guaranteed since 1997 and was reinforced in IDEA 2004, the requirement that state content standards be reflected in IEP goals is new with AA-MAS (Thurlow, 2008). States have taken various approaches to interpreting the requirement for standards-based IEPs (Ahearn, 2006). Students' present levels of academic performance are evaluated on the basis of their mastery of state content standards and areas in which they have not yet mastered those standards. Some states then require the IEP team to write goals that emphasize the skills the student will need in order to make progress in those content standards that have not yet been mastered. Other states require IEP teams to consider academic content standards broadly when evaluating present levels of performance and setting goals, but do not require teams to base those decisions on specific grade-level standards (Ahearn, 2006).

With the standards-based approach to IEPs, it is clear that these documents now play a much different role in educational planning in

2009 than they did in 1975. As states consider how to address the regulatory requirements for AA-MAS, it is important to keep in mind that the IEP cannot be a map of the entire academic curriculum for a student. It cannot contain documentation of all instructional strategies used with a student in a given year. It can, however, drive a purposeful planning process and ensure that good decisions about educational goals, grounded in a clear understanding of student needs, are established. Thus, before addressing IEPs directly, this chapter first considers implications for the planning, delivery, evaluation, and adjustment of instruction for this population of students.

EFFECTIVE CURRICULUM AND INSTRUCTION

One common criterion for determining eligibility for the AA-MAS is that the student will not attain proficiency on grade-level assessment in the *current year,* despite having received appropriate instruction all year. In reality, some students who are eligible for AA-MAS have probably not been proficient on grade-level assessments for *multiple years*—they are what some states call "persistently low-performing." Thus the target population may vary in their patterns of past performance, depending on how states define eligibility for the AA-MAS. Eligibility decisions based on past performance will be tied to states' guiding philosophies and theories of action about the AA-MAS (see Chapters 1 and 8). Regardless of past performance patterns, the assumption is that these students are unlikely to achieve proficiency on the general assessment despite having had instruction in grade-level academic content. Based on surveys and focus groups from teachers in several states, Perie (2009) synthesized findings from several focus groups on students who may be eligible for AA-MAS and provided a potential list of their characteristics:

- Require intensive, specially designed instruction and individualized supports
- Require repeated instruction in varied ways to make progress
- May be characterized as passive learners or non–risk takers
- Learning and meta-cognitive deficits (e.g., poor generalization, difficulty transitioning between topics, applying learned strategies) (slides 19–20)

Although this list is not exhaustive and may not represent the characteristics of students eligible for AA-MAS in all states, these types of characteristics reinforce the notion that highly effective instruction is the lynchpin for this population. Without meaningful access to the general curriculum, these students will have little hope of working toward grade-level expectations. What is essential in designing an instructional program that will help students meet these high expectations for growth? The Access Center (2006) offered the following as characteristics of educational programs that provide meaningful access to the general curriculum:

- The general education curriculum includes appropriate, standards-based instructional and learning goals for individual students with disabilities, as well as reflects an appropriate scope and sequence.

- Materials and media being used are appropriate, research-based, and documented as being effective in helping students with disabilities learn general education content and skills.

- Appropriate, research-based instructional methods and practices that have a track record for helping students with disabilities learn general education content and skills are being used.

- Research-based supports and accommodations that have a track record of helping students with disabilities learn general education content and skills are being used.

- Appropriate tools and procedures for assessing and documenting whether students with disabilities are meeting high standards and achieving their instructional goals are being used (pp. 4, 6).

This section of the chapter describes several characteristics of highly effective curriculum and instruction for students who present with the challenges described previously.

Students Are Given Access to Grade-Level Content

As noted earlier, ensuring access to grade-level content standards is a fundamental expectation in the federal regulations on AA-MAS [U.S. Department of Education, 2007b, § 200.1(f)(2)(iii)]. State content standards are often organized around content knowledge and processes reflected in standards or frameworks from national groups (e.g., National Council of Teachers of Mathematics, 2000; National Reading Panel, 2000). States differ in the grain size (i.e., level of specificity) and sequences of content area skills and knowledge when articulating their content standards. (See Chapter 4 for additional discussion on state content standards.)

By law, students eligible for AA-MAS are to be taught a curriculum that is based on chronologically appropriate, grade-level standards. Unlike AA-AAS, where students receive instruction in content that "links" to grade-level content standards, students who take AA-MAS are expected to be working "in" grade-level content standards. That does not mean they are taught the state standards directly; instead, they are provided with a curriculum that is aligned to state standards. In Chapter 4, Pugalee and Rickelman define *curriculum* as "a set of planned instructional activities that are designed to allow students to document achievement of their knowledge and skills" (p. 114).

One of the challenges in targeting academic goals for this target population of students is that they may lack foundational skills from earlier grade levels upon which the current grade-level content standards are based. Teachers will walk a fine line between helping the student master skills from earlier grades while also being taught a curriculum based on current grade-level standards. Ahearn (2006) offered the following for how students might work toward IEP goals based on content standards from an earlier grade:

> Such students are expected to make more than one year of progress through standards-based instruction because the needed skills are targeted by the teacher. Teachers scaffold instruction (i.e., provide supports as necessary) and prerequisite skills are used to work toward the grade-level standards. For example, a student who cannot read 6th grade materials may work toward a grade-level standard that calls for analyzing written materials. The cognitive processes associated with that higher level reading skill can still be taught while the student accesses the grade-level materials in a different way. (p. 8)

The caution here is that, according to the AA-MAS regulations, IEP goals must be based on the current (chronologically appropriate) grade-level content standards. In order to plan an effective curriculum based on remediation of missing skills and progress in current skills, teachers will have to be knowledgeable about how topics within a strand (e.g., algebra, writing) relate to each other within a grade level and how they build across grades. Teachers also will need to make choices about how best to sample content from within a standard. Clear alignment between assessment and instruction is essential if student assessment scores are to allow for valid inferences about proficiency against a set of standards (American Educational Research Association [AERA], American Psychological Association [APA], & National Council on Measurement in Education [NCME], 1999). General education teachers with expertise in content areas may play a critical role in helping special educators select content and design instruction for this population. These content experts will be fluent in their state's grade-level content standards and national standards for the discipline, know how instruction is designed to promote learning in that skill, and understand how the components relate to and build upon each other (see Chapter 4).

Curriculum materials can make it easier (or more difficult) for teachers to deliver grade-level curriculum. Adaptations of grade-level materials may be increasingly necessary the farther away from grade-level proficiency a student is working, and the more unique or complex the student's learning needs. The accessibility issue related to curriculum materials becomes increasingly important as students enter upper grade levels. In middle schools, textbooks are more like reference books and contain vocabulary that is above grade level; factual knowledge is emphasized over procedural knowledge (Hill & Erwin, 1984; Jitendra et al., 2001). There may be a tendency for special educators working with students eligible for AA-MAS to significantly adapt materials, potentially jeopardizing access to grade-level content if the adaptations stretch too far.

Instruction Consists of Proven Practices that Allow Teachers to Set a Trajectory Toward Performance that Can Be Evaluated Against Grade-Level Achievement Standards

Meaningful progress toward grade-level achievement requires accurate assessment of the student's current level of performance—using multiple, high-quality assessments that are appropriate for the student and provide valid inferences about strengths and areas for growth [34 C.F.R. § 200.1(e)(2)(ii)(B)]. When states determine eligibility for AA-MAS based on a pattern of low performance across years (versus a single year), baseline performance may also be investigated retrospectively to help teachers determine how firmly established a pattern of limited or no progress has been. Armed with this information, teachers would then also draw on their knowledge about how students learn in order to plan instruction. (See Chapter 3 for an extensive description of student cognition.)

Once present levels of performance are known, teachers will then adopt research-based strategies—those that work with the type of student whose IEP they are designing. The What Works Clearinghouse (WWC; http://ies.ed.gov/ncee/wwc/) is one source of information about which interventions have evidence of effectiveness. However, one pitfall is that the strict evidence standards set by the WWC means that when the evidence base is sparse or based on less rigorous designs (e.g., those without a comparison group), emerging evidence is not synthesized. For example, in a March 2009 search of the middle school math interventions listed by WWC, only 12 of 50 interventions had reports available. (Two more reports were pending.) The rest were not synthesized because of a lack of studies that met the criteria. Even when the WWC offers helpful syntheses, teachers will need to consider whether the interventions "work" for students who are eligible for AA-MAS based on their state's criteria. When WWC evidence is lacking, the field may look to other sources of evidence for state-of-the-art practice (see the Spring 2009 issue of *Exceptional Children* [Cook,

Tankersley, & Landrum, 2009], for example, or literature syntheses and meta-analyses published in journals such as *Review of Educational Research* [e.g., Slavin, Lake, Chambers, Cheung, & Davis, 2009]). Teachers may also rely on evidence related to particular instructional strategies if content-specific intervention evidence is not yet available. For instance, there is evidence that frequent opportunities to respond during instruction increases the rate of correct responses and frequency of on-task behaviors (Haydon, Mancil, & Van Loan, 2009). Increasing the amount of instructional time devoted to key concepts also has an impact on learning for students who may be at risk for academic failure (Harn, Linan-Thompson, & Roberts, 2008). Instructional pacing may need to vary depending on familiarity of content and the extent to which learning activities follow a routine (Ylvisaker, 2006). Sources such as the *Journal of Applied Behavior Analysis,* which publish single-subject research on discrete instructional techniques for students with particular learning needs, are another source of evidence for effective strategies.

Selecting research-based strategies and applying them indiscriminately will not automatically boost student learning. Teachers also use their knowledge of content and how skills link and build upon one another toward a goal for performance that year. Concepts such as learning progressions and learning maps will be discussed in detail later in this volume (Chapters 3, 4, 6, and 8), but it is worth mentioning them briefly here. Where research exists to support cognitive models of learning, teachers may use those models to plan for a sequence of instruction. Where such evidence does not yet exist, familiarity with typical content sequences may guide planning. Previous years' large-scale assessment scores, interpreted at the strand or topic level, along with state-provided guidance about how content is expected to build across grades, may be useful. Because all students do not learn in the same sequence, awareness of when skills really are (or are not) prerequisite or foundational concepts will also be important. Regardless of whether the teacher thinks in terms of progressions, maps, or sequences, identifying baseline knowledge and skills at a fine-grained level (e.g., a student's specific content knowledge within strands and process skills within a subject area) rather than coarse-grained level (e.g., the student scored below basic in English language arts the previous year), the foundation will be set for a meaningful path for teaching and learning.

If teachers have accurately identified present levels of performance and effective instructional strategies for that skill and that student, and have a solid understanding of how to build skills in that area, what should be the target for that student? One option would be to consider the state's modified achievement level descriptors and evaluate how much progress the student would need to make in order to move from his or her current AA-MAS achievement level to the next highest one (see Chapter 6 for a discussion of modified achievement standards). Over a period of years, long-term planning for the student could include annual goals for certain skills with a multiyear goal of transitioning back to eligibility for assessment options based on grade-level achievement standards. IEP teams will make decisions about how to set interim achievement targets at lower levels while also maintaining the highest possible performance expectations. General educators with deep content expertise may be helpful in setting reasonable interim targets. The concepts of learning progressions or learning maps may also guide decisions about interim targets. IEP teams may wish to guard against setting lower targets for several consecutive years, as there may be a point at which the student is unintentionally tracked into a level of performance that precludes his or her later participation in assessments based on grade-level achievement standards.

Assuming a growth trajectory has been set and the student makes progress during the academic year, there is a risk that the student will lose momentum—and perhaps even lose ground that was gained—during long breaks (i.e., summer vacation on a 9-month calendar or intersession on a year-round calendar). IEP teams have the option to include extended school year (ESY) services as part of the student's plan in order to prevent loss of the skills and knowledge that the student built during the academic year.

Instruction Is Flexible and Responsive to Student Progress

Even with a well-designed, long-term plan for instruction, teachers cannot just assume the student will progress according to that plan. They will need to monitor progress closely and know when to make decisions to adjust instruction. A vague plan to monitor progress using "teacher observation" will not be sufficient. Teachers need to know how to design or identify, and use, effective formative assessment methods.

Established techniques such as curriculum-based measurement (CBM) and progress monitoring can help teachers track student progress. CBM offers a way to periodically assess student progress toward long-term goals using assessments that are technically sound but easy to use in everyday instruction (Deno, 2003; Stecker, Fuchs, & Fuchs, 2005). Stecker (n.d.) provides a concise overview of how to use CBM for progress monitoring, including how to use CBM data to set IEP goals and short-term objectives. One option for monitoring progress is for teachers to chart performance on a graph with a super-

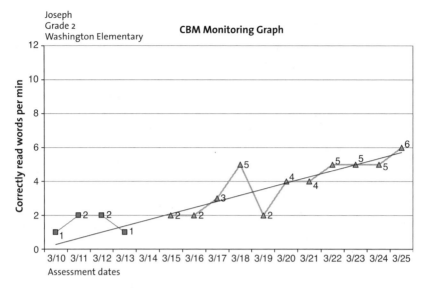

Figure 2.1. Example of a graph for tracking student progress against a trajectory. (*Key:* triangles, monitoring correctly read words [CRW]; squares, baseline CRW; line, curriculum-based measurement [CBM] trend line.)

imposed trend line (see an example in Figure 2.1). Establishing the trend line between present level of performance and target level of performance helps the teacher monitor interim progress. There are numerous resources available on the internet for teachers to customize and create graphs for tracking student progress using Excel or web-based forms (e.g., http://www.easycbm.com and http://www.jimwrightonline.com/php/rti/rti_wire.php). A synthesis report published by the National Center on Educational Outcomes (NCEO; Quenemoen, Thurlow, Moen, Thompson, & Morse, 2004) places short-term CBM in the broader context of progress monitoring linked to summative assessments and improvement across years.

As the literature base on CBM and progress monitoring grows, new studies emerge that may help teachers refine their practice to maximize benefit while minimizing effort. For example, Jenkins, Graff, and Miglioretti (2009) determined that *reading growth* (defined as words read correctly) could be determined with less frequent measurement but that it was important to obtain sufficient baseline data and an appropriate number of measurements at each data collection period. Benefits may also be realized by designing instruction that features alternating treatments in order to compare the efficacy of two approaches for teaching the same skill.

Teachers may effectively set a goal, collect data to measure progress using technically sound measures, and recognize when students are not progressing as they had hoped. The other critical skill is how to determine *why* that progress has not been made. If present levels of performance and student needs were correctly identified in the planning stages, the teacher may be reasonably satisfied that there were no unidentified deficits in prerequisite concepts. However, the teacher may find weaknesses in student knowledge of certain components of the target skill or may be able to uncover the source of the problem through error analysis and identification of the student's faulty thinking. Although the adjustment of instruction is dealt with extensively in the progress monitoring and response to intervention (RTI) literature, Nitko (2004) offered several general recommendations for how to conduct diagnostic assessments of students' problems in learning targeted content. The ability to monitor and adjust instruction requires creativity and persistence by teachers who design and deliver the instructional program.

Decisions about adjusting instruction may also emerge if groups of teachers collaborate to review student assessment data. Through grade-level team meetings or a professional learning community model, teachers could evaluate previous large-scale assessment results to plan for instruction. By examining individual student data for an entire grade level, teachers may uncover similarities in student performance and learning approaches across classrooms. Using a systematic process to pose questions about the data, analyze the data, and articulate the findings from that analysis, teams would be equipped with more information to then plan instructional changes for targeted groups of students. The types of questions to be asked of large-scale data will vary depending on the needs in the school. In a description of one process taught to teacher leaders, Henning (2006) identified four general categories of analysis for large-scale assessment scores, including 1) comparisons to the norm, 2) analysis of trends over time, 3) correlations between test performance and other measures, and 4) disaggregating data to examine subgroups. These approaches might also be used in conjunction with one another (e.g., analysis of trends for subgroups). Fisher, Lapp, Frey, Flood, and Moore (2007) also suggested conducting basic item analysis to identify popular distractors and evaluate potential sources underlying those misconceptions. If the state provides interim benchmark tests that give formative feedback on progress toward mastery of the content standards, or if teachers agree to use common formative assessments across classes, their capacity to identify successful strategies and share that information with other teachers is also enhanced. By collaborating to analyze and interpret test scores, rather than working in isolation, teachers create instructional goals that are more coherent across classrooms and better aligned to state content standards (Fisher et al., 2007).

The Instructional Program Minimizes Barriers and Provides the Full Range of Supports Necessary to Promote Growth

To provide effective instruction, teachers need to determine what aspect of student performance represents the student's actual mastery level and skill deficits and what aspects may be related to the disability or other barriers to learning. IEP teams are responsible for determining what types of accommodations are appropriate in instruction and assessment on the basis of how the student's disability impedes his or her ability to learn in the general curriculum. (See "State Guidance to Individualized Education Program Teams" later in this chapter for a full discussion of accommodations.) If the student has characteristics considered under IDEA to be special factors that interfere with learning (behavior, limited English proficiency, visual impairment, hearing impairment, or the need for assistive technologies), those areas must also be addressed. As the options for assistive technologies expand, teachers will need good resources for identifying appropriate devices that minimize barriers stemming from specific student needs. Teachers may also want to consider how environmental variables, such as instructional setting and grouping, may influence students' access to the general curriculum (Soukup, Wehmeyer, Bashinski, & Bovaird, 2007).

Given the diversity of students who may be eligible for AA-MAS, not all students in a class will need the same learning supports. It is possible that students eligible for AA-MAS can receive learning supports as a matter of standard practice for *all* students. Differentiated instruction allows teachers to identify how each eligible student will access grade-level content, respond to student progress and adjust instruction accordingly, and incorporate learning supports needed as a result of student disabilities. For students who may be eligible for AA-MAS because of a pattern of low achievement despite appropriate instruction, Harn, Linan-Thompson, and Roberts (2008) noted

> That they need "more intensive intervention" is the common refrain, but what features do we intensify? Do we increase time, explicitness of instruction, opportunities to respond? Do we decrease group size, the number of instructional components taught, or some combination of all these features? (p. 116)

Differentiation is more than just grouping—it involves variation in the curriculum (i.e., different materials) and how it is taught (i.e., individual work, small group, whole group; Gibson & Hasbrouck, 2008). Depending on students' prior knowledge and different ways of learning, it may also require targeting different expectations for depth of learning. However, differentiation for the target population cannot involve teaching to lower grade-level standards.

There are two more promising options for minimizing barriers and providing supports that are worth mentioning here. Both are applicable to broader ranges of students and may be useful beyond the target population for AA-MAS. Universal design for learning (UDL) offers a framework for reducing barriers by allowing for multiple means of representation, expression, and engagement (CAST, 2008). UDL is offered as a way to build flexibility and differentiation into instruction from the outset, thereby avoiding the need to adapt curriculum after the fact. RTI focuses on prevention of long-term failure through early assessment and intervention, with frequent progress monitoring and adjustment (National Center on Response to Intervention, n.d.). Although described in IDEA 2004 as a means of identifying and serving students with specific learning disabilities, RTI can be applied to an entire student body for multitiered interventions rather than a single subpopulation with identified disabilities. For more information on RTI, readers are encouraged to review Chapter 1 and visit the web site http://www.rti4success.org.

This section provides just an overview of principles that may guide effective instruction. States and LEAs will determine how best instructional practices translate locally, given state policies and local norms. However, the practices described here offer alternatives to help students who need to demonstrate substantial progress if they hope to reach grade-level proficiency. In many ways, the principles described here are suggestions for operationalizing the IDEA requirement for specifically designed instruction [20 U.S.C. § 1401(29)]. At the same time, principles such as UDL reflect the idea that good instruction for all students requires some level of differentiation to target strengths and needs.

USING THE IEP TO PROMOTE QUALITY INSTRUCTION

The federal guidance that requires the IEP to contain goals based on grade-level content standards implies that what gets documented is what gets taught. However, the IEP cannot reflect a student's entire academic curriculum in detail. How does the IEP meet the letter of the law while also providing a blueprint for the student's broader educational needs? This section offers suggestions for how to use the IEP to guide high-quality academic instruction by identifying needs, writing goals, and monitoring progress. It concludes with a discussion on how IEP teams can discuss and select optimal supports based on individual needs.

Reviewing Present Levels of Performance and Identifying Need

When planning an IEP, teams carefully consider present levels of performance and prioritize needs in order to support growth toward grade-level achievement. Present levels of performance may be described using recent assessment data (collected using sound measures) that are specific about student performance and areas for growth. For example, an IEP team will be better able to target goals in areas of need with detailed description (e.g., "Joey can read fifth grade texts with 70% accuracy and 85 words per minute but has difficulty inferring meaning of unfamiliar words using context clues") than with generalities (e.g., "according to the Woodcock-Johnson, Joey is reading at grade level 4.2"). CBM may be useful in determining present levels of performance, as a series of baseline measures can be used to describe student performance in specific ways that promote good goal-setting (Stecker, n.d.).

Selecting and Writing Academic Goals

The final regulations for AA-MAS indicate that the IEP must contain goals "based on the academic content standards for the grade in which the student is enrolled" [U.S. Department of Education, 2007a, p. 9; 200.1(e)(2)(iii)]. Because the AA-MAS must cover the same range of content as the typical grade-level assessment (U.S. Department of Education, 2007b, p. 21), IEP teams will need to consider the full range of grade-level content standards for each subject to determine what strands or objectives represent priorities for instruction. Besides data from individually administered, standardized or unstandardized assessments, teams may also wish to review the student's performance on the previous year's large-scale assessment. Ideally, the team could examine competencies within strands or domains if the state provides feedback on achievement within those smaller units of content. It is important to remember that if a student takes an AA-MAS in one subject but is eligible for assessment against grade-level achievement standards in other subjects, the IEP is not required to include those areas assessed against grade-level standards. In other words, IEP goals are only required for areas in which the student's disability is interfering with participation in the grade-level achievement test. However, the

IEP team may choose to write goals for subjects in which the student is assessed against grade-level achievement standards.

In subjects the IEP team has determined will be assessed using the AA-MAS, the target for instruction is the student's chronologically age-appropriate, grade-level content standards. Even if a state has designed its content standards as vertical progressions that build across grade levels, it is not acceptable to base IEP goals on academic standards at a lower grade level (NCEO, 2007).

Annual IEP goals represent priorities in the student's curriculum that year. That does not mean that the content of a goal statement must match the wording of a state content standard. IEP teams may identify essential skills that support general curriculum access in that area. Indeed, teams may identify pivotal skills—those that cross academic subjects and promote growth across the curriculum (Browder, Spooner, Wakeman, Trela, & Baker, 2006). For example, the team may write a goal for the student to learn certain strategies for monitoring comprehension of a reading passage. This self-evaluation skill may not be part of a reading content standard in that grade level, but a student who can monitor comprehension may make better progress in reading as well as other content areas. As Pellegrino notes in Chapter 3, metacognitive skills are most effective if taught in specific content areas rather than outside the context of a content area. A team may determine that a specific content goal is the best choice to support the student's growth toward grade-level proficiency, but the team should be discouraged from treating the content standards as an à la carte menu.

Once the priorities for IEP goal contents have been determined, the team then follows best practices for writing effective IEP goals. Good IEP goals are measurable, which means they cannot be vaguely written and need to reflect an observable behavior. They also specify the conditions under which the behavior will be demonstrated and the criterion for performance. There are numerous guides for writing effective IEP goals. Two excellent examples are Bateman and Herr (2006) and Courtade-Little and Browder (2005).

Monitoring Goal Attainment

With IDEA 2004, IEP teams are no longer required to write short-term objectives (STOs) for each goal [except for students who will be assessed using AA-AAS; see U.S. Department of Education, 2007b, p. 29; IDEA, 614(d)(1)(A)(I)(cc)]. Without this requirement, IEP teams will need to be diligent in thinking through and planning for progress monitoring. Progress must be reported at least as frequently as it is for students without disabilities (which typically translates to a report card cycle). It is hard to imagine that students eligible for AA-MAS can successfully accelerate their learning if teachers are doing the bare minimum to meet the letter of the law for monitoring progress. Bateman and Herr (2006) offer a convincing argument that teams should write STOs to operationalize the broader goal, even though that step is no longer federally required. Teams may also develop and document other methods in accordance with their state's interpretation of the federal requirement to monitor progress.

Regardless of whether teams write STOs for students eligible for AA-MAS, it is important that the criterion reflected in the goal be based on projected growth from present level of performance, in a given period of time, with a target that sets the student on a path toward grade-level achievement. Ideally, methods for monitoring goal attainment would follow some of the CBM or progress monitoring approaches described earlier in this chapter. Again, these methods would be based on technically sound, appropriate assessment instruments administered at a frequency that allows teachers to monitor and report progress and adjust instruction without becoming a burdensome process that detracts from instruction.

Choosing and Designing Supports

As mentioned previously, IEP teams will design educational programs for students eligible for AA-MAS that allow for achievement based on modified rather than grade-level achievement standards while also building toward eventual participation in assessments based on grade-level achievement standards. IEP teams will decide how to design appropriate supports for learning without setting the standard so low that the student is not held to the highest expectations possible that year. The IEP can provide clear markers about what supports are needed, in which parts of the curriculum, and under what conditions. If the team instead provides blanket coverage of certain supports across all subject areas and settings (including accommodations, positive behavior support plans, and ESY services), the team may end up overcompensating for the student's disability and providing supports that are not needed or even serve to limit student growth.

One decision support tool IEP teams can use to plan for academic instruction is provided in Table 2.1 (Quenemoen, 2009). Teams can ask themselves a series of questions to consider individual student strengths and needs within the context of his or her educational system. These questions would be asked and answered differently for each student, because each student may have different priorities for the academic year.

Table 2.1.   Question guide to support individualized education program (IEP) team decision-making process

System opportunities and challenges (representatives from school and district must provide this information and support)	Student strengths and needs (IEP team grapples with data-based decision making to identify services, supports, and specialized instruction so that the student will be successful)
1. What is the required content in the next grade level?	1. What are the student's current strengths and needs in the academic content areas? What data do we have to make that determination? What accelerated or remedial services and supports are necessary to ensure success in the content for the next grade level?
2. Where and when during the school year is the required content taught in Math? English Language Arts? Science? Social Studies? Other? How is it taught?	2. What adaptations and accommodations can the student use to access the grade-level content regardless of specific deficit basic skills in reading or mathematics or English language? What data do we have to support these choices? How will we determine whether their use is effective or needs changing?
3. What instructional and curricular options are currently available in this school to allow all students to achieve proficiency in the goals and standards set for all students?	3. What specific instructional strategies work well for this student? What types of curricular materials work well for this student? If the needs of this student and the options available don't align well, what aids, services, supports, and instruction does the student need to be successful despite gaps? How can the current options be changed?
4. What array of services does the school provide to meet the students' other needs?	4. What specific nonacademic needs does this student have? What goals and objectives will address those needs? How do these relate to the student's academic success?
5. What is the curricular map into the future, and what are essential understandings every student needs to achieve this year?	5. How can we set priorities to ensure the essential understandings are mastered by this student, but still allow the time the school and the student need to address all needs?
6. How does all this go together, with professional development, support, continuous improvement, community linkages ... so that all children are successful?	6. How do we align curriculum, instruction, supports, services, and needs so that this child is successful at grade level?

From Quenemoen, R. (2009). *Success one student at a time: What the IEP team does*. Minneapolis, MN: University of Minnesota, National Center on Educational Outcomes. Retrieved April 20, 2009, from http://www.nceo.info/Tools/StandardsIEPtool.pdf; reprinted by permission.

It will be important for IEP teams to carefully consider the implication of choosing a particular type of adaptation for the student's educational program and progress. If the content is significantly modified, teachers run the risk of unintentionally lowering expectations for the student. If the student is eligible for the AA-MAS because his or her disability precluded success in assessments based on grade-level achievement standards [as required in 34 C.F.R. § 200.1(e)(2)(i)], designing instruction that changes the construct may lead teachers to continue a pattern of working around the disability (i.e., modification) rather than eliminating its influence through effective supports (i.e., accommodation). Again, the educators on IEP teams will need to be very skilled in choosing adaptations and evaluating their impact on the student.

STATE GUIDANCE TO IEP TEAMS

Just as teachers design supports for student learning, states offer supports to IEP teams so educators can effectively meet the lofty goals described earlier. As a matter of routine, states already provide guidance to IEP teams on how to manage the "paperwork" aspect of IEPs (i.e., adhering to procedural aspects of IDEA, appropriate documentation of required IEP components). However, now that the IEP is a living document rather than a bureaucratic formality (Sopko, 2003), states have opportunities to provide a wide array of guidance to help teams design effective instructional programs as well. Recognizing that districts and individual schools act as a filter to interpret state guidance, this section highlights supports that states may wish to provide IEP teams planning for this target population of students.

Decisions About Participation in AA-MAS

Federal regulations to guide eligibility for AA-MAS are detailed in the final AA-MAS regulations and elsewhere in this volume (see Introduction). At a minimum, states are responsible for clearly conveying to the IEP team

- That a student from any disability category may be eligible for AA-MAS [34 C.F.R. § 200.1(f)(1)(ii)]
- Various options for students with disabilities to participate in statewide assessment (including assessments based on grade level, modified, or alternate achievement standards), including the impact of assessment choice on the student's educational options according to state or local policy [34 C.F.R. § 200.1(f)(1)(iii)]
- Clear and appropriate guidelines to determine when AA-MAS is the appropriate assessment option [34 C.F.R. § 200.1(f)(1)(i)]
- That students may be assessed against modified achievement standards in one or more subjects for which assessments are administered under § 200.2 [34 C.F.R. § 200.1(f)(2)(i)]

Teams must also use of a pattern of data to determine the appropriate assessment participation option (U.S. Department of Education, 2007b, p. 18). States may also wish to give IEP teams guidance on when it would be appropriate for a student to resume participation in state assessments on the basis of grade-level achievement standards.

Regardless of states' eligibility criteria, IEP teams will need clear guidance that allows them to differentiate in rather nuanced situations. Specific criteria and supporting rationales will help IEP teams understand how the criteria apply to each student. States may find that a flowchart, checklist, or other decision support tool may help teams correctly apply the criteria to arrive at appropriate eligibility determinations. Lazarus, Rogers, Cormier, and Thurlow (2008) reviewed states' AA-MAS participation guidelines and found 15 categories of criteria across nine states that had an operational AA-MAS. Most frequently occurring were criteria based on the regulatory language (e.g., must have an IEP; decision not made based on a specific disability label; not progressing at a rate at which the student would be expected to reach grade-level proficiency within the year; the use of multiple measures to determine previous performance; student cannot demonstrate knowledge on grade-level assessment even with appropriate accommodations). Some states also provided exclusion criteria, such as not being based on placement setting, not being eligible for AA-AAS, and not having a pattern of past performance attributable to excessive absences or other noninstructional factors (e.g., cultural, language, economic).

Lazarus et al. (2008) also compiled the materials they reviewed from the nine states into their synthesis report. As states think about how to provide clear guidance to IEP teams about appropriate assessment participation decisions, they may wish to adapt some of these published examples for their own use. For example, Maryland provides an IEP Team Decision-Making Process Eligibility Tool that teams can use to compile past assessment data, past instruction, and clear evidence of specific content-area interventions and relevant IEP goals in the past years. That type of tool could be helpful to teams in determining that the student really had received effective instruction in prior years. As another example, North Dakota provides an eight-item checklist with an accompanying flowchart to guide teams to the most appropriate large-scale assessment option for the student. As more states move closer to deciding whether and how to provide AA-MAS options, additional examples will likely be forthcoming.

Decisions About Accommodations

IEP teams make choices about what accommodations are appropriate under which circumstances. Accommodations remove the influence of a disability on a student's ability to show what she or he knows and can do. Accommodations should not be confused with modifications, which are adaptations that change the construct being taught or assessed. IEP teams determine appropriate accommodations based on how the disability influences the individual student's participation in the educational program. Accommodation needs may differ by subject area or type of learning activity and are determined separately for instruction, classroom assessment, and statewide assessment. Accommodations typically fall into one of four categories: presentation format, response format, timing, and setting (AERA et al., 1999). IEP teams are to choose the right kinds of accommodations for the right student in order to reduce construct-irrelevant variance and allow for valid inferences about student performance on assessments. The chosen accommodations should also provide sufficient support for the student to fully participate in instruction. (Accommodations are discussed in more detail in Chapter 7).

Unfortunately, there is a history of IEP teams having difficulty correctly interpreting accommodations (Byrnes, 2008) and choosing and applying accommodations (Shriner & Destefano, 2003) using best-practice principles. There may be confusion on the team about issues such as when to use accommodations and the difference between an accommodation and a modification. When choosing accommodations for AA-MAS, IEP teams are required to avoid accommodations that would, if used on the grade-level assessment, invalidate the score (U.S. Department of Education, 2007b, p. 27).

IEP teams will also consider the match between accommodations given for instructional purposes and in large-scale assessments. There is extensive literature supporting the correspondence between these two, but IDEA gives IEP teams latitude to allow instructional accommodations that would be considered necessary "for a student to advance toward attaining his or her annual goals, to be involved in and make progress in the general curriculum, and to be educated alongside his or her nondisabled peers" [U.S. Department of Education, 2007b, pp. 32–33; see also 34 C.F.R. § 300.320(a)(4)(i–iii)]. In other words, there is no legislation that precludes the use of accommodations in instruction that would invalidate results if used on a statewide assessment. Conversely, states may prohibit the use of accommodations on an assessment if they have not also been given in instruction. Given this potential mismatch, IEP teams will need to be deliberate in their choice of instructional accommodations beyond those that will be allowable for the assessment the student will take.

States can support the appropriate choice of accommodations in several ways. They can provide full descriptions of the types of accommodations, with examples, organized by category and with indications about where their use is appropriate. They may offer guiding questions for IEP teams to consider when choosing appropriate accommodations.

The Council of Chief State School Officers *Accommodations Manual* (Thompson, Morse, Sharpe, & Hall, 2005) includes a framework for each of these types of supports. States may also develop decision support materials or even computer-based tools, such as those described by Kopriva, Koran, and Hedgspeth (2007).

Regardless of which accommodations a state approves, the decisions should be made using the best data available. NCEO offers an online accommodation bibliography (http://www2.cehd.umn.edu/NCEO/accommodations/), which is a searchable database with annotated bibliographies that allow for quick scanning of outcomes across studies. As states deliberate which accommodations to allow under which conditions, they will need a process to review those potential accommodations. One such process, using a panel review, is described in Almond and Karvonen (2007). Finally, Thurlow, Christensen, and Lail (2008) summarized a review of reviewer comments made about accommodations practices described in states' peer review materials. Lessons learned from past peer reviews may be informative to states that implement new accommodations policies or options for AA-MAS–eligible students.

Other Guidance

State and local educational agencies coordinate and sponsor professional development for teachers on a wide array of topics. They may not be able to cover every topic described in this chapter, but an effective needs assessment could reveal areas to prioritize in planning professional development on topics related to students eligible for AA-MAS. Special education bureaus may be able to sponsor professional development on topics such as determining academic priorities, interpreting large-scale assessment data for instructional decision making, designing learning progressions, differentiating and adjusting instruction, CBM, and progress monitoring. As new technologies or teaching strategies become available, professional development plans may be adjusted to incorporate promising practices. Job-embedded professional development (e.g., professional learning communities, instructional coaches) may be the best approach to support teachers as they develop these instructional skills (Joyce & Showers, 2002).

Also, because the instructional implications associated with AA-MAS are relatively new, states should not overlook the importance of addressing teacher beliefs about what this population of students can do and how to hold them to high expectations (see Chapter 1). States may wish to provide guidance to IEP teams on how to set interim achievement targets that are lower without precluding students from being eligible for assessments based on grade-level achievement standards by the time they would need to take assessments linked to high school graduation requirements. The Access Center (2004) provides several other suggestions for how states can offer training on IEP writing.

States may also be able to warehouse on their web sites a wide variety of sample materials, including well-structured IEP goals and objectives, links to information on research-based curricula, assistive technologies, and data collection materials for formative assessment. One example is the site developed by the Georgia Department of Education for teachers of students who take the state's AA-AAS (http://gadoe.georgiastandards.org/impairment.aspx). These web sites may also offer a way for teachers to exchange their own created materials through a community working toward the same goal— figuring out how to do what nobody has yet done for these students. State-level assessment departments could coordinate resources related to large-scale assessment. Assessment and special education divisions could collaborate to provide guidance on how to link formative and summative assessments.

Finally, states and LEAs may provide guidance and professional development to strengthen collaboration among IEP team members. Successful instruction for students eligible for AA-MAS will require effective collaboration between general educators and special educators. In schools where the responsibility for educating this population still lays solely with the special education staff, administrators may want to guide a shift toward the philosophy that the whole school is responsible. The principal, as instructional leader for all students, may need to send a strong message in order to prompt this shift.

One other aspect of collaboration should not be neglected. Parents are partners on the IEP team and must be equipped to be meaningful contributors to the planning that will take place. They will need to understand what the AA-MAS is and what participation means for their children [§ 200.1(f)(1)(iv)]. If the instructional program under AA-MAS represents a fork in the road leading away from past practices, parents will also need to understand what to expect differently in terms of progress monitoring, reporting progress to families, and mid-year instructional changes. One excellent resource for this information is a parent guide published by the NCEO (Cortiella, 2007).

VALIDITY EVIDENCE

This chapter has addressed standards-based IEPs as vehicles for designing effective curriculum and instruction in order to help students eligible for AA-MAS access grade-level content and make progress toward grade-level proficiency. This section describes how instructional issues contribute to the validity argument for AA-MAS.

The clearest link between instruction and assessment validity is OTL. If scores on the AA-MAS are intended to reflect modified achievement of grade-level content standards, one premise is that students have had the opportunity to learn the content that is assessed. Marion (Chapter 8) offers two sample theories of action that illustrate how states might articulate the role of instruction in their validity arguments. One premise in his first example is that "teachers provide instruction that is aligned with these high academic expectations and ensure that students get the supports necessary to allow them to succeed with grade-level content" (p. 255). If this statement was supported by evidence, low scores would reflect limited achievement in the target domain, rather than lack of instruction in that domain.

For students who take AA-MAS, OTL requires instruction in the targeted content domain, with supports that remove barriers related to the disability. OTL is a matter of degree rather than an absolute dichotomy and can be difficult to measure (AERA et al., 1999, Standard 13.5). Alignment studies provide one way of assessing correspondence between curriculum and assessment. Teacher-reported curriculum measures such as Surveys of Enacted Curriculum (Porter & Smithson, 2001) or the Curriculum Indicators Survey (Karvonen, Wakeman, Flowers, & Browder, 2007) are a way of incorporating curricular data in alignment studies.

IEPs also offer a source of evidence related to OTL and can be used for other validity investigations as well. Content analysis can yield data such as the following:

- Curricular priorities reflected in the IEP, which can then be evaluated against grade-level content standards to document instruction in the intended content. Curricular priorities may also be compared with AA-MAS content, although that type of comparison does not yield strong "alignment" evidence.

- The quality of the instruction program for providing general curriculum access through

  —Links between present levels of performance and annual goals

  —Correspondence between accommodations provided for instruction and assessment

  —Evaluative judgments about criteria for performance specified in the academic goals and whether the expected growth from present level of performance to end-of-year goal reflects reasonable (and high) expectations

  —Appropriate use of other learning supports to promote meaningful access and remove barriers (e.g., ESY services, behavior intervention plans)

- Evidence of appropriate decisions made about student participation in AA-MAS

Investigators may determine whether the student's past pattern of instruction really does point to eligibility based on poor performance despite effective instruction, especially through use of retrospective analysis of multiple IEPs or the IEP decision support tools described in the eligibility section earlier in this chapter.

Two investigations of this nature are being conducted at the time of this writing, although the studies have not yet reached the data analysis phase (Karvonen, 2009).

Finally, evidence of the instructional program may be linked to student test scores and desired student outcomes (AERA et al., 1999, Standard 13.9). Although this type of investigation addresses validity evidence in cases where the score leads to high-stakes decisions for the individual student (e.g., promotion, graduation), one could argue that the stakes for students taking the AA-MAS are high every year if they are to reach grade-level proficiency in the future. The comment on Standard 13.9 relative to special education is as follows:

> When test scores are used in the development of specific educational objectives and instructional strategies, evidence is needed to show that the prescribed instruction enhances students' learning. When there is limited evidence about the relationship among test results, instructional plans, and student achievement outcomes, test developers and users should stress the tentative nature of test-based recommendations. (p. 147)

Thus, if a state chooses a model in which performance on an AA-MAS leads automatically to a decision about provision of different services or a change in test eligibility, it would be important to know whether the educational program was designed to promote learning in the content that was assessed.

CONCLUSION

The federal guidance on AA-MAS places a greater responsibility for results on the quality of instruction compared with other types of alternate assessment. Fortunately, the role of the IEP has become more central and is no longer seen as a compliance document (Sopko, 2003). A good, standards-based IEP can guide educators to support meaningful learning so students can work toward grade-level proficiency. States have noted benefits to using a standards-based approach to IEPs, including higher levels of student achievement, integration of special and general education, and benefits to parents who participate in the IEP process (Ahearn, 2006). Aside from representing the concept of OTL, there is some evidence that having IEPs aligned with state academic content standards makes a difference for instruction

(McLaughlin, Nolet, Rhim, & Henderson, 1999) and achievement (Karvonen & Huynh, 2007).

This chapter has presented suggestions for IEP teams to set curricular priorities, build services and supports into the educational program, and guide teachers in developing effective instruction. The chapter also offers suggestions to states on providing guidance and support to IEP teams in order to promote highly effective practices for students who are not achieving at grade level. These recommendations are intended to help the field move forward toward optimal practices that help students meet high expectations. In some areas, educators may be prepared to enact these strategies immediately. For example, there is an extensive body of practice on how to design and implement formative assessment. In other areas, there is still a significant gap between current, realistic practice and the ideal. These gaps exist at the state, local, and school/teacher levels.

States have many competing priorities and will need to decide what is pragmatic in the systems and supports they establish. State and local agencies may begin to set paths toward ideal practice by evaluating where they are and how to reach the next logical step. For example, existing IEP monitoring systems could be reviewed in light of the AA-MAS regulations to evaluate what elements of the system would need to be changed in order to meet federal requirements. In order to move the system forward, state stakeholders could define *ideal* practice as it relates to IEP content. They could then develop and pilot that system on a limited basis using early data for formative purposes before scaling up.

The largest challenges at the school level lie in the lack of research—both on cognitive models of learning and content progressions for this population and on effective instructional practices. Where there is a longer history of research (e.g., CBM practices), it may be challenging to distill and disseminate these strategies to teachers in ways that promote change in their practices. When resources are limited, instructional leaders at the state and local level may have less time to analyze promising new strategies that are worth disseminating to their teachers. Even when strong evidence exists for particular strategies and that evidence is shared with teachers, there is still the conundrum of interpreting the AA-MAS requirement that students be taught in grade-level content standards even when they may not have mastered prerequisite or foundational content. Local agencies may wish to weigh the potential benefits of focusing their professional development on a broad view for designing and using IEPs in effective instructional planning versus professional development on separate topics related to good instruction (e.g., detailed support on translating academic content, how to collect formative data, how to choose accommodations). Predominant needs may vary by district or school.

As teachers develop IEPs that are consistent with federal mandates for AA-MAS, it is important to remember that academics are part of the broader educational program. Instructional time is finite, and there are many competing priorities for these students (Thurlow, 2008). Where possible, teachers will need to think creatively about how to capitalize on relationships with other parts of the program (e.g., academics embedded in therapeutic or transition goals; a focus on learning strategies or academic goals that support growth across the curriculum) and provide instruction that combines academics with other values for the population. Without these combinations, the risk is that instruction will become more fragmented. This fragmentation may be detrimental to the goal of moving the student toward being prepared for assessment against grade-level achievement standards.

The final AA-MAS regulations emphasize the need for this target population of students to access grade-level content standards rather than modified content standards in order to maintain high expectations for student learning (U.S. Department of Education, 2007b, see p. 17,755). There are still many questions left unanswered about how students can access grade-level content, make more progress than they have made previously, and have their achievement measured against modified standards using assessments that allow for valid inferences about what they know and can do. If students who are eligible for AA-MAS remain identified as persistently low-performing over several years, what are the consequences for those students in the future? Are they permanently disadvantaged? Although participation in AA-MAS is not supposed to preclude participation in requirements for a high school diploma [34 C.F.R. § 200.1(f)(2)(iv)], what are the long-term consequences if the educational program does not help students make up for earlier learning deficits? Aside from the social justice implications, what are the economic costs for failing to help students be adequately prepared for successful completion of high school graduation requirements (Levin, 2009)? As described in Chapter 1, the population of low-performing students also includes many students without disabilities. If educators successfully design and implement effective instructional programs for struggling students with disabilities, they also have the potential to lead the way on instruction for all students who are persistently low-performing—not just those with disabilities. Individual growth or learning plans would allow teachers to translate the ideas behind the IEP as a means of instructional planning to the rest of the population of low-performing students in order to promote success for all struggling students.

REFERENCES

Access Center. (2004). *Aligning IEPs with state standards and accountability systems.* Washington, DC: American Institutes for Research. Retrieved April 22, 2009, from http://www.k8accesscenter.org/training_resources/aligningieps.asp

Access Center. (2006). *Teaching matters: The link between access to the general education curriculum and performance on state assessments.* Washington, DC: American Institutes for Research. Retrieved April 22, 2009, from www.k8accesscenter.org/documents/TeachingMattersBrief_001.pdf

Ahearn, E. (2006, May). *Standards-based IEPs: Implementation in selected states.* Alexandria, VA: Project Forum, National Association of State Directors of Special Education. Retrieved April 21, 2009, from http://www.projectforum.org/docs/Standards-BasedIEPs-ImplementationinSelectedStates.pdf

Almond, P., & Karvonen, M. (2007). *Accommodations for a K to 12 standardized assessment: Practical implications for policy.* In C. Cahalan Laitusis & L.L. Cook (Eds.), *Large-scale assessment and accommodations: What works?* (pp. 117–136). Arlington, VA: Council for Exceptional Children.

American Educational Research Association (AERA), American Psychological Association, & National Council on Measurement in Education. (1999). *Standards for educational and psychological testing.* Washington, DC: AERA.

Bateman, B.D., & Herr, C.M. (2006). *Writing measurable IEP goals and objectives* (2nd ed.). Verona, WI: Attainment Company.

Browder, D.M., Spooner, F., Wakeman, S., Trela, K., & Baker, J.N. (2006). Aligning instruction with academic content standards: Finding the link. *Research and Practice for Persons with Severe Disabilities, 31*(4), 309–321.

Byrnes, M. (2008). Educators' interpretations of ambiguous accommodations. *Remedial and Special Education, 29*(5), 306–315.

California Department of Education. (2008, December 18). Educational benefit activity. Sacramento, CA: Author.

CAST. (2008). *Universal design for learning (UDL) guidelines, version 1.0.* Wakefield, MA: Author. Retrieved April 21, 2009, from http://www.cast.org/publications/UDLguidelines/version1.html

Cook, B., Tankersley, M., & Landrum, T. (Eds.). (2009, Spring). Evidence-based practice for reading, math, and behavior [Special issue]. *Exceptional Children, 75*(3).

Cortiella, C. (2007). *Learning opportunities for your child through alternate assessments: Alternate assessments based on modified achievement standards.* Minneapolis, MN: University of Minnesota, National Center on Educational Outcomes. Retrieved April 21, 2009, from http://cehd.umn.edu/nceo/OnlinePubs/AAMASParentGuide.pdf

Courtade-Little, G., & Browder, D. (2005). *Aligning IEPs to academic standards for students with moderate and severe disabilities.* Verona, WI: IEP Resources.

Deno, S.L. (2003). Developments in curriculum-based measurement. *Journal of Special Education, 37*(3), 184–192.

Fisher, D., Lapp, D., Frey, N., Flood, J., & Moore, K. (2007). Putting the CIA system to work: Linking curriculum, instruction, and assessment to improve student achievement. In J.R. Paratore & R.L. McCormack (Eds.), *Classroom literacy assessment: Making sense of what students know and do* (pp. 280–293). New York: Guilford Press.

Gibson, V., & Hasbrouck, J. (2008). *Differentiated instruction: Grouping for success.* Boston: McGraw-Hill.

Hardman, M.L., & Dawson, S. (2008). The impact of federal public policy on curriculum and instruction for students with disabilities in the general classroom. *Preventing School Failure, 52*(2), 5–11.

Harn, B.A., Linan-Thompson, S., & Roberts, G. (2008). Intensifying instruction: Does additional instructional time make a difference for the most at-risk first graders? *Journal of Learning Disabilities, 41*(2), 115–125. doi:10.1177/0022219407313586

Haydon, T., Mancil, G.R., & Van Loan, C. (2009). Using opportunities to respond in a general education classroom: A case study. *Education and Treatment of Children, 32*(2), 267–278.

Henning, J.E. (2006). Teacher leaders at work: Analyzing standardized achievement data to improve instruction. *Education, 126*(4), 729–737.

Hess, K. (2008, June). *Developing and using learning progressions as a schema for measuring progress.* Paper presented at 2008 CCSSO National Conference on Student Assessment, Orlando, FL. Retrieved March 31, 2009, from http://www.nciea.org/cgi-bin/pubspage.cgi?sortby=pub_date

Hill, W., & Erwin, R. (1984). The readability of content textbooks used in middle and junior high schools. *Reading Psychology, 5*(1), 105–117.

Individuals with Disabilities Education Act Amendments (IDEA) of 1997, PL 105-17, 20 U.S.C. §§ 1400 *et seq.*

Individuals with Disabilities Education Improvement Act (IDEA) of 2004, PL 108-446, 20 U.S.C. §§ 611–614.

Jenkins, J.R., Graff, J.J., & Miglioretti, D.L. (2009). Estimating reading growth using intermittent CBM progress monitoring. *Exceptional Children, 75*(2), 151–163.

Jitendra, A.K., Nolet, V., Xin, Y.P., Gomez, O., Renouf, K., Iskold, L., et al. (2001). An analysis of middle school geography textbooks: Implications for students with learning problems. *Reading & Writing Quarterly, 17*(2), 151–173.

Joyce, B.R., & Showers, B. (2002). *Student achievement through staff development* (3rd ed.). Alexandria, VA: Association for Supervision and Curriculum Development.

Karger, J. (2004). *Access to the general education curriculum for students with disabilities: The role of the IEP.* Wakefield, MA: National Center on Accessing the General Curriculum. Retrieved February 21, 2010, from http://www.cast.org/publications/ncac/ncac_iep.html

Karvonen, M. (2009). *IEP content analysis protocols.* Cullowhee, NC: Western Carolina University.

Karvonen, M., & Huynh, H. (2007). The relationship between IEP characteristics and test scores on alternate assessments for students with significant cognitive disabilities. *Applied Measurement in Education, 20,* 273-300.

Karvonen, M., Wakeman, S.L., Flowers, C.P., & Browder, D.M. (2007). Measuring the enacted curriculum for students with significant cognitive disabilities: A preliminary investigation. *Assessment for Effective Intervention, 33*(1), 29–38.

Kopriva, R., Koran, J., & Hedgspeth, C. (2007). Addressing the importance of systematically matching student needs and test accommodations. In C. Cahalan Laitusis & L.L. Cook (Eds.), *Large-scale assessment and accommodations: What works?* (pp. 145–165). Arlington, VA: Council for Exceptional Children.

Lazarus, S.S., Rogers, C., Cormier, D., & Thurlow, M.L. (2008). *States' participation guidelines for alternate assessments based on alternate achievement standards*

(AA-MAS) in 2008 (Synthesis Report 71). Minneapolis, MN: National Center on Educational Outcomes.

Levin, H.M. (2009). The economic payoff to investing in educational justice. *Educational Researcher, 38*(1), 5–20. doi:10.3102/0013189X08331192

McLaughlin, M.J., Nolet, V., Rhim, L.M., & Henderson, K. (1999). Integrating standards: Including all students. *TEACHING Exceptional Children, 31*(3), 66–71.

National Association of State Directors of Special Education. (2007). *A seven-step process for creating standards-based IEPs.* Retrieved February 21, 2010, from http://cehd.umn.edu/nceo/Teleconferences/AAMASteleconferences/SevenStepProcess.pdf

National Center on Educational Outcomes [NCEO]. (2007, May 17). *Teleconference notes. Standards-based IEPs and IEP goals based on grade-level standards.* Retrieved February 21, 2010, from http://www.education.umn.edu/NCEO/USED2percentTele051707.pdf

National Center on Response to Intervention. (n.d.) *What is RTI?* Retrieved April 21, 2009, from http://www.rti4success.org/

National Council of Teachers of Mathematics. (2000). *Principles and standards for school mathematics.* Reston, VA: Author.

National Reading Panel. (2000). *Report of the National Reading Panel, teaching children to read: An evidence-based assessment of the scientific research literature on reading and its implications for reading instruction.* Washington, DC: National Institute for Literacy.

New York State Education Department. (2008, December 23). *Special education quality assurance: IDEA effective instructional practices focused review manual.* Albany, NY: New York State Education Department, Office of Vocational & Educational Services for Individuals with Disabilities.

Nitko, A.J. (Ed.). (2004). Formative evaluation using informal diagnostic assessments. In *Educational assessment of students* (4th ed., pp. 288–303). Upper Saddle River, NJ: Pearson Education.

No Child Left Behind Act of 2001, PL 107-110, 115 Stat. 1425, 20 U.S.C. §§ 6301 *et seq.*

Pellegrino, J., Chudowsky, N., & Glaser, R. (Eds). (2001). *Knowing what students know: The science and design of educational assessment.* Washington, DC: National Academies Press.

Perie, M. (2009, February). *Understanding the AA-MAS: How does it fit into a state assessment and accountability system?* Presentation to the SCASS groups, Orlando, FL. Retrieved March 26, 2009, from http://www.nciea.org/publications/CrossSCASS_MAP09.pdf

Porter, A.C., & Smithson, J.L. (2001, December). *Defining, developing, and using curriculum indicators* (CPRE Research Report Series RR-048). Retrieved April 22, 2009, from http://www.cpre.org/images/stories/cpre_pdfs/rr48.pdf

Quenemoen, R. (2009). *Success one student at a time: What the IEP team does.* Minneapolis, MN: University of Minnesota, National Center on Educational Outcomes. Retrieved April 20, 2009, from http://www.nceo.info/Tools/StandardsIEPtool.pdf

Quenemoen, R., Thurlow, M., Moen, R., Thompson, S., & Morse, A.B. (2004). *Progress monitoring in an inclusive standards-based assessment and accountability system* (Synthesis Report 53). Minneapolis, MN: University of Minnesota, National Center on Educational Outcomes. Retrieved April 20, 2009, from http://education.umn.edu/NCEO/OnlinePubs/Synthesis53.html

Shriner, J., & Destefano, L. (2003). Participation and accommodation in state assessment: The role of Individualized Education Programs. *Exceptional Children, 69*(2), 147–161.

Slavin, R.E., Lake, C., Chambers, B., Cheung, A., & Davis, S. (2009). Effective reading programs for the elementary grades: A best-evidence synthesis. *Review of Educational Research, 79*, 1391–1466.

Sopko, K.M. (2003). *The IEP: A synthesis of current literature since 1997.* Alexandria, VA: National Association of State Directors of Special Education, Project FORUM. Retrieved April 21, 2009, from http://www.projectforum.org/docs/iep.pdf

Soukup, J.H., Wehmeyer, M.L., Bashinski, S., & Bovaird, J.A. (2007). Classroom variables and access to the general curriculum for students with disabilities. *Exceptional Children, 74*(1), 101–120.

Stecker, P.M. (n.d.). *Monitoring student progress in individualized educational programs using curriculum-based measurement.* Washington, DC: National Center on Student Progress Monitoring. Retrieved April 21, 2009, from http://www.studentprogress.org/library/monitoring_student_progress_i n_individualized_educational_programs_using_cbm.pdf

Stecker, P.M., Fuchs, L.S., & Fuchs, D. (2005). Using curriculum-based measurement to improve student achievement: Review of research. *Psychology in the Schools, 42*(8), 795–819. doi:10.1002/pitts.20113

Thompson, S.J., Morse, A.B., Sharpe, M., & Hall, S. (2005). *Accommodations manual: How to select, administer, and evaluate use of accommodations for instruction and assessment of students with disabilities* (2nd ed.). Washington, DC: Council of Chief State School Officers. Retrieved September 30, 2009, from http://www.ccsso.org/content/pdfs/AccommodationsManual.doc

Thurlow, M.L. (2008). Assessment and instructional implications of the alternate assessment based on modified academic achievement standards (AA-MAS). *Journal of Disability Policy Studies, 19*(3), 132–139. doi:10.1177/1044207308327473

Thurlow, M.L., Christensen, L.L., & Lail, K.E. (2008). *An analysis of accommodations issues from the standards and assessments peer review* (Technical Report 51). Minneapolis, MN: University of Minnesota, National Center on Educational Outcomes. Retrieved April 20, 2009, from http://cehd.umn.edu/NCEO/ OnlinePubs/Tech51/index.htm

U.S. Department of Education. (2007a, April 9). Final Rule 34 C.F.R. Parts 200 and 300: Title I—Improving the academic achievement of the disadvantaged; Individuals with Disabilities Education Act (IDEA). 72 Fed. Reg. 67. Retrieved February 21, 2010, from http://www.ed.gov/admins/lead/account/saa.html#regulations

U.S. Department of Education. (2007b, July 20). *Modified academic achievement standards: Non-regulatory guidance.* Washington, DC: Office of Elementary and Secondary Education, U.S. Department of Education. Retrieved February 21, 2010, from http://www.ed.gov/admins/lead/account/saa.html#regulations

Ylvisaker, M. (with Hibbard, M., & Feeney, T). (2006). *Mini-tutorial: Instructional pacing.* Albany, NY: The Brain Injury Association of New York State. Retrieved September 30, 2009, from http://www.bianys.org/learnet/tutorials/instructional_pacing.html

3

The Challenges of Conceptualizing What Low Achievers Know and Assessing that Knowledge

James W. Pellegrino

This chapter considers some of the most important issues surrounding the "what" and "how" of assessment as applied to any population of students, but especially those students who fall in the range of low academic achievement as measured by the typical achievement tests used for purposes of No Child Left Behind Act of 2001 (PL 107-110) accountability. It is intended as a bridge between the prior two chapters, with their focus on identification of those students whose academic performance is such that assessment relative to modified achievement standards may be appropriate, and the next section of the book, with its focus on issues regarding the content and design of any such assessment.

This chapter moves from understanding relationships among assessment, curriculum, and instruction and conceptualizing assessment as a process of reasoning from evidence that should be driven by theories and data on student cognition to specific examples of the development of student cognition in reading and math. It then considers the implications for assessment design and concludes by considering the validity of assessment practices that might be considered for the population of students targeted by the alternate assessments based on modified achievement standards. It also suggests some things we still need to know to make progress in the design of valid assessments based on modified achievement standards.

TWO CRITICAL ISSUES FOR
CONCEPTUALIZING STUDENT ASSESSMENT
The Curriculum–Instruction–Assessment Triad

Whether we recognize it or not, assessment does not and should not stand alone. Rather, it is one of three central components in the educational enterprise—curriculum, instruction, and assessment. The three elements of this triad are linked, although the nature of their linkages and reciprocal influence is often less explicit than it should be. Furthermore, the separate pairs of connections are often inconsistent, which can lead to an overall incoherence in the educational enterprise.

Curriculum consists of the knowledge and skills in subject matter areas that teachers teach and students are supposed to learn. The curriculum generally consists of a scope or breadth of content in a given subject area and a sequence for learning (see Chapter 4, this volume). Content standards in each subject matter area typically outline the goals of learning, whereas curriculum sets forth the more specific means to be used to achieve those ends. *Instruction* refers to methods of teaching and the learning activities used to help students master the content and objectives specified by a curriculum. Instruction encompasses the activities of both teachers and students. It can be carried out by a variety of methods, sequences of activities, and topic orders. *Assessment* is the means used to measure the outcomes of education and the achievement of students with regard to important competencies. Assessment may include both formal methods, such as large-scale state assessments, and less formal classroom-based procedures, such as quizzes, class projects, and teacher questioning.

A precept of educational practice is the need for alignment among curriculum, instruction, and assessment (e.g., National Council of Teachers of Mathematics [NCTM], 1995, 2000; Webb, 1997). Alignment, in this sense, means that the three functions are directed toward the same ends and reinforce each other rather than working at cross-purposes. Ideally, an assessment should measure what students are actually being taught, and what is actually being taught should parallel the curriculum one wants students to master. If any of the functions are not well synchronized, it will disrupt the balance and skew the educational process. Assessment results will be misleading, or instruction will be ineffective. Alignment is difficult to achieve, however. Often what is lacking is a central theory about the nature of learning and knowing around which the three functions can be coordinated.

Most current approaches to curriculum, instruction, and assessment are based on theories and models that have not kept pace with modern knowledge of cognition and how people learn (e.g., Bransford, Brown, & Cocking, 1999; Bransford, Brown, Cocking, Donovan, & Pellegrino, 2000; Donovan, Bransford, & Pellegrino, 1999; Pellegrino, Chudowsky, & Glaser, 2001; Pellegrino, Jones, & Mitchell 1999; Shepard, 2000). They have been designed on the basis of implicit and highly limited conceptions of cognition and learning. Those conceptions tend to be fragmented, outdated, and poorly delineated for domains of subject matter knowledge. Alignment among curriculum, instruction, and assessment can be better achieved if all three are derived from a scientifically credible and shared knowledge base about cognition and learning in subject matter domains. The model of learning would provide the central bonding principle, serving as a nucleus around which the three functions would revolve. Without such a central core, and under pressure to prepare students for the accountability tests, teachers may feel compelled to move back and forth between instruction and external assessment and teach directly to the items on a state test. This approach can result in an undesirable narrowing of the curriculum and a limiting of learning outcomes. Such problems can be ameliorated if, instead, decisions about both instruction and assessment are guided by a model of learning in the domain that represents the best available scientific understanding of how people learn (Bransford et al., 2000).

Assessment as a Process of Reasoning from Evidence

Educators assess students to learn about what they know and can do, but assessments do not offer a direct pipeline into a student's mind. Assessing educational outcomes is not as straightforward as measuring height or weight; the attributes to be measured are mental representations and processes that are not outwardly visible. Thus an assessment is a tool designed to observe students' behavior and produce data that can be used to draw reasonable inferences about what students know. Deciding what to assess and how to do so is not as simple as it might appear.

The process of collecting evidence to support inferences about what students know represents a chain of reasoning from evidence about student learning that characterizes all assessments, from classroom quizzes and standardized achievement tests, to computerized tutoring programs, to the conversation a student has with her teacher as they work through a math problem or discuss the meaning of a text.

In the 2001 report issued by the NRC, *Knowing What Students Know: The Science and Design of Educational Assessment*, the process of reasoning from evidence was portrayed as a triad of three interconnected elements—the *assessment triangle* (Pellegrino et al., 2001). The vertices of the assessment triangle represent the three key elements underlying any assessment: a model of student *cognition* and learning in the domain of the assessment, a set of beliefs about the kinds of *observations* that will provide evidence of students' competencies, and an *interpretation* process for making sense of the evidence. These three elements may be explicit or implicit, but an assessment cannot be designed and implemented without some consideration of each. The three are represented as vertices of a triangle because each is connected to and dependent on the other two. A major tenet of the *Knowing What Students Know* report is that for an assessment to be effective and valid, the three elements must be in synchrony. The assessment triangle provides a useful framework for analyzing the underpinnings of current assessments to determine how well they accomplish the goals we have in mind, as well as for designing future assessments.

The *cognition* corner of the triangle refers to a theory or set of beliefs about how students represent knowledge and develop competence in a subject domain (e.g., fractions). In any particular assessment application, a theory of learning in the domain is needed to identify the set of knowledge and skills that is important to measure for the task at hand, whether that be characterizing the competencies students have acquired thus far or guiding instruction to further increase learning. A central premise is that the cognitive theory should represent the most scientifically credible understanding of typical ways in which learners represent knowledge and develop expertise in a domain. More will be said in the next section about what we know about the nature of cognition and the development of subject matter competence.

Every assessment is also based on a set of beliefs about the kinds of tasks or situations that will prompt students to say, do, or create something that demonstrates important knowledge and skills. The tasks to which students are asked to respond on an assessment are not arbitrary. They must be carefully designed to provide evidence that is linked to the cognitive model of learning and to support the kinds of inferences and decisions that will be made on the basis of the assessment results. The *observation* vertex of the assessment triangle represents a description or set of specifications for assessment tasks that will elicit illuminating responses from students. In assessment, one has the opportunity to structure some small corner of the world to make observations. The assessment designer can use this capability to maximize the value of the data collected as seen through the lens of the underlying beliefs about how students learn in the domain.

Every assessment is also based on certain assumptions and models for interpreting the evidence collected from observations. The *interpretation* vertex of the triangle encompasses all the methods and tools used to reason from fallible observations. It expresses how the observations derived from a set of assessment tasks constitute evidence about the knowledge and skills being assessed. In the context of large-scale assessment, the interpretation method is usually a statistical model, which is a characterization or summarization of patterns one would expect to see in the data, given varying levels of student competency. In the context of classroom assessment, the interpretation is often made less formally by the teacher and is usually based on an intuitive or qualitative model rather than a formal statistical one.

A crucial point is that each of the three elements of the assessment triangle not only must make sense on its own, but also must connect to each of the other two elements in a meaningful way to lead to an effective assessment and sound inferences. Thus to have an effective assessment, all three vertices of the triangle must work together in synchrony. Central to this entire process, however, are theories and data on how students learn and what students know as they develop competence in aspects of the curriculum.

FUNDAMENTAL COMPONENTS OF COGNITION AND SOME IMPLICATIONS FOR ASSESSMENT

This section begins the process of specifying some of what we know about the nature of human cognition that has implications for instruction, learning, and assessment.

Working Memory

One of the chief theoretical advances to emerge from cognitive research is the notion of *cognitive architecture*—the information processing system that determines the flow of information and how it is acquired, stored, represented, revised, and accessed in the mind. One of the most critical components of the cognitive architecture is *working memory*. It has been conceptualized as the system we use to process and act on information that is immediately before us and that we are consciously processing (Baddeley, 1986). Rather than viewing working memory as a "place" in the cognitive system, contemporary theoretical work has conceptualized working memory as a kind of cognitive energy level or "resource" that exists in limited amounts, with substantial individual variations. It is a well-established fact that there are reliable developmental and individual differences in working memory capacity that predict a range of cognitive outcomes, including scores on conventional tests of intelligence and achievement (e.g., Unsworth & Engle, 2007).

A significant aspect of the construct of working memory is that it plays a central role in virtually any cognitive activity we can imagine, determining the success or failure of many if not most of our intellectual endeavors. The range of activities that are impacted by the capacity and efficiency of one's working memory includes such things as executing a procedure like multicolumn addition or subtraction while monitoring the products of the process and the sequential steps, the act of representing and learning a new procedure like learning to "borrow across zero" in multicolumn subtraction, and the process of reading and comprehending a piece of narrative or expository text, including activities such as resolving issues of reference and making inferences (e.g., Miyake, Just, & Carpenter, 1994).

Metacognition

The term *metacognition* (literally "thinking about thinking") is commonly used to refer to the selection and monitoring processes, as well as to more general activities of reflecting on and directing one's own thinking. Good learners have strong metacognitive skills (Hatano, 1990). They monitor their problem solving, question limitations in their knowledge, and avoid oversimplistic interpretations of a problem. In the course of learning and problem solving, such individuals display certain kinds of regulatory performance, such as knowing when to apply a procedure or rule, predicting the correctness or outcomes of an action, planning ahead, and efficiently apportioning cognitive resources and time.

There is ample evidence that metacognition develops over the school years; for example, older children are better than younger ones at planning for tasks they are asked to do. Metacognitive skills can also be taught. For example, people can learn mental devices that help them stay on task, monitor their own progress, reflect on their strengths and weaknesses, and self-correct errors. It is important to note, however, that the teaching of metacognitive skills is often best accomplished in specific content areas because the ability to monitor one's understanding is closely tied to domain-specific knowledge and expertise.

Types of Knowledge and Processes of Acquisition

Long-term memory contains two distinct types of information—information about the way the world is (*declarative knowledge*) and procedural information about how things are done (*procedural knowledge*). It is one thing to know what it means to throw a 90-mile-per-hour fastball for a strike in baseball and quite another to be able to actually do it! Knowing about something (making a soufflé) is not the same as actually being able to do that thing. Much of what we would like students to learn in school is a combination of both declarative and procedural knowledge, and for both types of knowledge, we want them to access and use that knowledge in a highly fluent and relatively automatic fashion.

Unlike working memory, long-term memory is, for all practical purposes, an effectively limitless store of information. What matters most in learning situations is not the capacity of working memory—although that is often a factor in the speed and/or accuracy of processing—but how well one can evoke the knowledge stored in long-term memory and use it to reason efficiently about information and solve problems in the present.

As part of studying the nature of knowledge in long-term memory, researchers have probed deeply the nature of competence and how people acquire large bodies of knowledge over long periods of time. Studies have revealed much about the kinds of mental structures that support problem-solving and learning in various domains, what it means to develop competence in a domain, and how the thinking of high achievers differs from that of novices (e.g., Chi, Feltovich, & Glaser, 1981). What distinguishes high from low performers is not simply general mental abilities, such as memory or fluid intelligence, or general problem-solving strategies. High performers have acquired extensive stores of knowledge and skill in a particular domain. But perhaps most significant, their minds have organized this knowledge in ways that make it more retrievable and useful. Because their knowledge has been encoded in a way that closely links it with the contexts and conditions for its use, high achievers do not have to search through the vast repertoire of everything they know when confronted with a problem. Instead, they can readily activate and retrieve the subset of their knowledge that is relevant to the task at hand (Glaser, 1992). Such findings suggest that teachers should place more emphasis on the conditions for applying the facts or procedures being taught and that assessment should address whether students know when, where, and how to use their knowledge.

Considerable effort has also been expended on understanding the characteristics of persons and of the learning situations they encounter that foster the development of expertise. Much of what we know about the development of expertise has come from studies of children as they acquire competence in many areas of intellectual endeavor, including the learning of school subject matter. (This is further discussed in the section "Domain-Specific Aspects of Cognition and Learning.") From a cognitive standpoint, *development* and *learning* are not the same thing. Some types of knowledge are universally acquired in the course of typical development, whereas other types are learned only with the intervention of deliberate teaching (which includes teaching by any means, such as apprenticeship, formal schooling, or self-study). Infants and young children appear to be predisposed to learn rapidly and readily in some domains, including language, number, and notions of physical and biological causality. Infants who are only 3 or 4 months old, for example, have been shown to understand certain concepts about the physical world, such as the idea that inanimate objects need to be propelled in order to move (Massey & Gelman, 1988). By the time children are 3 or 4 years old, they have an implicit understanding of certain rudimentary principles for counting, adding, and subtracting cardinal numbers (Gelman, 1990).

In math, the fundamentals of ordinality and cardinality appear to develop in all human infants (who do not have any cognitive disability) without instruction. In contrast, however, such concepts as mathematical notation, algebra, and Cartesian graphing representations must be taught. Similarly, the basics of speech and language comprehension emerge naturally from millions of years of evolution, whereas mastery of the alphabetic code necessary for reading typically requires explicit instruction and long periods of practice (Geary, 1995). Much of what we want to assess in educational contexts is the product of such deliberate learning.

With respect to assessment, one of the most important findings from detailed observations of children's learning behavior is that children do not move simply and directly from an erroneous to an optimal solution strategy (Kaiser, Proffitt, & McCloskey, 1985). Instead, they may exhibit several different but locally or partially correct strategies (Fay & Klahr, 1996). They also may use less advanced strategies, even after demonstrating that they know more advanced ones, and the process of acquiring and consolidating robust and efficient strategies may be quite protracted, extending across many weeks and hundreds of problems (Siegler, 1998). Moreover, these studies have found that short-term transition strategies often precede more lasting approaches and that generalization of new approaches often occurs very slowly.

The Role of Social Context, Cultural Norms, and Student Beliefs

Much of what humans learn is acquired through discourse and interactions with others. For example, science, mathematics, and other domains are often shaped by collaborative work among peers. Through such interactions, individuals build communities of practice, test their own theories, and build on the learning of others. For example, those who are still using a naïve strategy can learn by observing others who have figured out a more productive one. This situation contrasts with many school situations, in which students are often required to work independently or even competitively. Yet the display and modeling of cognitive competence through group participation and social interaction is an important mechanism for the internalization of knowledge and skill in individuals (Rogoff, 1990). Studies suggest that much of knowledge is also highly *situated*—it is embedded within systems of representation, discourse, and physical activity. A part of developing competence is learning to participate in communities of practice, which in turn serve as sites for developing identity as a member of various communities and what happens in those communities as enabled by a variety of artifacts and tools (Lave, 1988).

The beliefs students hold about learning are another social dimension that can significantly affect learning and performance (e.g., Dweck & Legitt, 1988). For example, many students believe, on the basis of their typical classroom and homework assignments, that any math problem can be solved in 5 minutes or less, and if they cannot find a solution in that time, they will give up. Many young people and adults also believe that talent in mathematics and science is innate, which gives them little incentive to persist if they do not understand something in these subjects immediately. Conversely, people who believe they are capable of making sense of unfamiliar things often succeed because they invest more sustained effort in doing so. If mathematics is presented by a teacher as a set of rules to be applied, students may come to believe that "knowing" math means remembering which rule to apply when a question is asked (usually the rule the teacher last demonstrated) and that comprehending the concepts that underlie the question is too difficult for ordinary students. In contrast, when teachers structure math lessons so that important principles are apparent as students work through the procedures, students are more likely to develop deeper understanding and become independent and thoughtful problem solvers (Lampert, 1986).

Some Implications for Low-Achieving/Performing Students

What are some possible implications of the cognitive architecture and the nature of knowledge and its development for understanding the performance of low-achieving students? It would nice if we could provide definitive answers to such a question, but in many cases, we lack a research base that allows us to do so. Nevertheless, we can speculate

on some of the possible causes of low performance and the implications for both instruction and assessment. For example, some of the
problem may be an information processing bottleneck issue, especially
in regard to the capacity of working memory and the management of
attentional resources. Such a bottleneck has implications for the
processes of learning and knowledge acquisition, as well as for performance in a testing complex. It may well be the case that the ability
to integrate content and to proceduralize knowledge, which are key
aspects of the process of learning, are slowed or impaired by limitations in basic processing capacities. This is not to say that individuals
cannot acquire the knowledge that is intended, but rather that the
speed and conditions needed to do so may differ. Similarly, differences
in performance in a testing situation may have less to do with the availability of the appropriate knowledge than the load on working memory that taxes the person's capacity to manage the situation within the
time demands of the testing situation. Similar issues arise regarding
aspects of metacognition and the capacity to develop and/or exercise
such skills in a given learning or performance situation.

Without convincing evidence that it is the architecture per se that
contributes to low achievement, it is reasonable to assume that much of
the problem of low achievement represents a deficit in the nature of the
forms of knowledge that are demanded by different areas of the
curriculum. This almost sounds tautological—low achievement by
definition means lack of knowledge. But low achievement may not be
associated with a lack of knowledge per se but rather a failure to develop the forms of knowledge that are associated with higher levels of
competence and performance. If students perform poorly on tests of
domain-specific achievement, it is appropriate to ask how much of the
problem may result from a failure of sufficient opportunity to learn the
content required to attain higher levels of competence. In turn, much of
that deficiency might be a function of the failure to make explicit for
such students that which is often tacit in the learning situation and
more readily discerned or inferred by students without disabilities.
Learning is a process of constructing knowledge, and such a construc-
tive process occurs regardless of the forms of instruction—from guided discovery and hands-on experiences to collaborative learning to
direct instruction to rote memorization. Because knowledge is constructed rather than delivered, there is always a potential gap between
what was intended in the instructional environment and what was
actually understood and represented by the student.

As noted earlier, the development of knowledge is constituted
within particular contexts and situations—an *interactionist* perspective
of development (Newcombe & Huttenlocher, 2000). Accordingly,

assessment of children's development in contexts of schooling should include attention to the nature of classroom cultures and the practices they promote, as well as to individual variation. For example, the kinds of expectations established in a classroom for what counts as a mathematical explanation or what serves as a summarization or interpretation of a text affect the kinds of strategies and explanations that children pursue and the kinds of responses they are likely to give in an assessment context. Because knowledge is constructed from experience, we may need to pay more attention to the nature of the experiences that low-achieving students encounter as the conditions of learning and how those experiences align with the conditions and expectations for performance in an assessment context. In essence, any assessment or testing situation is a test of transfer (Ruiz-Primo, Shavelson, Hamilton, & Klein, 2002). What is near transfer for some students may be far transfer for others given the conditions of learning and the situated as well as sociocultural nature of their knowledge (e.g., Hickey & Pellegrino, 2005; Pellegrino & Hickey, 2006).

Despite all we know about cognition, we must remind ourselves that there are many questions yet to answer about the ways in which low-achieving students differ from their regular education peers and the possible causes as well as consequences. Some of the possible answers lie in a better understanding of the nature of knowledge and skill in specific curricular domains and how that develops over time and with instruction.

DOMAIN-SPECIFIC ASPECTS OF COGNITION AND LEARNING

Detailed models of cognition and learning in specific curricular areas can be invaluable for evaluating the progress of any individual or group, as well as for informing teaching and learning. In other words, a well-developed and empirically validated model of thinking and learning in an academic domain can be used to design and select assessment tasks that support the analysis of various kinds of student performance. Models with power highlight the main determinants of and obstacles to learning and include descriptions of students' conceptual progressions as they develop competence and expertise. Consistent with these ideas, there has been a recent spurt of interest in the topic of *learning progressions* (Duschl, Schweingruber, & Shouse, 2007; Wilson & Bertenthal, 2005). Learning progressions describe "successively more sophisticated ways of reasoning within a content domain that follow one another as students learn" (Smith, Wiser, Anderson, & Krajcik, 2006).

Duncan and Hmelo-Silver (2009) provided a description of essential features of learning progressions that attempts to capture an emerging consensus derived from panel discussions organized by the Center on Continuous Instructional Improvement and the Consortium for Policy Research in Education (Corcoran, Mosher, & Rogat, 2009). As described by Duncan and Hmelo-Silver, there are four essential features that define something as a learning progression. First, learning progressions are focused on a few foundational and generative disciplinary ideas and practices. Several researchers have argued that it is the combined focus on content and practice that is unique to the current definition of learning progressions and central to the development of scientific literacy (Smith et al., 2006). Second, these progressions are bounded by an upper anchor describing what students are expected to know and be able to do by the end of the progression and by a lower anchor describing assumptions about the prior knowledge and skills of learners as they enter the progression. The upper anchor is informed by analyses of the domain as well as societal expectations. Third, they describe varying levels of achievements as the intermediate steps between the two anchors. These levels are derived from syntheses of existing research on student learning in the domain as well as empirical studies of the progression (such as cross-sectional studies and teaching experiments). Levels of achievement are provided in the form of learning performances that can serve as evidence of students' level of understanding and competency. Fourth, learning progressions are mediated by targeted instruction and curriculum. They are not developmentally inevitable and as such do not describe learning as it naturally develops in the absence of scaffolded curriculum and instruction.

Next we consider some of what we currently know about the components of competence and the progression of learning in the domains of mathematics and reading. We are not offering these descriptions as learning progressions that meet the criteria outlined previously, but as illustrations of what we do know about how knowledge and competence develops over time and with instruction for certain aspects of the domains of reading and mathematics. In considering the information that is provided about the sequence of learning and cognitive development, we must remind ourselves that two pertinent questions, which we need to answer empirically, are whether low-performing students can be characterized as simply lagging behind in the pace of their development and whether they follow the same or different progressions. Clearly, being able to answer such questions is essential to the process of better educating these students, as well as for providing valid and fair assessments that are tied to appropriately modified achievement standards that in turn have coherence within and across grade levels.

K–8 Reading

There is an unusual degree of consensus regarding the goals of early reading instruction. The consensus is captured in the National Research Council Report, *Preventing Reading Difficulties in Young Children* (Snow, Burns, & Griffin, 1998), and in the report of the National Reading Panel, *Teaching Children to Read* (National Institute of Child Health and Human Development [NICHD], 2000). The goals are often expressed in terms of the competencies children should be able to demonstrate at the end of third grade: 1) read age-appropriate literature independently with pleasure and interest; 2) read age-appropriate explanatory texts with comprehension for the purpose of learning; and 3) talk and write about those texts in age-appropriate ways. Achieving these goals requires simultaneous development of an interdependent set of abilities: decoding skills, reading fluency, oral language development, vocabulary development, comprehension skills, and the ability to encode speech into writing.

The foundation for early reading lies in the earlier, informal acquisition of language. With little effort, children with intact neurological systems acquire the sounds of their language, its vocabulary, and its methods of conveying meaning (Snow et al., 1998). The path that children travel in acquiring language is predictable (Snow et al., 1998), though the age at which particular skills and abilities are mastered varies somewhat. As proficiency with language use grows, children develop the ability to think about language. Before that ability develops, children do not distinguish between the word and the object to which it refers. Children can begin to develop rudimentary metalinguistic skills as early as age 3. Acquiring this ability allows children to play with, analyze, and pass judgment on the correctness of language.

The trajectory of language development as described previously is universal, though the richness of the environment affects the pace and extent of language development powerfully (Hart & Risley, 1995; Huttenlocher, 1998). For example, Graves and Slater (1987) found that first-graders from higher-income families had a vocabulary that was double the size of those from low-income families. The differences are highly relevant because verbal ability generally, and vocabulary development particularly, are good predictors of success in early reading.

Although typical language development supports reading acquisition, other abilities required for effective reading mastery are unlikely to develop unless children receive formal instruction. With few exceptions, children need systematic instruction in the alphabetic principle to learn to decode words and to learn how to encode words in writing (Adams, Treiman, & Pressley, 1998). This instruction is what is referred to as *phonics*. But successful phonics instruction rests on a

more fundamental ability: phonemic awareness. This is the awareness, for example, that the word *cat* consists of three separable
sounds—/k/ /a/ /t/. The distinction is important because phonics
instruction that teaches the mapping of separate sounds onto letters
requires for success that a student hear those separate sounds.

Learning the alphabetic principle is prerequisite to reading. However, it is not nearly sufficient to help children reach the desired
third-grade competencies. Phonics instruction must be integrated with
comprehension instruction, opportunities to develop fluency in reading through practice, instruction to enhance and practice oral and written language abilities, and opportunities to acquire rich vocabulary
and background knowledge. The failure of any one of these will result
in falling short of the third-grade goals. If fluency does not develop,
little meaning is taken from a text that a student must plod through. If
background knowledge is inadequate, even a fluent reader will be
unable to engage with and learn from the text. The components of successful reading are tightly intertwined.

In addition to understanding the contributors to successful reading acquisition, there is also an extensive research base on the typical
hurdles that children encounter (NICHD, 2000; Snow et al., 1998). It is
now well established that a significant number of children have difficulty learning the alphabetic principle because they have not developed phonemic awareness. Among children who learn to decode
words but do not comprehend well, fluency is often the culprit; if children struggle slowly through a text, their comprehension when they
have finished will be poor. Fluency can suffer if children spend too little time actively engaged in effective reading practice or if vocabulary
and background knowledge are too weak to allow the student to read
with understanding (Lesgold & Perfetti, 1981).

In contrast, in the area of reading comprehension, much remains
to be known, as reflected in an assessment of research needs by the
RAND Reading Study Group (RRSG; RAND, 2002a), as well as in the
report of the National Reading Panel (NICHD, 2000). Those reports
make clear that with regard to both student learning and teacher
preparation, the research base to support practice is weak.

What should children know and be able to do? The answer to this
question is sometimes given in terms of state or national standards for
reading and language arts, but such answers are often inadequate
when it comes to development over time (see the discussion of standards for reading in Chapter 4). An answer to this question is implied
by the RRSG in its definition of reading comprehension as "the process
of simultaneously extracting and constructing meaning through interaction and involvement with written language" (RAND, 2002a). To

extract meaning requires the reader to decode the words and form a mental representation of what the text actually says, at both a local (sentences, phrases, and their interconnections) and global level (the "gist" of the text's meaning). To *construct* meaning requires that the reader create a *situation model*, or an understanding of the intended meaning conveyed with these words that is informed not just by the text, but by the knowledge and experience that the reader brings (Kintsch, 1998). The situation model is the foundation from which inferences are drawn. Consider the sentence, "The sky was a clear, bright blue the day she first saw Charles." The sentence does not state that it is not raining, but the reader can infer this from the bright blue sky. More importantly, it says nothing about whom Charles might be to the referenced woman, but we infer that he will be significant and memorable—not a plumber who will fix her drain and then disappear.

We would be pleased if a 6-year-old student could read the sentence mentioned previously, and understand it semantically. But we would expect a 16-year-old student to develop a situation model that is more complex due to greater developmental maturity, more experience with texts and text genres, and the benefits of instruction. The high school student might appreciate the expectation created by the author with two very simple phrases and might productively reflect on how that expectation might change if the sky were dark and the wind threatened to carry away all in its path. And yet our understanding of the typical progression of student reading comprehension between ages 6 and 16 is poorly mapped, with a consequence that our instructional support for comprehension is poorly defined as well. As the RRSG argues, "Without research-based benchmarks defining adequate progress in comprehension, we as a society risk aiming far too low in our expectations for student learning."

K–8 Mathematics

Investment in recent decades by federal agencies and private foundations has produced a wealth of knowledge about the development of mathematical understanding and correspondingly has led to the development of curricula that incorporate such knowledge (e.g., Carpenter, Fennema, & Franke, 1996; Ginsburg, Greenes, & Balfanz, 2003; Griffin, Case, & Siegler, 1994; National Mathematics Advisory Panel, 2008). Much of contemporary research and theory is synthesized in a report on elementary mathematics (Kilpatrick, Swafford, & Findell, 2001) and in the work of a RAND study group that produced a mathematics research agenda (RAND, 2002b). The NRC 2001 report (Kilpatrick et al., 2001) presents a view of what elementary school children should know and be able to do in mathematics that draws on a solid research base in cognitive psychology and mathematics education, some of which is described in the next section. It includes mastery of procedures as a critical element of mathematics competence, but places far more emphasis on understanding when and how to apply those procedures than is common in many mathematics classrooms. The latter is rooted in a deeper understanding of mathematical concepts and a facility with mathematical reasoning.

The NRC committee summarized its view in five intertwining "strands" that constitute mathematical proficiency:

- *Conceptual understanding*—comprehension of mathematical concepts, operations, and relations
- *Procedural fluency*—skill in carrying out procedures flexibly, accurately, efficiently, and appropriately
- *Strategic competence*—ability to formulate, represent, and solve mathematical problems
- *Adaptive reasoning*—capacity for logical thought, reflection, explanation, and justification
- *Productive disposition*—habitual inclination to see mathematics as sensible, useful, and worthwhile, coupled with a belief in diligence and one's own efficacy (Kilpatrick et al., 2001)

In Chapter 4, Pugalee and Rickelman provide an excellent discussion of the mathematics content and process strands that have been articulated in the NCTM standards (NCTM, 2000) and that have in turn served as the basis for National Assessment of Educational Progress and state assessments. Much of that discussion aligns with aspects of the NRC's five areas of mathematical proficiency previously mentioned. It is far beyond the scope of this chapter to try to capture what is known empirically about the multiple aspects of mathematical proficiency, including their development as a consequence of instruction. The literature on mathematical cognition and its development covers a diversity of topics, ranging from geometry problem solving to infant perception of numerosity (e.g., Greeno, 1978; Starkey & Cooper, 1980). More recently, the final report of the National Mathematics Advisory Panel (2008) stated that algebra is the gateway to all higher mathematics. They cite research showing that students who complete Algebra II are more than twice as likely to graduate from college as compared with students with less mathematical preparation. However, for purposes of discussing learning issues of low achievers, it may be useful to consider some of what is known about early acquisition of mathematical knowledge and competence. Accordingly, we have limited the discussion to current cognitive science accounts of performance on relatively basic aspects of mathematics, those that figure prominently in the early elementary school curriculum (see Carpenter, Moser, & Romberg, 1982; Kalchman, Moss, & Case, 2001; Lesh & Landau, 1983; Schoenfeld, 1985).

The discussion that follows considers in some detail what we know about the basics of addition and subtraction, including computational procedures. The goal of doing so is to help those outside the research arena understand that even the "simplest" cognitive acts and instructional domains imply complicated forms of knowledge that are slowly acquired through experience and instruction. Furthermore, just as knowledge is not random, neither is performance, especially erroneous performance. This section concludes with a consideration of the potential value of all this detailed information for instruction and assessment.

Basic Addition

For many basic mathematics skills, expertise is necessarily defined in terms of the knowledge, processing activities, and performance of adults. Thus, to begin a discussion of cognitive analyses of basic mathematics, we need to focus on theories of how adults do mental addition when faced with problems containing addends from 0 to 9 (e.g., Ashcraft, 1982, 1983, 1987). The theory assumes that adults have two basic types of mathematical knowledge. One type is an interrelated knowledge network containing the basic addition facts. As described earlier, such knowledge is referred to as declarative knowledge (i.e., knowledge of things that are true or false, such as $2 + 3 = 5$). The facts stored in this network have different strengths that determine how long it takes to activate a piece of information. Thus, if the fact $2 + 3 = 5$ has greater associative strength than the fact $7 + 5 = 12$, it will take less time to retrieve (activate) the answer to the first of these two problems. The theory also assumes the existence of a second type of knowledge, specifically, methods that can be used to derive answers for problems lacking pre-stored answers (e.g., 14×36 versus 4×6). As described earlier, this is referred to as procedural knowledge (i.e., knowledge of how to do something). For single-digit addition, it might include procedures such as counting up from one of the addends an amount equal to the other addend. Adults actually have a variety of procedures for calculating answers, including shortcuts that make use of stored facts. An example is computing the answer to $28 + 25$ by retrieving the sum of $25 + 25$ and then adding 3 to 50.

This theory may seem to be nothing more than a restatement of what is intuitively obvious to any adult. For most of us, the process of adding single-digit numbers is essentially the automatic retrieval of specific facts from memory. This process is rapid, automatic, effortless, and largely error-free. What is less obvious is that such a theory of stored knowledge and retrieval processes provides the basis for explaining several phenomena observed in adults' time to produce or verify basic addition facts. One phenomenon is that adults produce answers very quickly, typically in less than a second (e.g., Ashcraft, 1987; Groen & Parkman, 1972). This can be attributed to the process of activating stored knowledge, a relatively rapid and automatic process, as opposed to computing answers by way of sequential procedures, a relatively slow and controlled process.

A second phenomenon is that the time to produce an answer systematically varies across problems. The slowest responses are for problems with "large" sums such as 9 + 8, with intermediate times for problems with medium sums, such as 4 + 7, and relatively fast responses for problems with small sums, such as 2 + 1 and 3 + 2 and for "ties" such as 4 + 4, 7 + 7, and so forth, and these problems are relatively homogeneous in time to respond (Ashcraft & Stazyk, 1981; Groen & Parkman, 1972). As noted earlier, such differences in retrieval time are attributed to differences in the strength of specific facts. Stronger associations in the knowledge network are faster to activate.

A third phenomenon is that the time to reject a fact such as 4 + 3 = 12 is substantially slower than the time for 4 + 3 = 10, even though the first answer is actually further from the correct answer (Winkelman & Schmidt, 1974). Such effects are attributed to associative confusions between addition and multiplication facts.

The aforementioned theory of expert solution of simple addition problems relies heavily on the assumption of differential associative strengths across the basic facts formed by the digits 0–9. An obvious question is whether this assumption is arbitrary or whether the assumed pattern of strength differences can be related to experiential phenomena. According to the law of frequency, items accrue strength through use and practice. Analyses of problem presentation frequency in children's mathematics texts indicate that those basic facts assumed to be stronger in the network actually appear more frequently in the texts (Ashcraft, 1987). Furthermore, analyses of multicolumn addition reveal that the frequency of adding 1, 2, or 3 is greater than that of adding 7, 8, or 9, consistent with strength patterns in the network.

Given that this theory is a plausible account of adult or expert performance, the question of developmental and instructional import concerns the nature of the progression from novice to expert. The acquisition of expertise in addition actually has its roots in the more general domain of number knowledge and quantitative understanding, acquisitions that are strongly tied to children's counting behavior (e.g., Gelman & Gallistel, 1978; Steffe, von Glaserfeld, Richards, & Cobb, 1983). Before school entry, most children have acquired relatively sophisticated counting sequences for the digits 1–20 (Fuson & Hall, 1983; Gelman & Gallistel, 1978). Children also have a basic understanding of the semantics of addition and subtraction in terms of the combining and separating of quantities (e.g., Carpenter, 1985; Resnick, 1982, 1984). Their understanding of addition, in concert with their knowledge of counting, permits the solution of addition problems even in the absence of directly stored facts (e.g., Starkey & Gelman, 1982). Substantial evidence now exists that initial knowledge of addition consists of procedures for representing, combining, and counting physical entities. Subsequently, addition can be performed as mental counting operations in the absence of physical objects. Such overt and covert operations constitute forms of procedural knowledge and processing that develop before and along with declarative knowledge and direct retrieval of addition facts (Fuson, 1982).

A developmental theory of the acquisition of expertise in addition includes specific assumptions about the state of both declarative and procedural knowledge at different points in time. It includes the assumption that there is a gradual acquisition and strengthening of the network structure of addition facts. There is also a gradual acquisition of counting procedures that permit the calculation of answers when facts are not of sufficient strength to be retrieved. Preschoolers primarily depend on overt counting procedures to solve addition problems (Siegler & Shrager, 1984). Given instruction and practice in the early grades, there is a transition to more sophisticated and efficient counting procedures, together with a transition from calculation via counting to direct retrieval. Thus, at any point in time from preschool age through at least fourth grade, a child will have some facts that can be retrieved and some that need to be calculated. From the fourth grade on through adulthood, simple addition problems are solved via retrieval with a continued strengthening of facts in the network resulting in further increases in the speed of retrieving all addition facts (Ashcraft, 1987; Svenson, 1975).

Subtraction

This discussion has concentrated on addition, but the issues raised about the nature of expertise and its acquisition are equally applicable to simple subtraction problems. A theory of expertise in subtraction and its acquisition is similar to the theory for addition. Both emphasize the gradual acquisition of declarative knowledge facts. These changes in knowledge and processing occur over a period of several years. The rate of change both within and between individuals will vary with the experiential history and learning rate of each person. Thus one must consider the possibility that the difficulties in mathematics manifested by some children are partially attributable to problems with basic facts. The facts may be sufficiently weak such that they cannot be retrieved and must therefore be computed, and the counting procedures for doing such computations may be slow and error-prone.

Data on basic addition and subtraction performance suggest that children with mathematics difficulties often must compute rather than directly retrieve answers to problems (e.g., Goldman, Mertz, & Pellegrino, 1988; Russell & Ginsburg, 1984). Connor (1983) reported results obtained by Fleishner and her colleagues from testing basic facts. Students with learning disabilities relied more on reconstructive counting strategies than the students without disabilities, who tended to rely on direct retrieval. This agrees with the results obtained by Russell and Ginsburg (1984), who compared a group of fourth graders with learning disabilities in mathematics to third and fourth graders without disabilities. They observed particular difficulties in retrieving addition facts by those students with mathematics-specific learning disabilities, with the children performing at a level below the third graders without disabilities. Svenson and Broquist (1975) also reported results indicating that fifth-grade children with low mathematics achievement are particularly slow at answering simple addition problems. Although available data are suggestive of difficulties in simple addition and subtraction, considerably more must be done to pursue these issues. The theory of expertise and its acquisition that has been outlined previously provides a framework for systematically pursuing issues regarding both the assessment and instruction of basic skills (see also Baroody, Bajwa, & Eiland, 2009).

Knowledge of subtraction can be conceptualized as a complex procedure with multiple parts, each of which represents a successive complication. The essential parts are 1) processing single columns in a right to left order, 2) borrowing when the bottom digit in a column is greater than the top digit, and 3) borrowing from zero. These three parts correspond to the typical sequence in learning how to subtract. The child first learns how to subtract a single column of numbers where the top number is always greater than the bottom number. Then this is expanded to multiple columns, but in problems where borrowing is never needed. The assumption is frequently made that the child subtracts two numbers in a column by retrieving a fact from memory, such as $7 - 5 = 2$. However, a child might actually perform the subtraction for single digits by a counting procedure. The next major stage is to introduce the borrowing part of the procedure. This involves a test to see if the top number is greater than the bottom number in a column. If it is, then borrowing is needed and the sequence of steps is taught. In beginning instruction, this usually takes the form of crossing out the top digit in the column to the left, decrementing it by one, and then writing the new digit in the top of that column. The child then writes a 1 in front of the top digit in the original column and then goes on to do the column subtraction by retrieving a fact such as $17 - 9 = 8$. Practice in borrowing is provided with a progression to problems with multiple columns that require borrowing. The final stage of instruction is the procedure for borrowing from zero. The original borrowing procedure is now expanded to include a test for whether the column to the left contains a zero. If a zero is present, then a new set of operations must be executed, which include changing zero to 9 and moving one column to the left, testing for zero again, and so forth. Analyses of children's errors in subtraction suggest that they often follow faulty procedures that preserve syntactic aspects of subtraction procedures, such as crossing things out or writing down a 1 while simultaneously violating the semantics of the procedures (e.g., Resnick, 1982, 1984).

Expertise can be defined as being able to solve any subtraction problem, which minimally implies knowledge of all the elements of the subtraction procedure. Lower levels of expertise are defined by the probability that errors will occur. Considerable effort has been expended on analyzing children's errors on subtraction problems (Burton, 1981; Brown & Burton, 1978; Brown & VanLehn, 1980; Friend & Burton, 1981; VanLehn, 1990; Young & O'Shea, 1981). It is now apparent that errors are not just random; in other words, they cannot be attributed primarily to slips. Instead, errors tend to be systematic and can be directly related to one or more of the elements of the major subprocedures of the complete subtraction procedure. As might be suspected, most of the systematic errors involve borrowing in general and borrowing from zero in particular. A common error is *smaller from larger,* in which the child subtracts the smaller digit in a column from the larger, regardless of which one is on top. This may be due to a child's lack of knowledge about how to borrow, a failure to incorporate a test for borrowing, or a carryover from simple subtraction where the smaller number is always "taken away" from the larger number and position doesn't matter.

One way to conceptualize the underlying source of these types of errors is in terms of slightly flawed procedural knowledge. The child has represented the procedures for performing subtraction, but one or more of the elements is incorrectly represented (i.e., the child has a "bug" in his program for doing subtraction). The term *bug* is taken from computer programming and reflects an algorithm that contains an incorrect operation. A systematic error is produced each time the program is run on the particular class of problems that requires execution of that operation. An alternative possibility is that the child is missing a piece of procedural knowledge, which is similar to a critical operation being omitted from a program. In a computer program, a missing operation will typically cause the program to crash and produce no output whatsoever. However, in the case of a child who knows that some response must be made, the child reaches an impasse. In order to move on, the child attempts to repair that impasse by doing something. The something he or she does is an operation that may mimic syntactic but not semantic constraints of subtraction.

It is almost a given that elementary school children experiencing difficulty in mathematics will demonstrate less than expert performance on problems requiring complex procedures. Concern then is whether the errors they make can be understood in terms of the theory of knowledge and performance described previously. One possibility is that such children have all the correct procedures and that errors are due to slips and miscalculations associated with their weak knowledge of basic facts (Russell & Ginsburg, 1984). A second possibility is that parts of the procedural knowledge are either missing or flawed, in which case the errors they make would be systematic. If there are systematic errors, then do these children exhibit bugs similar to those found in previous research, or are their errors more bizarre? There is little in the way of systematic data to address these questions. Russell and Ginsburg (1984) reported limited data indicating that fourth graders with learning disabilities in mathematics have bugs similar to those exhibited by younger children without disabilities. They offer a hypothesis of *essential cognitive normality,* in which children with learning disabilities in mathematics are at the lower levels of expertise representing the knowledge and performance of younger children. Considerably more needs to be done to explore such a hypothesis as it applies to complex procedural skills, as well as other important aspects of mathematical proficiency as identified by Kilpatrick and colleagues (2001).

Is All This Detail Necessary?

It is not uncommon for individuals to ask what useful purpose, beyond esoteric academic pursuits, is served by the foregoing consideration of what we know about the knowledge and cognitive processing underlying something as simple as basic reading or mathematics knowledge and skills. As mentioned earlier, the preceding was designed help those outside the research arena understand that even the supposedly simplest cognitive acts and instructional domains imply complicated forms of knowledge that are slowly acquired through experience and instruction. Furthermore, just as knowledge is not random, neither is performance, especially erroneous performance. In fact, some would argue that we can learn far more from mistakes than we do from correct answers.

Unfortunately, test content and test scores focus on just the opposite. For one thing, test items are often far removed from a theory of the knowledge underlying the performance of interest, and test scores provide little in the way of information that is directly useful to teachers to guide instructional decision making. In a typical test, the items are sampled from some universe of possibilities, and the emphasis is not on the individual problem, but on the score derived by aggregating over problems. This leads to a situation in which the same score can have very different meanings, but there is no way of knowing that, because the focus is on the total score rather than the way in which the score was produced. If the research within cognitive science has told us anything, it is that the process by which a response is produced is far more important than the product. The same products can often result from very different thinking processes, and testing procedures are frequently insensitive to such differences.

Consider, for example, a case in which two children have systematic but different misconceptions involving borrowing in multicolumn subtraction. They might well achieve the same score by missing different problems. Even if they miss the same problem, the nature of their errors might be different. Typical tests and test scoring procedures do not discriminate among these possibilities because they were not designed to do so, nor do they provide any information about the incorrect choices that were made. A similar situation could arise with respect to tests of basic math facts. Tests of basic addition and subtraction facts are usually timed. What matters is the number of correct answers within the time period allotted. What is often ignored is how the number correct relates to the number attempted and the nature of the errors made on those attempted. In this regard, the author is reminded of an actual situation that arose when one of his children brought home a test of addition and subtraction basic facts. All of the addition facts were correct, but almost all of the subtraction facts were wrong. The note on the test said that he should memorize his basic math facts. The child was clearly distressed because he didn't know what the teacher meant. I examined his test and noticed that for all the subtraction fact answers that were incorrect, they were off by 1. This suggested that he was not recalling his facts from memory but was using a counting scheme that had a systematic flaw or bug. I sat him down and got him to explain how he arrived at his answers and discovered that he was using a "counting down" procedure, but with an extra count. I showed him how to correct his "buggy" procedure, he practiced the new one for a while until it was reliable, and off he went, content that he wasn't stupid and that he could now get the right answers. It was true that he still didn't know his subtraction facts, but eventually he would, because the counting procedure would yield the right answers, and this in turn would give way to retrieval from memory once each of the facts was sufficiently strong to be associatively retrieved. The point of this little true example is that tests, testing procedures, and score interpretation need to be brought in correspondence with current theories of the nature of expertise in the domain of interest and the nature of the acquisition process. It is far more helpful to know that a child understands how to do subtraction and what it means, albeit he is less than fluent in fact retrieval, than to know that he misses 70% of all his subtraction facts.

There is an obvious challenge in translating theories about content knowledge and the acquisition of expertise into acceptable and workable instructional and testing procedures. To think that this is an easy task is to seriously underestimate the practical problems of the translation and implementation process. The problem is confounded with working with a group of students with learning and/or cognitive disabilities. Researchers must be willing to expend the time and effort needed to articulate their theories and assessment procedures in ways that are operationally feasible. Assessment developers must be willing to adopt new measurement models and scoring and reporting procedures. Educational practitioners must be willing to articulate their needs regarding the instructional monitoring functions they would like to perform and then find ways to incorporate new teaching and assessment technologies into daily classroom practices.

IMPLICATIONS FOR ASSESSMENT DESIGN

Existing guidelines for assessment design emphasize that the process should begin with a statement of the purpose for the assessment and a definition of the content domain to be measured (American Educational Research Association [AERA], American Psychological Association [APA], & National Council of Measurement in Education [NCME], 1999). A central thesis of this chapter is that the targets of inference should also be largely determined by a model of cognition and learning that describes how people represent knowledge and develop competence in the domain (the cognition element of the assessment triangle). Starting with a model of learning is one of the main features that distinguishes the proposed approach to assessment design from typical current approaches. The model suggests the most important aspects of student achievement about which one would want to draw inferences and provides clues about the types of assessment tasks that will elicit evidence to support those inferences (see also Pellegrino, 1988; Pellegrino, Baxter, & Glaser, 1999; Pellegrino et al., 2001).

The model of learning that informs assessment design should ideally have as many as possible of the following key features:

1. It should be based on empirical studies of learners in the domain.

2. It should identify performances that differentiate beginning and expert performance in the domain.

3. It should provide a developmental perspective, laying out typical progressions from novice levels toward competence and then expertise, and noting landmark performances along the way.

4. It should allow for a variety of typical ways in which children come to understand the subject matter.

5. It should capture some, but not all, aspects of what is known about how students think and learn in the domain. Starting with a theory of how people learn the subject matter, the designers of an assessment will need to select a slice or subset of the larger theory as the targets of inference.

6. It should lend itself to being aggregated at different grain sizes so that it can be used for different assessment purposes (e.g., to provide fine-grained diagnostic information as well as coarser-grained summary information).

As described earlier, research on cognition and learning has produced a rich set of descriptions of domain-specific performance that can serve as the basis for assessment design, particularly for certain areas of reading, mathematics, and science (e.g., American Association for the Advancement of Science, 2001; Bransford et al., 2000; Duschl et al., 2007; Kilpatrick et al., 2001; Snow et al., 1998; Wilson & Bertenthal, 2005). Yet much more research is needed, especially with regard to students who are low achievers and who may have various identifiable learning or cognitive disabilities. This is despite the fact that a significant body of work already exists regarding students with disabilities and their performance in aspects of mathematics (e.g., Baroody et al., 2009; Fuchs et al., 2005; Goldman et al., 1988; Miller, 1997; Russell & Ginsburg, 1984; Swanson & Jerman, 2006) and their performance in aspects of reading (e.g., Connor, 1983; Fletcher et al., 2002; Foorman & Torgesen, 2001; O'Connor & Jenkins, 1999; Torgesen, 2002; Wagner et al., 1997).

What follows are some of the implications of the knowledge we do have for multiple aspects of assessment design and use. We begin with a consideration of issues related to assessment purpose and move to implications of cognitive research and theory for assessment that occurs in the context of the classroom and for state-level, large-scale accountability assessment. Many of the specific topics in the following sections related to assessment design and use, including issues of validity and fairness, are developed in much greater depth in the chapters that follow in this book.

Assessment Purposes, Levels, and Timescales

Although assessments are currently used for many purposes in the educational system, a premise of the *Knowing What Students Know* report (Pellegrino et al., 2001) is that their effectiveness and utility must ultimately be judged by the extent to which they promote student learning. The aim of assessment should be *"to educate and improve student performance, not merely to audit it"* (Wiggins, 1998, p.7). Because assessments are developed for specific purposes, the nature of their design is very much constrained by their intended use. The reciprocal relationship between function and design leads to concerns about the inappropriate and ineffective use of assessments for purposes beyond their original intent. To clarify some of these issues of assessment purpose, design, and use, it is worth considering two pervasive dichotomies in the literature that are often misunderstood and conflated.

The first dichotomy is between *internal* classroom assessments, administered by teachers, and *external* tests, administered by districts, states, or nations. Ruiz-Primo et al. (2002) showed that these two very different types of assessments are better understood as two points on a continuum that is defined by the distance from the enactment of specific instructional activities. They defined five discrete points on the continuum of assessment distance: *immediate* (e.g., observations or artifacts from the enactment of a specific activity), *close* (e.g., embedded assessments and semiformal quizzes of learning from one or more activities), *proximal* (e.g., formal classroom exams of learning from a specific curriculum), *distal* (e.g., criterion-referenced achievement tests such as required by the federal No Child Left Behind legislation), and *remote* (broader outcomes measured over time, including norm-referenced achievement tests and some national and international achievement measures). Different assessments should be understood as different points on this continuum if they are to be effectively aligned with each other and with curriculum and instruction.

A second pervasive dichotomy is the one between *formative* assessments used to advance learning and *summative* assessments used to provide evidence of prior learning. Often it is assumed that classroom assessment is synonymous with formative assessment and that large-scale assessment is synonymous with summative assessment. What are now widely understood as different types of assessment practices are more productively understood as different functions of assessment practice and that summative and formative functions can be identified for most assessment activities, regardless of the level on which they function.

Drawing from the work of Lemke (2000), it is apparent that different assessment practices can be understood as operating at different *timescales*. The timescales for the five levels defined previously can be characterized as minutes, days, weeks, months, and years. Timescale is important because the different competencies that various assessments aim to measure (and therefore the appropriate timing for being impacted by feedback) are timescale-specific. The cycles, or periodicity, of educational processes build from individual utterances into an individual's lifespan of educational development. What teachers and students say in class constitute verbal exchanges; these exchanges make up the lesson; a sequence of lessons make up the unit; units form a curriculum, and the curricula form an education. Each of these elements operates on different cycles or timescales: second to second, day to day, week to week, month to month, and year to year.

The level at which an assessment is intended to function, which involves varying distance in "space and time" from the enactment of instruction and learning, has implications for how and how well it can fulfill various functions of assessment, be they formative, summative, or program evaluation (NRC, 2003). As argued elsewhere (Hickey & Pellegrino, 2005; Pellegrino & Hickey, 2006), it is also the case that the different levels and functions of assessment can have varying degrees of match with theoretical stances about the nature of knowing and learning. With this in mind, we now turn to the implications of cognitive theory and research for both classroom assessment practices and for large-scale assessment. These two contexts reflect some of the rich variation in assessment captured by the foregoing discussion of levels, functions, and timescales.

Implications of Cognitive Theory and Research for Classroom Assessment

Shepard (2000) discussed ways in which classroom assessment practices need to change to better support learning: The content and character of assessments need to be significantly improved to reflect contemporary understanding of learning; the gathering and use of assessment information and insights must become a part of the ongoing learning process; and assessment must become a central concern in methods courses in teacher preparation programs. Her messages are reflective of a growing belief among many educational assessment experts that if assessment, curriculum, and instruction were more integrally connected, student learning would improve (e.g., Pellegrino, et al., 1999; Stiggins, 1997).

Sadler (1989) provided a conceptual framework that places classroom assessment in the context of curriculum and instruction. According to this framework, three elements are required for assessment to promote learning:

- A clear view of the learning goals (derived from the curriculum)
- Information about the present state of the learner (derived from assessment)
- Action to close the gap (taken through instruction)

Furthermore, there are ongoing, dynamic relationships among formative assessment, curriculum, and instruction. That is, there are important bidirectional interactions among the three elements, such that each informs the other. For instance, formulating assessment procedures for classroom use can spur a teacher to think more specifically about learning goals, thus leading to modification of curriculum and instruction. These modifications can, in turn, lead to refined assessment procedures, and so on. The mere existence of classroom assessment along the lines discussed here will not ensure effective learning. The clarity and appropriateness of the curriculum goals, the validity of the assessments in relationship to these goals, the interpretation of the assessment evidence, and the relevance and quality of the instruction that ensues are all critical determinants of the outcome. Starting with a model of cognition and learning in the domain can enhance each of these determinants.

For most teachers, the ultimate goals for learning are established by the curriculum, which is usually mandated externally (e.g., by state content standards). However, teachers and others responsible for designing curriculum, instruction, and assessment must fashion intermediate goals that can serve as an effective route to achieving the ultimate goals, and to do so effectively, they must have an understanding of how students represent knowledge and develop competence in the domain. National and state content standards set forth learning goals, but often not at a level of detail that is useful for operationalizing those goals in instruction and assessment. By dividing goal descriptions into sets appropriate for different age and grade ranges, current content standards provide broad guidance about the nature of the progression to be expected in various subject domains. Whereas this kind of epistemological and conceptual analysis of the subject domain is an essential basis for guiding assessment, deeper cognitive analysis of how people learn the subject matter is also needed. Formative assessment should be based in cognitive theories about how people learn particular subject matter to ensure that instruction centers on what is most important for the next stage of learning, given a learner's current state of understanding.

It follows that teachers need training to develop their understanding of cognition and learning in the domains they teach. Pre-service training and professional development are needed to uncover teachers' existing understandings of how students learn and to help them formulate models of learning so they can identify students' naive or initial sense-making strategies and build on those to move students toward more sophisticated understandings. The aim is to increase teachers' diagnostic expertise so they can make informed decisions about next steps for student learning. This has been a primary goal of cognitively based approaches to instruction and assessment that have been shown to have a positive impact on student learning, including the Cognitively Guided Instruction program (Carpenter et al., 1996) and others (Cobb et al., 1991; Griffin & Case, 1997). Such approaches rest on a bedrock of informed professional practice.

Implications of Cognitive Research and Theory for Large-Scale Assessment

Large-scale assessments are further removed from instruction but can still benefit learning if well-designed and properly used. Substantially more valid, useful, and fair information could be gained from large-scale assessments if the principles of design set forth previously and described subsequently were applied. However, fully capitalizing on contemporary theory and research will require more substantial changes in the way large-scale assessment is approached and relaxation of some of the constraints that currently drive large-scale assessment practices.

Large-scale summative assessments should focus on the most critical and central aspects of learning in a domain as identified by content standards and informed by cognitive research and theory. Large-scale assessments typically will reflect aspects of the model of learning at a less detailed level than classroom assessments, which can go into more depth because they focus on a smaller slice of curriculum and instruction. For instance, one might need to know for summative purposes whether a student has mastered the more complex aspects of multicolumn subtraction, including borrowing from and across zero, rather than exactly which subtraction bugs lead to mistakes. At the same time, although policy makers and parents may not need all the diagnostic detail that would be useful to a teacher and student during the course of instruction, large-scale summative assessments should be based on a model of learning that is compatible with and derived from the same set of knowledge and beliefs about learning as classroom assessment.

As described previously, research on cognition and learning suggests a broad range of competencies that should be assessed when measuring student achievement, many of which are essentially untapped by current assessments. Examples are knowledge organization, problem representation, strategy use, metacognition, and participatory activities (e.g., formulating questions, constructing and evaluating arguments, contributing to group problem solving). Furthermore, large-scale assessments should provide information about the nature of student understanding, rather than simply ranking students according to general proficiency estimates.

Large-scale assessments not only serve as a means for reporting on student achievement, but also reflect aspects of academic competence societies consider worthy of recognition and reward. Thus large-scale assessments can signal worthwhile targets for educators and students to pursue. Whereas teaching directly to the items on a test is not desirable, teaching to the theory of cognition and learning that underlies an assessment can provide positive direction for instruction.

A major problem is that only limited improvements in large-scale assessments are possible under current constraints and typical standardized testing scenarios. Large-scale assessments are designed to meet certain purposes under constraints that often include providing reliable and comparable scores for individuals as well as groups, sampling a broad set of content standards within a limited testing time per student, and offering cost-efficiency in terms of development, scoring, and administration. To meet these kinds of demands, designers typically create assessments that are given at a specified time, with all students being given the same (or parallel) tests under strictly standardized conditions (often referred to as *on-demand assessment*). Tasks are generally of the kind that can be presented in paper-and-pencil format, that students can respond to quickly, and that can be scored reliably and efficiently. In general, competencies that lend themselves to being assessed in these ways are tapped, whereas aspects of learning that cannot be observed under such constrained conditions are not addressed. To design new kinds of situations for capturing the complexity of cognition and learning will require examining the assumptions and values that currently drive assessment design choices and breaking out of the current paradigm to explore alternative approaches to large-scale assessment, including innovative uses of technology (see Quellmalz & Pellegrino, 2009).

Design of Observational Situations

Once the purpose for an assessment, the underlying model of learning in the domain, and the desired types of inferences to be drawn from the results have been specified, situations must be designed for collecting evidence to support the desired inferences about what students know and can do.

Task Design

The focus should be on the cognitive demands of tasks (the mental processes and knowledge required for successful performance), rather than primarily on surface features, such as how tasks are presented to students or the format in which students are asked to respond. For instance, it is commonly believed that multiple-choice items are limited to assessing low-level processes such as recall of facts, whereas performance tasks elicit more complex cognitive processes. However, research shows that the relationship between item format and cognitive demands is not so straightforward (Baxter & Glaser, 1998; Hamilton, Nussbaum, & Snow, 1997).

Linking tasks to the model of cognition and learning forces attention to a central principle of task design—that tasks should emphasize the features that are relevant to the construct being measured and minimize extraneous features (AERA et al., 1999; Messick, 1993). Ideally, a task will not measure aspects of cognition that are irrelevant to the targeted performance. For instance, when assessing students' mathematical reasoning, one should avoid presenting problems in contexts that might be unfamiliar to a particular population of students. Similarly, mathematics tasks should not make heavy demands for reading or writing unless one is explicitly aiming to assess students' abilities to read or communicate about mathematics. Surface features of tasks do need to be considered to the extent that they affect or change the cognitive demands of the tasks in unintended ways.

Task Difficulty

The difficulty of tasks should be explained in terms of the underlying knowledge and cognitive processes required, rather than simply in terms of statistical item difficulty indices, such as the proportion of respondents answering the item correctly (which ignores that two tasks with similar surface features can be equally difficult, but for very different reasons). Beyond knowing that 80% of students answered a particular item incorrectly, it would be educationally useful to know why so many did so, that is, to identify the sources of the difficulty so they could be remedied.

Cognitive theory and analysis can be helpful here. For instance, cognitive research shows that a mathematics word problem that describes the combining of quantities and seeks the resultant total (e.g., John has 3 marbles and Mary has 5, how many do they have altogether?) is easier to comprehend than one that describes the same actors but expresses a comparison of their respective quantities (e.g., John has 3 marbles. He has 2 less than Mary. How many does she have?) (e.g., Morales, Shute & Pellegrino, 1985; Riley, Greeno, & Heller, 1983). Part of the difficulty for children is the conflict between the relational expression *less than,* which implies subtraction, and the operation required, which involves addition.

The point is not that such sources of difficulty should necessarily be avoided. Rather, these kinds of cognitive complexities should be introduced into the assessment tasks in principled ways in those cases in which one wants to draw inferences about whether students can handle them. There are many reasons why educators might want to assess students' abilities to apply integrated sets of skills (e.g., literacy and mathematics capabilities) to complex problems. That is entirely consistent with the approach being set forth here, as long as assessment design begins with a model of learning that describes the complex of skills, understandings, and communicative practices that one is interested in making inferences about, and tasks are specifically designed to provide evidence to support those inferences.

Scoring

Tasks and the procedures to be used for drawing the relevant evidence from students' responses to those tasks must be considered together. That is, the ways in which student responses will be scored should be conceptualized during the design of a task. A task may stimulate creative thinking or problem solving, but such rich information will be lost unless the means used to interpret the responses capture the evidence needed to draw inferences about those processes. Like tasks, scoring methods must be carefully constructed to be sensitive to critical differences in levels and types of student understanding identified by the model of learning. At times one may be interested in the quantity of facts a student has learned, for instance, when one is measuring mastery of the alphabet or multiplication table. However, a cognitive approach generally implies that when evaluating students' responses, the focus should be on the quality or nature of their understanding, rather than simply the quantity of information produced. In many cases, quality can be modeled quantitatively; that is, even in very qualitative contexts, ideas of order and orderliness will be present.

Task Sets and Assembly of an Assessment Instrument

An assessment should be more than a collection of items that work well individually. The utility of assessment information can be enhanced by carefully selecting tasks and combining the information from those tasks to provide evidence about the nature of student understanding. Sets of tasks should be carefully constructed and selected to discriminate among different levels and kinds of understanding that are identified in the model of learning. To illustrate this point simply, it takes more than one item or a collection of unrelated items to diagnose a procedural error in subtraction. If a student answers three of five separate subtraction questions incorrectly, one can infer only that the student is using some faulty process(es), but a carefully crafted collection of items can be designed to pinpoint the limited concepts or flawed rules the student is using.

Validation

Traditionally, validity concerns associated with achievement tests have tended to center around test content, that is, the degree to which the test samples the subject matter domain about which inferences are to be drawn. There is increasing recognition within the assessment community that traditional forms of validation—which emphasize expert appraisal of the alignment of tasks with content frameworks and their statistical consistency with other measures—should be supplemented with evidence of the cognitive or substantive aspect of validity (e.g., AERA et al., 1999; Messick, 1993). That is, the trustworthiness of the interpretation of test scores should rest in part on empirical evidence that the assessment tasks actually tap the intended cognitive processes and knowledge.

As described by Messick (1993) and summarized by Magone, Cai, Silver, and Wang (1994), a variety of techniques can be used to examine the processes examinees use during task performance to evaluate whether prospective items are functioning as intended. These techniques include *protocol analysis,* in which students are asked to think aloud as they solve problems or to describe retrospectively how they solved the problems. Another method is *analysis of reasons,* in which students are asked to provide rationales for their responses to the tasks. A third method is *analysis of errors,* in which one draws inferences about processes from incorrect procedures, concepts, or representations of the problems.

Situative and sociocultural research on learning suggests that validation should be taken a step further. This body of research emphasizes that cognitive processes are embedded in social practices. From this perspective, performance of students on tests is understood as an activity in the situation that the test presents, and success depends on abilities to participate in the practices of test taking (Greeno, Pearson, & Schoenfeld, 1996). It follows that validation should include the collection of evidence that test-takers possess the communicative practices required for their responses to be actual indicators of their abilities, for instance, to understand and reason. This has been demonstrated to be false in many cases (e.g., Cole, Gay, & Glick, 1968).

Reporting

Although reporting of results occurs at the end of an assessment cycle, assessments must be designed from the outset to ensure that reporting of the desired types of information will be possible. The familiar distinction between norm-referenced and criterion-referenced testing (Glaser, 1963) is salient in understanding the central role of a model of learning in the reporting of assessment results. The notion of criterion-referenced testing has gained popularity in the last several decades, particularly with the advent of standards-based reforms in the 1990s. As a result of these reforms, many states are implementing tests designed to measure student performance against standards in core content areas.

Because criterion-referenced interpretations depend so directly on a clear explication of what students can or cannot do, well-delineated descriptions of learning in the domain are key to their effectiveness in communicating about student performance. Test results should be reported in relation to a model of learning. The ways people learn the subject matter and different states of competence should be displayed and made as recognizable as possible to educators, students, and the public to foster discussion and shared understanding of what constitutes academic achievement.

Fairness

Fairness in testing is defined in many ways (see AERA et al., 1999), but at its core is the idea of comparable validity: A fair test is one that yields comparably valid inferences from person to person and group to group (Heubert & Hauser, 1999). An assessment task is considered biased if construct-irrelevant characteristics of the task result in different meanings for different subgroups. Currently, bias tends to be identified through expert review of items. Such a finding is merely judgmental, however, and in and of itself may not warrant removal of items from an assessment. Also used are statistical differential item functioning (DIF) analyses, which identify items that produce differing results for members of particular groups after the groups have been matched in ability with regard to the attribute being measured. However, DIF is a statistical finding and again may not warrant removal of items from an assessment. Some researchers have therefore begun to supplement existing bias-detection methods with cognitive analyses designed to uncover the reasons why items are functioning differently across groups in terms of how students think about and approach the problems (e.g., Lane, Wang, & Magone, 1996; Zwick & Ercikan, 1989).

A particular set of fairness issues involves the testing of students with disabilities. A substantial number of children who participate in assessments do so with accommodations intended to permit them to participate meaningfully. For instance, a student with a severe reading and writing disability might be able to take a chemistry test with the assistance of a computer-based reader and dictation system. Unfortunately, little evidence currently exists about the effects of various accommodations on the inferences one might wish to draw about the performance of individuals with disabilities (McDonnell, McLaughlin, & Morison, 1997), although some researchers have taken initial steps in studying these issues (Abedi, Hofstetter, Baker, & Lord, 2001). Therefore, cognitive analyses are also needed to gain insight into how accommodations affect task demands, as well as the validity of inferences drawn from test scores obtained under such circumstances.

CONCLUSIONS AND CAVEATS

A major thesis of this chapter is that the task of developing assessments tied to modified achievement standards needs to take seriously what we know about aspects of human cognition and its development, especially in domains of academic achievement and performance. This is much easier said than done, especially when we try to consider students who are hard to define and classify (see Chapter 1) and whose performance in the regular education context and on general academic achievement tests consistently leaves much to be desired. Many of the issues raised in this chapter pertain to the assessment of any and all students. It would behoove us to pay as much attention to a careful definition of academic achievement standards and assessments for the majority of students as we might propose to give to a subgroup of the population for whom we wish to define modified achievement standards and develop appropriate assessments. Although there is much we know about aspects of the development of competence in the regular education population, there is much that we don't know about cognition in selective parts of the school-age population. This knowledge gap has major implications for defining appropriate assessment targets and appropriate modes of assessment.

Given that we can never really know all that we need to know, and that there are pragmatic problems to be solved in the design of assessments for students with typical low levels of achievement, it is perhaps useful to consider some of the modifications that have been proposed for the assessment of this group of students and whether such design features can be justified. One such example is reducing cognitive load in questions through various means, such as presenting a smaller number of distracters. Although such a modification might well reduce construct irrelevant variance associated with working memory or metacognitive monitoring issues, it is a far cry from the type of deep engagement with assessment design issues related to the measurement construct that one would like to see. Such modifications may in fact change the nature of the construct assessed, but they do little to engage the issue of what the targets for learning should be and how such targets are manifested in the types of knowledge tapped by specific test items. Furthermore, work needs to be done to establish the cognitive processing validity of such modifications, which includes ruling out the possibility that improved performance has little to do with the nature of the knowledge and skill that is the intended achievement target. This is not to say, however, that attention to issues of processing load and construct irrelevant variance should not be considered in the design of assessment situations for students who may experience these types of processing issues.

A second example is choosing items that have a lower level of cognitive difficulty or depth of knowledge but that still represent the appropriate grade-level content standards. Aside from the fact that item difficulty can be driven by multiple factors that vary in their relationship to the construct one proposes to measure, it is important that any such efforts grapple in some detail with precisely what is meant by depth of knowledge. This can only be done by taking seriously an analysis of the nature of domain knowledge and competence and then selecting items that are purposely designed to assess some restricted aspects of the domain. Such a choice can be done in a principled way, and it necessarily brings with it the implication that the new assessment has a different construct representation than the general education assessment. Regardless of how one chooses to approach the process of changing difficulty, decisions cannot be made on the basis of a superficial level of analysis of the nature of knowledge and skill desired at a particular grade level nor a similarly superficial analysis of how it articulates with some progression of knowledge and skill at both higher and lower grade levels.

A third possible approach is to use a dynamic assessment procedure, with varying levels of prompting and scaffolding. Such a procedure might well be justifiable when assessment is viewed as a test of transfer and the goal is to see how far a student is capable of transferring his or her knowledge. As was noted previously, one must still engage deeply with an analysis of what defines competence and acceptable achievement at the particular grade level. On that basis, one can determine how a dynamic assessment or scaffolding process can be used to provide an estimate of the intended construct at the desired level of attainment.

One way to view the preceding is as a plea for states, and the field in general, to move cautiously in the development of modified achievement standards and in the implementation of assessments designed to provide valid measures of those standards. Clearly, there is much that we still need to know. A design-based research strategy (e.g., Kelly, Lesh, & Baek, 2008), in which there are serious, small-scale attempts to design and validate such assessments through iterative cycles of empirical testing, redesign, and refinement, may be the most appropriate and cost-effective model for the field at this point in time. Such an approach has multiple advantages, including avoiding considerable investment in an approach to assessment that may have limited validity and utility. One critical goal of the pursuit of modified achievement standards should be to provide resources and information that allow educators to engage in a better integration of curriculum, instruction, and assessment for precisely those students whose achievement is characteristically well below desired levels.

REFERENCES

Abedi, J., Hofstetter, C., Baker, E., & Lord, C. (2001). *NAEP math performance and test accommodations: Interactions with student language background* (CSE Technical Report 536). Los Angeles: National Center for Research on Evaluation, Standards, and Student Testing (CRESST), University of California, Los Angeles.

Adams, J., Treiman, R., & Pressley, M. (1998). Reading, writing, and literacy. In I.E. Sigel & K.A. Renninger (Eds.), *Handbook of child psychology: Vol. 4. Child psychology in practice* (5th ed., pp. 275–355). New York: Wiley.

American Association for the Advancement of Science. (2001). *Atlas of science literacy.* Washington, DC: Author.

American Educational Research Association, American Psychological Association, & National Council of Measurement in Education. (1999). *Standards for educational and psychological testing.* Washington, DC: American Educational Research Association.

Ashcraft, M.H. (1982). The development of mental arithmetic: A chronometric approach. *Developmental Review, 2,* 213–236.

Ashcraft, M.H. (1983). *Simulating network retrieval of arithmetic facts* (Report No. 1983/10). Pittsburgh: University of Pittsburgh, Learning Research and Development Center.

Ashcraft, M.H. (1987). Children's knowledge of simple arithmetic: A developmental simulation. In J. Bisanz, C. Brainerd, & R. Kail (Eds.), *Formal methods in developmental psychology* (pp. 302–338). New York: Springer-Verlag.

Ashcraft, M.H., & Stazyk, E.H. (1981). Mental addition: A test of three verification models. *Memory & Cognition, 9,* 185–196.

Baddeley, A. (1986). *Working memory.* Oxford, England: Oxford University Press.

Baroody, A.J., Bajwa, N.P., & Eiland, M. (2009). Why can't Johnny remember the basic facts? *Developmental Disabilities Research Reviews, 15*(1), 69–79.

Baxter, G.P., & Glaser, R. (1998). Investigating the cognitive complexity of science assessments. *Educational Measurement: Research and Practice, 17*(3), 37–45.

Bransford, J.D., Brown, A.L., & Cocking, R.R. (Eds.). (1999). *How people learn: Brain, mind, experience, and school.* Washington, DC: National Academies Press.

Bransford, J.D., Brown, A.L., Cocking, R.R., Donovan, M.S., & Pellegrino, J.W. (Eds.). (2000). *How people learn: Brain, mind, experience, and school* (Expanded ed.). Washington, DC: National Academies Press.

Brown, J.S., & Burton, R.R. (1978). Diagnostic models for procedural bugs in mathematics. *Cognitive Science, 4,* 379–426.

Brown, J.S., & VanLehn, K. (1980). Repair theory: A generative theory of bugs in procedural skills. *Cognitive Science, 4,* 379–426.

Burton, R.B. (1981). DEBUGGY: Diagnosis of errors in basic mathematical skills. In D.H. Sleeman & J.S. Brown (Eds.), *Intelligent tutoring systems.* London: Academic Press.

Carpenter, T.P. (1985). Learning to add and subtract: An exercise in problem solving. In E.A. Silver (Ed.), *Teaching and learning mathematical problem solving: Multiple research perspectives* (pp. 17–40). Mahwah, NJ: Lawrence Erlbaum Associates.

Carpenter, T.P., Moser, J.M., & Romberg, T.A. (Eds.). (1982). *Addition and subtraction: A cognitive perspective.* Mahwah, NJ: Lawrence Erlbaum Associates.

Carpenter, T., Fennema, E., & Franke, M. (1996). Cognitively guided instruction: A knowledge base for reform in primary mathematics instruction. *Elementary School Journal, 97*(1), 3–20.

Chi, M.T.H., Feltovich, P.J., & Glaser, R. (1981). Categorization and representation of physics problems by experts and novices. *Cognitive Science, 5,* 121–152.

Cobb, P., Wood, T., Yackel, E., Nicholls, J., Wheatley, G., Trigatti, B., et al. (1991). Assessment of a problem-centered second-grade mathematics project. *Journal for Research in Mathematics Education, 22*(1), 3–29.

Cole, M., Gay, J., & Glick, J. (1968). Some experimental studies of Kpelle quantitative behavior. *Psychonomic Monograph Supplements, 2*(10), 173–190.

Connor, F.P. (1983). Improving school instruction for learning disabled children: The Teachers College Institute. *Exceptional Education Quarterly, 4,* 23–44.

Corcoran, T.B., Mosher, F.A., & Rogat, A. (2009). *Learning progressions in science: An evidence-based approach to reform.* New York: Consortium for Policy Research in Education, Center on Continuous Instructional Improvement, Teachers College, Columbia University.

Donovan, M.S., Bransford, J.D., & Pellegrino, J.W. (Eds.). (1999). *How people learn: Bridging research and practice.* Washington, DC: National Academies Press.

Duncan, R.G., & Hmelo-Silver, C. (2009). Learning progressions: Aligning curriculum, instruction, and assessment. *Journal for Research in Science Teaching, 46*(6), 606–609.

Duschl, R.A., Schweingruber, H.A., & Shouse, A.W. (Eds.). (2007). *Taking science to school: Learning and teaching science in grade K–8.* Washington DC: National Academies Press.

Dweck, C., & Legget, E. (1988). A social-cognitive approach to motivation and personality. *Psychological Review, 95,* 256–273.

Fay, A., & Klahr, D. (1996). Knowing about guessing and guessing about knowing: Preschoolers' understanding of indeterminacy. *Child Development, 67,* 689–716.

Fletcher, J.M., Foorman, B.R., Boudousquie, A., Barnes, M., Schatschneider, C., & Francis, D.J. (2002). Assessment of reading and learning disabilities: A research-based, treatment-oriented approach. *Journal of School Psychology, 40,* 27–63.

Foorman, B.R., & Torgesen, J.K. (2001). Critical elements of classroom and small-group instruction promote reading success in all children. *Disabilities Research and Practice, 16,* 202–211.

Friend, J., & Burton, R. (1981). *A teacher's manual of subtraction bugs* (working paper). Palo Alto, CA: Xerox Palo Alto Research Center.

Fuchs, L.S., Compton, D.L., Fuchs, D., Paulsen, K., Bryant, J.D., Hamlett, C.L. (2005). The prevention, identification, and cognitive determinants of math difficulty. *Journal of Educational Psychology, 97*(3), 493–513.

Fuson, K.C. (1982). An analysis of the counting-on procedure in addition. In T.P. Carpenter, J.M. Moser, & T.A. Romberg (Eds.), *Addition and subtraction: A cognitive perspective* (pp. 67–81). Mahwah, NJ: Lawrence Erlbaum Associates.

Fuson, K.C., & Hall, J.W. (1983). The acquisition of early number word meanings: A conceptual analysis and review. In H.P. Ginsburg (Ed.), *The development of mathematical thinking* (pp. 49–107). New York: Academic Press.

Geary, D. (1995). Reflections of evolution and culture in children's cognition: Implications for mathematical development and instruction. *American Psychologist, 50*(1), 24–37.

Gelman, R. (1990). First principles organize attention to and learning about relevant data: Number and the animate-inanimate distinction as examples. *Cognitive Science, 14,* 79–106.

Gelman, R., & Gallistel, C.R. (1978). *The child's understanding of number.* Cambridge, MA: Harvard University Press.

Ginsburg, H.P., Greenes, C., & Balfanz, R. (2003). *Big math for little kids.* Parsippany, NJ: Dale Seymour.

Glaser, R. (1963). Instructional technology and the measurement of learning outcomes: Some questions. *American Psychologist, 18,* 519–521.

Glaser, R. (1992). Expert knowledge and processes of thinking. In D.F. Halpern (Ed.), *Enhancing thinking skills in the sciences and mathematics* (pp. 63–75). Mahwah, NJ: Lawrence Erlbaum Associates.

Goldman, S.R., Mertz, D., & Pellegrino, J.W. (1988). Extended practice of basic addition facts: Strategy changes in learning disabled students. *Cognition & Instruction, 5*(3), 223–265.

Graves, M.F., & Slater, W.H. (1987, April). *Development of reading vocabularies in rural disadvantaged students, intercity disadvantaged students and middle class suburban students.* Paper presented at the conference of the American Educational Research Association, Washington, DC.

Greeno, J.G. (1978). A study of problem solving. In R. Glaser (Ed.), *Advances in instructional psychology, Vol. 1* (pp. 13–75). Mahwah, NJ: Lawrence Erlbaum Associates.

Greeno, J.G., Pearson, P.D., & Schoenfeld, A.H. (1996). *Implications for NAEP of research on learning and cognition. Report of a study commissioned by the National*

Academy of Education. Panel on the NAEP Trial State Assessment, Conducted by the Institute for Research on Learning. Stanford, CA: National Academy of Education.

Griffin, S., & Case, R. (1997). Re-thinking the primary school math curriculum: An approach based on cognitive science. *Issues in Education, 3*(1), 1–49.

Griffin, S.A., Case, R., & Siegler, R.S. (1994). Rightstart: Providing the central conceptual prerequisites for first formal learning of arithmetic to students at risk for school failure. In K. McGilly (Ed.), *Classroom lessons: Integrating cognitive theory and classroom practice* (pp. 1–50). Cambridge, MA: The MIT Press/Bradford Books.

Groen, G.J., & Parkman, J.M. (1972). A chronometric analysis of simple addition. *Psychological Review, 79,* 329–343.

Hamilton, L.S., Nussbaum, E.M., & Snow, R.E. (1997). Interview procedures for validating science assessments. *Applied Measurement in Education, 10*(2), 181–200.

Hart, B., & Risley, T.R. (1995). *Meaningful differences in the everyday experience of young American children.* Baltimore: Paul H. Brookes Publishing Co.

Hatano, G. (1990). The nature of everyday science: A brief introduction. *British Journal of Developmental Psychology, 8,* 245–250.

Heubert, J.P., & Hauser, R.M. (Eds.). (1999). *High stakes: Testing for tracking, promotion, and graduation.* Washington, DC: National Academies Press.

Hickey, D., & Pellegrino, J.W. (2005). Theory, level, and function: Three dimensions for understanding transfer and student assessment. In J.P. Mestre (Ed.), *Transfer of learning from a modern multidisciplinary perspective* (pp. 251–293). Greenwich, CO: Information Age Publishing.

Huttenlocher, J. (1998). Language input and language growth. *Preventive Medicine, 27,* 195–199.

Kaiser, M.K., Proffitt, D.R., & McCloskey, M. (1985). The development of beliefs about falling objects. *Perception & Psychophysics, 38*(6), 533–539.

Kalchman, M., Moss, J., & Case, R. (2001). Psychological models for development of mathematical understanding: Rational numbers and functions. In S. Carver & D. Klahr (Eds.), *Cognition and instruction: Twenty-five years of progress* (pp. 1–38). Mahwah, NJ: Lawrence Erlbaum Associates.

Kelly, A.E., Lesh, R.A., & Baek, J.Y. (Eds.). (2008). *Handbook of design research methods in education: Innovations in science, technology, engineering, and mathematics learning and teaching.* New York: Routledge.

Kilpatrick, J., Swafford, J., & Findell, B. (Eds.). (2001). *Adding it up: Helping children learn mathematics.* Washington, DC: National Academies Press.

Kintsch, W. (1998). *Paradigms of comprehension.* Oxford, England: Oxford University Press.

Lampert, M. (1986). Knowing, doing, and teaching multiplication. *Cognition and Instruction, 3,* 305–342.

Lane, S., Wang, N., & Magone, M. (1996). Gender-related differential item functioning on a middle-school mathematics performance assessment. *Educational Measurement: Issues and Practice, 15*(4), 21–28.

Lave, J. (1988). *Cognition in practice.* Cambridge, England: Cambridge University Press.

Lemke, J.L. (2000). Across the scale of time: Artifacts, activities, and meaning in ecosocial systems. *Mind, Culture, and Activity, 7*(4), 273–290.

Lesgold, A., & Perfetti, C.A. (Eds.). (1981). *Interactive process in reading.* Mahwah, NJ: Lawrence Erlbaum Associates.

Lesh, R., & Landau, M. (Eds.). (1983). *Acquisition of mathematics concepts and processes*. New York: Academic Press.

Magone, M.E., Cai, J., Silver, E.A., & Wang, N. (1994). Validating the cognitive complexity and content quality of a mathematics performance assessment. *International Journal of Educational Research, 21*(3), 317–340.

Massey, C.M., & Gelman, R. (1988). Preschoolers decide whether pictured unfamiliar objects can move themselves. *Developmental Psychology, 24,* 307–317.

McDonnell, L.M., McLaughlin, M.J., & Morison P. (Eds.). (1997). *Educating one and all: Students with disabilities and standards-based reform*. Washington, DC: National Academies Press.

Messick, S. (1993). Validity. In R.L. Linn (Ed.), *Educational measurement* (3rd ed., pp. 13–103). Phoenix, AZ: Oryx Press.

Miller, S.P. (1997). Educational aspects of mathematics disabilities. *Journal of Learning Disabilities, 30*(1), 47–56.

Miyake, A., Just, M.A., & Carpenter, P.A. (1994). Working memory constraints on the resolution of lexical ambiguity: Maintaining multiple interpretations in neutral contexts. *Journal of Memory and Language, 33*(2), 175–202.

Morales, R., Shute, V., & Pellegrino, J.W. (1985). Developmental differences in understanding and solving simple mathematics word problems. *Cognition and Instruction, 2,* 41–57.

National Council of Teachers of Mathematics. (1995). *Assessment standards for school mathematics*. Reston, VA: Author.

National Council of Teachers of Mathematics. (2000). *Principles and standards for school mathematics*. Reston, VA: Author.

National Institute of Child Health and Human Development. (2000). *Teaching children to read: An evidence-based assessment of the scientific research literature on reading and its implications for reading instruction*. Report of the National Reading Panel. NIH Publication No. 00-4769. Washington, DC: U.S. Department of Education.

National Mathematics Advisory Panel. (2008). *Foundations for success: The final report of the National Mathematics Advisory Panel*. Washington, DC: U.S. Department of Education.

National Research Council. (2003). *Assessment in support of learning and instruction: Bridging the gap between large-scale and classroom assessment*. Committee on Assessment in Support of Learning and Instruction. Washington, DC: National Academies Press.

Newcombe, N.S., & Huttenlocher, J.E. (2000). *Making space*. Cambridge, MA: The MIT Press.

No Child Left Behind Act of 2001, PL 107-110, 115 Stat. 1425, 20 U.S.C. §§ 6301 *et seq.*

O'Connor, R.E., & Jenkins, J.R. (1999). The prediction of reading disabilities in kindergarten and first grade. *Scientific Studies of Reading, 3,* 159–197.

Pellegrino, J.W. (1988). Mental models and mental tests. In H. Wainer & H.I. Braun (Eds.), *Test validity* (pp. 49–60). Mahwah, NJ: Lawrence Erlbaum Associates.

Pellegrino, J.W., Baxter, G.P., and Glaser, R. (1999). Addressing the "two disciplines" problem: Linking theories of cognition and learning with assessment and instructional practice. In A. Iran-Nejad & P.D. Pearson (Eds.), *Review of research in education, Vol. 24* (pp. 307–353). Washington, DC: American Educational Research Association.

Pellegrino, J.W., Chudowsky, N., & Glaser, R. (Eds.). (2001). *Knowing what students know: The science and design of educational assessment.* Washington, DC: National Academies Press.

Pellegrino, J.W., & Hickey, D. (2006). Educational assessment: Towards better alignment between theory and practice. In L. Verschaffel, F. Dochy, M. Boekaerts, & S. Vosniadou (Eds.), *Instructional psychology: Past, present and future trends. Sixteen essays in honour of Erik De Corte* (Advances in Learning and Instruction Series, pp. 169–189). Oxford, England: Elsevier.

Pellegrino, J.W., Jones, L.R., & Mitchell, K.J. (Eds.). (1999). *Grading the nation's report card: Evaluating NAEP and transforming the assessment of educational progress.* Washington, DC: National Academies Press.

Quellmalz, E., & Pellegrino, J.W. (2009). Technology and testing. *Science, 323,* 75–79.

RAND. (2002a). *Toward an R and D program in reading comprehension.* RAND Reading Study Group, Catherine Snow, Chair. Santa Monica, CA: RAND.

RAND. (2002b). *Mathematical proficiency for all students: Toward a strategic research and development program in mathematics education.* RAND Mathematics Study Panel, Deborah Loewenberg Ball, Chair. DRU-2773-OERI. Santa Monica, CA: RAND.

Resnick, L.B. (1982). *Syntax and semantics in learning to subtract.* Report No. LRDC-1982/8. Pittsburgh, PA: Learning Research and Development Center, University of Pittsburgh.

Resnick, L.B. (1984). Beyond error analysis: The role of understanding in elementary school arithmetic. In H.N. Creek (Ed.), *Diagnostic and prescriptive mathematics: Issues, ideas, and insight* (pp. 181–205). Kent, OH: Research Council for Diagnostic and Prescriptive Mathematics.

Riley, M., Greeno, J., & Heller, J. (1983). Development of children's problem-solving ability in arithmetic. In H. Ginsburg (Ed.), *The development of mathematical thinking* (pp. 153–196). New York: Academic Press.

Rogoff, B. (1990). *Apprenticeship in thinking: Cognitive development in social context.* New York: Oxford University Press.

Ruiz-Primo, M.A., Shavelson, R.J., Hamilton, L., & Klein, S. (2002). On the evaluation of systemic science education reform: Searching for instructional sensitivity. *Journal of Research in Science Teaching, 39,* 369–393.

Russell, R.L., & Ginsburg, H.P. (1984). Cognitive analysis of children's mathematics difficulties. *Cognition and Instruction, 1,* 217–244.

Sadler, R. (1989). Formative assessment and the design of instructional systems. *Instructional Science, 18,* 119–144.

Schoenfeld, A.H. (1985). *Mathematical problem solving.* Orlando, FL: Academic Press.

Shepard, L.A. (2000). The role of assessment in a learning culture. *Educational Researcher, 29*(7), 4–14.

Siegler, R.S. (1998). *Children's thinking* (3rd ed.). Upper Saddle River, NJ: Prentice Hall.

Siegler, R.S., & Shrager, J. (1984). Strategy choices in addition and subtraction: How do children know what to do? In C. Sophian (Ed.), *Origins of cognitive skills* (pp. 229–293). Mahwah, NJ: Lawrence Erlbaum Associates.

Smith, C., Wiser, M., Anderson, C.W., & Krajcik, J. (2006). Implications of children's learning for assessment: A proposed learning progression for matter and the atomic molecular theory. *Measurement, 14*(1–2), 1–98.

Snow, C.E., Burns, M., & Griffin, M. (Eds.). (1998). *Preventing reading difficulties in young children.* Washington, DC: National Academies Press.

Starkey, P., & Cooper, R.G. (1980). Perception of numbers by human infants. *Science, 210,* 1033–1035.

Starkey, P., & Gelman, R. (1982). The development of addition and subtraction abilities prior to formal schooling in arithmetic. In T.P. Carpenter, J.M. Moser, & T.A. Romberg (Eds.), *Addition and subtraction: A cognitive perspective* (pp. 99–116). Mahwah, NJ: Lawrence Erlbaum Associates.

Steffe, L.P., von Glaserfeld, E., Richards, J., & Cobb, P. (1983). *Children's counting types: Philosophy, theory, and application.* New York: Praeger Scientific.

Stiggins, R.J. (1997). *Student-centered classroom assessment.* Upper Saddle River, NJ: Prentice-Hall.

Svenson, O. (1975). Analysis of time required by children for simple additions. *Acta Psychologica, 39,* 289–302.

Svenson, O., & Broquist, S. (1975). Strategies for solving simple addition problems: A comparison of normal and subnormal children. *Scandinavian Journal of Psychology, 16,* 143–151.

Swanson, H.L., & Jerman, O. (2006). Math disabilities: A selective meta-analysis of the literature. *Review of Educational Research, 76*(2), 249–274.

Torgesen, J.K. (2002). The prevention of reading difficulties. *Journal of School Psychology, 40*(1), 7–26.

Unsworth, N., & Engle, R.W. (2007). The nature of individual differences in working memory capacity: Active maintenance in primary memory and controlled search from secondary memory. *Psychological Review, 114*(1), 104–132.

VanLehn, K. (1990). *Mind bugs: The origins of procedural misconceptions.* Cambridge, MA: The MIT Press.

Wagner, R.K., Torgesen, J.K., Rashotte, C.A., Hecht, S.A., Barker, T.A., Burgess, S.R., et al. (1997). Changing relations between phonological processing abilities and word-level reading as children develop from beginning to skilled readers: A 5-year longitudinal study. *Developmental Psychology, 33,* 468–479.

Webb, N.L. (1997). *Criteria for alignment of expectations and assessments in mathematics and science education.* National Institute for Science Education and Council of Chief State School Officers Research Monograph No. 6. Washington, DC: Council of Chief State School Officers.

Wiggins, G. (1998) *Educative assessment: Designing assessments to inform and improve student performance.* San Francisco: Jossey-Bass.

Wilson, M.R., & Bertenthal, M.W. (Eds.). (2005). *Systems for state science assessments.* Washington DC: National Academies Press.

Winkelman, H.J., & Schmidt, J. (1974). Associative confusions in mental arithmetic. *Journal of Experimental Psychology, 102,* 734–736.

Young, R.M., & O'Shea, T. (1981). Errors in children's subtraction. *Cognitive Science, 5,* 153–177.

Zwick, R., & Ercikan, K. (1989). Analysis of differential item functioning in the NAEP history assessment. *Journal of Educational Measurement, 26*(1), 55–66.

II

Test Design: Understanding Content and Achievement Standards and Incorporating Appropriate Item Modifications

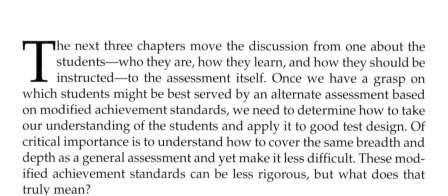

The next three chapters move the discussion from one about the students—who they are, how they learn, and how they should be instructed—to the assessment itself. Once we have a grasp on which students might be best served by an alternate assessment based on modified achievement standards, we need to determine how to take our understanding of the students and apply it to good test design. Of critical importance is to understand how to cover the same breadth and depth as a general assessment and yet make it less difficult. These modified achievement standards can be less rigorous, but what does that truly mean?

Chapter 4, by David K. Pugalee and Robert J. Rickelman, bridges us from the discussions of Section I to lay the foundation for good test design. It focuses on content standards and curriculum and describes how content standards are developed. Then it moves to the key issue of how to maintain the same content, only modifying the achievement standards. It ends with some suggestions on ways to enhance or revise items to provide scaffolding for students who may need additional supports in order to show what they know and can do. The authors point out that the scaffolds described only work if they are incorporated both in instruction and assessment.

Chapter 5, by Catherine Welch and Stephen B. Dunbar, picks up where Chapter 4 leaves off, focusing on types of modifications that can be made to the general assessment to make it more appropriate for low-achieving students with disabilities. It also provides an overview of best item and test development practices and uses these considerations to frame the discussion of areas for modification. The authors then address the psychometric consequences of test modifications as they play out in the assembly of test forms and in the analysis of technical characteristics of items and test forms.

Then, in Chapter 6, by Marianne Perie, the focus turns to the modified achievement standards. Here, the issue of rigor and what standard students are measured against is addressed. This chapter focuses on the main components of achievement standards—numbers and names of levels, achievement level descriptors, and cut scores—and provides guidance on how to develop each component. The theory is brought back to match the test design from Chapter 5, the content from Chapter 4, and student cognition from Chapter 3.

4

Understanding the Content

A Focus on Reading and Mathematics

David K. Pugalee and Robert J. Rickelman

In order to understand the assessment process, whether discussing general assessments or alternate assessments, it is essential to have a good basic understanding of the content learning that is being assessed. The content domain, as explicated in state standards, must be the continued focus of assessment and the underlying force that drives instruction. For alternate assessments based on modified achievement standards (AA-MAS), students' work must align with the published state grade-level standards. But how are these standards developed? How do they link to the curriculum approved for use in schools? How do these standards come into play when developing IEP goals? This chapter builds upon Chapters 2 and 3 by focusing on how the content standards reflect these content domains and provide a framework for both testing and instruction for students who meet the AA-MAS criteria.

This chapter defines curriculum, explains the link to content standards, and describes how content standards are developed by states. It is important to understand the difference between *content standards* and *achievement standards,* so this differentiation is made. Finally, issues surrounding links between the general content and modified assessments are discussed, including examples related to mathematics and English/language arts. A discussion related to the effects of scaffolding on instruction and assessment concludes this chapter.

WHAT IS THE CURRICULUM?

At a very basic level, a curriculum is a set of planned instructional activities that are designed to allow students to document achievement of their knowledge and skills, including how these skills can be applied to real-life situations. The goal of a curriculum is to provide a comprehensive focus for instruction and learning within a school, a school system, and/or across a state. They also provide a scope and sequence of skills within and across grade levels. The curriculum generally drives the important factor of materials that will be used to implement the curriculum, and often there are several choices among state-approved materials developed by different sources within the state or at the national level. In short, the curriculum is the glue that holds the pieces together, informing both teaching and learning, which should then link to the content standards assessed and any subsequent interpretation of the assessment. This, in turn, should then drive instruction. In this continuous improvement loop (instruction → assessment → interpretation → instruction), the curriculum lays out a scope and sequence of skills aligned to the content standards that will be taught, learned, and assessed in different subjects across different grade levels.

For example, a state may approve five different programs to be used to inform the mathematics curriculum across the K–12 grade levels. In order to purchase materials with state funding, a school district would have to choose from among the state-approved materials. It is common for states to have textbook adoption committees, made up of experts within the content field, who make decisions about the quality of the options and how well they align to the state curriculum goals and approved content standards. At the school district level, it is also common to have textbook adoption committees who make choices among the five state-approved sets of materials.

A less common option is that a set of materials can be developed at a much smaller scale to be used with smaller populations of students. For instance, in a grade level where a specific state history is the focus for a course, related materials will likely be developed by in-state experts, because the content would not appeal to anyone in other states. It is common for individuals to develop these materials around a curriculum that will guide decision making at a local district or even individual school level.

To link this discussion on curriculum back to the AA-MAS, it is important to recognize that students must document that they can meet the state grade-level content standards. What this means is that they must be given the opportunity to learn and be assessed using the same curriculum as the population of students who are assessed using general assessments. In other words, they cannot be accountable for learning a different set of standards or for using a curriculum that is not available to the general population of students within that state. Not only must they have access to the general curriculum, but they must take part in an AA-MAS that is aligned to grade-level content standards. Therefore, a student in the ninth grade could not be assessed on standards established for fifth grade, even though that might be the grade level most representative of that student's observed skill.

HOW ARE CONTENT STANDARDS DEVELOPED?

Content standards are generally developed in one of two ways. In some subject areas, standards are established at the national level, and these subsequently drive the development of individual state standards. For instance, in mathematics, the National Council of Teachers of Mathematics (NCTM; 2000) has developed a set of standards for grades prekindergarten (pre-K) through 12th grade. According to the Executive Summary of the 2000 *Principles and Standards for School Mathematics* (available at http://www.nctm.org/uploadedFiles/Math_Standards/12752_exec_pssm.pdf), these standards were developed by a set of national content experts, with broad opportunities for input from teachers and others, on the basis of an extensive study of curriculum materials, state documents, and best practice research, to

- Set forth a comprehensive and coherent set of learning goals for pre-K–12 math
- Serve as a resource for educators and policy makers
- Guide the development of curriculum frameworks, assessments, and instructional materials
- Stimulate ideas and ongoing conversations at the national, state, and local levels about how best to help students gain a deep understanding of important mathematics (p. 1)

These standards are used extensively to guide state standards committees, which often shape the NCTM standards to the needs of the specific state, including aligning them to state content and assessments required of all students. Therefore, although there may be minor differences in the details of specific standards across states, the general standards themselves are very consistent from state to state.

The second way that content standards are developed is within states, when national-level standards have not been developed or when national-level content standards are fairly generic and perhaps not specifically aligned to grade levels. These standards are considered to be more generic guiding principles and can be helpful in developing an overall philosophy of the goals for standards, but more specific, focused, and assessable statements must be crafted by state-level experts to make sense of the continuous improvement cycle mentioned earlier.

The reading and English/language arts (ELA) content area provides an example of this type of standards development. In 1996, the National Council of Teachers of English (NCTE) and the International Reading Association (IRA) published *Standards for the English Language Arts*. This document was the result of 5 years of collaboration between these two professional organizations. However, unlike the NCTM standards, which are broken down into specific content and process standards across grade levels, these ELA standards are more generic. For instance, Standard 1 states that a goal for ELA instruction should be that

> Students read a wide range of print and nonprint texts to build an understanding of texts, of themselves, and of the cultures of the United States and the world; to acquire new information; to respond to the needs and demands of society and the workplace; and for personal fulfillment. Among these texts are fiction and nonfiction, classic and contemporary works. (p. 3)

It is up to each individual state to determine how this general recommendation is actualized within and across grade levels within the state. As such, these can be considered more like guiding principles for content standard development rather than actual grade-level content standards.

It is easy to see that, unlike the NCTM standards, these are not grade-band specific standards, but rather 12 general standards supported by research and classroom vignettes of what might happen in a classroom in which the recommendations were being implemented. States must craft their own more detailed grade-level standards using committees made up of experts in the field who work in state departments of public instruction, colleges and universities, and public and private schools. Typically, these committees meet for several days to write the pre-K–12 state standards in each subject area using (much like NCTM did on a national level) previous state standards and current state and national policy, along with scientific research in best practices, to put together a detailed list of standards for each grade level. These standards are then generally widely disseminated among stakeholders for additional input before being officially approved and implemented by the state department.

States vary greatly in how often these committees meet to update standards, regardless of whether they come from national or state sources. Many states update grade-level content standards every 5 years, but this cycle is often interrupted by new federal or state laws so that standards may be changed more than once every 5 years to adhere to new mandates or even less than every 5 years if major mandates are expected to be forthcoming and states want more guidance before proceeding with this tedious task.

States also vary widely in how they organize the adopted standards. For instance, in California (1998/2009), each main standard provides a generic overview of the goals within the standard. Then each is divided into more specific substandards, which form the basis for instruction and assessment. So, in grade 3, Standard 1 relates to "Word Analysis, Fluency, and Systematic Vocabulary Development." It outlines that "Students understand the basic features of reading. They select letter patterns and know how to translate them into spoken language by using phonics, syllabication, and word parts. They apply this knowledge to achieve fluent oral and silent reading" (p. 16). This generic standard is broken down into eight substandards (e.g., "Decode regular multisyllabic words"). Overall, grade 3 ELA guidelines include 8 main standards, but 51 individual substandards must be learned.

Hawaii standards (1999), on the other hand, are organized much differently:

> The eighteen Language Arts Content Standards are organized into six strands across three components of the language arts. The standards represent a necessary mix of the cognitive, intellectual, academic, and practical dimensions of learning. While the standards emphasize the academic performance and intellectual accomplishments of Hawaii's students, they also acknowledge that learning has a social and emotional component. (p. 5)

The standards are presented in five grade-level bands (K–1, 2–3, 4–5, 6–8, 9–12).

The ways that state standards are organized can have a profound effect on how the standards are interpreted (broad versus specific) in terms of organizing a curriculum and how they are assessed. If the standards are fairly broad (e.g., "Use facts, information, and ideas from research and own experience that take into account the knowledge and experience of listeners," Hawaii, p. 19) teachers and assessment developers have much more leeway to design items to test for mastery of this skill. That can be both good and bad. A similar standard from California (1998/2009) for the same grade-level range is much more specific: "Develop an interpretation exhibiting careful reading, understanding, and insight" (p. 41). Ideally, when standards are developed within states, attention should be paid to how easy or difficult the standards are to assess for general, as well as special, education students.

Several important points must be made concerning the development of content standards, especially in subject areas for which national standards have not been developed. First, the published content standards, critically important to the assessment process, are assumed to be the gold standard within states—reference points of knowledge to which students must achieve. But often there is no clear, scientific methodology behind the development of these standards, as mentioned earlier. In fact, when one state was recently working on its modified achievement standards and developing learning maps for each content standard in each grade level, the teams working on developing the maps struggled to understand what some of the state content standards actually meant and how they could be taught and assessed and interpreted across the general, modified, and alternate assessment systems. After much struggle, frustration, and consultation, the teams decided that some of the state standards were just poorly written, and some team members expressed a strong interest in being named to content standard writing committees in the future. Another point is that when these content standards are being developed by content expert teams, there is often no deliberate thought about how each content standard will be assessed, which was one problem that these teams discovered (as highlighted previously).

In other words, the development of this gold standard is sometimes quite unscientific and can be heavily influenced by one or two strong committee members who may or may not espouse a certain ideology of what should be taught and learned within the state. Therefore, although the process of developing content standards obviously has to take place, understanding both how these standards are developed and how they may be unduly influenced by individual committee members is important to keep in mind. Sending out drafts of standards to a broad variety of stakeholders can be helpful in terms of quality control, but it remains, by nature, an imperfect system.

As mentioned in Chapter 3, *learning progressions* can provide guidance about how a typical skill will be developed on a theoretical level, but these learning progressions have limited usefulness, because some students (perhaps many) do not follow typical learning patterns. Some states use the term *learning maps,* which should not be confused with learning progressions, to offer suggested pathways in which a student can learn and be assessed across achievement standards, with the understanding that, just like a road map, these pathways are meant to offer guidance, but can (and often must) allow for deviation to account for individual differences. This flexibility is especially important for students being assessed against alternate and modified achievement standards, because they may be more atypical than their peers in adhering to both theoretical and practical expectations for learning and developing expertise for both declarative and procedural knowledge.

In other words, there is little solid evidence that there is only one way in which all students acquire knowledge. There are, more likely, multiple pathways, and learning maps offer practical guidance into how these might develop, especially in terms of depth of knowledge of the standards. These would generally be developed for each grade-level standard, and appropriate assessment measures subsequently need to be developed to allow students the opportunity to show performance across the levels. These maps can also link to achievement standards, often by taking into account depth of knowledge, with the assumption that more depth can demonstrate a higher achievement level. The effectiveness of such maps in positively impacting student learning is dependent on a rich system of formative assessment processes aligned to instruction that provides pictures of what students are able to do on multiple tasks related to the standard. Examples of learning or progress maps in ELA and mathematics can be seen in Table 4.1.

Table 4.1.   Examples of learning or progress maps in ELA and mathematics
Published State Standard: Student will be able to understand simile and metaphor.

Developing	Proficient	Target	Advanced
Student will be able to correctly label figurative language and literal language given lists of statements.	Student will be able to correctly identify a simile and a metaphor embedded in a paragraph of text.	Student will be able to use an appropriate simile or a metaphor in their own written work.	Student will be able to use a simile or a metaphor in their own written work and will be able to discuss the relevant characteristics of the word(s) being compared.

Hawaii State Standard: Patterns and Functions: Demonstrate and explain the difference between repeating patterns and growing patterns (see Ban, Holt, & Kurizaki, 2008)

Less complex	More complex	Proficient
Student **can** describe a growing pattern by using objects, pictures, and numbers.	Student **can** describe repeating AND growing patterns by paying attention to how each element in the pattern relates to each other.	Student **can** describe repeating AND growing patterns. Student **can** use appropriate vocabulary to explain/justify the growing pattern.
Student **can** use appropriate vocabulary to describe the growing pattern.	Student **can** use appropriate vocabulary to explain/justify the growing pattern.	Student **can** use comparison/contrast and cause-effect language to describe similarity and differences among patterns.

DIFFERENCE BETWEEN CONTENT
STANDARDS AND ACHIEVEMENT STANDARDS

The *Modified Academic Achievement Standards* document (U.S. Department of Education, 2007) defines academic content standards as "statements of the knowledge and skills that schools are expected to teach and students are expected to learn" (pp. 12–13). These content standards are mandated for all students, regardless of ability, and are meant to drive instruction and assessments. These are the content standards discussed earlier, established at the national or state level by teams of experts and stakeholders. On the other hand, academic achievement standards "are explicit definitions of how students are expected to demonstrate attainment of the knowledge and skills of the content standards" (p. 13). They further state that academic achievement standards must have the following elements:

- At least three achievement levels, which are labels that convey the degree of achievement in a given subject area (e.g., proficient, developing, not proficient)

- Achievement descriptors, which are descriptions of content-based competencies associated with each of the achievement levels established (what students at each level know and can demonstrate)

- Cut scores, which separate one level of achievement from another (e.g., how is a proficient student different from a developing student)

More will be said about establishing achievement standards in Chapter 6. This differentiation is important, because within an AA-MAS system, only the achievement standards may be modified, not the content standards. In order for assessments to provide meaningful information about students' academic progress and promote accountability, there must be a clear alignment between the assessments and grade-level content standards. Readers may refer to the discussion of the assessment triangle in Chapter 3 for more information.

BARRIERS IN PROVIDING
ACCESS TO THE GENERAL CURRICULUM

Ideally, all students must have access to the general curriculum used in their school and be able to be assessed with the same assessment that all students use in such a way as to document learning through performance within a general assessment system. However, with the broad diversity of skills and language that are typical in most schools, this ideal is very difficult to fully implement, which is why states are allowed alternate assessments for a limited population of students. In the not-so-distant past, students with severe disabilities were not allowed to attend school. When the Individuals with Disabilities Education Act was originally passed by Congress in 1975 (as the Education of All Handicapped Children, PL 94-142), school-based placements were mandated and generally occurred in segregated settings within the school. More recently, students with disabilities (both those with severe and mild disabilities) were able to be excluded from the general assessments used for other students in the school who did not have documented disabilities. However, in the most recent era of high-stakes assessments and after the passage of the No Child Left Behind Act of 2001 (PL 107-110), school administrators no longer have free reign to exclude certain students from being counted in the standardized assessment system. All students have to be included in adequate yearly progress (AYP) reporting to the state and federal government.

These changes are helpful in that all students now count in terms of AYP. Schools are no longer able to exclude a student because of severe disabilities, and they must document that the content being taught and learned in the school setting has direct or indirect links to the general curriculum being studied by peers. In the past, there were concerns that some administrators tried to exclude any student thought to be detrimental in bringing down the school's overall achievement level, which may impact their ability to meet their AYP goals. Now schools must find ways to create meaningful links to the curriculum for students with even the most significant cognitive disabilities. But this requirement also highlighted challenges, or barriers, to inclusion that have been around for years.

One barrier is the way that many teachers are trained, both at the in-service and preservice levels. In a nutshell, special education teachers (especially those working with students who have the most severe disabilities) are rarely trained to think about the general state standards and required curriculum and are not shown how to link their teaching and student learning directly to those grade-level standards (Brownell, Ross, Colon, & McCallum, 2005). Historically, students with disabilities were expected to work on nonacademic, more functional skills, which are important in terms of day-to-day living, and this is what teachers were trained to teach. On the other hand, general education teachers and teacher candidates, who were generally much better versed in understanding how their teaching was driven by the state content standards expected within the different subject areas, had little or no idea how to apply that information to students with disabilities. In fact, it was common in most schools to find that general education and special education teachers rarely, if ever, interacted professionally within a school setting. So the information necessary to successfully navigate the new federal mandates were generally not shared among the two sets of teachers (Brownell et al., 2005).

Why is this important? General education and special education professionals must find ways to align their points of view, with general education teachers providing help in understanding mandated grade-level standards for learning and special education teachers providing expertise in how to teach the necessary skills to achieve these standards for students with disabilities. There is a synergy when special and general education teachers work together that is not possible when they work in isolation. General education teachers are able to address the "what" questions surrounding student learning: What is meant by a state standard? What are higher-level thinking skills? Process writing skills? What does it look like in a classroom setting? Special education teachers are able to better address the "how" questions: How do I teach a student who is nonverbal to understand algebraic principles? How can I teach a student with a visual or hearing impairment to read? Both kinds of expertise are needed in order to ensure that all students have access to good teaching and learning. However, in most teacher training schools and many pre-K–12 schools, these teachers continue to work in isolation.

To create professional development models that break these barriers, certain processes need to be in place. First, it is essential that teacher training institutions consider developing teacher candidates with dual expertise in both general education and special education. The good news is that a few teacher training programs are either mandating or allowing undergraduates to finish a degree program with dual licensure in special education and a field of general education, typically elementary education. This idea needs to be expanded, however, to more teacher education programs. Second, these partnerships between general and special educators must be fostered to allow for the design of meaningful assessments, including the challenging work of designing an assessment that is less difficult but that maintains the same levels of breadth and depth of content. In addition, these teams can help develop learning maps and/or curricula that utilize best practices in teaching, thereby allowing for alternate ways to teach students skills and processes related to content standards.

By working together and negotiating this fine line between content integrity and less difficult assessments, the synergy mentioned earlier can be maintained. These experts must work with assessment experts as well, with the general education teachers making judgments about fidelity of assessment items to the learning domain, and special education experts making judgments about accessibility to testing for students who may need supports in order to show what they know.

Ideally, all three voices (general education, special education, and educational assessment) are important in terms of establishing coherent content standards, writing quality achievement standards, and helping assess and interpret data to maintain the continuous improvement loop mentioned earlier.

THE CONTENT STANDARDS FOR MATHEMATICS

The majority of states have mathematics content standards that align to *Principles and Standards for School Mathematics,* the content standards document published by the NCTM (2000). This document presents key mathematics goals for students in pre-K through 12th grade. The document describes 10 standards, 5 content and 5 process standards, that represent a comprehensive and connected organization of key mathematical understandings and competencies of what students should know and be able to do. The content standards include number and operations, algebra, geometry, measurement, and data analysis and probability. The five process standards underscoring ways of acquiring and using mathematics content knowledge include problem solving, reasoning and proof, communication, connections, and representation. For the five content standards, broad goals are presented for all students pre-K–12, with specific expectations explicated for the various grade bands: pre-K–grade 2, grades 3–5, grades 6–8, and grades 9–12. Table 4.2 presents the goals for each of the content standards for all students grades pre-K–12.

Each of the five content standards is broken down by grade-level bands, providing greater specificity regarding what is expected of students at that particular grade level. This elaboration is provided for each of the goals listed in Table 4.2. For example, the algebra standard includes "analyze change in various contexts" as one of the goals. Table 4.3 presents the expectations at various grade bands for this goal.

Similarly, the process standards for mathematics provide general guidelines that assist in describing the types of mental processes that are inherent in a well-balanced mathematics curriculum. Though more difficult to specify in terms of concrete and measurable behaviors, the process standards present key ideas about what is valued in the discipline. Table 4.4 lists the goals for each of the five process standards for pre-K–12. The *Principles and Standards for School Mathematics* (NCTM, 2000) does not further delineate grade-band expectations for the goals. Later in this section, the process standards will be revised in reference to their use in designing state assessments.

Recognizing that states and local educational agencies were often challenged in implementing rigorous assessment and accountability sys-

Table 4.2.   Goals for prekindergarten through grade 12 for five content standards

Number and operations	Algebra	Geometry	Measurement	Data analysis and probability
Understand numbers, ways of representing numbers, relationships among numbers, and number systems	Understand patterns, relations, and functions	Analyze characteristics and properties of two- and three-dimensional geometric shapes and develop mathematical arguments about geometric relationships	Understand measurable attributes of objects and the units, systems, and processes of measurement	Formulate questions that can be addressed with data and collect, organize, and display relevant data to answer them
Understand meanings of operations and how they relate to one another	Represent and analyze mathematical situations and structures using algebraic symbols	Specify locations and describe spatial relationships using coordinate geometry and other representational systems	Apply appropriate techniques, tools, and formulas to determine measurements.	Select and use appropriate statistical methods to analyze data
Compute fluently and make reasonable estimates	Use mathematical models to represent and understand quantitative relationships	Apply transformations and use symmetry to analyze mathematical situations		Develop and evaluate inferences and predictions that are based on data
	Analyze change in various contexts	Use visualization, spatial reasoning, and geometric modeling to solve problems		Understand and apply basic concepts of probability

From National Council of Teachers of Mathematics. (2000). *Principles and standards for school mathematics* (pp. 392–401). Reston, VA: Author; reprinted by permission.

Table 4.3. Grade band expectations for the algebra standard

PreK–grade 2	Grades 3–5	Grades 6–8	Grades 9–12
Describe qualitative change, such as a student's growing taller	Investigate how a change in one variable relates to a change in a second variable	Use graphs to analyze the nature of changes in quantities in linear relationships	Approximate and interpret rates of change from graphical and numerical data
Describe quantitative change, such as a student's growing 2 inches in 1 year	Identify and describe situations with constant or varying rates of change and compare them		

From National Council of Teachers of Mathematics. (2000). *Principles and standards for school mathematics* (pp. 394–395). Reston, VA: Author; reprinted by permission.

tems, and to assist teachers in identifying consistent priorities and focus, the NCTM (2006) developed *Curriculum Focal Points for Prekindergarten through Grade 8 Mathematics.* In this document, NCTM asserts that

> Organizing a curriculum around these described focal points, with a clear emphasis on the processes that *Principles and Standards* addresses in the Process Standards—communication, reasoning, representation, connections, and, particularly, problem solving—can provide students with a connected, coherent, ever expanding body of mathematical knowledge and ways of thinking. (p. 1)

It is clear that these documents offer a comprehensive picture of the domain of school mathematics. It is further evidence that such documents can provide the core for developing curriculum and informing instructional and assessment priorities.

Professional specialty organizations, such as NCTM, and various government-sponsored enterprises, including the National Mathematics Advisory Panel, provide an articulation of the content domain for mathematics. This articulation is a broad framework providing state educational agencies with a launching point from which to develop grade level–specific mathematics competencies. States use different processes to develop academic standards for grade-level content, as mentioned earlier. The resulting documents become the critical focus as states develop assessments, including modified achievement standards, to measure students' proficiency toward meeting those state competencies.

SAMPLING MATHEMATICS

Important mathematics that should be reflected in assessments includes "both the necessary content and the interconnectedness of topics and process" (Mathematical Sciences Education Board [MSEB],

Table 4.4. Process standards for prekindergarten through grade 12

Problem solving	Reasoning and proof	Communication	Connections	Representation
Build new mathematical knowledge through problem solving	Recognize reasoning and proof as fundamental aspects of mathematics	Organize and consolidate their mathematical thinking through communication	Recognize and use connections among mathematical ideas	Create and use representations to organize, record, and communicate mathematical ideas
Solve problems that arise in mathematics and in other contexts	Make and investigate mathematical conjectures	Communicate their mathematical thinking coherently and clearly to peers, teachers, and others	Understand how mathematical ideas interconnect and build on one another to produce a coherent whole	Select, apply, and translate among mathematical representations to solve problems
Apply and adapt a variety of appropriate strategies to solve problems	Develop and evaluate mathematical arguments and proofs	Analyze and evaluate the mathematical thinking and strategies of others	Recognize and apply mathematics in contexts outside of mathematics	Use representations to model and interpret physical, social, and mathematical phenomena
Monitor and reflect on the process of mathematical problem solving	Select and use various types of reasoning and methods of proof	Use the language of mathematics to express mathematical ideas precisely		

From National Council of Teachers of Mathematics. (2000). *Principles and standards for school mathematics* (p. 401). Reston, VA: Author; reprinted by permission.

1993, p. 42). The National Assessment of Educational Progress (NAEP) employs a unique way to characterize the learning domain and the corresponding assessment that utilizes a lattice structure, allowing a more interconnected view of mathematics. Since 1995, items reflect five content categories: number and operations; measurement; geometry; data analysis, probability, and statistics; and algebra and functions. Also included are mathematical abilities categories: conceptual understanding, procedural knowledge, and problem solving. These ability categories are considered throughout the test development process to confirm that there is balance among the three categories, though not necessarily within each content category (MSEB, 1993).

These different frameworks are carried over to state content standards. New York, for example, includes five content strands: number sense and operations, algebra, geometry, measurement, and statistics and probability. Items are distributed across those strands in predetermined weights and aligned to both content and process strands in order to provide tests that "assess students' conceptual understanding, procedural fluency, and problem-solving abilities, rather than solely addressing their knowledge of isolated skills and facts" (New York State Education Department, 2007a, p. 5). This process is similar to that followed in the majority of states in which there is an effort to align state curricular frameworks to the standards published by NCTM.

THE CONTENT STANDARDS
FOR ENGLISH/LANGUAGE ARTS

As mentioned at the beginning of this chapter, there are no specific grade-level content standards in ELA at the national level, as there are in mathematics. So the manner of teaching, learning, and assessing ELA is, not surprisingly, also different. Part of the issue was discussed earlier in Chapter 3. Although it is fairly easy to observe and draw inferences about how a child might develop skills in and learn long division, it is much more difficult to make inferences about how a child might learn to comprehend information, and, as also mentioned earlier, even these inferences from commonly used measures can be misleading. This is likely one reason why there is less consensus among experts about how competency in ELA develops. Rather, there are the general recommendations from the NCTE/IRA publication mentioned earlier, which are somewhat outdated but still sound.

It might be easy to assume, given what has already been discussed, that the ELA standards across different states are quite different, especially compared with areas like math, for which there are national guidelines for standard setting. But an examination of ELA standards by grade level and across different states reveals that they are actually comparable. Part of the reason for this general consensus relates to the extensive research that is available in ELA (Leu, 2007). So there does tend to be much general consensus, framed by this research, around the standards that need to be taught in different grades, with an initial focus on "learning to read" being gradually replaced by an emphasis on "reading to learn."

This distinction is important and first surfaced in the early 1970s (Herber, 1970). In the first few years of school, especially at the preschool through second grade levels, much ELA instruction is focused on learning to read, which involves learning the requisite skills that lead to more complex reading skills, in phonics, phonemic awareness, and so forth, and also developing fluency practicing and using these skills on both narrative and informational texts. As students begin to move into third grade, in general, and even more dramatically as they move into the middle grades and then into high school, the emphasis shifts farther and farther away from these core basics, since the assumption is that they have been taught and learned in the earlier grades. The emphasis then shifts to reading to learn. This means that students become more and more accountable for using the earlier developed skills to read in order to learn content information—mathematics, science, social studies, and so forth. Although there is not a clean break between the two, and there is indeed much overlap as students work to learn to read and read to learn at the same time as they progress through higher grades, the skills expected to be learned become much more intangible, making them more difficult to assess. Although it is fairly simple to teach and assess a student's ability to put letters and sounds together to make words, it is much more difficult to teach and assess a student's ability to utilize higher-order thinking and critical comprehension skills. So the task of developing content standards, curricula, and assessments tends to be much more straightforward in the earlier grades, in which the skills can be demonstrated in a much more concrete way, and much more difficult as students move into the higher grade levels, and documenting learning of the skills becomes much less of a concrete process.

Much attention has been paid to the report of the National Reading Panel (2000) (www.nationalreadingpanel.org). For instance, the findings of the panel were used in establishing the Reading First program, a $5 billion initiative introduced during the George W. Bush administration. Many curricular materials and school professional development activities are developed around the "Big Five" or the "Essential Five" skills highlighted in the report—phonemic awareness, phonics, fluency, vocabulary, and comprehension. Some advocates of the report suggest that these Big Five are the only skills that are research-based, and so these are the only ones that should be a part of the state ELA standards.

In terms of how the work of the National Reading Panel influences state standards in ELA, it is safe to say that the Big Five should certainly be included, because there is strong evidence that they are indeed essential for allowing students to access the curriculum in other content subjects, especially during the learning to read phase. However, it is not safe to assume that if a topic was not included in the report, there is no scientific evidence that it is worth learning.

ALIGNING STATE STANDARDS TO ASSESSMENTS

Using curriculum documents, such as content maps, developed at the state level, assessments are designed to sample skill learning and knowledge within the content domain. *Content match* and *depth match* are two dimensions considered when aligning the assessments to the curriculum (LaMarca, 2001). Content match is the degree to which the assessment content matches to the subject area content, as identified in the state academic standards. Content match may be further delineated through an analysis of broad content coverage, range of coverage, and balance of coverage. Broad content coverage, or the categorical congruence of the assessment, addresses whether the test content links to the broad content standards. Range of coverage asks whether the test items address the specific objectives related to each content standard. Balance of coverage is concerned with whether the assessment items reflect the major emphases and priorities found within the academic standards. The second dimension of alignment, depth match, is related to the degree to which the test items match the skills and knowledge specified in the state's academic standards in terms of cognitive complexity. Once items are developed, there should be a systematic analysis of the alignment that includes a determination of what objective an item measures and the degree of cognitive complexity for that item (LaMarca, 2001; Webb, 1999).

GUIDANCE ON TEST SPECIFICATIONS

Ketterlin-Geller (2008) proposed a model of assessment development that extends the model created by the National Research Council (Pellegrino, Chudowsky, & Glaser, 2001) in order to better meet the needs of students with cognitive disabilities. Ketterlin-Geller's model is guided by the concept of *universal design* as applied to educational testing. Students with cognitive disabilities may not interact with a test in the same way as general population students. This difference involves "construct-irrelevant variance" that could produce an inaccurate assessment of "domain-specific knowledge" (Ketterlin-Geller, 2008, p. 4). Universally designed tests assess the same constructs but allow greater flexibility in the format or delivery of the test, thus rendering them more useful and accessible to a greater percentage of the student population. Ketterlin-Geller argues that "applying the principles of universal design to academic assessments provides a mechanism for reducing the impact of construct-irrelevant variance on test-score interpretation, thereby, increasing the validity of the uses of test results" (p. 4).

Assessment must also consider the interaction between observation, cognition, and interpretation in the assessment design (Pellegrino et al., 2001). Ketterlin-Geller (2008) elaborated on some basic ideas of how this model might inform the design of assessment tools. In this model, within the assessment triangle detailed in Chapter 3, the cognition aspect represents the theories and beliefs of learning within the domain. Cognitive models should reflect the ways that children learn content within the targeted domain. Such targets include broad constructs, such as analytic reasoning, as well as narrow components, such as the unit of length in mathematics. The observation aspect involves collecting student behaviors, which become the basis for interpretations about the cognitive targets. The features of assessments should reflect and align with the construct. Students with significant disabilities may interpret and respond to items as a result of their disability, contributing to construct-irrelevant variance. Assessment features such as test platform, item format, problem context, administration procedures, and scoring systems should be considered when determining the characteristics of assessment tools. The interpretation aspect grounds decisions made about student skills and knowledge in the domain. Student characteristics, the cognitive model, and the observational tool interact in ways that influence the interpretation of student performance. Failure to consider these interactions may lead to problems with the validity of score-based interpretations.

Part of creating a universally designed test is to incorporate a cognitive task analysis for each test item (alongside the content of the domain targeted). Ketterlin-Geller proposed a cognitive task analysis along four levels of cognitive engagement: knowledge and application of general facts and procedures, knowledge and application of concepts and procedures, strategic thinking, and extended thinking. Furthermore, delineation between target and access skills should be clear. Target skills include both the cognitive and content components that the test is designed to actually measure. Access skills, on the other hand, include cognitive and content components that are needed to attain the target skills, but which the test is not designed to measure. Explicitly analyzing and articulating the cognitive tasks underlying a given problem can lead to better test accommodations for students with cognitive disabilities. For instance, a cognitive task analysis for a given mathematics problem may reveal that a test taker must be familiar with the concept of a calendar. If familiarity with a calendar is classified as an access skill, and the student has a limited concept of a calendar, an accommodation may be made (e.g., eliminate the calendar reference or embed an explanation of the concept of a calendar in the problem).

As the assessment system is further developed, review of items for assessments should follow a structured protocol and be reviewed by content and grade-level experts. Such review should be sensitive to the interaction between cognition, observation, and interpretation. Item review might include the following elements:

- Accuracy and grade-level appropriateness
- Mapping of the items to performance indicators
- Accompanying exemplar responses (for constructed-response items)
- Appropriateness of the correct response and distracters
- Conciseness, preciseness, clarity, and readability
- Existence of ethnic, gender, regional, or other possible bias

Such procedures are imperative, particularly for AA-MAS, so that students have access to a range of academic content specified in the state's academic grade-level curriculum. Procedures minimize clustering of assessment items in isolated content strands and further guarantee that assessments are not over-reliant on items that align to processes, such as procedures in mathematics and decoding skills in reading.

It is essential that reviews consider the interpretation aspect of the assessment model. Messick (1989) put forth the idea of a unified view of validity that takes into consideration the ethical underpinnings of the test interpretation and use. He argues that the way content validity has been defined, as "evidence in support of the domain relevance and the representativeness of content of the test instrument" (p. 7), does not consider the inferences that may be made from the test. Messick argued that "we must inquire whether the potential and actual social consequences of test interpretation and use are not only supportive of the intended testing purposes, but at the same time are consistent with other social values" (p. 8). Only through systematic and comprehensive analysis of the assessment program will all of the issues related to the assessment model (observation, cognition, and interpretation) be an integral part of the test design process.

JUDGING THE ALIGNMENT BETWEEN EXPECTATIONS AND MODIFIED ASSESSMENTS

Webb (1997a) offered five categories for judging the alignment between expectations and assessments. The first, content focus, states that the focus should consistently be on developing students' knowledge of content. This consistency is primarily emphasized in four components: categorical concurrence, depth of knowledge consistency, range of knowledge correspondence, and balance of representation.

1. *Categorical concurrence* allows for differences in the level of detail but expects the same categories of content (such as content headings and their subheadings) to appear in the expectations and the assessment. For example, an assessment in mathematics would need to reflect the five content strands from the NCTM.

2. *Depth of knowledge consistency* can vary on a number of dimensions, such as level of cognitive complexity, and describes how well students should be able to transfer the knowledge to different contexts and how much prerequisite knowledge is necessary in order to understand more difficult concepts. For example, using a state standard mandating that the student will "Create and explain patterns and algebraic relationships (e.g., 2, 4, 6, 8...) algebraically: 2n (doubling)," if students are only required to identify the next item in the pattern, the depth of knowledge is not aligned for this performance indicator. The learning map related to figurative language presented earlier in this chapter provides another example of how the depth of knowledge can vary across content achievement standards.

3. *Range of knowledge correspondence* refers to the degree to which expectations and assessments cover comparable topics and ideas within categories. For example, the California (California Department of Education, 1998/2009) grade 4 performance indicators for ELA include the following: Identify the main events of the plot, their causes, and the influence of each event on future actions. Assessments that only focus on identifying the main events in a plot would not meet the range of knowledge correspondence, because the other skills are left out. Although it is tempting to create learning maps related to achievement standards that are additive (i.e., if students can identify the main events in a plot, they are in the developing level, and if they can identify the main events and list their causes, they are at the target level), this methodology does not adhere to the intent of the content standard, which requires knowledge of all of the skills mentioned.

4. *Balance of representation* means that similar emphasis is given to different content topics, instructional activities, and tasks. Assessments must reflect shifts in emphasis in content. Figure 4.1, a visual from the NCTM (2000), emphasizes this shifting emphasis for the five content strands. Typically, alternate assessments

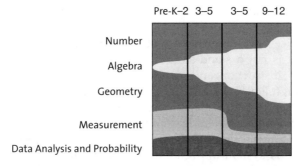

Figure 4.1. Shift in emphasis in math content from prekindergarten through grade 12. (From National Council of Teachers of Mathematics. [2000]. *Principles and standards for school mathematics.* Reston, VA: Author; reprinted by permission.)

have focused on number and measurement, even for students at the middle and secondary levels. Such emphasis would not be consistent with the shifting emphasis in content. Similarly, in language arts, the example stated previously relating learning to read and reading to learn document this shifting emphasis across grade levels.

The second category for determining alignment is articulation across grades and ages. Expectations and assessments should reflect views about how students develop and learn at different stages. This view from Webb (1997b) includes "cognitive soundness as determined by best research and understanding" (p. 23) and "cumulative growth in knowledge during students' schooling" (p. 25). The underlying structure of knowledge in content domains influences how instructional experiences for students should be organized. Specialty professional associations such as NCTM, NCTE, IRA, and the National Council for the Social Studies exist as organizations to support the articulation of this body of research and understanding.

The third component is equity and fairness. Assessments that align to this criterion provide every student with a reasonable opportunity to demonstrate their level of attainment relative to what is expected. High expectations are reflected in all learning standards. Multiple forms of assessment provide a better alignment based on students' level of knowledge, culture, social background, and experiences.

The fourth category is pedagogical implications. Classroom practice is related to the learning of students. Review of assessments must consider the implications for classroom practice. Teachers might be asked to interpret expectations and assessments and consider how their classroom practices fit with their interpretations. Two critical elements to consider when taking pedagogical influences into account are the active engagement of students in learning and effective class-room practice, including the use of technology, materials, and tools. Assessment is not a stand-alone component of educational practice. Curriculum, instruction, and assessment should be linked in a coherent and meaningful fashion. Further, assessment is an ongoing process that should inform instruction; therefore, effective practices align all three components so that student learning is promoted as a coherent whole.

The fifth category for determining alignment of expectations and assessments is system applicability. Programs must be realistic and manageable. Policy must be constructed so that it is applicable to teach-ers and administrators in their day-to-day efforts and does not present an additional burden outside of what is considered "normal" school activities.

CONSIDERING COGNITIVE COMPLEXITY IN ASSESSMENTS

The Council of Chief State School Officers recognizes three models for evaluating the alignment between curricular expectations and assess-ments: Webb's alignment model (Webb, 1999), the Surveys of Enacted Curriculum (SEC) model (Porter & Smithson, 2001), and the Achieve model (Roach, Niebling, & Kurz, 2008). The Webb alignment model is the primary model that has been applied to alternate assessments and will be the focus of this discussion (see also Chapter 8); however, SEC provides an additional framework for considering cognitive complexi-ty and is also described in the following paragraphs.

The SEC includes a common language framework for examining the content and visual displays of alignment analysis (see Porter & Smithson, 2001). The common language framework provides general categories under which a series of topics is organized. For example, addition and subtraction of whole numbers would be under the larger category of "Operations." Other topical content categories for K–12 include number sense/properties/relationships, measurement, con-sumer applications, basic algebra, advanced algebra, geometric concepts, advanced geometry, data displays, statistics, probability, analysis, trigonometry, special topics, functions, and instructional tech-nology. Content areas for reading and language arts for K–12 include phonemic awareness, phonics, vocabulary, awareness of text and print features, fluency, comprehension, critical reading, author's craft, writ-ing processes, writing components, writing applications, language study, listening and viewing, and speaking and presenting. All content areas will not be present at every grade level. Comparing the content categories with levels of cognitive demand (see Tables 4.5 and 4.6)

Table 4.5. Surveys of enacted curriculum cognitive demand categories for mathematics

Memorize	Perform procedures	Demonstrate understanding	Conjecture, generalize, prove	Solve nonroutine problems, make connections
Recite basic mathematical facts	Use numbers to count, order, denote	Communicate mathematical ideas	Determine the truth of a mathematical pattern or proposition	Apply and adapt a variety of appropriate strategies to solve nonroutine problems
Recall mathematics terms and definitions	Do computational procedures or algorithms	Use representations to model mathematical ideas	Write formal or informal proofs	Apply mathematics in contexts outside of mathematics
Recall formulas and computational procedures	Follow procedures/instructions	Explain findings and results from data analysis	Recognize, generate or create patterns	Analyze data, recognize patterns
	Solve equations/formulas/routine word problems	Develop/explain relationships between concepts	Find a mathematical rule to generate a pattern or number sequence	Synthesize content and ideas from several sources
	Organize or display data	Show or explain relationships between models, diagrams, and/or other representations	Make and investigate mathematical conjectures	
	Read or produce graphs and tables		Identify faulty arguments or misrepresentations of data	
	Execute geometric constructions		Reason inductively or deductively	

Sources: Porter, 2001; Roach, 2008.

Table 4.6. Surveys of enacted curriculum cognitive demand categories for English language arts/reading

Memorize/recall	Perform procedures/explain	Generate/ create/demonstrate	Analyze/investigate	Evaluate
Reproduce sounds or words	Follow instructions	Create/develop connections among text, self, world	Categorize/schematize information	Determine relevance, coherence, internal consistency, logic
Provide facts, terms, definitions, conventions	Give examples	Recognize relationships	Distinguish fact and opinion	Assess adequacy, appropriateness, credibility
Locate literal answers in text	Check consistency	Dramatize	Compare and contrast	Test conclusions, hypotheses
Identify relevant information	Summarize	Order, group, outline, organize ideas	Identify with another's point of view	Synthesize content and ideas from several sources
Describe	Identify purpose, main ideas, organizational patterns	Express new ideas (or express ideas newly)	Make inferences, draw conclusions	Generalize
	Gather information	Develop reasonable alternatives	Predict probable consequences	Critique
		Integrate with other topics and subjects		

Sources: Porter, 2001; Roach, 2008.

allow for a coarse-grain view of what students are expected to do with their knowledge of content. A fine-grained view breaks the content into more discrete descriptions. Algebra, for example, includes such components as absolute value, multistep equations, factoring, and so forth.

The SEC model involves raters, including individual teachers and an alignment panel of three or more content area specialists. Teachers complete surveys at the end of the year, rating level of coverage for topics and subtopics and the level of cognitive demand for tasks in each of the topic areas. The model provides useful descriptors of cognitive demand that can serve as a guide in considering the design of assessments.

Application of Webb's model requires members of a trained alignment panel, consisting of educators and curriculum experts, to

1. Recognize and apply depth-of-knowledge (DOK) level rating for each objective in the state content standards

2. Rate the DOK level for each assessment task

3. Identify the objective(s) from the content standards to which the assessment item corresponds

The central feature of this model is the DOK rating given to each assessment item. There are four DOK levels: recall, skill/concept, strategic thinking, and extended thinking. Once an analysis of each assessment item is completed, analyses of the ratings allow for computing descriptive statistics for each of the four criteria in Webb's alignment model: categorical concurrence, range of knowledge, balance of representation, and depth of knowledge, which were described earlier in this chapter.

These models provide useful descriptions to inform the development of AA-MAS and modified achievement level descriptors (see Table 4.7). The descriptions can also guide assessment development and ensure the assessments cover the same breadth and depth of content as the general assessment.

LEVELS OF COGNITIVE COMPLEXITY IN MATHEMATICS

State assessment frameworks articulate performance indicators listed for content strands and are intended to provide teachers with guidance in determining the outcomes of instruction. Table 4.8, an example from Wyoming, illustrates how state standards can be addressed through items with different depth of knowledge levels, with the items still directly related to the content standard.

This grade 6 geometry strand includes the goal that "Students apply geometric concepts, properties, and relationships in a problem solving situation" and more specifically to ". . . classify, describe, compare,

Table 4.7.   Webb's general descriptions for depth-of-knowledge (DOK) level

Level	Description
Level 1: Recall	Recalling information such as facts, definitions, terms, or simple procedures; performing simple algorithms or applying formulas
Level 2: Skill/Concept	Requires some decision regarding how to approach a problem or activity; classifying, organizing, estimating, making observations, collecting and displaying data, comparing data
Level 3: Strategic Thinking	Requires reasoning, planning, using evidence, and a higher level of thinking than recall or skill/concept; explaining one's thinking, making conjectures, determining solutions to a problem with multiple correct outcomes
Level 4: Extended Thinking	Requires complex reasoning, planning, developing, and thinking often over an extended period of time. Cognitive demand for tasks is high and work is complex. Requires making connections within and between subject domains. Includes designing and conducting experiments, making connections between a finding or outcome and related concepts, combining and synthesizing ideas into new concepts, critiquing literary pieces and designs of experiments.

Source: Webb (1999).

and draw representations of 1- and 2-dimensional objects and angles" (indicator MA6.2.1). This indicator requires that students demonstrate skills and understanding of coordinate geometry by, for example, plotting points in the context of identifying and classifying basic geometric shapes. The indicator contains multiple content-related targets, suggesting that a modified standard could be constructed by breaking relevant tasks into multiple components. Depth of knowledge can be considered by changing the complexity of assessment tasks related to the indicator. The guiding principle is that assessment tasks must be aligned to content for the grade-level standards. How specific assessment items contribute to a student's level of proficiency is discussed later in this chapter.

Table 4.8.   Content standard 2. Geometry: Students apply geometric concepts, properties, and relationships in a problem-solving situation

Code	Grade 6 benchmarks
MA6.2.1	Students classify, describe, compare, and draw representations of 1- and 2-dimensional objects and angles.
MA6.2.2	Students identify and classify congruent objects by properties appropriate to grade level.
MA6.2.3	Students communicate the reasoning used in identifying geometric relationships in problem-solving situations appropriate to grade level.

From Wyoming State Board of Education. (2008). *Wyoming mathematics content and performance standards* (p. 45). Cheyenne, WY: Wyoming Department of Education; reprinted by permission.
Note: Students communicate the reasoning used in solving these problems. They may use tools/technology to support learning.

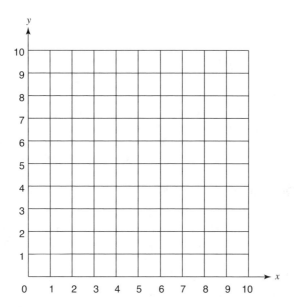

Figure 4.2.   Mathematics goals for students K–12.

Consider Figure 4.2, with each of the examples of depth of knowledge offered by Webb (1999), as an example of developing items that reflect this indicator.

1. *Recall and Reproduction.* Present student with the following points graphed on a coordinate plane: A (1, 5), B (3, 2), C (6, 2), and D (?, ?). Students are asked to give the coordinates for point D. Next, present a similar diagram with points A (1, 1), B (1, 5), C (5, 5), and D (5, 1) connected to form a quadrilateral. The student is required to identify the type of quadrilateral formed by connecting the points. Students might be given possible choices such as square, rectangle, and trapezoid.

2. *Skills and Concepts/Basic Reasoning.* Presented with a coordinate grid, students are asked to plot points A (1, 1), B (1, 5), C (5, 5), and D (5, 1). They are then asked to connect A, B, C, and D in order and to identify the quadrilateral that is formed. Students might be asked to explain or describe how they determined the type of quadrilateral that was formed. The assessment item might include scaffolds to guide the students in this process, such as "Describe the characteristics of the sides and angles that helped you decide what type of figure was formed."

3. *Strategic Thinking/Complex Reasoning.* The student is asked to plot points A (1, 1), B (1, 5), and C (5, 5). They are then asked to plot point D such that the figure formed by connecting the points A, B, C, and

D, in order, forms a square. Name the coordinates for point D. Give two reasons why the figure has to be a square.

4. *Extended Thinking/Reasoning.* The student is asked to plot point A (1, 1). Students are then asked to plot three additional points and connect them such that the figure formed is a rectangle. To extend their thinking, the student is asked to describe a process for forming a rectangle in a coordinate grid given one point as a vertex. Instead of a rectangle, the student might be asked to discuss the process for constructing a trapezoid given one point as a vertex.

ITEM MODIFICATIONS

Additional modifications can be accomplished by changing the format of the assessment items, reducing the complexity of the language used in the item, and providing additional information or scaffolding to reduce the cognitive load for the student; however, the items must maintain alignment to the grade-level content in the standard, as discussed earlier. Hess, McDivitt, and Fincher (2008) conducted a pilot study about the effects of providing scaffolds for students within test items and across state assessments to determine whether these scaffolds allowed students to better document knowledge that they possessed related to content standards. Some of the scaffolds that they studied included using graphic organizers, chunking or segmenting longer texts into shorter pieces, and adding graphics to illustrate a term. They also examined item simplification techniques, such as restricting the use of pronouns, left justifying text, shortening or simplifying test item stems, and paying attention to the physical presentation of the assessment material by examining typeface, spacing on the page, line length, and the use of blank space (or leading) around paragraphs or between columns of numbers to make them more legible. A goal of these modifications was to provide students better access to the information on the assessment without cuing them to correct answers. These methods, if effective, could meet the AA-MAS guidelines of "less difficult" but adhering to the fidelity of the grade-level standard. In this study, teachers were also asked to use the scaffolding supports in their lessons, so that students were used to seeing them before the actual assessment. The results of this pilot study indicate that providing scaffolding that supports both teaching and assessments could provide a valid way to assess students on the AA-MAS test. Although the scaffolds discussed are research-based, there are some inconsistent findings about their effectiveness in improving student performance. For instance, Abedi et al. (2008) found that students with disabilities did not perform significantly better on reading comprehension assessments that utilized segmented text, although the reliability of the tests improved. Further studies and appropriate field testing are necessary to justify the choice and use of proper scaffolds at the state level.

Some more specific examples of scaffolding and item simplification are provided in the following sections.

Common Stimulus

The approach of a common stimulus has been used on the NAEP (Kenney, 2000). The common stimulus might be a table, graph, or chart. A series of items draws from previously presented information or a common context. Anderson and Morgan (2008) offered some guidelines for constructing items that have a common stimulus:

- Items should be independent. A student's response on one question should not be dependent on getting the correct answer for a previous item.
- Items should refer to a clearly different aspect of the stimulus to avoid overlap.
- Items should assess a range of skills.
- Items should have a range of difficulty with the easier items appearing first.
- Information given in a stem or answer choice should not assist the student in correctly answering another item.
- Items should appear on the same page or on a facing page.

Such simple approaches reduce the cognitive load required to comprehend and process multiple items presented with varying contexts or information.

Replace Text with Relevant
Pictures, Diagrams, Tables, and Graphics

In the item in Figure 4.3, the student is presented with a diagram that may assist him or her in visualizing the relationship between the sides of the scale and representing that relationship symbolically. This NAEP item received mostly exemplary comments from raters because of the scaffolding provided by the visual; however, one rater argued that the item was inauthentic and imposed as a testing convention because the item could be solved by visual inspection and did not require the construction of a number sentence (Daro, Stancavage, Ortega, DeStefano, & Linn, 2007). Despite this criticism, the item demonstrates how visuals might assist a student in understanding the relationship

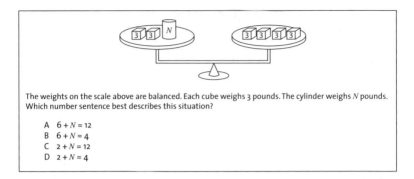

The weights on the scale above are balanced. Each cube weighs 3 pounds. The cylinder weighs N pounds. Which number sentence best describes this situation?

A $6 + N = 12$
B $6 + N = 4$
C $2 + N = 12$
D $2 + N = 4$

Figure 4.3. Mathematics expectations for students by grade band. (From U.S. Department of Education, National Center for Education Statistics. [2007]. *National Assessment of Education Progress [NAEP] 2007 Mathematics assessment.* Grade 4, Block B1M7, #4. Washington, DC: Author; reprinted by permission.)

and thus be able to focus on the task of identifying an equivalent symbolic representation. The diagram did not change the underlying skill of being able to identify a relationship symbolically.

Reduce Complexity of Stem

The question and its modification (Elliott, Kurz, Beddow, & Frey, 2009) shown in Figure 4.4 illustrate how items might be modified to reduce the complexity of the item stem while preserving the alignment to the

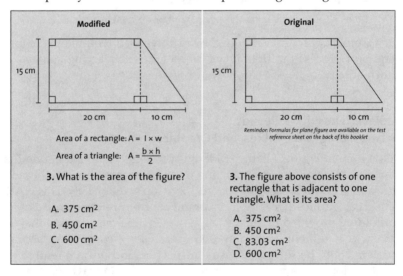

Figure 4.4. Mathematical process goals for students. (From Elliott, S.N., Kurz, A., Beddow, P., & Frey, J. [2009]. *Cognitive load theory and universal design principles: Applications to test item development.* Paper presented at the annual meeting of the National Association of School Psychologists, Boston; reprinted by permission.)

Table 4.9. Levels of cognitive demand

Original stem and distractors	Modified stem and distractors
The United States eventually reduced the number of immigrants allowed to enter the country because	Why did the United States reduce the number of immigrants?
A. the United States already had too many people	A. The United States already had too many people.
B. the immigrants were taking away jobs from American workers	B. The immigrants were taking away jobs from American workers.
C. the immigrants had too many hardships to face in America	C. The immigrants had too many hardships to face in America.
D. the country that the immigrants came from was angry about their leaving	D. The country that the immigrants came from was angry about their leaving.

content standard. The modified item requires the student to evaluate a formula to find the area of a complex figure consisting of a rectangle and a triangle. The revised format removes the requirement that the student either recall the appropriate formula or identify it from the list provided in the booklet. Both items assess a student's ability to evaluate a geometric formula using data from a figure. Both items also require the student to differentiate between a rectangle and a triangle and to understand the basic concept of area. The modified item removes extraneous information (i.e., adjacent) while also maintaining depth of knowledge.

Hess et al. (2008) provide a similar example of simplifying the stem and making the distractors complete sentences, as shown in Table 4.9.

Grouping Questions by Content or Topic

Clustering items according to the particular standard that they link back to or by specific learning targets or objects is another way of modifying the assessment without changing the content focus of the item. For example, if an assessment in mathematics has four items that link to the state standard "Apply ratios and proportions in solving real-world problems," then clustering those items (preferably by level of difficulty, with easier items first) will facilitate the student being focused on specific content for a longer period of time without having to adjust to changes in content from item to item. The student will be working with similar thinking processes as proportional reasoning is applied to situations such as rates of change, percentages, unit pricing or rates, and so forth. Such measures reduce anxiety and may generate more interest, thus improving concentration.

Breaking Up Questions and Providing Hints

Another set of modifications involves breaking complex tasks into components that may contain hints or supports to assist the test taker. A longer task may be broken into parts that are matched to a specific indicator or expectation (Suurtamm, Lawson, & Koch, 2008). Suurtamm and her colleagues do warn, however, that such modifications potentially lead to specific approaches to solving a problem and may diminish students' opportunities to participate in complex problem solving. In modified assessments, such practices are likely to reduce the overall complexity of the problem-solving situation while retaining a link to the content standard.

Another aspect of this type of modification is providing hints. For example, if a student is asked to define a compound word ("noninterference," for example), they might be prompted to "Break the word into parts." Hess et al. (2008) showed how thought balloons, similar to what you might see in a comic strip, might be used to provide these hints. However, the test developer will need to exercise caution to ensure that these additional features assist the test taker and do not provide distracting clutter on the page.

Summary of Modifications

These illustrations demonstrate that item modifications can be made while preserving the fidelity of the content. Such modifications reduce cognitive load and simplify language features that can sometimes obscure the intent of the assessment item. Simplifying language features is important in making assessment items accessible to a larger population of students, including those with learning difficulties and those for whom English is not their native language (see also Chapter 7). Scaffolding, item simplification, and related practices are good instructional tools and should not be used only during assessments. Remember that there should be a coherent link between the curriculum, instruction, and assessment.

HOW DO WE LINK CONTENT TO CURRICULUM AND INSTRUCTION APPROPRIATE FOR THIS POPULATION?

Curriculum access, data collection, and instructional effectiveness are issues that have been identified as variables that potentially influence student outcomes (Spooner, Dymond, Smith, & Kennedy, 2006). As emphasized throughout this chapter, linking assessment to content standards increases the likelihood that students with learning difficulties will have access to relevant grade-level academic content. The importance of curriculum access has been the focus of this chapter. Continued monitoring through data collection and analysis of student performance will provide greater alignment between instruction and assessment outcomes. Linking the curriculum and instruction to assessment outcomes is crucial in focusing the instructional design system on planning, implementing, and assessment of student learning.

The teacher is a critical factor in linking curriculum and instruction. Browder, Karvonen, Davis, Fallin, and Courtade-Little (2005) found that when teachers were trained on sound instructional practices, students' scores on alternate assessments improved. Fuchs et al. (2008) identified seven instructional principles that promote mathematical learning for students with disabilities. These instructional principles also provide an important set of guidelines for application to other content domains. First, instructional explicitness refers to instruction in which the teacher provides explicit and didactic teaching, sharing information focused on the goals of instruction. The authors reported that a meta-analysis of 58 math studies showed that although developing students advance from programs with constructivist and inductive styles, students with mathematics difficulties do not profit in meaningful ways. Second, instructional design to minimize the learning challenge anticipates and eliminates misunderstandings with precise details and the utilization of intentionally sequenced and integrated instructions focused on addressing gaps in achievement. The use of learning tools such as manipulatives and visuals enhance mathematics instruction, reducing confusion and the inability to maintain content. Third, a strong conceptual basis situates the procedures being taught in order to provide a strong conceptual foundation. Fourth, drill and practice is critical to maintaining skills through daily lessons, review, and computerized supports. Fifth, cumulative review reinforces practice and review, building a continued reliance on foundational skills being taught. Sixth, instruction must include motivators to help students regulate their attention and behavior and work hard integrating systematic self-regulation and motivation supports, including tangible reinforcers. The seventh principle, considered the most essential, is ongoing progress monitoring to establish whether a strategy is effective for a particular student.

In the next chapter, these ideas regarding modifying the content will be actualized into test design theory. However, it is important to remember that the best test design will not produce the desired results if the understandings about human cognition applied to the item development are not also carried into the classroom through curriculum and instruction.

REFERENCES

Abedi, J., Kao, J.C., Leon, S., Sullivan, L., Herman, J.L., Pope, R., et al. (2008). *Exploring factors that affect the accessibility of reading comprehension assessments for students with disabilities: A study of segmented text.* Los Angeles: National Center for Research on Evaluation, Standards, and Student Testing. Retrieved March 21, 2009, from http://www.cse.ucla.edu/products/reports/R746.pdf

Anderson, P., & Morgan, G. (2008). *Developing tests and questionnaires for a national assessment of educational achievement.* Washington, DC: The World Bank.

Ban, P., Holt, L., & Kurizaki, V. (2008). *Hawaii progress maps.* Presentation made at the Council of Chief State School Officers Conference, National Conference on Student Assessment Resources, Orlando, FL.

Browder, D.M., Karvonen, M., Davis, S., Fallin, K., & Courtade-Little, G. (2005). The impact of teacher training on state alternate assessment scores. *Exceptional Children, 71,* 267–282.

Browder, D.M., Spooner, F., Wakeman, S., Trela, K., & Baker, J. (2006). Aligning instruction with academic content standards: Finding the link. *Research & Practice for Persons with Severe Disabilities, 31*(4), 309–321.

Brownell, M.T., Ross, D.D., Colon, E.P., & McCallum, C.L. (2005). Critical features of Special Education teacher preparation: A comparison with general teacher education. *The Journal of Special Education, 38,* 242–252.

California Department of Education. (1998, relisted in 2009). *English-language arts content standards for California public schools: Kindergarten through grade twelve.* Sacramento, CA: California Department of Education.

Daro, P., Stancavage, F., Ortega, M., DeStefano, L., & Linn, R. (2007). *Validity study of the NAEP Mathematics Assessment: Grades 4 and 8.* Washington, DC: NAEP Validity Studies Panel, U.S. Department of Education.

Education for All Handicapped Children Act of 1975, PL 94-142, 20 U.S.C. §§ 1400 *et seq.*

Elliott, S.N., Kurz, A., Beddow, P., & Frey, J. (2009). *Cognitive load theory and universal design principles: Applications to test item development.* Paper presented at the annual meeting of the National Association of School Psychologists, Boston.

Fuchs, L.S., Fuchs, D., Powell, S.R., Seethaler, P.M., Cirino, P.T., & Fletcher, J.M. (2008). Intensive intervention for students with mathematics disabilities: Seven principles of effective practice. *Learning Disability Quarterly, 31*(2), 79–92.

Hawaii Department of Education. (1999). *Language arts content standards: Moving from the Blue Book to HCPS II.* Honolulu, HI: Hawaii Department of Education. Retrieved March 18, 2009, from http://www.hcps.k12.hi.us/PUBLIC/contst1.nsf/2be12f699cdba2840a2567830069239d/fbc32f9bf7fcc6bd0a2567e000146fc7/$FILE/Language%20Arts%20Booklet.pdf

Herber, H.L. (1970). *Teaching reading in the content areas.* Englewood Cliffs, NJ: Prentice Hall.

Hess, K., McDivitt, P., & Fincher, M. (2008). *Who are the 2% and how do we design test items and assessments that provide greater access to them? Results from a pilot study with Georgia students.* National Center for the Improvement of Educational Assessment. Retrieved April 1, 2009, from http://www.nciea.org/publications/CCSSO_KHPMMF08.pdf

International Reading Association and National Council of Teachers of English. (1996). *Standards for the English Language Arts.* Newark, DE: Authors.

Kenney, P.A. (2000). Families of items in the NAEP mathematics assessment. In N.S. Raju, J. W. Pelligrino, M.W. Bertenthal, K.J. Mitchell, & L.R. Jones (Eds.), *Grading the nation's report card: Research from the evaluation of NAEP* (pp. 5–43). Washington, DC: National Academies Press.

Ketterlin-Geller, L.R. (2008). Testing students with special needs: A model for understanding the interaction between assessment and student characteristics in a universally designed environment. *Educational Measurement: Issues and Practice, 27*(3), 3–16.

LaMarca, P.M. (2001). Alignment of standards and assessments as an accountability criterion. *Practical Assessment, Research & Evaluation, 7*(21). Retrieved March 20, 2009 from http://PAREonline.net/getvn.asp?v=7&n=21

Leu, D. (2007). *The literacy web: Literacy standards.* Retrieved February 23, 2010 from http://www.literacy.uconn.edu/litstan.htm

Mathematical Sciences Education Board. (1993). *Measuring what counts: A conceptual guide for mathematics assessment.* Washington, DC: National Academies Press.

Messick, S. (1989). Meaning and values in test validation: The sciences and ethics of assessment, *Educational Researcher, 18*(2), 5–11.

National Center for Educational Statistics. (2003). *Mathematics framework for the 2003 National assessment of educational progress.* Washington, DC: Author.

National Council of Teachers of Mathematics. (2000). *Principles and standards for school mathematics.* Reston, VA: Author.

National Council of Teachers of Mathematics. (2006). *Curriculum focal points for prekindergarten through grade 8 mathematics: A quest for coherence.* Reston, VA: Author.

National Reading Panel. (2000). *Report of the National Reading Panel, teaching children to read: An evidence-based assessment of the scientific research literature on reading and its implications for reading instruction.* Washington, DC: National Institute for Literacy.

New York State Education Department. (2006). *Mathematics Core Curriculum: MST Standard 3.* New York: The University of the State of New York & New York State Education Department.

New York State Education Department. (2007a). *New York State testing program 2007: Mathematics, grades 3-8. Technical report.* Monterey, CA: CTB/McGraw-Hill.

New York State Education Department. (2007b). *New York State testing program 2007: English language arts, grades 3-8. Technical report.* Monterey, CA: CTB/McGraw-Hill.

No Child Left Behind Act of 2001, PL 107-110, 115 Stat. 1425, 20 U.S.C. §§ 6301 *et seq.*

Pellegrino, J.W., Chudowsky, N., & Glaser, R. (Eds.). (2001). *Knowing what students know: The science and design of educational assessment.* Washington, DC: National Academies Press.

Porter, A.C., & Smithson, J.L. (2001). *Defining, developing, and using curriculum indicators* (CPRE Research Report Series RR-048). Philadelphia: University of Pennsylvania, Consortium for Policy Research in Education.

Roach, A.T., Niebling, B.C., & Kurz, A. (2008). Evaluating the alignment among curriculum, instruction, and assessments: Implications and applications for research and practice. *Psychology in Schools, 45*(2), 158–175.

Shanahan, T. (2003). Research-based reading instruction: Myths about the National Reading Panel report. *The Reading Teacher, 56,* 646–655.

Spooner, F., Dymond, S.K., Smith, A., & Kennedy, C.H. (2006). What we know and need to know about accessing the general curriculum for students with significant cognitive disabilities. *Research and Practice for Persons with Severe Disabilities, 31,* 277–283.

Suurtamm, C., Lawson, A., & Koch, M. (2008).The challenge of maintaining the integrity of reform mathematics in large-scale assessment. *Studies in Educational Evaluation, 34,* 31–43.

U.S. Department of Education. (April, 2007). *Modified academic achievement standards.* Washington, DC: Author.

U.S. Department of Education, National Center for Education Statistics. (2007). *National Assessment of Education Progress (NAEP) 2007 Mathematics assessment.* Grade 4, Block B1M7, #4. Washington, DC: Author.

Webb, N.L. (1997a). Determining alignment of expectations and assessments in mathematics and science education. *NISE Briefs, 1*(2), 1–11.

Webb, N.L. (1997b). *Criteria for alignment of expectations and assessments in mathematics and science education* (Research monograph No. 6). Washington, DC: Council of Chief State School Officers.

Webb, N.L. (1999). *Alignment of science and mathematics standards and assessments in four states.* Washington, DC: Council of Chief State School Officers.

Wyoming State Board of Education. (2008). *Wyoming mathematics content and performance standards.* Cheyenne, WY: Wyoming Department of Education.

5

Developing Items and Assembling Test Forms for the Alternate Assessment Based on Modified Achievement Standards

Catherine Welch and Stephen B. Dunbar

In many respects, the development of items and assembly of test forms for specific populations involves no special process considerations other than those required of any professional test development activity. This chapter begins with an overview of best practices in item and test development in K–12 achievement testing in the context of the content domains of English language arts (ELA) and mathematics. Although the processes involved may be similar, the specific accountability context established by the alternate assessment based on modified achievement standards (AA-MAS) guidelines, the potentially diverse characteristics of students in the AA-MAS population, and the fact that states are approaching AA-MAS designs in the presence of existing accountability tests developed under federal guidelines for technical quality mean that certain steps in the test development process may deviate from typical best practice.

Nothing in the federal guidelines for the AA-MAS program specifies that the design and development of the 2% assessment be approached as a modification of an existing general assessment or as an alternate assessment developed as a separate endeavor (U.S. Department of Education, 2007b). Given the position of the AA-MAS assessment in a difficult-to-define gray zone between two existing assessments in each state, one can imagine its design and development to follow an approach already established by a state (or by its contractors) for any existing assessment, including an alternate assessment based on grade-level achievement standards (e.g., Massachusetts). Alternatively, an AA-MAS assessment might be developed as a kind of hybrid, consisting of features and materials from the general assessment and, where required by considerations of accessibility, for example, measurement approaches adopted in the state's alternate assessments based on alternate achievement standards program.

One could imagine how informative a typology of successful approaches states used to design tests for their AA-MAS program might be. That typology might span the range from direct modification of existing items or item pools to full custom design of task types and assessment items tailored specifically to the AA-MAS population. At the time of this writing, however, only one state has received U.S. Department of Education approval for its AA-MAS program. Early efforts by states have focused on changes to their general education assessment through the inclusion of one or more of the following strategies (Ahearn, 2009; Lazarus, Thurlow, Christensen, & Cormier, 2007):

- Removing one distractor from multiple-choice items
- Reducing the number of items on the test
- Simplifying language of the items
- Using shorter reading passages or segmenting them
- Putting fewer items on a page
- Using larger font size
- Underlining or bolding key text

Only a handful of states appear to be modifying an alternate assessment or designing a brand new assessment from scratch, and information on the success of these approaches was not available at the time of this writing. Given the limited data and incomplete development activities at the state level at this time, a best-practice approach is taken to the topic of design and development of assessments for the AA-MAS population.

This chapter discusses test development processes in general that apply to whatever approach is taken by a state. Professional standards for test development and for the assessment of students with disabilities (American Educational Research Association [AERA], American Psychological Association [APA], & National Council on Measurement in Education [NCME], 1999) provide guidance regardless of the approach. Much of the discussion in this chapter, however, presumes the AA-MAS approach taken by most states is to modify the existing general assessment. In most settings, the general assessment (its essential measurement features, its alignment to state content standards, its methods of scaling and reporting student achievement and mapping onto achievement levels) establishes the technical standards to be evaluated for purposes of reliability, validity, and comparability in the federal peer review process. Modification of the general assessment is likely to be cost effective as well. Thus the argument to support inferences from the AA-MAS for purposes of accountability is likely to be structured with a state's general assessment in mind. This provides states with a logical starting point for developing the many justifications for resource allocation that set the foundation for validity and comparability arguments (Kane, 2006; Marion, 2007; see also Chapter 7, this volume) as articulated in federal guidelines.

This chapter begins with a discussion of best practice in test development. The purpose of this discussion is to clarify key processes in development that contribute to the technical qualities of any assessment. Specific aspects of the process prominent in K–12 achievement testing for the No Child Left Behind Act of 2001 (NCLB; PL 107-110) are noted, as they represent key procedural steps that may be altered for the AA-MAS. Special considerations for the AA-MAS context are discussed in order to clarify the implications of modified achievement standards and performance level descriptors (Perie, 2008) for item and test development. In this discussion, the advantages and disadvantages of various options for modification are highlighted. Because a very real aspect of development for the AA-MAS is modification of items from the general assessment, examples of item analysis results from the latter are presented to illustrate approaches to identifying items for modification. Finally, psychometric consequences of test modifications are discussed, as they play out in the assembly of test forms and in the analysis of technical characteristics of items and test forms. This chapter closes with consideration of how best to document modifications during test development so the case can be made for validity and comparability as well as for interpretation of test results for both reporting on the achievement of individual students and the use of results for adequate yearly progress purposes.

BEST PRACTICE IN ITEM DEVELOPMENT AND FORMS ASSEMBLY

Test development plays a key role in validation, and validity considerations play a key role in test development. The procedures to develop and revise test materials and interpretive information lay the foundation for test validity. Meaningful evidence related to inferences based on test scores can only provide scores with utility if test development produces meaningful test materials. Content quality is the essence of arguments for test validity (Linn, Baker, & Dunbar, 1991). Test development is undeniably important to the proper interpretation of test scores and the inferences that are drawn from them (Kane, 2006). Users of test scores should study the specifications for the test, how they were derived, and the process by which the test is developed. Test development influences many aspects of validity (most importantly, content validity) and many types of inferences. The purpose of this section is to discuss the issues and considerations associated with best practice in developing tests. The considerations that are provided in this chapter are consistent with the *Standards for Educational and Psychological Testing* (AERA et al., 1999). The *Standards* constitute a seminal guide for proper test design and development.

Key to proper test design and development is the incorporation of universal design principles for all types of test items. These principles suggest an approach to assessment development based on principles of accessibility for a wide variety of end users. These principles are as applicable to the general assessment population as they are to a student population preparing to take an AA-MAS. Thompson, Johnstone, and Thurlow (2002) described seven elements of universally designed assessments, including inclusive test population; precisely defined constructs; accessible, nonbiased items; tests that are amenable to accommodations; simple, clear, and intuitive procedures; maximum readability and comprehensibility; and maximum legibility. Further guidance for states on universally designed assessments is provided by Lazarus et al. (2007).

Test Domain

A critical stage in the development of a statewide assessment is the design stage. In the design stage, important overall decisions about the test are made, including establishing a validation foundation for the test based on the state's academic content and achievement standards; designing test specifications that align with those standards; and reviewing, refining, and reaffirming validity evidence for test design.

Before test design can take place, it is important that the test developer understand the link between test purpose and test domain. The NCLB Act requires all public school students to participate in statewide assessments. The primary purposes of these assessments (given annually in certain grades and subjects) is to measure student progress toward state achievement standards and to hold schools, districts, and states accountable to bring all students to a proficient level in reading and mathematics. *Test domain* is used to refer to the various attributes used to define what a test should measure, including content topics, tasks, and process levels. In the NCLB context, states' content and achievement standards provide this definition of test domain. Understanding this connection between purpose and domain allows developers to determine what should and what should not be included on a statewide assessment. To be able to develop items that measure the test domain, developers need to define the test domain explicitly (i.e., which of the state's content standards are eligible for inclusion on the statewide assessment and which are not).

One of the major struggles with current statewide assessments is the large number of standards that most of the states have adopted and the need to align content standards with curriculum and statewide assessments. There are many issues in alignment, stemming from the wide variation in the specificity and clarity of state standards in defining what students need to know and be able to do, an imbalance between the number of standards and the testing time available, and the lack of agreement about the relative importance of the standards and the emphasis each receives in the statewide assessment. Several methods for evaluating alignment have been developed in recent years (Bhola, Impara, & Buckendahl, 2003; Rothman, Slattery, Vranek, & Resnick, 2002; Webb, 1999). Using empirical validation strategies that focus on alignment can help identify, through more objective means, those standards that are the most important priorities for inclusion on the assessment.

Another important consideration at the early stages of test design, and particularly important for the AA-MAS, is defining the examinee population(s) for whom the test is intended (see Chapter 1, this volume). It is important to define the characteristics of the students who will constitute the examinee population for the test. Specifying the examinee population must take into account examinee characteristics that fall outside of the requirements of the test, but may constrain or confound the examinee's performance on the test.

Test Specifications

The next step in test design is to specify the important attributes of the items and test forms. Test specifications are often called blueprints because they specify how the test is to be constructed. Derived directly from test philosophy, test purpose and use, test audience, and empirical validity evidence gathered for the test, test specifications delineate the requirements for the subsequent stages of development, review, field testing, assembly, and evaluation of the end product. The test specifications should identify the content domain, cognitive processes, the number and balance of items, the technical characteristics of the test, and the appropriate item formats (AERA et al., 1999, Standard 3.3). Each of these is presented in the following sections.

Content Domain

The empirical methods previously described can be used to define the content topics to be included in the domain measured by a test. The ideal level of specificity of content topics in test specifications is that which ensures adequate control of all crucial elements of the content standards. In defining the content domain, the test developer must understand the structure of the content domain, how topics within the domain relate to each other, and how students build their knowledge over time.

Processes

It is equally important to specify the process requirements of the items in the test. These cognitive requirements represent the breadth, depth, and range of complexity that students have been taught to use within the context of the content domain. There are multiple approaches to the classification of items by cognitive demand (see Chapter 4, this volume, for more detail).

Distribution of Content and Processes

Each content area and process needs to have a weight assigned to it in the test specifications that represents the relative emphasis to be placed on the topic or skill in a test form or item pool. These weights are important to the assembly of multiple, parallel test forms, and they are especially relevant in establishing comparability of an AA-MAS and the general assessment.

Item Formats

After the specification of test content and processes, the next aspect of the test specifications involves identifying the type(s) of items to be developed. At this point, the test developer needs to define the item format features that are required by the content and process specifications, specify the item types that possess those features, and comparatively evaluate each item type to identify those that might be preferred for reasons of coverage, economy, precision, response time, development and scoring costs, delivery constraints, and feasibility. The content and skills to be measured should drive the choice of item type. Selected-response (also known as multiple choice) items may be significantly more efficient in the amount of information they gather per unit of testing time, but constructed-response items can add a performance dimension to observed scores and can be scored reliably, although not as inexpensively as selected-response items (Welch, 2006). Lindquist (1951) argued that the item type should match the criterion of interest. He indicated that the test developer should make the item format as similar to the criterion format as possible, recognizing the constraints of efficiency, comparability, and economy. As noted in Chapter 3 (this volume), there is no necessary connection between response format and cognitive level (e.g., multiple choice items can be used to assess higher-order thinking, and some performance tasks only measure surface knowledge).

Test Length

The next substantive consideration is length. The optimum test length is one that is accurate enough to support the inferences that will be made on the basis of the test results. Test length is a function of many concerns, most of which have been described, including content coverage and item formats. However, in addition to such concerns, test length is also a practical constraint of testing time. Testing time may be influenced by constraints such as class periods or the age of the student examinees.

Technical Characteristics

The test developer must consider the specifications for the test(s) as a whole. This includes consideration of statistical specifications such as estimates of reliability, distribution of content and processes across the test form, test organization, administrative plan, and special accommodations.

To the extent the test specifications are well specified, the test forms produced will be far more parallel than they would be if developed from general specifications. By developing detailed specifications, the test developer considers many specifics of the test development process before that process is begun. By carefully considering the major aspects of the testing process, the test developer can identify inconsistent or conflicting specifications early in the design process.

Well-developed test specifications drive the entire item-development and test-assembly process and serve as helpful directions to item writers, reviewers, and test users. Kane (2006) notes the importance of linking test specifications, item development, and forms assembly with the interpretive argument that will be used in attaching meaning to test scores. In this sense, validity is grounded in the test development process itself.

The content validation process is also ongoing. Evidence supporting the test specifications should be reaffirmed on a regular basis. If state assessments are to reflect the curriculum and the expectations of teachers regarding what their students need to be ready to learn or what they should have learned, test developers need to engage in a regular process to collect evidence to adjust or reaffirm the test specifications. Test design is at best an iterative process, one that repeatedly cycles through information gleaned through item development, test administration, and evaluation.

Item Development

Sound test development depends on well-defined, defensible item development. Sound item development is critical for providing the quality and consistency necessary to produce reliable test scores upon which validated test-score inferences can be made.

The development process should include considerations of universally designed assessments. Thompson et al. (2002) identify specific questions for test developers to take into account as they develop items and design assessments. The considerations of universal design appropriate for all stages of test development include the following:

1. Incorporate elements of universal design in the early stages of test development.

2. Include disability, technology, and language acquisition experts in item reviews.

3. Provide professional development for item developers and reviewers on use of the considerations for universal design.

4. Present the items being reviewed in the format in which they will appear on the test.

5. Include standards being tested with the items being reviewed.

6. Try out items with students.

7. Field test items in accommodated formats.

8. Review computer-based items on computers.

Item Writing

Item writing is very much an iterative process, but it can be undertaken in a standardized manner. Item development processes need to establish principles and procedures that take into account the various audiences and purposes of the program. Item development processes for constructed-response items may also include the initial drafting of the scoring rubric simultaneously with the item writing. The qualifications of the item writers, the security of the process, and the training are all essential considerations for the item development process.

The process adopted for developing items in any testing program is critical and must be considered in relation to issues of validity, reliability, and interpretability. The determination of the source of the item content depends on test purpose and the inferences that need to be made on the basis of that content. Identifying those individuals who are qualified to develop items will be dependent on the requirements of a particular assessment. Common procedures reflect a concern for demographic characteristics, such as representation of the racial/ethnic backgrounds and gender of the examinee population.

Item Reviews

Once items have been developed, they should be subjected to a multistage, multipurpose review for content accuracy, fairness, universal design, and psychometric concerns. As with item writers, it is critical that item reviewers be experts in the area for which they are being recruited, that they be representative of the examinee population, and that they receive standardized training on the item attributes they are being recruited to evaluate.

The content reviewers should then be asked to review the items according to a set of established criteria. These criteria include scrutinizing items to ensure that they:

1. Align with the specified content standards

2. Match to the specified processes

3. Are technically correct

4. Include effective distractors for multiple-choice items

5. Include draft scoring rubrics for constructed-response items

6. Show clarity in response options (keyed option correct, distractors incorrect)

7. Adhere to the specified item format

Reviewers should also provide guidance on how to rephrase item stems, propose alternative keys and distractors, clarify scoring criteria, and identify ambiguous or confusing language in order to improve item quality. This guidance could be informed by cognitive interviews, think-aloud protocols, and piloting the items in individual administrations to examine their cognitive demands (Almond et al., 2009).

All item development should be attended to fairness both in principle and in practice. Both the *Code of Fair Testing Practices in Education* (2004) and the AERA/APA/NCME *Standards* (1999) include obligations for ensuring fairness to test takers. The *Standards* also address obligations to ensure fairness through all stages of test development, test administration, and test use.

Assessments should also be reviewed for consistency with universal design principles to help ensure that optimal, standardized conditions are available for all students and that the test materials students encounter do not present unnecessary complexity in surface appearance.

Although content reviews are critical in consideration of internal qualities of a test, fairness reviews are equally essential in large-scale assessment programs, as they are designed to ensure that all test takers have a comparable opportunity to demonstrate what they know and can do. Test fairness starts with design of the test and its specifications. It then continues through every stage of the test development process, including item writing and review, item field testing, item selection and forms construction, and forms review. These reviews help to ensure that items are evaluated from diverse viewpoints, not least of which are based on multicultural and gender-related perspectives (Camilli, 2006; Schmeiser & Welch, 2006).

Field Testing

Once the items have been reviewed and problems with them addressed, the items are typically prepared for field testing. After the field test, item evaluations should be conducted using the field test data. Statistical analyses of field test data typically include item analysis that is used to identify items that may be problematic. For constructed-response items, analyses may include 1) descriptive statistics, such as the mean performance, standard deviation of the mean performance, range of responses, and frequency distribution of responses; 2) rater consistency and reliability estimates; and 3) correlations with multiple-choice items. For multiple-choice items, analyses may include difficulty and discrimination indices. It may also include an analysis of the distractors, student response patterns, and indications of speediness.

Items that appear statistically flawed should be carefully reviewed for possible content-related problems and for structural problems with the item (e.g., inadvertent cues to the key or distractors that are too close to the key).

Test Assembly

This stage of the development activity includes the process of selecting and organizing a particular set of items that will constitute a given form of a test. Test form assembly requires expert-level knowledge and skills in test construction, including an understanding of the relationships between the content and statistical characteristics of the items in a test and the test's measurement properties. Though test assembly is guided by test specifications, it also requires the well-reasoned decisions of a test developer who understands the relevant measurement principles and the judgments of content experts.

TEST SPECIFICATIONS, ITEM DEVELOPMENT, FORMS ASSEMBLY, AND ITEM-LEVEL STATISTICS FOR THE AA-MAS

The primary purpose of this section is to describe approaches and strategies and identify various considerations that test developers of AA-MAS should take into account as they develop or modify general state assessments to create new alternate assessments. The intention is to focus on various steps of the development process, as outlined in the section on best practice, particularly those that are most relevant or available for modifications.

Several major assumptions guide the discussion in this section:

1. Modified achievement standards do not imply that the content standards are being modified. Rather, AA-MASs must adhere to the state content standards and must cover the same breadth and depth as the general assessment. The AA-MAS must be aligned to the content standards with respect to the content and process specifications but may be less difficult.

2. Given the substantial investment that states have made in the design and development of their testing programs, states may elect to modify existing assessments as a preferred approach to developing an AA-MAS.

3. The AA-MAS must satisfy reasonable technical requirements in terms of validity and reliability (Sato et al., 2007). In order to maximize the validity of the AA-MAS, test developers must follow the same rigorous and iterative approach that has been established as best practice in test development.

Figure 5.1 implies that there is a parallel relationship between content and achievement standards and test specifications and cut scores. The content standards define what students need to know. The achievement standards define how well the students know the content standards and determine which students are proficient and which are not.

The test specifications are the translation of the content standards into assessment language (what will be on the test that the students need to know). The cut score on the assessment determines the minimum score that indicates proficiency.

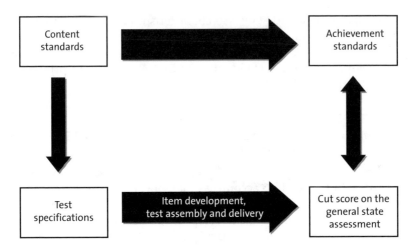

Figure 5.1.   Schematic diagram of interplay among test design components.

If test developers are not allowed to modify the content standards, then the test development effort for the AA-MAS should focus on test specifications (and item and test development) for allowable modifications. Depending on the extent of these modifications, the AA-MAS may require either a new standards-setting process to locate the cut score representing the modified achievement standards or a validation study to examine the fidelity of the existing cut score given the extent of the modifications to test specifications and items. If the achievement descriptors for the modified achievement standards are rewritten to reflect a changed definition of proficiency, a new cut score study would also be necessary.

Special Considerations for Test Specifications

As with any assessment, the establishment of the test domain for the AA-MAS is the first consideration. State content standards and achievement standards define the test domain in the assessments being used to meet the requirements of NCLB and in the AA-MAS. The content standards are not to be modified. However, a review of the state content standards would be an appropriate first step. Grade-level content standards could be reviewed to ensure that students have an opportunity to achieve grade-level content. Students must have access to and must have received instruction in the grade-level content.

As discussed earlier, test specifications should include articulation of the content areas, process skills, and the balance between the two. They also include decisions about the item format, test length, and technical characteristics of the assessment. Careful consideration of modifications introduced in the test specifications phase of development may produce assessments that more closely model the range of grade-level content appropriate for students eligible for this assessment. This may provide students with a better opportunity to be assessed on the same grade-level content standards as all other students, but with modifications to the expectations for the mastery of the content. Access to these modified assessments based on these changes to test specifications will ideally provide a better estimate of the student's achievement. However, making these modifications is not without compromise. Changes to the test specifications can result in modified assessments that are less comparable, less reliable or even less valid than the original assessment. Table 5.1 provides an overview of modifications that would be viable based on changes to test specifications. The advantages of making these changes and the potential limitations of such changes are also provided.

Whenever modifications such as these are considered, experts who possess knowledge of the student population, can access relevant information, and are familiar with the state content standards are a critical part of the process. These experts need to address the complex interactions of the various approaches. For example, reducing the number of higher-order process items may benefit this particular student population, but may not be consistent with the state content standards.

Any modifications to test specifications must be consistent with the guiding assumptions cited previously in this chapter. That is, AA-MASs must adhere to the state content standards and must cover the same breadth and depth as the general assessment.

Using information from the *New York State Testing Program 2007 Technical Report for Mathematics, Grades 3-8* (New York State Education Department, 2007, December), the example shown in Table 5.2 illustrates a hypothetical modification of content specifications and the relative weights of item format for the grade 5 mathematics. The entries in Table 5.2 in regular type are the number of items for each content standard for the general assessment in 2007, whereas the entries in italics are proposed modifications for a potential AA-MAS.

The modification to the test specifications preserves (as closely as possible given fixed counts of items and points in the general assessment) the proportion of items aligned to each content standard as well as the proportion of items in each format based on a one-third reduction in the total number of items. It should be emphasized that the one-third reduction in this example does not represent an arbitrary selection of items to remove from a general assessment, such as the most difficult items, but instead items whose removal does not alter the content balance nor detract from the technical quality of the resulting AA-MAS.

Table 5.1. Proposed modifications to test specifications

Test specification	Proposed modification	Advantages	Possible limitations
Content	Reduce the number of items per content standard.	Maintains alignment with content standards	Comparability of test specifications of the AA-MAS to the general assessment
Process (or cognitive level)	Reduce the number of items per process standard.	Maintains alignment with content standards	May alter proportional representation of tested construct(s)
	Reallocate the process skills to reflect a more appropriate match to student abilities in terms of breadth, depth, and complexity.	Ensures accessibility of test materials Reduces difficulty	
Content by process weighting	Adjust the relative weights of the content and process dimensions.	Improves match of content strand to appropriate level of cognitive processes	The interaction between process and content is often difficult to quantify.
Item formats	Diversify the item formats to maximize inclusion of those that are preferable for content and process coverage.	Allows for partial credit to be given for short-answer, extended responses, and other types of open-ended items	Comparability of the test specifications of the AA-MAS to the general assessment
		Allows for fewer items to cover more content and process standards if the appropriate items are written and appropriate adjustments made to scoring rubrics	Comparability of the scores from the AA-MAS to the general assessment
			New scales may need to be established.
			Additional open-ended items would require additional resources for scoring, additional time for reporting.
			Exposure of items and need for additional forms of the assessment
			Designing scoring rubric to be aligned with content standards while improving accessibility for students of interest
			Field testing of open-ended items on appropriate student population

Test length	Reduce the reading load of the assessment but maintain the number of items.	Allows students more time per item	Reduces reliability
	Reduce the overall number of items in the test.	Decreases speediness impact of the assessment Reduces impact of student fatigue	Reduces precision of the cut-score decisions
Technical characteristics	Reduce the overall difficulty of the assessment by eliminating the most difficult items proportional to content standards.	Increases proportion of students with IEPs exceeding the cut score	Reduces reliability
	Replace the most difficult items with simpler items covering the same content standards.	Increases information about total score per-item included	Reduces precision of the cut-score decisions
	Increase the overall discrimination of the assessment by adding appropriate items.		May alter construct representation
	Reduce the overall difficulty of the assessment by eliminating higher-order process items.		Increases costs associated with item development

Key: AA-MAS, alternate assessments based on modified achievement standards; IEPs, individualized education programs.

Table 5.2.   Implications based on modifications to test specifications

Content standard	Multiple choice	Constructed response	Points allocated
Number sense and operations	14 *(9)*	1 *(1)*	16 *(11)*
Algebra	3 *(2)*	1 *(1)*	6 *(4)*
Geometry	4 *(2)*	3 *(2)*	12 *(8)*
Measurement	2 *(1)*	2 *(1)*	6 *(4)*
Statistics and probability	3 *(2)*	1 *(1)*	6 *(4)*
Total	26 *(16)*	8 *(6)*	46 *(31)*

Note: Entries in regular type are for the general assessment, whereas entries in italics and parentheses are for a potential alternate assessment based on modified achievement standards.

The guiding principle is to remain true to the overall specifications while reducing the length (i.e., number of items) of the test.

An additional dimension that may be considered at this stage is process or cognitive level of the items in the AA-MAS. NCLB guidelines require evaluation of cognitive level, and test specifications in many states reflect this aspect of items, as well as content strand. Although cognitive level may not be specified on an item-by-item basis during test assembly, a distribution of items is often identified for three or more levels of a cognitive hierarchy, and attention to these features of items is important in proposed modifications for AA-MAS. Because constructed-response items (and the rubric specifications for high scores on those items) typically define higher levels of a cognitive hierarchy, their proportional representation in the AA-MAS is critical.

Proportional representation of content specifications, cognitive levels, and item formats is intended to preserve certain aspects of test validity to yield comparability. The reduction in total-score points and number of items can have a predictable effect on reliability. In the example, the New York State Education Department math assessment had a reported reliability coefficient of 0.93. The reliability estimate of the modified assessment depicted in the table is 0.87.

Special Considerations for Item Development

The item development process involves many varied, yet related, considerations. In this context, item development refers to the three major processes of item writing, item reviewing, and field testing. Although many of the processes are similar for both selected-response and constructed-response items, there are also characteristics of these two item types that would suggest they should be discussed separately.

Tables 5.3 and 5.4 present possible modifications and their advantages and limitations for these two categories of items.

Consistent with needs for the design of the test specifications, item development for the AA-MAS will involve the identification of experts who are familiar with the student population and who are expert in providing appropriate and sufficient access to the general curriculum to prepare students to complete this assessment. Identifying experts to assist in the drafting or revising of items and reviewing these items for a variety of issues related to the student population needs will be critical. It will be critical that the role of these experts remain very central throughout the entire development process. Guidelines for use by the item writers and reviewers should include strategies for adapting items for students eligible for the AA-MAS. Frequent iterations of items should be expected in this process. All newly created items will need to be generated, reviewed, and revised throughout the development process by experts. All modified items should be subjected to the same rigorous review and refinement process. Reviews should take place as early in the process as possible, maximizing the benefits of the reviews before field testing.

Research on Item Modifications

Since the first draft regulations for the AA-MAS were issued by the U.S. Department of Education, ideas for item and test modification have appeared in white papers and plans submitted by states for peer review. Some of these ideas are included in this discussion. Much like the early years of work on testing accommodations for students with special needs, students with disabilities, and English language learners, ideas and innovations grow out of administrative imperatives and policy considerations for inclusion of all students in assessment and accountability programs. Empirical studies of the effects of accommodations on comparability of test score interpretations tend to lag behind the innovations themselves.

Although some research on adapting learning and assessment tasks for students with mild disabilities has been completed (American Institutes for Research, 2000; Bergeson, Wise, Gill, & Barlett, 2001) that would provide support for these suggestions, it would be misleading to assert that the suggestions offered here for modifications of existing items for accessibility in the AA-MAS context have a strong research base or have been shown empirically to justify the spirit and intentions of the law with regard to comparability of test-based inferences or fidelity to the accountability provisions of NCLB. Rather they should be understood as rational approaches to the challenges of the AA-MAS

Table 5.3. Proposed modifications to item development process for multiple-choice items

Process	Proposed modification	Advantages	Possible limitations
Item writing	Prepare reading passages and related items with as much scaffolding as possible.	Increases accessibility of items Maximizes students' ability to demonstrate what they know	Increased development time Increased development budget Comparability issues Alignment issues Increased chance of correct response by guessing
	Control stimulus complexity to allow for the minimum level of complexity while remaining aligned with the content standards.	Reduces effects owing to distractibility and fatigue	
	Write items with effective distractors for the AA-MAS population.	Removes construct-irrelevant variance owing to visual acuity and linguistic complexity	
	Use figures, pictures, and graphs to aid students in understanding the items.		
	Remove irrelevant language from items that may distract students.		
Item reviews	Review items for the possible revision of distractors that are attracting a very limited number of students.	Ensures distractors are contributing to student information	Increased development time Increased development budget Comparability issues
	Review items for the possible revision of distractors that are misleading to students.	Ensures relevance to classroom experiences and consistency with everyday learning supports	
	Review items for irrelevant language.	Graphics aid understanding	
	Review figures, pictures, and graphs for appropriate contributions and relevance.		
Field testing	Conduct cognitive interviews, cognitive labs, and think-alouds.	Provides preliminary analysis of processing levels	Increased development budget Limited access to appropriate students
	Field test items on student populations that are representative of students eligible for the AA-MAS to investigate the	Provides relevant statistics for use in forms assembly Provides statistics on both the AA-MAS	

appropriateness and feasibility of the modifications.

Field test all new or revised items on the appropriate sample of students.

Field test parallel variations of items (i.e., with various levels of scaffolding, with various levels of instruction, with various levels of language complexity) to identify those working most appropriately.

Beta test items on small samples of students. Conduct think-alouds with students to identify characteristics that are benefiting students and could be duplicated in future item.

Generate DIF statistics from the field test to help make item selection.

Generate item analysis statistics from the field test to help evaluate an item's ability to discriminate for the students of interest.

and general assessment students to identify different response patterns

---

Key: AA-MAS, alternate assessments based on modified achievement standards; DIF, differential item functioning.

Table 5.4. Proposed modifications to item development process for constructed response items

Process	Proposed modification	Advantages	Possible limitations
Item writing	Develop items that lend themselves to scaffolding, allowing students the opportunity to work through controlled sections of the items. Use figures, pictures, and graphs to aid students in understanding the items. Articulate the scoring criteria when the item is unusually drafted.	Increases accessibility of items Maximizes students' opportunity to fully demonstrate what they know	Generalizability of results may be reduced Reliability of the assessment may be reduced
Item reviews	Review scoring criteria for content, fairness, and universal design considerations.	Increases appropriate difficulty of items	
Field testing	Conduct cognitive interviews, cognitive labs, and think-alouds. Field test items on student populations that are representative of students eligible for the AA-MAS to investigate the appropriateness and feasibility of the modifications. Beta test items on small samples of students. Conduct think-alouds with students to identify characteristics that are benefiting students and could be duplicated in future items.	Provide preliminary analysis of processing levels Solicitation of responses from representative students to be used establish the scoring criteria.	Costs of studies Exposure of items Security of items

Scoring	Allow for partial credit of responses (based on scaffold items structure).	Provides relevant statistics for use in forms assembly
	Evaluate item responses separately for both content and process skills.	Maximizes the unique information available from constructed-response items
	Apply different types or scoring rubrics to the same item responses.	Generalizability of results may be reduced
	Generate distributional statistics for all constructed-response items for the AA-MAS and general assessment students.	Reliability of the assessment may be reduced
		Comparability to general assessment may be weaker

Key: AA-MAS, alternate assessments based on modified achievement standards.

that should be validated as any other aspect of an accountability system should be validated.

Empirical studies need to be conducted in order for test developers to provide the information necessary for appropriate interpretation. For example, studies that demonstrate a consistency between scores on a child's AA-MAS with other types of information about the child (individualized education program team evaluations, classroom performance) should be conducted. Studies that examine the relationship between the AA-MAS and other measures of the same constructs that are not necessarily used for state accountability purposes (performance on formative assessments, performance on diagnostic assessments) should also be planned. Research should also be planned to examine the internal structure for the AA-MAS as compared with that of the general assessment. Results from factor analysis for the AA-MAS could be compared with factor analysis results on the general assessment.

Modifications in Item Development

Consistent with the previous section "Research on Item Modifications," the effect of item modifications should be empirically studied. The methods used to modify the items should be thoroughly described as part of the validation process. Empirical and logical evidence should also be provided. Table 5.5 illustrates the application of item modifications to several sample items. Modifications such as those recommended for items 2 and 3 employ the principles of universal design. Such principles are most appropriately included in the standard development procedures for all new item development. When the selected approach is the modification of an existing assessment, universal design principles are critical to inclusion in the modification process.

Special Considerations for Forms Assembly

Table 5.6 presents similar modifications for the forms assembly and administration of the AA-MAS. As with the previous sections, advantages and limitations exist for every type of modification. After items have been developed, field tested, revised, and deemed eligible for inclusion on an operational form, the test developer selects the operational items from the pool of field-tested items, using all available data (item-level statistics for difficulty, discrimination, differential item functioning [DIF], item response theory [IRT] parameter estimates). In general, test developers will be more successful in assembling forms if an item pool exists that allows for some degrees of freedom in the selection of items for inclusion on the operational form. Although building such a pool would require additional time and resources from the state, the benefit of such efforts would be realized in the assembly process.

Table 5-5. Examples of modifications in development

Original item	Revised item	Description of modification
Anna baked 6 of 10 cupcakes for her classmates. Which number sentence describes how many more cupcakes Anna has to bake? A $10 + 6 = \square$ B $10 + 6 = \square$ C $10 \times 6 = \square$ D $10 \div 6 = \square$	Anna needs to bake 10 cupcakes for her classmates. She has baked 6. **Which number sentence describes how many more cupcakes Anna needs to bake?** A $10 + 6 = \square$ B $10 - 6 = \square$ C $10 \times 6 = \square$ D $10 \div 6 = \square$	Simpler sentence structure Use of additional space between distractors Use of bold text to highlight question
Recycling brought to Green River Recycling Plant last month: Week 1: 1,178 pounds Week 2: 1,065 pounds Week 3: 1,879 pounds Week 4: 1,997 pounds **The closest estimate of the total recycling taken to Green River Recycling Plant was** _____. A 4,000 pounds B 6,000 pounds C 8,000 pounds D 10,000 pounds	**Green River Recycling** | Weeks:	Pounds
---	---
1	1,178
2	1,065
3	1,879
4	1,997 | **What is the best estimate of the total recycling taken to Green River Recycling last month?** A 4,000 pounds B 6,000 pounds C 8,000 pounds D 10,000 pounds	Table with title, clear headings, and reduced verbiage Alignment of numerals Less text in title Question format changed from incomplete sentence
Sarah and her family went to the grocery store. At the store Sarah and her brother Kyle went up and down the aisles looking for their favorite snacks. They each bought 2 snacks. One snack costs $2. **How much did the children pay for the snacks altogether?** A $4 B $8 C $12 D $24	Sarah and her brother bought 2 snacks each at the grocery store. One snack costs $2. **How much did the children pay for the snacks altogether?** A $4 B $8 C $12 D $24	Reduced demands on working memory Use of additional space between distractors Alignment of numerals

(continued)

Table 5.5. *(continued)*

How do the authors portray Luis in the second paragraph? A As an eager student with many interests B As a popular boy with many friends C As someone who preferred performing to schoolwork D As someone who had trouble deciding what he wanted to do	How is Luis described in paragraph 2? A A student with many interests. B A boy with many friends. C Someone who didn't like schoolwork. D Someone who couldn't decide what he liked.	Simpler sentence structure Less irrelevant detail Use of additional space between distractors
According to the passage, what is a dory? A A wild bird B A large pail C A small boat D A body of water	In the line marked with ✓, what is a dory? A A wild bird B A large pail C A small boat D A body of water	Visual aid introduced to help focus student on appropriate place in the reading passage Example of the use of a support Potential for scaffolding

Table 5.6. Proposed modifications to test assembly process

Process	Proposed modification	Advantages	Possible limitations
Selecting items for inclusion on the operational form	Assemble forms from the least difficult to the most difficult item. Assemble items to reduce the number of items within any one test section. Assemble items to minimize changing from one content standard to another (e.g., within a math test, group the geometry items together, then group the measurement items together).	Increases accessibility for students	Comparability to general assessment
Test layout	Maximize white space in the test booklet. Follow principles of universal design. Limit the number of items per page or screen presentation.	Eliminates distractions for students	Comparability to general assessment
Test administration	Minimize the number of items presented in any separately timed section of the assessment (e.g., if a 44-item math test could be divided into two 22-item sections, assemble and administer in the shorter blocks). Minimize the transferring of information from a test booklet to an answer document by offering online delivery, consumable test booklets, or other mechanisms for capturing the student responses.	Reduces fatigue Reduces examinee error	May differ from general assessment administration format

Test developers should complete a match-to-specifications report based on the final assembled form. This process ensures the alignment of the modified assessment to the content standards, the test design and specifications, and the guidelines for item selection. This process also provides documentation of the overall characteristics of the form and how these characteristics compare with the target test specifications. Comparisons of distributions of item difficulties and discriminations from the field test statistics to the target technical distributions should be made. Estimates of reliability for the assembled form and estimates of the standard error of measurement should also be included in the match-to-specifications report. This is critical information to the review and approval of the assembled form. This information provides one last opportunity for the test developer to make changes to the composition of the assessment before an operational administration.

The greater the change in development, selection, presentation and administration of items change, the less likely it will be that states can "link" the performance on the AA-MAS to performance on the general assessment. However, one strategy, the reduction of the number of items proportional to the test specifications for the general assessment, offers the possibility of relating or linking the reduced version of the assessment to the full length of the assessment. In such instances, the modified assessment may be structured to maintain the intuitive understanding of the standard score scale used for the general assessment. This approach may offer some utility with respect to the interpretability of the results. Table 5.7 offers a quick summary of the impact on comparability and the scale for three tiers of change.

Special Considerations for Evaluating
Statistical Characteristics of AA-MAS Items

A standard activity in any test development context is the statistical evaluation of items for an assessment. In the AA-MAS context, this might happen in various places in the item and test development workflow as different types of item statistics become available. Preliminary data might exist, for example, from small samples in which item modifications are pilot-tested for accessibility and feasibility of administration. Field test data on larger samples may be reviewed after formal content and sensitivity reviews take place and before test form assembly. In test development processes using item-response theory, item- and person-fit statistics on larger samples may be needed. A significant challenge in the AA-MAS context, however, is the fact that item statistics may not be readily available at ideal times from ideal samples of students from the population.

Table 5.7. Impact of AA-MAS strategy on comparability and scale

Possible strategy	Comparability to general assessment	Scale considerations
Develop new assessment	None	New standard setting New scale necessary
Modify items (i.e., shift in item formats, number of distractors, scaffolding)	Limited	New standard setting New scale possible
Reduce number of items (proportional to content standards)	Linked	Retention of scale Validation of cut scores with standard-setting study

A reasonable approach to developing an empirical basis for item selection and modification is to examine conventional item analysis statistics for items in the general assessment. Because states have been administering their general assessment to all students except the 1% with the most severe disabilities since 2006, item-level data for students who might be deemed eligible for the AA-MAS assessment presumably exist. Statistical characteristics of items in this target population may provide some insights for item selection and modification.

Item Analyses for Contrasting Groups

Conventional item analyses for dichotomous, multiple-choice items produce observed percent correct or p values to measure item difficulty, correlations between items and total scores to measure item discrimination, as well as more detailed indicators of item functioning, such as the percentage of examinees choosing each multiple-choice option and correlations between option choice and total score as measures of distractor discrimination. Also informative for the latter concept is the percentage of high- and low-scoring examinees choosing each distractor. In addition, many state assessments are likely to have similar item statistics based on item-response theory. Test developers use indicators of item difficulty to assemble test forms appropriately matched to the achievement level of the examinee population and indicators of discrimination to ensure some degree of homogeneity in the selected items. Both item characteristics influence the reliability and internal validity of the assembled test form.

Of interest to the present discussion is the extent to which item statistics might provide insight into the performance of items in the target population for the AA-MAS. The specification of that population means that p values are likely to be, by definition, smaller in the AA-MAS population than in the full examinee population, as that population consists of students not likely to be proficient on the general

Table 5.8. Mean (standard deviation) difficulty and discrimination for items in an AA-MAS and general assessment

Population	Reading		Math	
	Difficulty	Discrimination	Difficulty	Discrimination
General	0.67 (0.14)	0.57 (0.12)	0.68 (0.13)	0.57 (0.13)
AA-MAS	0.37 (0.15)	0.27 (0.09)	0.35 (0.10)	0.30 (0.10)

Key: SD, standard deviation; AA-MAS, alternate assessments based on modified achievement standards.

assessment. One might also expect item-total correlations to be smaller as a result of the restricted range of total scores in the AA-MAS group. A full array of item analysis statistics can provide test developers with some guidance on the relative performance of items in the 2% population. For example, items with marked differences in difficulty and markedly low discrimination for the AA-MAS group could be argued to contribute to low scores without contributing to observed score variance for the students of interest. Such item statistics combined with poorly performing distractors could support the elimination of these types of items from the 2% assessment.

Table 5.8 provides a concrete example of distributions of *p* values and item-total correlations on grade 5 state math and reading assessments in an examinee group identified as potentially eligible for the AA-MAS in a given state and the general student population. The AA-MAS group consisted of students who had individualized education programs and who were deemed not proficient in 2 consecutive years of the general assessment. The results in the table are based on the second of those years.

As can be seen from the entries in Table 5.8, the mean difference between item difficulty in the two student populations is substantial and translates into effect sizes of 2.5 and 2.1 for math and reading, respectively. Standardized mean differences of this magnitude are extremely rare in typical comparisons of subgroups in educational testing and suggest that whatever modifications of the general assessment are introduced for the AA-MAS population, their impact on performance must indeed be great if the AA-MAS form is expected to alter adequate yearly progress results. Proposed modifications of items during AA-MAS test development must attend to characteristics of items in such a way that the modification effort will have a measurable impact on test results in the context of accountability. Specific modifications based on item statistics will be considered next.

The distributions of *p* values and item-total correlations are shown in the stem-and-leaf plots in Figure 5.2. Each statistic is expressed on a scale from 0 to 1. The plots show the 10ths digit in bold and the 100ths digit in regular type. Hundredths digits to the right in italics are for the

Item Difficulty

Mathematics		Reading comprehension
	.9 5	.9
	.9 022	.9
	.8 699	.8 5568
	.8 00012334	.8 1233444
86	.7 689	.7 6778
2	.7 00001233344	.7 122
7	.6 56667789	.6 567779
32	.6 0011223	.6 0122234
8765	.5 5567788	65 .5 579
11	.5 0023	42 .5 1223444
977655	.4 89999	97665 .4 5
43321	.4 2234	4310 .4
998888876	.3 6	9876655 .3 9
33222221100	.3	443222211000 .3
97666655	.2	9865 .2
4433211100	.2	332221 .2
9999	.1	.1
0	.1	4 .1
	.0	.0
	.0	.0

Item Discrimination

Mathematics		Reading comprehension
	.8	.8 0
	.7 55	.7 9
	.7 0001111334	.7 02234
	.6 5556799	.6 57889
	.6 01112333444	.6 01112334
5	.5 5566678889	.5 55669
4	.5 001111122233444	.5 123455
77665	.4 6677	6 .4 6666779
00112444	.4	433 .4 0124
9876	.3 7999	88665 .3 689
44433221110	.3 03	43332211 .3
99998777776555	.2	998655 .2
444433322	.2	44432222110 .2
9998888885	.1	88775 .1
42	.1	442 .1
9	.0	6 .0
	.0 0	.0

Figure 5.2. Stem-and-leaf plots of item difficulty (proportion correct) and discrimination (item–total correlation). (*Note:* Italics indicates general population; regular font indicates alternate assessment based on modified achievement standards examinee population.)

general student population, and those to the left are for students eligible for the AA-MAS. As can be seen from the figure, the distributions of p values and item-total correlations are generally symmetrical in both the general population and the group identified for the AA-MAS. The p values for math in the AA-MAS sample are somewhat positively skewed. The distinctive feature of these distributions is the small degree of overlap. This is of particular interest in the case of the item discrimination indices. Ideally test developers would like the distribution of discrimination indices to be similar. However, range restriction on total score is likely to systematically lower item-total correlations in the AA-MAS population. The dramatic separation of the distributions of these correlations suggests there may be additional reasons for low discrimination. Understanding why would be an important part of AA-MAS test development if modification of items from the general assessment is the selected approach. The item-total correlations suggest that even within the AA-MAS population, items in these sets, irrespective of content, possess idiosyncratic characteristics that reduce their overall correlation with total scores. If these characteristics can be isolated by content or statistical analyses of item keys and distractors, for example, then perhaps target modifications at the item level could at once make items less difficult and increase their internal consistency and correlations with total test scores. Some illustrations of these ideas are presented next.

Table 5.9 gives an example of a distractor analysis from a statewide mathematics assessment given to nearly 40,000 students in fifth grade. The item measures a student's ability to compute total length of six objects and to convert inches to feet. Data marked "AA-MAS" are from a group identified previously as eligible for a modified assessment.

Table 5.9. Illustration of distractor analysis
A brick is 9 inches long. If 6 bricks are lined up, one after the other, in a row, how long is the row of bricks?

	Options	General performance (%)	AA-MAS performance (%)
A	1 foot 3 inches	9	17
B*	4 feet 6 inches	42	19
C	5 feet 4 inches	35	25
C	6 feet 9 inches	14	39
Item statistics:			
Sample size		37,223	2,432
Difficulty		0.42	0.19
discrimination		0.53	0.12

Key: AA-MAS, alternate assessments based on modified achievement standards; *correct answer.

This item has reasonable statistical properties in the general population (difficulty = 0.42, discrimination = 0.53). In that population, 35% are drawn to the combination of numbers, 5 and 4, that reflect correct calculation of total length, but no conversion from inches to feet (54 inches, thus 5 feet 4 inches). A simple distractor analysis shows the nature of the error most common in the general student population.

The students in the AA-MAS–eligible group were drawn to option C as well. Those students demonstrated a similar misunderstanding. However, option D (6 feet 9 inches) was the most frequent (39%) response in the AA-MAS group. This distractor simply repeats the specific numbers used in the item stem and indicates no calculation and no conversion of units. The summary statistics (difficulty = 0.19, discrimination = 0.12) indicate this item to be providing very little information about total test scores for the AA-MAS population. On the basis of such information, the test developer could choose to replace distractor D with a different option, eliminating the repetition of specific numbers used in the stem, or reduce the number of distractors by eliminating D.

This concrete example highlights the complexities involved in modification strategies such as elimination of distractors. Eliminating the most popular distractor in the total group would do little to change the behaviors of this item in the AA-MAS group. Moreover, such a strategy would eliminate the distractor that carries a meaningful message in an error analysis. Distractor elimination is clearly going to alter the construct interpretation of item performance and perhaps do so without any gain in relative item difficulty and impact. This concrete example is designed to illustrate that eliminating distractors can have untold effects on the meaning of resulting test scores. Cases such as this might be better addressed by the elimination of entire items that can be arguably shown to contribute little to total scores in the AA-MAS population.

Differential Item Functioning

An apparently straightforward analysis for identification of items for modification in the AA-MAS context would be differential item functioning (DIF). DIF methods are designed to detect items with different item characteristic curves in two populations, in other words, systematic differences in the item performance of examinees in groups matched on general achievement in the domain. As discussed in Chapter 7 (this volume), DIF methods are routinely used as part of the test development process to screen items for psychometric appropriateness with respect to background characteristics of examinees, such as gender, ethnicity, socioeconomic status, native language, and disability status. DIF methods have the potential to provide insight into facets of item design that may unknowingly create a relative advantage or disadvantage to examinees that is unrelated to the construct measured by the test.

In the AA-MAS, DIF methods might be thought to offer insight into differential performance at the item level. As noted in Chapter 7, however, when DIF methods are used in an assessment context with multiple focal groups of interest (e.g., students with disabilities, linguistic minorities, ethnic minorities), it can become difficult to find consistency in the flagging of items. Moreover, the statistical limitations of DIF methods have necessitated the development of judgmental criteria for evaluating the magnitude of DIF (e.g., its expected influence on total scores; Zieky, 1993) to supplement statistical criteria used in testing null hypotheses of no DIF. In particular, DIF methods tend to perform poorly when groups differ markedly in overall test performance and when the variable used for matching (typically total test score) does not allow adequate matching throughout its range. Given the effect sizes presented previously, as well as the distributions of p values in a prospective AA-MAS population relative to the general population, DIF methods are likely to prove difficult to apply in the test development process for the AA-MAS. Large mean differences between groups and sparseness of scores in the upper ranges of total score distributions are likely to produce spurious DIF in the AA-MAS context (Camilli, 2006; Holland & Thayer, 1988).

Validating the AA-MAS

Validity remains the most fundamental consideration in developing and interpreting any assessment. Although this chapter has been devoted to the development of a sound AA-MAS, it is the use and interpretation of these scores that must be validated. There are numerous sources of evidence that might be used to evaluate a proposed interpretation. One critical type of validity evidence is based on the test content. As defined in the *Standards* (AERA et al., 1999), content refers to the themes, wording, and format of the items, tasks, or questions on a test, as well as the guidelines for procedures regarding development, administration, and scoring. This chapter has attempted to discuss issues about differences in meaning or interpretations of test scores for an AA-MAS as compared with a general assessment. Of particular concern is the extent to which construct-irrelevant components could be eliminated to avoid disadvantaging students eligible for an AA-MAS to create an assessment that provides students an opportunity to demonstrate what they know and can do. Consistent with Marion (see Chapter 8, this volume), content-related evidence requires evaluating the interaction of both content and process required of the test items and documenting that the interaction is what is expected.

The responsibility for validating the AA-MAS is shared between test developers, users and education policy makers. An important aspect of test validation in this regard is the documentation of the test and item development processes used for the AA-MAS; the specific steps followed in the test development workflow; the types of item modifications chosen; the expert analysis of the cognitive demands of the items; the impact measured through think-aloud protocols, cognitive interviews, and field testing; studies examining differences in performance on items; and the changes to test specifications and distributions of items across formats, content strands, and cognitive levels. Education policy makers are likely to weigh in on general parameters of AA-MAS development, such as the representation of subject matter included, the process of setting standards, and the budget allocated for test development, delivery, and reporting. More specific aspects of validation are a joint responsibility of test developers and users. In statewide assessment, state education agencies (SEAs) are both developers and users, but SEAs typically work with one or more contractors who carry out the activities associated with item and test development. If the goal is to develop the foundation for a validity argument in support of proficiency-related inferences based on the AA-MAS (Kane, 2006), then the outline of the argument needs to be formulated in the joint work of an SEA and its contractors.

REFERENCES

Ahearn, E. (2009). *The alternate assessment based on modified achievement standards: An initial review of state implementation.* Alexandria, VA: National Association of State Directors of Special Education. Retrieved October 9, 2009 from http://www.projectforum.org/docs/TheAABasedonMAS AnInitialReviewofStateImplementation2.pdf

Almond, P.J., Cameto, R., Johnstone, C.J., Laitusis, C., Lazarus, S., Nagle, K., et al. (2009). *Cognitive interview methods in reading test design and development for alternate assessments based on modified academic achievement standards (AA-MAS)* (white paper). Dover, NH: Measured Progress, and Menlo Park, CA: SRI International.

American Educational Research Association, American Psychological Association, & National Council on Measurement in Education. (1999). *Standards for educational and psychological testing.* Washington, DC: American Psychological Association.

American Institutes for Research (AIR). (2000). *Effects of item scaffolding on student responses: A cognitive laboratory study.* Washington, DC: AIR for Institutes for Research for the National Assessment Governing Board in support of contract # RJ97153001.

Assessment and Accountability Comprehensive Center. (2007, November). *Assessments based on modified achievement standards: Critical considerations and implications for implementation.* San Francisco: WestEd.

Bergeson, T., Wise, B.J., Gill, D.H., & Bartlett, K.M. (2001). *Adaptations are essential: A resource guide for adapting learning and assessment tasks for students with mild disabilities.* Olympia, WA: Special Education Section of the Office of the Superintendent of Public Instruction. Retrieved February 21, 2010, from http://www.k8accesscenter.org/accessinaction/documents/EARLYwritin gADAPTATIONS.pdf

Bhola, D.S., Impara, J.D., & Buckendahl, W. (2003). Aligning tests with states' content standards: Methods and issues. *Educational Measurement: Issues and Practice, 22*(3), 21–29.

Camilli, G. (2006). Test fairness. In R.L. Brennan (Ed.), *Educational measurement* (4th ed., pp. 221–256). Westport, CT: American Council on Education/ Praeger.

Code of fair testing practices in education. (2004). Washington, DC: Joint Committee on Testing Practices.

Filbin, J. (2008). *Lessons from the initial peer review of alternate assessments based on modified achievement standards.* Washington, DC: U.S. Department of Education, Office of Elementary and Secondary Education.

Holland, P.W., & Thayer, D.T. (1988). Differential item performance and the Mantel-Haenszel procedure. In H. Wainer & H. Brown (Eds.), *Test validity* (pp. 129–145). Mahwah, NJ: Lawrence Erlbaum Associates.

Johnstone, C.J., Altman, J., & Thurlow, M. (2006). *A state guide to the development of universally designed assessments.* Minneapolis, MN: University of Minnesota, National Center on Educational Outcomes.

Kane, M.T. (2006). Validation. In R.L. Brennan (Ed.), *Educational measurement* (4th ed., pp. 17–64). Westport, CT: American Council on Education/Praeger.

Lazarus, S.S., Thurlow, M.L., Christensen, L.L., & Cormier, D. (2007). *States' alternate assessments based on modified achievement standards (AA-MAS) in 2007* (Synthesis Report 67). Minneapolis, MN: University of Minnesota, National Center on Educational Outcomes.

Lindquist, E.F. (1951). Preliminary considerations in objective test construction. In E.F. Lindquist (Ed.), *Educational measurement* (pp. 119–158). Washington, DC: American Council on Education.

Linn, R.L, Baker, E.L., & Dunbar, S.B. (1991). Complex, performance-based assessment: Expectations and validation criteria. *Education Researcher, 20*(8), 15–21.

Marion, S. (2007). *A technical design and documentation workbook for assessments based on modified achievement standards working draft.* Minneapolis, MN: University of Minnesota, National Center on Educational Outcomes.

Perie, M. (2008). A guide to understanding and developing performance-level descriptors. *Educational Measurement: Issues and Practice, 27*(4), 15–29.

New York State Department of Education (2007, December). *New York State testing program 2007: Mathematics, grades 3-8, technical report.* Albany, NY: Author.

No Child Left Behind Act of 2001, PL 107-110, 115 Stat. 1425, 20 U.S.C. §§ 6301 *et seq.*

Rothman, R., Slattery, J.B., Vranek, J.L., & Resnick, L.B. (2002). *Benchmarking and alignment of standards and testing* (CSE Technical Report 566). Los Angeles: UCLA Center for Research on Evaluation, Standards and Student Testing.

Sato, E., Rabinowitz, S., Worth, P., Gallagher, C., Lagunoff, R., & Crane, E. (2007, September). *Evaluation of the technical evidence of assessments for special student populations* (Assessment and Accountability Comprehensive Center Report). San Francisco: WestEd.

Schmeiser, C.B., & Welch, C.J. (2006). Test development. In R.L. Brennan (Ed.), *Educational measurement* (4th ed., pp. 307–353). Westport, CT: American Council on Education/Praeger.

Thompson, S.J., Johnstone, C.J., & Thurlow, M. (2002). *Universal design applied to large-scale assessments* (NCEO Synthesis Report 44). Minneapolis, MN: University of Minnesota, National Center on Educational Outcomes.

U.S. Department of Education. (2007a, April 9). *Final Rule 34 CFR Parts 200 and 300: Title I—Improving the academic achievement of the disadvantaged: Individuals with Disabilities Education Act (IDEA). 72 Fed. Reg. 67,* Washington DC: Author. Retrieved February 26, 2010, from http:// www2.ed.gov/legislation/FedRegister/finrule/2007-2/040907a.html

U.S. Department of Education. (2007b, July 20). *Modified academic achievement standards: Non-regulatory guidance.* Washington, DC: Office of Elementary and Secondary Education, U.S. Department of Education. Retrieved February 26, 2010, from http://www2.ed.gov/admins/lead/account/saa .html#regulations

U.S. Department of Education. (2007c, December 21). *Standards and assessment peer review guidance: Information and examples for meeting requirements of the No Child Left Behind Act of 2001.* Washington, DC: Office of Elementary and Secondary Education, U.S. Department of Education. Retrieved February 26, 2010, from http://www.ed.gov/policy/elsec/guid/saaprguidance.pdf

Webb, N.L. (1999). *Alignment of science and mathematics standards and assessments in four states.* (Research Monograph No. 18). Madison, WI: National Institute for Science Education.

Welch, C. (2006). Item and prompt development in performance testing. In S.M. Downing & T.M. Haladyna (Eds.), *Handbook of test development* (pp. 303–327). Mahwah, NJ: Lawrence Erlbaum Associates.

Zieky, M. (1993). Practical questions in the use of DIF statistics. In P.W. Holland & H. Wainer (Eds.), *Differential item functioning* (pp. 337–347). Mahwah, NJ: Lawrence Erlbaum Associates.

6

Developing Achievement Level Descriptors and Setting Cut Scores on the Alternate Assessment Based on Modified Achievement Standards

Marianne Perie

In developing an alternate assessment based on modified achievement standards (AA-MAS), test developers can improve the design process by paying close attention to those modified achievement standards. By collaborating with policy makers, they can together work through the issues of what proficiency means for this group of students, what type of modified achievement standards are appropriate, and how best to measure them. In fact, it is most important for policy makers to work directly with test developers in defining the achievement standard to ensure coherence so that what is intended as a state standard and goal is actualized through the assessment and interpretive materials. As discussed previously, the U.S. Department of Education (2007) regulation requires that the modified achievement standards:

- Be aligned with a state's academic content standards for the grade in which the student is enrolled

- Be challenging for eligible students, but may be less difficult than grade-level academic achievement standards
- Be developed by grade level, not grade span
- Include at least three achievement levels
- Be developed through a documented and validated standard-setting process that includes broad stakeholder input

The only other guidance that policy makers are given from the federal government in defining modified achievement standards is that they are expected to represent a "less difficult expectation of grade-level content standards." Inherent in this guidance is a tension between ensuring that the tests measure the same breadth and depth while being less difficult. This chapter examines how the achievement standards work within that tension to provide a less difficult performance target. It will analyze the different dimensions of modified achievement standards, describe the various components, and provide suggestions for drafting descriptors and setting cut scores.

DEFINING ACHIEVEMENT STANDARDS

An achievement standard defines a level of performance and includes both a minimum cut score and a written description that distinguishes the level of performance from other defined levels. It consists of four components: number of levels, names of levels, a descriptor for each level, and a cut score for each level.

Numbers

According to the federal regulations, the number of modified achievement levels to be defined includes a minimum of three: one distinguishing proficient performance, one above, and one below. However, some states may want to add one or two more levels to meet the goals of their assessment. The majority of states have four performance levels for the general assessment. It may be desirable to mimic the structure of the general assessment by including the same number of achievement levels for the modified assessment so that report cards and interpretive material can be standardized as much as possible. Or, as is the case for some states that use a performance index, it may be necessary to include the same number of levels to more easily incorporate the results of these assessments into the state accountability model. However, it is also an option to consider these levels extensions of the lowest grade-level achievement standard, in which case a parallel number would not be necessary. In this case, a state would need to consider the number of levels necessary to convey the message intended by these modified achievement standards.

Caution is urged in developing more than four levels. As noted in Perie (2008), it can be difficult to describe meaningful differences across more than four levels. In addition, any particular test has a fixed amount of measurement power that depends primarily on the number and quality of the questions in the test. "The more cut scores there are in any given test, the less measurement power the test developer can devote to each cut score, and the less information there is around each cut score" (p. 17). Given the nature of the AA-MAS and the typical rationales for developing one (i.e., school accountability), it seems unlikely that more than four levels would be needed.

Names

Beck (2003) indicated that naming conventions should be developed as the first step in defining performance. With modified achievement levels, the first question in naming them is whether the names should be the same or different from the levels used in the general assessment. Although it may be tempting to assign the levels the same names, state policy makers could also consider using different names to avoid confusion and simply designate one level to be the equivalent of *proficient* for purposes of adequate yearly progress. In fact, some states that developed an AA-MAS for the purposes of federal accountability received feedback from their peer reviewers advising them to select names for their modified achievement levels that are different from those of the grade-level achievement levels.

Policy makers can also consider how these modified standards relate to grade-level standards and portray that in the name. That is, if these modified achievement standards are truly downward extensions of the grade-level achievement standards, the names should reflect their relationship with the general assessment. For instance, some state policy makers have considered naming the levels relative to the general assessment, such as *not ready for the general assessment, almost ready for the general assessment,* and *ready for the general assessment.* Or, the same idea could be used to talk about achievement relative to grade-level standards (e.g., *near grade-level proficiency*). Some state policy makers have also chosen not to call any modified achievement level *advanced,* as they believe student performance needs to be measured against grade-level standards before it can be called advanced. It is important to keep in mind that the names of the modified achievement levels often express the values of the policy makers or the intent of the assessment.

Descriptors

Achievement level descriptors put into words how good is good enough. That is, they qualitatively describe the performance expected of a student at the *proficient* level or the *basic* level. They must be aligned with the state academic content standards and describe breadth and depth of the standards appropriate to the assessment so that they represent knowledge and skills that are evaluated by the assessment. The descriptors are essential to articulating what modified proficiency means. For purposes of meeting 2007 federal regulations, these modified descriptors may be written to a less difficult level, even though the breadth and depth of the assessment must be parallel to the general assessment. That is, although the assessment must measure similar levels of depth of knowledge, perhaps competency of a lower depth of knowledge is all that is needed to be proficient using the modified achievement standards.

Ideally, the descriptors will be written so that they clearly differentiate among levels and progress logically across levels. That is, to improve articulation across levels, write the proficient descriptor to be appropriately more rigorous than the basic descriptor. In addition, considering the entire assessment program will help ensure that the descriptors also progress logically across grade levels (e.g., the descriptor for grade 5 proficient is sufficiently more challenging than the descriptor for grade 4 proficient). It is important to take great care in writing the descriptors because they drive not only the standard-setting process, but also the reporting, score interpretation, and, potentially, the item-writing process. In fact, many in the field claim that the descriptors are instrumental to the validity and defensibility of the standard-setting process (cf. Cizek & Bunch, 2007; Hambleton, 2001). More detail about this step is provided later in this chapter.

Cut Scores

The fourth component of achievement standards is the cut score. *Cut scores* define the number of points necessary to reach each performance level based on a total test score. They are typically set after the assessment has been field tested so that statistics are available to inform the process. Then recommended cut scores come from a committee using any of a number of possible methodologies to determine the best cutoff points. The regulations require the use of a documented and validated methodology, but the choice of methods is left up to the test developers and policy makers. Ideally, a broad range of stakeholders would be involved in the process, typically including both special educators and content experts. It is important to fully document the process, including a rationale for selecting a particular methodology and the process for selecting the committee. More detail on the methods, procedures, and documentation will be provided later in this chapter.

DEFINING PROFICIENCY

The biggest issue that state policy makers will wrestle with is what proficiency means for these lower-achieving students with disabilities. That is, we need to determine what we mean by modified achievement standards. Defining the levels is an important step in standard setting. Berk (1996) discussed the importance of providing explicit behavioral descriptions of each level, saying "the interpretation of the final cut scores hinge on the clarity of the behavioral definitions" (p. 224). Previous chapters discussed issues related to the interaction of cognition, instruction, and assessment and offered some insights into providing this clarity. Understanding cognition and improving instruction can have large implications for determining what proficient means on a given assessment. It is here that policy makers will wrestle with making a test of similar breadth and depth less difficult.

Taking information from earlier chapters on how students learn the content and ways in which the content increases in difficulty provides some insights into writing meaningful descriptors. If there was one learning progression that all students followed, the task of writing achievement level descriptors would be greatly simplified, as we could simply identify points on the learning continuum that represent basic, proficient, or advanced achievement. However, as discussed previously (see Chapters 3 and 4), there is little to no agreement on standard learning progressions for any population, let alone a population of students with disabilities.

With this population, which may include all disability types and different learning progressions, it is vitally important to clearly define the population and understand why the students are not achieving at grade level before we can describe proficient performance for them. By considering the grain sizes (depth and breadth) of learning targets along a continuum (Gong, 2007), instructional scaffolding that best supports how they learn, and an appropriate level of cognitive challenge for their grade level, we can better understand achievement of these students as compared with students without disabilities. These differences will greatly influence the writing of performance level descriptors (PLDs).

For example, in Chapter 3, Pellegrino discusses the possibility that low achievers may have a similar set of knowledge and skills as high achievers but may not have cognitively organized that information as efficiently, so they are not able to access it as readily. One solution is to design a test that reduces the burden on working memory or that includes supports to help students better organize information or more easily determine the best strategy to solve a problem. This type of theory would need to be captured both in the test design and in the definition of proficiency. As another example, in Chapter 4, Pugalee and Rickelman discuss ways of modifying the domain targets systematically within each depth of knowledge level. This approach could again be explored in both the test design and the descriptors. Most importantly, there should be a guiding philosophy about the model of learning for students with disabilities who are low achievers and thus eligible for this assessment. That guiding philosophy should drive the definition of proficiency and the test design simultaneously.

As discussed in Perie, Hess, and Gong (2008), it is usually important to consider the definition of proficiency for the AA-MAS (or any assessment) long before standard setting, as it should influence the design of the assessment. That is, test developers can work to design items that measure the features that policy makers have determined are important to distinguish proficient performance from performance below that level. However, as discussed by Welch and Dunbar in Chapter 5, it is also possible to modify the general assessment using statistical information gathered from an administration of the general assessment to the target population. If, as they suggest, a test developer takes the option of creating an AA-MAS by simply eliminating the most difficult items proportional to the content standards, the cut score could be mapped from the general assessment to the AA-MAS. Then, the descriptor would be modified after the fact—focusing on the general knowledge and skills measured by the items that appear to map to each achievement level.

One issue that several states are considering is whether the AA-MAS is at the lower end of some continuum that includes the general assessment or whether it is a completely separate test that measures the same content standards but to a less rigorous extent. For instance, policy makers need to decide whether they see the AA-MAS as a stepping stone for students to move toward grade-level achievement standards or whether they believe that a student's disability will require a different type of assessment for the foreseeable future. One implication for this decision is the definition of proficiency. Should proficiency be defined in terms of how ready a student is to be assessed on grade-level assessments, or should it be defined simply as proficient on this separate assessment, with no explicit or implicit link to performance on the general assessment?

Another similar consideration is how this AA-MAS fits between the alternate assessment based on alternate achievement standards (AA-AAS) and the general, grade-level assessment. Most states appear to be developing an AA-MAS that is closer in design to the general assessment than to the AA-AAS. But how should the achievement standards compare? One possibility is to consider proficiency as being just below proficiency on the general assessment—that is, somewhere between basic and proficient performance on the general assessment. Another possibility is to simply shift down the levels one step, so that proficient performance on the AA-MAS will be similar in nature to basic performance on the general assessment. This approach is one way to keep the breadth and depth similar across the two assessment types while still making the AA-MAS less difficult by requiring less knowledge and fewer skills to reach proficiency. This type of relationship among the assessments would have implications for the intended comparability of the assessments. (See Chapter 7 for more details on comparability.) It also has implications for the development of the modified achievement level descriptors. In this case, the committees would start with the grade-level descriptors for both basic and proficient and try to write a modified proficient descriptor that falls in between the two, or perhaps closer to the basic level.

Other possible strategies emerge depending on state policy makers' beliefs and values, which come into play as they consider whether students who would take this assessment are capable of learning grade-level materials to the grade-level standard. One possible theory is that these students can learn grade-level material as well as students without disabilities, but they take longer to master each unit and thus do not complete the curriculum by the end of the year. Following this theory would lead to a description of proficiency that is similar to grade-level proficiency for material learned earlier in the year, but requires less of students on material learned later in the school year. However, this approach could be difficult to defend as it may violate the mandate that the breadth must remain equivalent across the two assessments and only the difficulty may be modified. The breadth described by the modified proficient descriptor should not be narrower than the breadth of the grade-level proficient descriptor.

Another theory is that these students can learn grade-level material as well as students without disabilities, but they require specific supports to do so. That is, the ultimate goal for reaching proficiency may be the same, but it includes conditions. For example, the proficiency standard may include clauses that describe the scaffolds available on the test, such as segmenting text, providing strategies, supplying definitions, and so forth. Then the descriptor could indicate that the student measured against the modified achievement standard has similar knowledge as the proficient student measured against grade-level achievement standards, but he or she may require more supports (e.g., less vocabulary load in the test item, use of graphic organizers to organize information before solving a problem) to demonstrate that knowledge.

Regardless of which theory drives the process, it is important to articulate that theory and clearly state the inferences policy makers and educators wish to draw from the AA-MAS. Fitting this context with the design decisions made and the definition of proficiency is central to forming a coherent validity argument (discussed more fully in Chapter 8).

Applying Theories of Learning to Modified Achievement Level Descriptors

If state policy makers start with the perspective that the modified achievement level descriptors are closer in nature to the grade-level achievement standards than to the alternate achievement standards, then one strategy for drafting the descriptors is to start with the grade-level descriptors and modify them appropriately.[1] These modifications can take several forms depending on the theory one is following, as described in the previous section.

The first question that needs to be answered is whether the knowledge and skills required for proficiency within the modified achievement standard are the same as with the grade-level achievement standard, but with more supports and scaffolding, or whether the knowledge and skills are actually different. If those drafting the descriptors believe the first description is true, that the standards are the same but students require appropriate supports, then they can modify the grade-level descriptor for proficient accordingly. For example, a grade-level standard may state "student is able to read a fictional text and identify key elements of the story," whereas a modified standard may state "when the text is chunked meaningfully, the student is able to read a fictional text and identify key elements of the story." Other examples of adding scaffolds to the descriptors include: "A proficient student can comprehend the main message within segmented grade-level text. With suggested reading strategies or graphic organizers, students are able to generate and/or answer inferential questions." These statements only differ from grade-level descriptors through the addition of the scaffolds. Note that it is important to ensure that these scaffolds are included in the test design if they are included in the descriptor. Furthermore, these scaffolds will only be helpful on the test to the extent that they have been used during instruction. (See Chapter 4 for more information on scaffolding.)

---

[1]Note that although it is also possible to start with the alternate achievement level descriptors and modify them to make them more difficult, this approach may be more challenging, because many alternate achievement standards do not cover all content standards and are often based on extended content standards rather than grade-level content standards.

Other strategies for modifying descriptors apply if those designing the test believe that the knowledge and skills required of these students should be different. First of all, under the current federal regulations, *different* means less difficult, as the content must stay the same. There are several ways to make grade-level achievement standards less difficult. One option is to focus on the cognitive complexity of the requirement and reduce it appropriately. For instance, a grade-level descriptor at grade 8 may state that a student can "evaluate algebraic expressions," whereas the modified descriptor could require the student to "identify algebraic expressions." Likewise, if the grade-level descriptor says a student can solve two-step problems, a possible modification is to require students to solve one-step problems.[2] For English language arts, we can reduce the complexity either by reducing the depth of knowledge required (e.g., move from *analyze* to *describe*) or qualifying broader statements of knowledge. For instance, if the grade-level standard requires students to identify various parts of speech, including "nouns, verbs, pronouns, adjectives, adverbs, conjunctions, and interjections," one could modify that standard by reducing the number of parts of speech required, such as removing the requirement of identifying conjunctions and interjections. Both standards require students to identify parts of speech, but the modified standard reduces the difficulty by only requiring students to identify simpler parts of speech. These modifications to the descriptors make the achievement standards less difficult to reach by reducing cognitive complexity, which complies with federal regulations as long as the depth and breadth of the assessment itself remains similar to that of the general assessment. It is important to note, however, that lowering the depth of knowledge is an appropriate adjustment only if the depth of knowledge has not been specified in the content standard. For example, if the content standard specifically says that students must solve multistep problems, reducing the requirement to a one-step problem would cause the descriptors to be out of alignment with the content standards.

In practice, those drafting the modified achievement level descriptors could choose to adopt more than one of these strategies. That is, they could choose to reduce the depth of knowledge required for proficiency on some of the skills, add scaffolds to the statements about other skills, and provide specific examples to others indicating that the student is required to perform a narrower range of the tasks than what

---

[2]Note that this modification is only allowable if it maps to the content standards. If the content standards explicitly state that students must master two-step problems, then this would not be an appropriate modification.

is required in the grade-level standards, as long as that narrower range still matches the content standards and indicators. Of course, there is always the option of drafting new descriptors that are not linked to the general descriptors, but there must be a rationale for doing so and a clearly articulated statement of how the AA-MAS relates to the general assessment. Again, referring back to Chapter 4 will provide insights on how to target each of four levels of depth of knowledge within a single indicator. Specifics on writing achievement level descriptors are discussed in the next section.

Procedures for Drafting Modified Achievement Level Descriptors

Regardless of the type of assessment, it is usually preferable to start considering achievement level descriptors early in the test development process. In the case of the AA-MAS (and all assessments developed under the No Child Left Behind Act of 2001 [PL 107-110]), the most important distinction is between achieving proficient and not, and so a strong understanding of proficiency is needed. By considering this definition early, test developers can start an iterative process of using the descriptors to help design the test and then refining the descriptors as needed to match the final test blueprint.[3] When the descriptors are used to drive the test design, test developers can ensure that the test blueprint supports the desired judgments and that the items themselves provide opportunities for students to show what they know and can do relative to the achievement standards. Consideration can be given to distinguishing items that would likely be answered correctly by students who met the definition for proficiency and incorrectly by those who did not.

A recommended approach for drafting achievement level descriptors is to involve a committee of people who know the content and the students (Perie, 2008). However, this committee will always need some direction from the policy makers regarding the intent of the assessment program. In the case of modified achievement level descriptors, the committee will typically include both special education teachers as well as content specialists for each subject area (e.g., reading and mathematics). Content specialists could be subject area teachers, curriculum supervisors, or members of the general public with a specialty in that subject (e.g., a mathematician). Approximately 5–8 participants are

---

[3]If the test developer is shortening the test by eliminating the most difficult items proportional to the content standards, then the descriptors will be considered after the test is administered. This process will be discussed further in this section.

needed per subject area, but if descriptors are being developed for multiple grade levels, more participants can be invited and then split into teams. That is, a group of eight participants can write the descriptors for grade 4, and then they can separate into two groups of four, with one group working on grade 3 and the other on grade 5.

The direction required from the policy makers will include the assumptions made about the population, such as who the students are and what the barriers are to their ability to achieve grade-level proficiency on the general assessments. The committee members will also need to understanding the theory behind the revisions and enhancements made to the assessment as well as see examples of those revisions and enhancements or the plans for such revisions and enhancements if the PLD writing meeting is occurring before the assessment is developed. They also need to understand the type of modifications that will not be permitted, such as providing below grade-level passages on a reading assessment. In addition, if any data analyses have been done on the performance of these students on other assessments, such as those suggested in Chapter 1, the committee could be informed by concrete information about what was learned from these analyses, including specific examples of items this population seemed to perform well on and those they did not.

Once the committee members have sufficient background information, the real work drafting the descriptors begins. The majority of those developing modified achievement level descriptors are starting from the grade-level descriptors and editing them rather than starting new descriptors from scratch. However, some may start writing the descriptors directly from the grade-level content standards and test blueprints without referring to the grade-level achievement standards. Regardless of the approach taken, Perie et al. (2008) recommend that the committee discuss several issues, including:

- Interactions of process and content
- How students move both across performance levels and across grade levels
  - Whether the knowledge and skills required of proficient on the modified achievement standard are the same as those of the general assessment, but some scaffolding is needed, or whether the knowledge and skills are different
  - If they are different, whether they are so in terms of content or processes (e.g., grade-level achievement standards require that the same-level inferences are made in a more complex context than the modified achievement standards, or grade-level achievement standards require students to make inferences, whereas modified achievement standards require students to only draw a lower level conclusion)

—How students move across grades; for example, how proficient in one grade compares with proficient in the next

- Transition from this assessment to the general assessment—how they are linked

—Whether the proficient level of the modified achievement standards should be an indicator of readiness for achievement on grade-level standards

—Whether the state should adopt a policy regarding the modified achievement standards, such as students scoring at the advanced level on the modified achievement standards must take the general grade-level test the following year

Given their answers to these questions and the theories regarding appropriate revisions to the test design, the committees can then draft descriptors. Recall from the previous section that some of the modifications could include 1) reducing the cognitive complexity of the required skill, 2) decreasing the number of elements required, or 3) adding appropriate supports and scaffolds to the description of the knowledge and skills required. Table 6.1 shows an example of a fifth-grade reading descriptor for a general assessment and the modified version that includes all three types of modifications.

Table 6.1.   Example of a fifth-grade reading descriptor for a general assessment and the modified version

Grade-level descriptor	Modified descriptor
Proficient students comprehend the message within grade-level text. Using supporting details, they are able to analyze information from the text and summarize main ideas. Before, during, and after reading, students generate and/or answer questions at the literal, inferential, interpretive, and critical levels. Students interpret and use organizational patterns in text (e.g., description, cause/effect, compare/contrast, fact/opinion) in order to gain meaning. They use informational text features (e.g., index, maps, graphs, headings) to locate information and aid in comprehension. Students are able to identify and analyze elements of narrative text (e.g., characters, setting, and plot). In addition, Level II students can identify author's purpose and recognize how author's perspective influences the text.	Proficient students comprehend the message within segmented grade-level text. Students are able to identify the main idea and retell information from the passage with supports (e.g., a web, 5 Ws chart, timeline), when appropriate. During and after reading, students are able to generate and/or answer questions at a literal level. Students identify and use organizational patterns in text (e.g., sequence, compare/contrast, fact/opinion) in order to gain meaning. They use informational text features (e.g., index, maps, graphs, charts) to locate information and aid in comprehension. When given supports (e.g., story maps, character web, illustrations), students are able to identify basic elements of narrative text (characters, setting, beginning/middle/end). In addition, Level II students identify author's purpose when given the definitions.

Having similar structure between the grade-level and modified descriptors helps teachers, administrators, and parents see the difference between grade-level proficiency and modified proficiency, providing useful information on what it takes to move a student from the AA-MAS to the general assessment based on grade-level achievement standards.

Earlier, a different approach to modifying descriptors was introduced, following from the suggestion by Welch and Dunbar (see Chapter 5) that an AA-MAS could be designed by eliminating the most difficult item proportional to the content standards. This approach would result in an AA-MAS that was similar to the general assessment in scope but shorter. The two assessments could be statistically linked together because there are common items across both populations. Then, the cut score could be mapped directly onto the AA-MAS. As discussed by Welch and Dunbar in Chapter 5, a standards validation would need to be conducted to ensure the cut scores divide student performance meaningfully into the achievement levels. Once the cut scores have been validated, the grade-level descriptors can be modified by taking into consideration the items that map to each achievement level. Different rules have been used to identify items within each level, usually focusing on the likelihood that a student within that level would answer the item correctly compared with the likelihood of a student below that level answering the item correctly. Items that are distinct between these two groups are identified as mapping to that level. Then, content experts can summarize the types of knowledge and skills represented by those items and use those summaries to write descriptors. This approach focuses solely on the item specifications, as scaffolds have not been used in this test design. However, caution must be taken to avoid writing descriptors that are too specific to one test form. In addition, there would still need to be a guiding philosophy driving this approach, including defining proficiency. The philosophy should relate to our understanding of how reducing difficulty in this manner addresses some of the concerns about the cognitive processing of low achievers (as discussed in Chapter 3).

Regardless of what approach to writing modified descriptors is taken, the articulation across grades should be considered. Often when committees are working on drafting modified achievement level descriptors, they are split into smaller groups to work on specific grade levels. If this occurs, it will be important to spend time at the end of the workshop examining the descriptors across all grades. Articulation will be improved if the committee members are asked to consider whether they can see a clear progression across levels and how well these descriptors translate to instruction.

Once the modified achievement level descriptors have been drafted, they will need to be finalized by the state department of education and then approved by the state policy maker (typically a board of education). When the state department of education is reviewing the draft descriptors, they typically consider them as a whole, analyzing the consistency in rigor across grades and subjects, the natural progression of difficulty from one grade to the next, and the alignment between the descriptors and the test blueprints.

SETTING CUT SCORES

At first glance, it appears that any standard-setting method that a state uses for its general assessment would work for the modified assessment, particularly because most states appear to be starting with their general assessment and applying various types of modifications. However, there are additional considerations that come into play when selecting an appropriate method for setting cut scores.

Keeping in mind that there may be some state policy makers who choose to develop a brand-new assessment or to modify their alternate assessment based on grade-level achievement standards, we will start with the scenario that a state has modified the general assessment. Almost all state general assessments are comprised primarily of multiple-choice items, with some states choosing to include some open-ended items as well. With these types of tests, a test-based approach to standard setting is typically used. Test-based approaches are those where the judgments are made about the test itself—usually about individual items—rather than about the students or their actual performance. Another way to think about the type of methods is based on the type of judgment required. According to Zieky, Perie, and Livingston (2008), there are four types of standard-setting judgments: 1) judgments of test questions, 2) judgments of profiles of scores, 3) judgments of people or products, and 4) judgments of groups of people. Examples of judgments of test questions include methods such as Angoff or bookmark. Methods involving judgment of profiles or scores include dominant profile or the performance profile method. Methods that require judgments of people or products include contrasting groups and body of work. Methods that involve judgments of groups of people are rarely used in the educational context.

Although any of the four prominent types of judgments could apply to an AA-MAS, the methods most appropriate for a test that is primarily composed of multiple-choice items with a few (or no) open-ended items include judgments of test items. This section will focus on the two most common test-based methods—Angoff and bookmark—and then discuss the feasibility of using methods based on judgments of profiles, people, or products.

Methods Based on Judgments of Test Items

Test-based approaches typically require standard-setting committees to make judgments about test items. The two most commonly used methods for K–12 educational assessments are the modified Angoff method and item mapping, typically the bookmark method. The applications of these two methods to set cut scores on the AA-MAS will be discussed in this section.

Modified Angoff

The modified Angoff method (Angoff, 1971) is probably the most widely used and best researched standard-setting method. In it, participants are asked to state the probability that a borderline test taker (e.g., someone who is just barely proficient) would answer each test item correctly. Summing the probabilities across all test items provides the test score for a borderline test taker, which becomes the cut score for that achievement level. Typically, for a multiple-choice test with four response options, we recommend that panelists limit their judgments of probability to a range of .25–.95. The reasoning is that even if the student has minimal ability to answer the item correctly, he will have a 25% probability of answering it correctly by chance (1-in-4). We limit the upper end to show that we never expect perfection from a student. The only exception that panelists are given is that if they think that one distractor will be so appealing to a student with minimal knowledge that he is likely to be drawn to that distractor to the point that he has a less than 25% chance of answering the item correctly, then they can provide a rating of less than .25.

Now consider an AA-MAS in which the revisions have included reducing the answer options from four to three. In this situation, the student has a 1-in-3 (33.3%) probability of answering the item correctly by chance, further restricting the range of possible judgments to .35–.95. This adjustment will almost certainly result in a higher cut score, which may not be desirable.

Another option for states wanting to stick to a modified Angoff approach is to use another modification of the Angoff method—the yes/no method (Impara & Plake, 1997). In this option, the judgment would be a simpler yes/no that the borderline test taker either would or would not answer this item correctly. There have been some concerns raised that the yes/no method rounds judgments inaccurately (cf. Reckase, 2006; Zieky et al., 2008). For instance, a panelist who feels that a borderline test taker has a 25% chance of answering the item correctly would record a 0. He would also likely record a 0 for an item he thought the borderline test taker had a 45% probability of answering correctly and another 0 for an item he thought a borderline test taker had a 40% chance of answering correctly, resulting in a cut score of 0 out of 3, whereas the traditional Angoff would calculate a cut score of 1 out of 3. Thus it would be reasonable to consider adding in a guessing factor.

For example, if on a 50-item test a group of panelists agrees that the borderline-proficient student would answer 23 items correctly, then the unadjusted raw cut score would be 23 out of 50 points. However, to adjust for guessing, we could then assume that of the remaining 27 items that the student does not have the ability to answer correctly, they would answer one third of them correctly by guessing (assuming three-option answer choices). Therefore, they would answer 23 items correctly through their ability and 9 items correctly by chance, making the adjusted cut score 32 points out of 50.[4] This raw score cut can then be transformed to a scale score cut if desired.

Note that no change would be needed for applying an Angoff methodology to an open-ended item on an AA-MAS. The method most commonly used in K–12 assessments for the open-ended items is the mean estimate method, where the panelists estimate the mean (or average) score a roomful of 100 borderline test takers would achieve. Those averages are then added to the probabilities for the multiple-choice items (which are, in fact, averages of 0/1 scores) or to the sum of 0s and 1s. Alternatively, the panelists could be asked whether or not a borderline test taker would receive 1 score point on the open-ended item (yes/no), two points, three points, and so forth. The highest number of points to which the panelists indicated *yes* would then be added to the total raw score cut score. Modification should not affect a panelist's ability to make this type of judgment, and no adjustment for guessing would be needed for the open-ended items.

Item Mapping

Item mapping approaches include item–descriptor matching (Ferrara, Perie, & Johnson, 2008) and the more commonly used bookmark method (Mitzel, Lewis, Patz, & Green, 2001). The bookmark method was developed to be used with tests that are scored using item response

---

[4]This adjustment could result in a cut score higher than the panelist intended if they are not confident in their judgment of the 1s. They should be instructed to record a 1 only if they feel the borderline test taker would have a strong probability of answering this item correctly. Another option would be to substitute the 1s and 0s with probabilities before summing the judgments to calculate a cut score. For instance, the 0s could be transformed to 0.33 and the 1s could be transformed to 0.95.

theory (IRT). It is now one of the most widely used cut score-setting methods for state K–12 assessments. To use this method as it was designed, the state will need a test that was calibrated using IRT and be able to order the items from easiest to most difficult based on the calibrations. The panelist uses an ordered-item booklet that displays the questions in order of difficulty from easy to hard and is asked to place a bookmark at the spot that separates the test items into two groups—a group of easier items that the borderline test taker would probably answer correctly (with a response probability of 67, meaning a chance of at least 2 out of 3, or .67) and a group of harder items that the borderline test taker would probably not answer correctly (i.e., the test taker would have a probability of less than .67 of answering correctly). The bookmark placement is then translated to an ability level of a student who has at least a .67 probability of answering the items before the bookmark correctly and a less than .67 probability of answering the items after the bookmark correctly. That ability level (or theta value) can be translated to a scale score and mapped back to a raw score.

A concern with using this (or any item mapping) method on an AA-MAS is in the item ordering. Typically, an ordered-item booklet reflects a large population of students with a wide degree of variance in their abilities. Although there may be some distance in the associated theta values at extreme ends of the booklet, the majority of items are close enough together that it is a fairly simple transformation to map a bookmark placement to an ability score. However, some states have experienced difficulties with an ordered-item booklet of an AA-MAS for which there were fewer items and less variation among test takers, resulting in some clumping of item difficulties and areas with large gaps in ability scores between the clumps.

To explain why the decreased variance might be problematic, let's suppose that in a traditional Bookmark item map, items 10–16 have associated theta values of 1.02, 1.04, 1.05, 1.05, 1.07, 1.08, and 1.10. Although there are different methods for selecting the actual cut point (theta value of the item that is bookmarked, the theta value of the item before it, or the mean of those two values), it is relatively straightforward to determine the cut score value for a bookmark that is placed at any of those items. But what if the items had theta values of 1.02, 1.02, 1.03, 1.42, 1.42, 1.43, and 1.67? If the bookmark is placed on item 13 (the fourth value in the string) indicating that the 13th item is the first one that a borderline test taker would not have a .67 probability of answering correctly, what should the cut score be? Given the three methods usually used to determine the cut score, this one cut score could be assigned a value of 1.42, 1.03, or 1.225. These are fairly disparate numbers and could result in very different scale score and raw score cuts.

Therefore, before choosing to use an item mapping approach, it is important to consider the size and variance of the population taking the AA-MAS. That is, be sure that there are enough students taking the test and enough variance in that population of students for the items to both scale well and order sensibly. Theoretically, it may be more feasible for a state the size of Texas to use an item mapping approach to set cut scores on the AA-MAS than a state the size of Delaware.

An alternative for states who are worried that their samples are too small or too homogeneous is to vary a traditional item mapping approach using classical measurement theory rather than IRT. Actually, the process described here is similar to a yes/no Angoff except that the items are ordered by difficulty, as in a traditional item mapping approach.

The approach involves ordering the items and placing them into an ordered-item booklet, as in the Bookmark approach; however, p values rather than IRT difficulties are used to determine the order. Then, the panelists are told to start with the easiest item and simply ask, "Would a borderline-proficient student be able to answer this item correctly?" If the answer is yes, then they move to the next item. When they reach an item to which they answer no, that is where they place their bookmark. As with all bookmark method procedures, we recommend that the panelists continue a little further into the booklet to ensure that the bookmarked item is truly the beginning of the more difficult items and not an anomaly. Then, rather than transforming the bookmark to a difficulty estimate, the panelists simply count the number of items before the bookmark and use that number as the initial raw score cut. For instance, in a 50-item booklet, if the panelist places their bookmark on item 22, then the initial cut score would be set at 22 out of 50 raw score points. Again, it is worth adjusting this cut score for guessing. If this booklet contained only multiple-choice items with 4-option answers, then a borderline test taker would have a 1-in-4 chance of answering the remaining 28 items correctly by guessing. So, we would add 7 raw score points to the cut score for a final cut score of 29 out of 50 points.[5]

Methods Based on Judgments of People, Products, and Profiles of Scores

As mentioned earlier, there are other standard-setting approaches

---

[5]Note that if the booklet contained open-ended items, they could not be answered correctly by chance and would not be figured into the adjustment. For instance, if 8 of the 28 remaining "items" in the booklet represented various point values for open-ended items, we would simply calculate the probability of guessing correctly on the 20 multiple-choice items, adding 5 points to the initial raw score cut.

that may be worth considering, particularly if the test design includes more than multiple-choice items. At least one state is developing an AA-MAS that involves collecting student evidence on each content standard assessed. The result will look more like a portfolio assessment than a traditional paper-and-pencil assessment. Therefore, it is important to consider other standard-setting methods for these alternate approaches. Four methods discussed here are the body of work (Kingston, Kahl, Sweeney, & Bay, 2001), analytic judgment (Plake & Hambleton, 2001), dominant profile (Plake, Hambleton, & Jaeger, 1997), and contrasting group (Livingston & Zieky, 1982) methods.

Body of Work

The body of work method falls under the category of judgments of people and products and requires some type of evidence for the panelists to consider. Zieky et al. (2008) listed this as a type of contrasting groups approach that focuses on categorizing student work rather than the students themselves. The method is designed for tests with performance tasks or tasks that yield observable products of a student's work, such as essays or recorded speech or science experiments. This is a popular method for the portfolios often used for the AA-AAS. It would also be suitable for a design that requires students to submit evidence of achievement for each assessed content standard. The method does not work well for tests that include large numbers of multiple-choice questions, but it will work if there are a few multiple-choice questions with the performance tasks.

The panelists are asked to review a full body of evidence (meaning the responses to all test questions) and make a single judgment about the entire set of responses, matching the knowledge and skills exhibited in the responses to the knowledge and skills required to be in an achievement level. The cut score between two performance levels is chosen by finding the point on the score scale that best distinguishes between the sets of evidence placed in each of the achievement levels.

Analytic Judgment

The analytic judgment method is also a method in which judgments are made on products; however, judgments are made on responses to individual items (or groups of related items) rather than on the product as a whole. It was designed to be used with tests made of several essay or performance tasks. The method will work for tests that include some multiple-choice items with the performance tasks so long as the items can be grouped into meaningful content clusters.

The analytic judgment method begins by asking panelists to review samples of test takers' work. As described in Zieky et al. (2008), it is similar to the body of work method, but there are two distinct differences:

1. Panelists make judgments on test takers' responses to individual items or to clusters of related items rather than to the entire body of evidence at once.

2. In addition to classifying a response into an achievement level, panelists further classify the responses at each performance level into *low, middle,* and *high* categories. For example, a response is not simply classified as proficient. It is, in addition, classified as low proficient, middle proficient, or high proficient.

The result is a cut score for each item or group of related items; this cut score is the score that most clearly distinguishes between the best responses in the lower achievement level and the worst responses in the higher achievement level (e.g., between responses classified as high basic and low proficient.) Those are the responses that are close to the borderline of each achievement level. The cut scores for all items or all groups of items are summed to get the cut score for the total test.

Dominant Profile

The dominant profile is a method based on profiles of scores and typically results in a conjunctive cut score. That is, the test is divided into meaningful parts that measure different knowledge and skills, and a cut score is determined for each part separately. Thus the outcome is not a single cut score but a set of rules. Those rules can specify separate cut scores for each content strand, or there can be a single cut score for the total score with a minimum score on certain components.

The panelists' task is to become familiar with the test, how it is scored, and the meanings of the different strands/components. They then work together to specify rules for determining which combinations of scores represent acceptable performance and which do not. The rules can combine information from the scores of different components in various ways, as in the following example:

A mathematics test is divided into five strands with 20 points per strand. The panelists determine the following set of rules to be used before classifying a student as proficient:

*   No score less than 10 on any component
*   At least one score of 15 or higher
*   A total score of at least 60 points

Contrasting Groups

Finally, what if a test developer is in a position in which cut scores need to be set, but the data are not yet available, and there is no rubric or student work to analyze? The original contrasting groups method involves judgments about test takers (Livingston & Zieky, 1982). The judgments can be made before the test administration and then compared with the actual scores received to calculate the cut score. The method involves identifying teachers familiar with the target population and then training them on the meaning of the achievement level descriptors, paying particular attention to differentiating between high performance on the lower level and low performance on the higher level. This training does not have to be done in person (videotapes work well), as the method typically works best when there are large numbers of teachers involved (at least 100 per cut score). Once the teachers have been trained, the test developer asks them to place each of their students who will be taking the AA-MAS into one of the achievement levels based on their experience with those students. Once the students have taken the test, they are assigned a total score (either a raw score or a scale score will work for this method). Then the distribution of scores across assigned achievement levels can be examined to determine the best cut score for each level. For instance, for each cut score, the percentage of students identified in each level can be plotted against the test score. That is, for the basic/proficient cut, a graph is plotted with the range in total test scores along the x-axis and the percentage of students at each of those levels categorized as proficient by their teachers on the y-axis. Then, the cut score for proficient is chosen based on the percentages. Zieky et al. (2008) recommended that "one reasonable choice for a cuts core would be the score at which 50 percent of the test takers are [categorized as] Proficient because that would represent the borderline of the Proficient performance level" (p. 78). Another procedure is to plot the distributions of scores for two adjacent levels (e.g., basic and proficient) and set the cut score at the point at which two distributions overlap.

Because this method is based on the judgments of teachers about students they know, it is a reasonable way to match students to achievement levels, but it also introduces some bias. Teachers may factor other considerations into their judgments, such as effort and likability, when the judgment should truly be about a student's knowledge, skills, and ability. This method is often used to check a cut score set through a method based on judgments of test items. This check can be done a couple of years after the initial standard-setting workshop, once teachers have become very familiar with both the test and the meaning of the achievement levels.

Linking Tests Through Cut Scores

A final option for consideration is linking the AA-MAS to the general assessment through the cut scores. Although this idea will be discussed more thoroughly in Chapter 7, it is worth introducing here. Some state policy makers have suggested linking the advanced or proficient level of the modified achievement levels to the basic level of the general grade-level achievement levels. One option would be to link the assessments statistically with common items taken by both populations (as described in Chapter 5), but another option is to link the assessments judgmentally.

A judgmental linking is where a standard-setting method is applied to make the advanced level of one test equivalent to the basic level of another (for example). There are several ways to do this, but the best is to use many of the same panelists in both standard settings. Start by having the panelists become thoroughly familiar with the basic level of the general assessment, both by reviewing the grade-level achievement level descriptor and by examining exemplar items and/or student work at that level. Then, the modified achievement level descriptor for advanced (or proficient) would need to be matched to the grade-level achievement level descriptor for basic. Preferably, the descriptors would be exactly the same, with only slight modifications to allow for the use of the scaffolds that may have been built into the assessment. The judgmental task most commonly used is an item mapping approach in which the panelists work through an ordered-item booklet to find the cut score that would allow for the same interpretation of knowledge and skills across the two assessments.

FINAL CONSIDERATIONS

Although the greatest challenges for developing modified achievement standards lie in defining proficiency for this population and applying an appropriate standard-setting methodology to set a cut score, it would be neglectful not to discuss the importance of documentation and validity studies. Proper documentation is important for any testing program and mandated by the peer review guidance. Likewise, test developers and users should always be thinking of the validity of the interpretations made using the achievement standards.

Documentation

It is important to document both the process of developing modified achievement level descriptors and the standard-setting procedures. Two professional standards (American Educational Research Association,

American Psychological Association, & National Council on Measurement in Education, 1999) directly address the importance of documenting the rationale, procedures, and results:

- Document the PLDs, selection of panelists, training provided, ratings, and variance measures (Standard 1.7)
- Document the rationale and procedures for the methodology used (Standard 4.19)

As discussed in Perie (2007), there are eight important components that need to be documented regarding the standard-setting process:

1. Achievement level descriptors

2. Panelists

3. Rationale

4. Training

5. Procedures

6. Ratings and variance

7. Any adjustments and adoption of cut scores

8. Validity evaluation

Most of these are fairly straightforward and are discussed in several texts on standard setting. Here, we highlight only two areas that may have particular sensitivities for modified achievement standards and have been discussed within this chapter.

Achievement Level Descriptors

Because of the challenges associated with describing proficiency using a modified achievement standard, it is vital that the test developer both describe and justify the process used, including the selection of participants who may have drafted the descriptors, the directions given to them, the data or information used to inform the process, and the number and type of reviews conducted before the descriptors were formally adopted. Providing a theory of who the students are and what the barriers are to their achieving grade-level standards will aid the understanding of how the descriptors were developed.

Rationale

It will be important to document the rationale for selecting the standard setting method used to set the cut scores. If the revisions or enhancements made to the assessments (e.g., the reduction of a response option) or the characteristics of the population (e.g., small variance in performance) affected the choice of available methods, this could be explained in writing to better help a reader understand the purpose and logic. Explaining the rationale behind any selection of a process helps inform the validity argument, as discussed in the next section and in Chapter 8. Finally, if any modifications to the traditional application of the standard-setting method—such as those described in this chapter—were made, these need to be documented as well, along with the rationale for these modifications.

Validation

Validity is a large topic that will be covered more completely in Chapter 8, but it is worth touching on the various types of evidence that can be collected during the standard-setting process here. Collecting the information discussed in the documentation section can provide evidence of internal validity of the achievement standards. Providing a rationale for the methods used, ensuring an appropriate panel composition, and comparing the results to other external sources can all provide validity evidence to the argument that the achievement standards were set appropriately. Then, thought should be given to how the interpretation and use of the achievement standards contribute to the consequential validity of the assessment.

In examining the validity of the use of the achievement standards, it is important to ask a series of questions about the basic components of those standards. Conducting appropriate studies over the first several years of the assessment can provide information to answer these questions on issues regarding appropriateness of the modified achievement level descriptors and the accuracy of the cut scores. For example, questions may include:

- Was the standard-setting procedure internally valid?
- Do the cut scores divide students reasonably in terms of achievement?
- How well does the test classify students compared with their achievement in the classroom?
- Do the effects of the achievement standards match what was intended?
- Have the modified achievement level descriptors had an impact on instruction?
- Have there been any negative consequences to using these achievement standards?

Some of these questions can be answered through the standard-setting process itself. It will be important to show that the panelists were qualified and representative of all possible panelists. Evaluation forms can be used to show that the panelists understood the process and were confident in the results. If feasible, working with two separate panels during the standard-setting process will also provide a measure of consistency in cut score recommendations and provide evidence of validity. To argue for the reasonableness of the cut scores, the test developer can compare the percentage of students categorized into each achievement level by the AA-MAS to the percentages in the equivalent categories by the general assessment and the AA-AAS. If all tests are intended to be developed to the same rigor for their specific populations, then one would expect the impact data to be distributed similarly across all assessments.

Other questions can be answered through teacher surveys and focus groups as well as classroom observations. Conducting a contrasting groups study 1 or 2 years after the cut scores are set can also provide useful interpretative information. Once the test developers are confident that teachers know and understand the modified achievement level descriptors, they could ask the teachers to classify their students into one of the four achievement levels before the assessment. Then the classifications determined by the assessment could be compared with the teacher classifications to determine whether the teachers would generally assign students into higher or lower categories or whether the two sources of data provide similar classifications.

As a final thought, it is important to keep in mind that the process of setting achievement standards does not end with the cut score study or even with state board approval of the descriptors and cut scores. Instead, consider designing a mechanism within an assessment program to continually monitor the effectiveness and appropriateness of the achievement level descriptors and the usefulness of the categories as defined by the cut scores. Particularly for this population, for which we expect instruction to continually improve and move closer to grade-level instruction, it is important to frequently monitor the efficacy of the modified achievement standards.

REFERENCES

American Educational Research Association, American Psychological Association, & National Council on Measurement in Education. (1999). *Standards for educational and psychological testing.* Washington, DC: American Educational Research Association.

Angoff, W.H. (1971). Scales, norms, and equivalent scores. In R.L. Thorndike (Ed.), *Educational measurement* (2nd ed., pp. 508–600). Washington, DC: American Council on Education.

Beck, M. (2003, April). *Standard setting: If it is science, it's sociology and linguistics, not psychometrics.* Paper presented at the annual meeting of the National Council on Measurement in Education, Chicago.

Berk, R.A. (1996). Standard setting: The next generation (where few psychometricians have gone before!). *Applied Measurement in Education, 9*(3), 215–235.

Cizek, G.J., & Bunch, M.B. (2007). *Standard setting: A guide to establishing and evaluating performance standards on tests.* Thousand Oaks, CA: Sage.

Ferrara, S., Perie, M., & Johnson, E. (2008, February). Matching the judgmental task with standard setting panelist expertise: The Item–Descriptor (ID) Matching procedure. *Journal of Applied Testing Technology, 9*(1), 1–22.

Gong, B. (2007). *Learning progressions: Sources and implications for assessment.* Presentation at the Council of Chief State School Officers Large-Scale Assessment Conference, Nashville.

Hambleton, R.H. (2001). Setting performance standards on educational assessments and criteria for evaluating the process. In G.J. Cizek (Ed.), *Setting performance standards: Concepts, methods, and perspectives* (pp. 89–116). Mahwah, NJ: Lawrence Erlbaum Associates.

Impara, J.C., & Plake, B.S. (1997). Standard setting: An alternative approach. *Journal of Educational Measurement, 34*(4), 353–366.

Kingston, N.M., Kahl, S.R., Sweeney, K.P., & Bay, L. (2001). Setting performance standards using the body of work method. In G.J. Cizek (Ed.), *Setting performance standards: Concepts, methods, and perspectives.* Mahwah, NJ: Lawrence Erlbaum Associates.

Livingston, S., & Zieky, M. (1982). *Passing scores: A manual for setting standards of performance on educational and occupational tests.* Princeton, NJ: Educational Testing Service.

Mitzel, H.C., Lewis, D.M., Patz, R.J., & Green, D.R. (2001). The Bookmark procedure: Psychological perspectives. In G.J. Cizek (Ed.), *Setting performance standards: Concepts, methods, and perspectives.* Mahwah, NJ: Lawrence Erlbaum Associates.

No Child Left Behind Act of 2001, PL 107-110, 115 Stat. 1425, 20 U.S.C. §§ 6301 *et seq.*

Perie, M. (2007). *Setting alternate achievement standards.* Lexington, KY: University of Kentucky, Human Development Institute, National Alternate Assessment Center. Retrieved from http://www.naacpartners.org/products/whitePapers/18020.pdf

Perie, M. (2008). A guide to understanding and developing performance level descriptors. *Educational Measurement: Issues and Practice, 27*(4), 15–29.

Perie, M., Hess, K., & Gong, B. (2008). *Writing performance level descriptors: Applying lessons Learned from the general assessment to the 1% and 2% assessments.* Dover, NH: National Center for the Improvement of Educational Assessment.

Plake, B.S., & Hambleton, R.K. (2001). The analytic judgment method for setting standards on complex performance assessments. In G.J. Cizek (Ed.), *Standard setting: Concepts, methods, and perspectives* (pp. 283–312). Mahwah, NJ: Lawrence Erlbaum Associates.

Plake, B.S., Hambleton, R.K., & Jaeger, R.M. (1997). A new standard setting method for performance assessments: The Dominant Profile Judgment method and some field-test results. *Educational and Psychological Measurement, 57,* 400–411.

Reckase, M.D. (2006). A conceptual framework for a psychometric theory for standard setting with examples of its use for evaluating the functioning of two standard setting methods. *Educational Measurement: Issues and Practice, 25*(2), 4–18.

U.S. Department of Education. (2007). Final Rule 34 CFR Parts 200 and 300: Title I—Improving the academic achievement of the disadvantaged. 72 *Fed. Reg., 67*, Washington DC: Office of Elementary and Secondary Education. Retrieved July 12, 2008, from http://www2.ed.gov/legislation/ FedRegister/ finrule/2003-4/120903a.html

Zieky, M., Perie, M., & Livingston, S. (2008). *Cutscores: A manual for setting performance standards on educational and occupational tests.* Princeton, NJ: Educational Testing Service.

Technical Considerations and Practical Applications

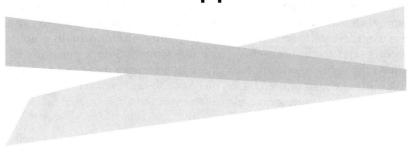

This final section incorporates the overarching themes of comparability and validity of alternate assessments based on modified achievement standards (AA-MAS) and then focuses on how the AA-MAS will fit into a state accountability system. Whereas a previous chapter (Welch & Dunbar, Chapter 5) began the discussion of technical adequacy, focusing on item analyses and psychometric characteristics of the test, these chapters focus on very specific aspects of technical quality. They focus not on the AA-MAS simply as a standalone assessment, but as it fits into a larger assessment program.

Chapter 7, by Jamal Abedi, discusses issues related to the comparability of the AA-MAS from the perspective of ensuring that students who take this assessment have the same opportunities for success and inclusion as students who take the general assessment. Several components of comparability are examined, including content and construct, psychometrics, scale and score, linguistic structure, basic text features, depth of knowledge, and accommodations used for students with disabilities based on their individualized education programs.

Chapter 8, by Scott F. Marion, discusses the importance of developing a validity argument for the implementation and use of the AA-MAS. It emphasizes the importance of articulating the theory of action, particularly in light of the uncertain conceptual framework supporting this AA-MAS initiative. The chapter then describes methods for evaluating the argument to provide information about how to improve the program and how to determine the value of AA-MAS in terms of the instructional and social benefits, given the costs.

Finally, in Chapter 9, by Chris Domaleski, the focus turns to the practical application of these ideas in a state assessment system. It describes issues of fitting this assessment into a preexisting state assessment and accountability system. The chapter considers the current state context in reviewing operational considerations and discusses ways to estimate reliability, produce informative score reports, and incorporate these new assessments into a performance index; thoughts regarding how these assessments relate to diploma eligibility are also offered.

7

Comparability Issues for the Alternate Assessment Based on Modified Achievement Standards

Jamal Abedi

The mandate of including students with disabilities in state and national assessments may not produce desirable results if the assessment outcomes for these students are not comparable with those of mainstream students. Thus, comparability issues must be given careful attention if these students are to be given a fair chance of inclusion in the assessment and accountability system. The principle of comparability and its related issues have long been debated. In this chapter, the concept of comparability is viewed and discussed in broader terms and from different perspectives, including content and construct, psychometrics, scale and score, linguistic structure, basic text features, depth of knowledge, and accommodations used for students with disabilities based on their individualized education program (IEP). It is indicated that comparability is not an "all-or-none" proposition; rather it is a continuum of varying degrees. Recommendations have been provided on how to view and evaluate comparability between alternate assessments based on modified achievement standards (AA-MAS) and general assessments.

RATIONALE

Recent legislation such as the Individuals with Disabilities Education Improvement Act (IDEA) of 2004 (PL 108-446) and the No Child Left Behind (NCLB) Act of 2001 (PL 107-110) mandates inclusion of students with disabilities in assessment and accountability systems (Gong & Blank, 2002; Lowrey, Drasgow, Renzaglia, & Chezan, 2009; Thompson, Lazarus, Clapper, & Thurlow, 2006; see also Chapter 9, this volume). This mandate is based on the assumption that the same, or at least comparable, assessments are used across groups of students, those with different types of disabilities and those without any apparent disabilities. In the context of assessment, comparability means that the inferences from the scores on one test can be psychometrically related to scores on another "comparable" test (Marion, 2006). In other words, comparability assumes equivalence between the assessments (Elosua & Lopez-Jauregui, 2008). Although these definitions provide one aspect of comparability, they emphasize the importance of comparability of AA-MAS with general assessments, as the policy of inclusion may not produce valid outcomes if the assessments used for different subgroups of students do not have the same meaning and do not lead to the same interpretation across these subgroups. In this chapter, issues concerning comparability of assessments for students with disabilities taking AA-MAS are discussed and methods for examining such comparability are described. The focus on comparability in this chapter centers on the application of the AA-MAS for students with disabilities. A comprehensive discussion of issues concerning comparability of scores from different variations of achievement tests has been presented in a recently published volume (Winter, 2009b). The discussion of comparability issues in this chapter is intended to help the reader understand the complex nature of comparability across forms of assessments and subgroups of students being assessed.

The majority of students with disabilities take the general state assessments, with or without accommodations. However, a small group of students with disabilities—who can make significant academic progress but who are not able to achieve grade-level progress—may not be able to show the full range of their knowledge and skills on the general assessments, even with accommodations. Therefore, they are offered alternate assessments (Lazarus, Rogers, Cormier, & Thurlow, 2008). These alternate assessments have been described as the "ultimate accommodation" for inclusion of students with significant disabilities in the accountability system (Roach, 2005; see also Chapter 9, this volume).

However, there are major questions and concerns regarding the purpose, design, development, implementation, and interpretation of the outcomes of these assessments. For example, Kettler and Almond (2009) raise many questions regarding these assessments: "First and foremost, which students should be eligible for an AA-MAS? Second, what are their unique learning characteristics, and how should an assessment be tailored to their needs based on a better understanding of their cognitive processing?" (p. 5)

The authors also raised questions related to item and test development, which include

> (a) What characteristics make an item or test more accessible? (b) How might changes in test delivery and format interact with altered items? (c) At what point does an alteration to an item affect the construct being measured? (d) How is alignment to the content standards affected by item and test alterations? (e) How do proficiency-level descriptions affect the development of AA-MAS? (f) What criteria should be used to judge student success? (g) How do alterations designed to change the complexity and difficulty of items affect the technical quality of AA-MAS as complete tests? (2009, p. 5)

There are also major issues with setting achievement standards for AA-MAS. For example, how comparable should the cut scores be for different performance level and how should these cut scores be defined (Olson, Mead, & Payne, 2002)? Answers to these questions require substantial efforts in conducting research in the area of alternate assessments for students with disabilities.

Different forms of alternate assessments have been proposed. Among them are 1) alternate assessments based on grade-level achievement standards (AA-GLAS), 2) alternate assessments based on alternate achievement standards (AA-AAS), which are often referred to as the 1% tests, and 3) AA-MAS, often referred to as the 2% tests (Gong, 2007). Elliot and Roach (2007) underscore the importance of determining effective strategies for including special needs students in the overall accountability for student achievement, stating

> Alternate assessments are used with a relatively small population of students with disabilities, yet demand a significant amount of time from educators and state assessment professionals to develop, implement, and evaluate. It appears the efforts of these professionals will need to be extended given the vast majority of states' have not met the [U.S. Department of Education's] requirements for alignment and technical soundness. (pp. 330–331)

Different chapters in this volume address some of the issues raised above. For example, in Chapter 1, Quenemoen discusses eligibility criteria for students taking AA-MAS. She distinguishes between low-performing students who have disabilities and those with no apparent disabilities. The chapter by Welch and Dunbar (Chapter 5) discusses issues concerning the development of AA-MAS and the advantages and disadvantages of various options for modifications, and this chapter focuses on the comparability aspect of AA-MAS.

CHALLENGES IN EVALUATING COMPARABILITY

Developing alternate assessments for students with disabilities is quite complex and requires special attention and planning. For example, Lowrey et al. (2009) suggest "adherence to the requirement to maintain an individualized, meaningful curriculum for students with severe disabilities complicates delivery of an assessment that is created to measure progress of students toward a standardized curriculum" (p. 250). The authors indicate that the use of different approaches by states (e.g., simplifying general education standards, redefining them as functional skills, or extending them through the use of foundational skills) brings further complications to the process of developing alternate assessments. Roach (2005) discussed and examined four challenges in designing and implementing alternate assessments for students with significant disabilities. These challenges include 1) deciding who should participate in alternate assessments, 2) determining the content area that alternate assessments should measure, 3) creating reliable and valid alternate assessments, and 4) defining proficient performance on alternate assessments. Although some of these challenges (such as challenge 2, which only applies to AA-AAS) may not apply to AA-MAS, they emphasize the difficulty in developing these assessments and interpreting their scores.

According to one U.S. Department of Education report from November 2008, eight states developed an AA-MAS for at least one grade level. This report by the National Technical Advisory Council indicated that "seven of these states have submitted evidence to the Department for peer review but none has met all the requirements" (p. 4). One of the main reasons that states were not able to provide sufficient evidence on the comparability of assessments for AA-MAS is that some of the students who face the most challenges in their educational careers belong to subgroups that are small in size. It would be extremely difficult for researchers to examine the factors affecting comparability between AA-MAS and general assessments using traditional research/psychometric methodologies due to such small group sizes. In order to do a comparison between students who take general assessments and those taking alternate assessments, large enough samples are needed to detect meaningful differences.

In some categories of low incidence disabilities, there are hardly enough subjects in a school, district, or even in most states to allow for meaningful analyses of data to examine comparability issues. In such cases, researchers may be required to combine some of these categories in order to obtain a large enough sample to conduct studies that are methodologically sound. However, research suggests that issues concerning assessment of students with disabilities might vary across different categories of disabilities; therefore, it may not be reasonable to aggregate findings from students in the different subgroups of disabilities (e.g., see Abedi, Leon, & Kao, 2008).

The *Standards for Educational and Psychological Testing* (American Educational Research Association [AERA], American Psychological Association [APA], & National Council on Measurement in Education [NCME], 1999) view comparability as a major foundation underlying valid and fair assessments and allocate an entire chapter to issues regarding comparability (Chapter 4, pp. 49–60). However, the main focus of the *Standards'* Chapter 4 is on *score comparability,* which can be established through approaches such as scaling test scores. The *Standards* state: "Scale scores may aid interpretation by indicating how a given score compares to those of other test takers by enhancing the comparability of scores obtained using different forms of a test, or in other ways" (p. 49). The *Standards* acknowledge the limitations on score comparability, particularly when implemented in terms of cut score: "Criterion-referenced interpretations based on cut scores are sometimes criticized on the grounds that there is very rarely a sharp distinction of any kind between those just below versus just above a cut score" (p. 50). (See also Chapter 6 in this volume for a detailed description of cut scores.)

APPROACHES TO COMPARABILITY

In order to address the current need and develop strategies to overcome the challenges, the discussion of comparability in this chapter goes beyond the traditional approach including those discussed in the *Standards*. In addition to score comparability, the chapter discusses comparability in several other areas. Specifically, this chapter proposes comparability in six major areas: a) content and construct, b) depth of knowledge, c) accommodation, d) psychometrics, e) linguistic structure, and f) basic text features. However, we acknowledge the challenging task of establishing comparability in all six areas. Therefore, we group these comparability features into two categories: 1) required comparability (features a through c) and 2) complementary or desired comparability (features d through f). To ensure comparability, test developers must present evidence on the first category, and if feasible, with supplemental (preferred) evidence from the second category. This recommendation of two broad categories is based on literature and experts' opinions (e.g., see Allen & Yen, 1979; Thorndike, 2005). However, in many cases, states determine where they would like the tests to be comparable. For example, the AA-MAS may be a better measure of achievement at the lower end of the scale, but states may want the *proficient* level to be comparable across AA-MAS and general assessments.

Content and Construct Comparability between AA-MAS and General Assessments

The first and most important criterion for examining comparability of different assessments is to establish content and construct comparability. Assessments that measure different content and constructs may not produce comparable outcomes even if they are shown to be comparable in terms of psychometric characteristics. The concept of content and construct comparability has been discussed from different points of view, including expert judgment, moderation, and alignment with the grade-level content standards. Thus comparability between AA-MAS and general assessments can be established through expert judgment, moderation by inspection, social moderation (Winter, 2009a), and alignment with the grade-level content standards.

The concept of cognitive demand in assessment is related to the discussion of content and construct comparability. The level of cognitive demand of an assessment (or of an item within an assessment) could be determined by different sources, some of which are relevant to the assessments and some of which may be due to the impact of nuisance variables or construct-irrelevant sources. For example, irrelevant or poorly labeled visuals may increase the cognitive load of perceiving information for students with disabilities. However, cognitive complexity might be a relevant factor in the assessment. Similarly, in reading comprehension, items that are inferential may significantly increase the cognitive load for students with disabilities and thus affect students' abilities to display their understanding of the passage. Assessing depth of knowledge reveals the level of the cognitive demands of the standards and the cognitive demands of the assessment items. Level 4 of depth of knowledge (extended thinking) requires the highest level of cognitive demand in Webb's model. This level demands complex reasoning, planning, developing, and thinking (Webb, Alt, Cormier, Vesperman, 2006).

Expert Judgment

Content comparability can be established through experts judgment (Mislevy, 1992). A team of experts, including content specialists, teachers, and linguistic experts, could judge the comparability of content across the two assessments. For expert judgment, a rubric is often developed and validated to help ensure more consistent judgment across a variety of experts with different backgrounds. To estimate interrater reliability, comparability between the two assessments may be examined by more than one person. Interrater reliability indices such as kappa and intraclass correlations can then be computed and can be compared across the two assessments.

Moderation

Moderation refers to the identification of local scoring instances that are overly stringent or overly lenient to "moderate" those scores to bring them more into line (Burton & Linn, 1994). Moderation techniques can be grouped into several categories. A commonly used approach is classified as moderation by inspection, or cross-moderation, which is mainly based on judgmental audits. Another moderation approach is based on statistical moderation. Under this approach, moderation is done on the basis of external criteria. The third approach is the enhancement of one of the two approaches mentioned above or a combination of the two approaches (Burton & Linn, 1994; Linn, 1993; Mislevy, 1992).

Alignment with the Grade-Level Content Standards

States conduct alignment studies to demonstrate how and to what extent their assessments are aligned with their content standards (e.g., see Moore & O'Neal, 2004). Alignment is conducted to examine the degree of correspondence between a set of educational standards—often referred to as state content standards—and the assessments that are developed to measure what students are expected to learn in relation to those standards (Moore & O'Neal, 2004; Webb, 1999, 2002). According to Webb (1999), there are several major criteria for alignment. These criteria include: 1) categorical concurrence, 2) depth-of-knowledge consistency, 3) range-of-knowledge correspondence, and 4) balance of representation. The Achieve model presents a slightly different approach to alignment. In this model, a panel of content experts evaluates the degree of alignment between assessment items and standards using the following five criteria: 1) content centrality, 2) performance centrality, 3) challenge, 4) balance, and 5) range. The content and performance centrality are defined based on the content and performance required by an individual assessment item to that of the related standard (Achieve, 2006).

Studies suggest that Webb's alignment model, used for the alignment of assessment content with the state content standards for regular state assessments, can be meaningfully applied to alternate assessments, which provide states a way to comply with the requirements of

IDEA and NCLB (Gong & Marion, 2006; Roach & Elliott, 2004; Tindal, 2005). Tindal (2005) describes procedures for alignment of alternate assessments using the Webb alignment model.

In fact, the report on the peer review results from six states suggests that test blueprints should provide evidence on the alignment between AA-MAS and grade-level content standards (Filbin, 2008; Kettler & Almond, 2009). These assessments are required to assess the same breadth and depth as the general assessments.

Psychometric Comparability Between AA-MAS and General Assessments

Psychometric comparability data can serve as complementary and supportive evidence to the content and construct comparability. In this section, psychometric comparability is discussed in the context of both classical and modern theory of measurement.

Classical Measurement Approach in Examining Comparability of Assessments

Under classical test theory, assessment outcomes can be considered comparable if they are from parallel or tau-equivalent tests. To consider different forms of assessments as parallel or tau-equivalent, certain assumptions underlying parallel and tau-equivalent tests must be met. The main assumption underlying classical test theory is that the measurement error is randomly distributed and that the correlation between measurement errors of two tests is zero ($\rho_{E1E2} = 0$). This implies that the correlation between the true scores of form 1 of the test with measurement error of form 2 of the test is zero ($\rho_{T1E2} = 0$). In addition, if two tests have observed scores of X and X' that satisfies the assumption of randomly distributed measurement error, and if for every population of examinees, the true score of test 1 (T) equals the true score of test 2 (T'), and if the variance of measurement error of test 1 (σ_E^2) equals the variance of measurement error of test 2 ($\sigma_{E'}^2$), then the tests are considered parallel tests (Allen & Yen, 1979; Thorndike, 2005).

However, as indicated by the U.S. Department of Education (2007) and in the literature, AA-MAS assessments differ from states' general assessments in many different aspects. Some of these assessments include fewer items with higher p values (less difficult items), have shorter and fewer reading passages, have less complex linguistic structures, and use fewer distractors in their multiple choice items (Cortiella, 2007; Kettler & Almond, 2009; Lazarus, Thurlow, Christensen, & Cormier, 2007). Such systematic differences between states' alternate and general assessments create major limitations on the comparability of the two assessments.

One question is whether a shorter version of the test can be considered as parallel (tau-equivalent) to the full version of the test. As indicated above, a test with fewer items, given all other parallel test assumptions are true (except for an additive constant, C_{12}), can be considered as a tau-equivalent test to the original version. However, in terms of alternate assessments, it is very difficult to assume that the two tests (the state's general assessment and the alternate assessment) meet any conditions of parallel tests. If the shorter version of the test is different than the full version of the test in terms of linguistic structure, item difficulty, or the number of choices (in multiple-choice format), then the shorter version of the test cannot be considered as a tau-equivalent test. For example, Karvonen and Huynh (2007) indicated that alternate assessment items typically require simple cognitive processes such as recall.

Reliability, Validity, and Standard Error of Measurement

Assessments used by states for accountability purposes are usually developed and field-tested for mainstream students. In the development process, many of the assessment needs of subgroups (e.g., students with disabilities) may not be adequately considered. Therefore, there may be many sources of nuisance variables that can impact the performance of students with disabilities. These sources, which are also referred to as extraneous variables (Linn & Gronlund, 1995), contaminants, or construct-irrelevant (Haladyna & Downing, 2004; Messick, 1984), may differentially impact the reliability and validity of assessments for students with disabilities. Linn and Gronlund (1995) indicated that "During the development of an assessment, an attempt is made to rule out extraneous factors that might distort the meaning of the scores, and follow-up studies are conducted to verify the success of these attempts" (p. 71). Furthermore, Zieky (1989) cautioned that a fairness review to identify construct-irrelevant sources is a major effort when constructing impartial tests. In Chapter 5, Welch and Dunbar address some of the issues concerning the development of AA-MAS by first discussing the best practice in test development and then highlighting the advantages and disadvantages of various options for modifications.

Reliability

The linguistic complexity of assessment and format and structure of test booklets (e.g., font size, complex and irrelevant charts and graphs, crowded text on pages) may cause fatigue and frustration for students with disabilities and may result in a higher level of measurement error that can substantially reduce the reliability of assessment outcomes for these students. For example, Abedi, Leon, and Mirocha (2003) found a gap of more than 0.32 in the internal consistency coefficient in scores of state assessments in math between students with disabilities and students without disabilities. The standard error of measurement was substantially larger in assessment outcomes for students with disabilities.

More importantly, some of these sources of construct-irrelevant variance may bring another dimension to the measurement model and make it multidimensional. This multidimensionality issue would then introduce more complexity into the comparability concept. For example, it would be a challenging task, both in terms of content and psychometric properties, to compare assessment outcomes that are unidimensional in nature (i.e., measuring only the construct-relevant aspects of assessment) with the outcomes that represent several dimensions of construct-irrelevant sources. Multidimensionality of assessment outcomes may directly impact internal consistency measures (such as alpha coefficient), as these measures are extremely sensitive to multidimensionality and severely underestimate reliability of multidimensional assessments when they are supposed to measure a single construct (Cortina, 1993).

Validity

Sources of construct-irrelevant variance previously discussed will not only impact the reliability of assessments, but they also directly affect the construct validity of the assessments. Content-based state tests are designed to measure constructs that are the target of the assessments. Therefore, items within a test are often highly correlated when they are used for students without disabilities for whom the assessments were constructed. For students with disabilities, however, different sources of construct-irrelevant variance may negatively impact the validity of these assessments. More importantly, it might be difficult to assess the validity of AA-MAS using external criteria, because finding valid external criteria for examining the validity of AA-MAS can be a major challenge.

As part of a comprehensive set of studies on score comparability, DePascale (2009b) examined the comparability of an AA-MAS (which he called a 2% test). The study addressed validity questions regarding the modified test by examining the relationship between the states' general test and the modified test. The goals of the study were:

> a) to determine that the 2% tests were less difficult than the general tests, and b) to determine that the 2% tests provide more reliable information than the general test in the area of interest for its target population of the 2% test. (p. 11)

As one of the major findings of the study, the author indicated that the 2% test provided reliable information at the extreme low end of the scale.

The findings of this study are very informative in terms of psychometric properties of the AA-MAS as compared with those for the general state assessments. Although it is true that the alternate assessments may generally have lower reliability and validity when considering the entire distribution of content knowledge, these assessments do what they set out to accomplish for the lower part of the ability distribution (see Chapter 8 for a comprehensive presentation of validity of AA-MAS).

Structural Equation Modeling Approach

Comparing the structural relationship between test items, item scores, and total test score and between different subscales of the tests across the two assessments (AA-MAS and the general state assessment) using a multiple group confirmatory factor analytic model can provide useful information (Abedi, 2002). Figure 7.1 presents a multiple group confirmatory model that provides comparability evidence. This model may include data from states with two groups of students: 1) students with disabilities taking AA-MAS, and 2) students without disabilities

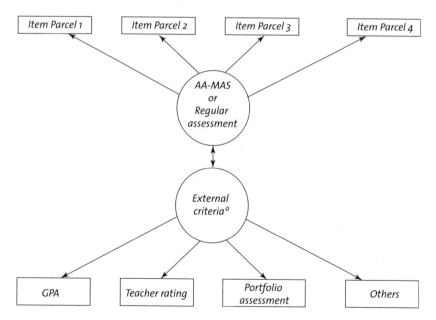

Figure 7.1. Multigroup confirmatory model. [a]External criteria include assessment outcomes other than state test scores.

taking general assessments, which can be used in content areas such as math, science, or reading/language arts. A set of item parcels can be constructed based on existing data from each group. Each parcel should include items representing different subscales, but items across parcels should be similar. These item parcels can then be used for creating a latent variable for the content-based assessment. A set of other assessment scores can then be used as external criteria for establishing criterion-based validity. This set of variables could include student grade point average, teacher's rating of student performance, and a score from the portfolio in the content being assessed. Thus the model includes two latent variables: one is the test scores, which is computed from the item parcel, and the other is the external criterion.

In this model, it is not necessary to have an equal number of items across the two assessments; however, the number of parcels across the two groups should be equal. A set of invariances across the two groups of students taking the two different assessments can be tested for significance. These include testing invariance of factor loadings of the item parcels with the overall test latent variables and the overall external criteria and invariance of correlations between the content assessment's latent variable with the external criteria latent variable. A significant outcome on the invariance hypotheses would be an indication of a lack of comparability between the two assessments.

Generalizability Approach

A G model can be used to examine comparability between AA-MAS and the general state assessments. A multifacet G design can be used to compare the two groups in terms of different sources of measurement error, such as variation between items and occasions. The model can be applied separately to each of the two groups. Sources of variability due to items and occasions (and interaction between items and occasions) can be compared across the two groups of students taking the two different assessments. The overall G coefficients as well as the percentage of variance explained by each of the sources (e.g., students, items, occasions, and interaction between items and occasion) can be compared across the two groups. Both relative and absolute decisions for computing G coefficient may be applied and comparisons can be made. For a more detailed discussion of the generalizability concept and instruction on how to conduct a G study, see Brennan (2001) and Shavelson and Webb (1991).

The structure and size of the variance components, the significance of the main and interaction effects, and effect sizes across the two assessments can also be compared for any significant differences. For example, if a linguistic complexity facet accounts for 25% of the variance in one assessment but explains less than 5% in the other assessment, then such a difference points to a lack of comparability in terms of the generalizability model.

Differential Item Functioning Approach

Test publishers and states often conduct differential item functioning (DIF) analyses to identify test items that differentially perform across subgroups of students. Different student background variables are used for grouping students. DIF analyses are usually conducted to examine any possible biases due to gender, ethnicity, student socioeconomic status, student disability status, and student language background. DIF analyses by student disability status using states' general and alternate assessments may shed light on comparability between the two assessments. For example, it would be informative to compare the trend of results of DIF on a state general assessment in a specific content (e.g., math or science) with the results of DIF on a corresponding AA-MAS assessment by some student background variables such as socioeconomic status (free/reduced price lunch program) for similarities and differences. One could identify the number of items labeled as A, B, or C DIF across AA-MAS and the general assessments. Similarly, comparing the pattern of uniform and nonuniform DIF across AA-MAS and general assessments could provide useful information. However, there are major limitations in such comparisons when used for comparability purposes.

First, the number of students (sample size) for the AA-MAS is a major challenge because it would be extremely difficult to find a large enough sample to compare with the focal and reference groups. Second, the literature clearly suggests that different procedures for computing DIF may provide quite different outcomes (Abedi, et al., 2008). This may be a major problem in using DIF as a criterion for judging comparability of different assessments because different approaches may perform differently across the assessments. Third, and most importantly, test items may perform differentially across students in different subgroups of disabilities. Results of a study on DIF by different subgroups of disabilities found that a substantial number of items were identified as DIF for different disability groups, but very few or almost none of the items were identified as DIF across all or several subgroups of disabilities (Abedi et al., 2008).

Scale and Score Comparability Between AA-MAS and General Assessments

According to the *Standards for Educational and Psychological Testing* (AERA et al., 1999), scale and score comparability between two assessments is required in order to provide similar interpretation of the outcomes measured by those assessments. Winter (2009a) discussed score comparability and indicates that "In general, test scores can be considered comparable if they can be used interchangeably" (p. 6). Winter argued, however, that comparability depends on the level of scores being used. For example, scores reported at the scale level or achievement score level can be compared only at that level. Additionally these scores must provide measures of the same set of knowledge and skills, present the same degree of achievement, and have similar technical properties (Winter, 2009a).

AA-MAS tests may have major differences from the general assessments, including the number and level of difficulty of test items. Even with such differences, some evidences of score comparability can be obtained. "For example, it may be desirable to interpret scores from a shortened (and hence less reliable) form of a test by first converting them to corresponding scores on the full-length version" (AERA et al., 1999, p. 52). Converting scores from the AA-MAS and general assessments on the same scale is extremely challenging because such conversions require comparability on many different aspects. As Mislevy (1992) indicated, "No simple statistical machinery can transform the results of two arbitrarily selected assessments so that they provide interchangeable information about all questions about students' competencies" (p. 91), particularly in the case of AA-MAS and the general assessments, for which there are such major and substantial differences. However, despite the limitations, such conversions could provide useful information.

Linguistic Comparability Between
AA-MAS and General State Assessments

Recent literature on the issues concerning assessments consistently demonstrates the impact of language factors on the assessment outcomes. These factors differentially impact the performance of subgroups of students such as English language learners and students with disabilities, particularly those with learning and reading disabilities. Several linguistic features have been identified in the literature that may have major impacts on the assessment outcomes for these students (Abedi, 2007, 2010; Abedi & Lord, 2001; Sato, 2007). Research literature also suggests that reducing the level of unnecessary linguistic complexity of assessments helps to close the gap between subgroups, such as students with disabilities and English language learner students, and the main group (Abedi, 2010; Abedi et al., 2003). The process of reducing the level of unnecessary linguistic complexity of assessments is often referred to as the linguistic modification of assessments. Although the linguistic modification process does not affect the performance of native speakers of English at the higher performance level (thus not affecting the validity of assessments), it helps reduce the performance gap between students with disabilities and students without disabilities.

One approach in examining comparability between AA-MAS and general state assessments is to compare their linguistic structures to see if the level of linguistic complexity is similar across the two assessments (DePascale, 2009a). In this comparison, a distinction must be made between linguistic features that are related and those that are not related to the content being measured. To promote comparability with the states' general assessments, the linguistic structure related to the content may not be changed, because changing linguistic structures that are content related may alter the construct being measured. Therefore, linguistic modification should only be applied to language that is not related to the construct being measured. The distinction between related and unrelated linguistic features to the content can be made by a team of experts that includes content and linguistic experts.

Literature provides clear guidelines and instructions on how to conduct linguistic modification of assessments and how to distinguish between necessary and unnecessary linguistic complexity in assessments (Abedi, 2007, 2010; Sato, 2007). These guidelines would help in two important contexts: 1) to identify which linguistic features should be considered in making judgments on comparability between state general and alternate assessments, and 2) to inform the development of alternate assessments when linguistic modification is considered as a factor in the alternate assessment process.

Once again, it is extremely important to distinguish between linguistic structure that is related to the content being measured and unnecessary linguistic complexity that is unrelated to the content. As indicated earlier, some states may choose to remove or reduce unnecessary linguistic complexity of the AA-MAS to make them more accessible for students with disabilities, which should be considered a reasonable practice. Reducing unnecessary linguistic complexity of assessments also makes them more accessible for students with no disability who are at the lower level of the achievement performance distribution.

Assessing the Level of Linguistic Complexity of the AA-MAS and General Assessment Test Items

Outcomes of the studies on the impact of linguistic factors on the assessment of English language learners and students with disabilities have led to identification of 48 linguistic features that make assessment more complex for these students (e.g., see Abedi, 2010; Abedi & Lord, 2001).

	Degree of complexity				
Linguistic feature	Not complex 1	2	3	4	Most complex 5
1. Word frequency/ familiarity					
2. Word length					
3. Sentence length					
4. Passive voice constructs					
5. Long noun phrases					
6. Long question phrases					
7. Comparative structures					
8. Prepositional phrases					
9. Sentence and discourse structure					
10. Subordinate clauses					
11. Conditional clauses					
12. Relative clauses					
13. Concrete versus abstract or impersonal presentations					
14. Negation					

Figure 7.2. Rubric for rating level of linguistic complexity. (From Abedi, J. [2006]. Language issues in item development. In S.M. Downing & T.M. Haladyna [Eds.], *Handbook of test development* [p. 391]. Mahwah, NJ: Lawrence Erlbaum Associates; adapted by permission.)

The first step in examining linguistic comparability is to identify which of the linguistic features are present in the item and the seriousness of their effects. A rating system for evaluating the level of linguistic complexity of test items was developed. The rating system consists of two different rating scales: 1) an analytical scale, and 2) a holistic scale. Test items in AA-MAS and general assessments may be rated on both scales, and then the ratings can be compared across the AA-MAS and the general assessment. We will elaborate on each of these rating approaches below:

Analytical Rating

Figure 7.2 presents a rubric for rating the level of complexity on each of the 14 features for each test item. The ratings are based on a 5-point Likert scale, with 1 indicating no complexity present with respect for that particular feature and 5 suggesting a high level of linguistic complexity with that feature. Abedi and Lord (2001) combined the 48 linguistic features mentioned above into 14 general categories for ease of rating linguistic complexities. Ratings were performed on the overall

14 categories. Each test item receives 14 ratings, one for each linguistic feature. For example, with respect to linguistic feature number 1 (word frequency/familiarity), if the words used in the item are very familiar and frequently being used, then the item receives a rating of 1 (*no complexity*). However, if the word is unfamiliar, or being used less frequently, then depending on the level of unfamiliarity and low frequency, it receives a rating of between 2 and 5. Judgments on the familiarity/frequency of the word can be made based on sources such as The *American Heritage Word Frequency Book* (Carroll, 1971) and the *Frequency Analysis of English Usage: Lexicon and Grammar* (Francis & Kucera, 1982). The highest rating of 5 in this example would refer to a word that is extremely unfamiliar and rarely occurring.

Holistic Rating

Similar to the ratings that are assigned based on the analytical procedure, this rating is on a 5-point Likert scale, with 1 representing items with no or minimal level of linguistic complexity and 5 showing an item with an extremely complex linguistic structure. Table 7.1 shows the holistic rating rubric. As Table 7.1 shows, a test item free of linguistic complexity (with a rating of 1) does not suffer from any of the 14 linguistic complexity threats. For example, the item uses familiar or frequently used words, the words as well as sentences in these items are generally shorter, there are no complex conditional and/or adverbial clauses, and there are no passive voices or abstract presentations. On the contrary, an item with a severe level of linguistic complexity contains all or many sources of threats.

Ratings on linguistic modification (both analytical and holistic) provide diagnostic information on the linguistic barriers present in test items. This information may help item writers or test developers to identify *problem* items. These items can then be corrected for such problems. Because linguistic modification ratings are on a Likert scale, median ratings can be computed and can be used for decisions on how the items should be modified. Different patterns of linguistic complexity across the two assessments may lead to the conclusion that the two assessments are not linguistically comparable (for a detailed description of linguistic complexity assessment, see Abedi, 2010).

Basic Text Features

Text Format and Text Features

This feature includes typeface and point size, passage and item placement on page(s), and the relevance and clarity of all visuals within a passage. It is important to consider typeface and point size when deter-

Table 7.1.   Holistic item rating rubric

	Quality
1	**Exemplary item** Sample features: • Familiar or frequently used words; word length generally shorter • Short sentences and limited prepositional phrases • Concrete item and a narrative structure • No complex conditional or adverbial clauses • No passive voice or abstract or impersonal presentations
2	**Adequate item** Sample features: • Familiar or frequently used words; short to moderate word length • Moderate sentence length with a few prepositional phrases • Concrete item • No subordinate, conditional, or adverbial clauses • No passive voice or abstract or impersonal presentations
3	**Weak item** Sample features: • Relatively unfamiliar or seldom used words • Long sentence(s) • Abstract concept(s) • Complex sentence/conditional tense/adverbial clause • A few passive voice or abstract or impersonal presentations
4	**Attention item** Sample features: • Unfamiliar or seldom used words • Long or complex sentence • Abstract item • Difficult subordinate, conditional, or adverbial clause • Passive voice/abstract or impersonal presentations
5	**Problematic item** Sample features: • Highly unfamiliar or seldom used words • Very long or complex sentence • Abstract item • Very difficult subordinate, conditional, or adverbial clause • Many passive voice and abstract or impersonal presentations

From Abedi, J. (2006). Language issues in item development. In S.M. Downing & T.M. Haladyna (Eds.), *Handbook of test development* (p. 392). Mahwah, NJ: Lawrence Erlbaum Associates; adapted by permission.

mining whether a test passage and its items are accessible to students with low visibility. Similarly, pages with excessive blank space or, conversely, with small margins may unfairly affect students with low visibility. Additionally, it is essential to determine whether the visuals (graphs, tables, charts, and pictures) within a passage are relevant, meaning that they are needed to answer the item, and if they are clearly labeled. Visuals that are not relevant or clearly labeled may increase the cognitive load of perceiving information for students with disabilities.

Type of Passage/Item in Reading Comprehension Assessment

This feature identifies the genre of the passage (descriptive, narrative, expository, poetry, or persuasive). This feature also determines whether a test item is informational or inferential. Items that are informational can be answered using only slightly paraphrased or verbatim information that is found in the passage, whereas items that are inferential require the student to combine information from the text together with their own background knowledge in order to recognize implicit relationships and outcomes. Therefore, items that are inferential may significantly increase the cognitive load for students with disabilities and thus hinder students' abilities to accurately display their understanding of the passage.

Comparability in Terms of Depth of Knowledge

Depth-of-knowledge (DOK) comparability is confirmed if what is elicited from students on the assessments is as cognitively demanding as what students are expected to know and do as stated in the state and national standards. DOK consistency is defined as the level of consistency between the cognitive demands of standards and the cognitive demands of the assessment items. If between 40% and 50% of the assessment items are at or above the DOK levels of the objectives, then the DOK consistency criterion is "weakly" met. Webb (1999) defined four levels of cognitive complexity when comparing the cognitive demands of the standards and assessment items. They are as follows: Level 1 (Recall), Level 2 (Skills and Concepts), Level 3 (Strategic Thinking), and Level 4 (Extended Thinking).

Level 1 (Recall)

Level 1 items require students to use simple skills or abilities. Examples include recall of information. Key words that signify Level 1 include *identify, recall, measure,* and *recognize.*

Level 2 (Skill/Concept)

Level 2 items demand a higher level of cognitive complexity as compared with Level 1 items. Assessment items at Level 2 require some decision making on how to approach problems or activities. For example, Level 2 key words for math include terms such as *classify, estimate, compare,* and *organize.* These actions imply more than one step.

Level 3 (Strategic Thinking)

Assessment items at this level require reasoning, planning, and using evidence, which are at a higher level of thinking than the previous two levels. In most instances, students are required to explain their thinking at this level. The cognitive demands at Level 3 are complex and abstract. An activity, for example, that has more than one possible answer and requires students to justify the response they give would most likely be at Level 3.

Level 4 (Extended Thinking)

Level 4 items require the highest level of cognitive demand in Webb's model of DOK. This level demands complex reasoning, planning, developing, and thinking. Assessment items at Level 4 may include activities such as designing and conducting experiments, analyzing and interpreting results, combining and synthesizing ideas into new concepts, and critiquing experimental designs (Webb et al., 2006).

Comparability Issues in the Accommodated Assessments for Students with Disabilities

Many different forms of accommodations are being used for students with different types of disabilities. However, some of these accommodations may alter the construct being measured; therefore, the issues concerning comparability of accommodated and nonaccommodated assessments are of paramount importance to this chapter because many of the features that are incorporated in AA-MAS are being used as a form of accommodation for students with disabilities.

The most commonly used accommodations for students with disabilities are using Braille, using computerized assessments, dictating of responses to a scribe, giving extended time, providing an interpreter for instructions, marking answers in test booklets, reading aloud test items, reading or simplifying test directions, and providing test breaks (Thurlow, House, Boys, Scott, & Ysseldyke, 2000). We present a summary of studies that have examined the validity of assessments under these accommodations. As can be seen from these summaries, research evidence suggests that some of these accommodations alter the construct being measured. For others, however, there is not much evidence to judge the validity of assessments using those accommodations. Issues concerning validity of accommodations are directly related to comparability of accommodated and nonaccommodated assessments. When an accommodation is not valid (i.e., when it alters the construct being measured), then the outcomes of assessments under this accommodation are not comparable with assessments conducted under standard conditions with no accommodations provided.

Braille is used for students with blindness or significant visual impairments. Developing a Braille version of the test may be more difficult for some items than others. It would be challenging to use Braille items with diagrams and special symbols (Bennett, Rock, & Kaplan, 1987; Bennett, Rock, & Novatkoski, 1989; Coleman, 1990). Thurlow and Bolt (2001) recommend using Braille for students with severe visual impairments. Also, Braille is recommended to be paired with extended time (Thurlow & Bolt, 2000).

Computerized assessment can be used for students with physical impairments who have difficulty in responding to items in paper-and-pencil format. Some studies suggest that this accommodation is effective in increasing the performance of students with disabilities (e.g., see Russell, 1999; Russell & Haney, 1997; Russell & Plati, 2001). Other studies did not find computerized assessment to be effective (MacArthur & Graham, 1987) or even as effective as traditional assessments (Hollenbeck, Tindal, Stieber, & Harniss, 1999; Thurlow & Bolt, 2001; Varnhagen & Gerber, 1984; Watkins & Kush, 1988).

Extended time is one of the most commonly used and most controversial forms of accommodation for students with different types of disabilities (SWD). Some studies found that extended time affects the performance of both SWD and non-SWD students and, therefore, makes the validity of this accommodation suspect. Similarly, Thurlow and Bolt (2001) expressed concern regarding the validity of this accommodation. Chiu and Pearson (1999) found extended time to be an effective accommodation for students with disabilities, particularly for those with learning disabilities. Some studies found extended time to help students with disabilities in math (Chiu & Pearson, 1999; Gallina, 1989). However, other studies did not show an effect of extended time on students with disabilities (Fuchs, Fuchs, Eaton, Hamlett, & Karns, 2000; Marquart, 2000; Munger & Loyd, 1991). Studies on the effect of extended time on language arts did not find this accommodation to be effective (Fuchs, Fuchs, Eaton, Hamlett, Binkley, & Crouch, 2000; Munger & Loyd, 1991). Thus research on this particular accommodation produced inconsistent results. More studies are needed to make a firm recommendation regarding the use of this accommodation.

The *interpreter for instructions* accommodation is recommended for students with hearing impairments. Ray (1982) found that adaptations in the directions help deaf children score the same as other students (see also Sullivan, 1982). Thurlow and Bolt (2001) recommended that using an interpreter for instructions may be beneficial to students with hearing impairments. However, not much information exists on the validity of this accommodation.

The *marking answers in test booklet* accommodation can be used for students with difficulties in mobility coordination. Some studies on the effectiveness of this accommodation did not find a significant difference between those tested under this accommodation and those using separate answer sheets (Rogers, 1983; Tindal, Heath, Hollenbeck, Almond, & Harniss, 1998). However, other studies found lower performance for students using this accommodation (Mick, 1989). Because a majority of studies did not show a performance increase as a result of this accommodation, it would be safe to say that this may not have much of an impact on the construct being measured.

A *read aloud test* is used for students with learning disabilities and students with physical or visual impairments. Although some studies found this accommodation to be valid in math assessments (Tindal et al., 1998), there have been concerns over the use of this accommodation in reading and listening comprehension tests (e.g., see Burns, 1998; Phillips, 1994), because the construct being measured may be changed and thus the validity of the assessment is affected (e.g., see Bielinski, Thurlow, Ysseldyke, Freidebach, & Freidebach, 2001; Meloy, Deville, & Frisbie, 2000).

The *reading or simplifying test directions* accommodation is appropriate for students with reading/learning disabilities. A study by Elliot, Kratochwill, and McKevitt (2001) suggested that this accommodation affects the performance of both students with disabilities (63.4%) and students without disabilities (42.9%), thus expressing concerns over the validity of this accommodation.

Test breaks can help students with different forms of disabilities. In a study, DiCerbo, Stanley, Roberts, and Blanchard (2001) found that students receiving test breaks obtained scores significantly higher than those obtained under standard testing conditions and that middle- and low-ability readers benefited more from this accommodation than high-ability readers. However, another study (Walz, Albus, Thompson, & Thurlow, 2000) found that students with disabilities did not benefit from a multiple-day test administration, whereas students without disabilities did benefit. These results show quite the opposite of what is expected of valid accommodations.

The summary of research presented above on some of the commonly used accommodations shows a lack of consensus regarding validity and comparability of accommodated assessments as compared with general assessments with no accommodations provided. As indicated earlier in this chapter, when accommodations alter the construct being measured, the accommodated assessment outcomes are not comparable with the nonaccommodated assessments.

The issues of comparability of accommodated and nonaccommodated assessments are relevant to our discussion of comparability between AA-MAS and regular state assessments for two main reasons.

First, with AA-MAS, some students with disabilities still need accommodations that are recommended by their IEP team. Therefore, knowledge of comparability of accommodated and nonaccommodated AA-MAS would help states to provide comparability evidence to peer reviewers and other authorities. Second, the concept of comparability is well defined in accommodation studies. Although there may not be sufficient literature on the comparability of all accommodations used by states, we have enough research to help us design comprehensive studies for examining comparability between various assessments.

SUMMARY AND CONCLUSIONS

Comparability of the outcome of AA-MAS with general state assessments is one of the most fundamental aspects of the assessment and accountability system for students with disabilities who are eligible for taking AA-MAS. The comparability issues may seriously impact many aspects of the academic careers of these students (often referred as the 2% group), including their instruction, promotion, and graduation. Literature presents the comparability argument mostly in terms of psychometric and content comparability (e.g., see AERA et al., 1999; DePascale, 2009b). Although content and psychometric comparability provides convincing evidence on the comparability of AA-MAS with the general state assessments, looking at a more comprehensive picture on comparability will provide states with the information they need to present a strong justification for development and use of AA-MAS.

In this chapter, we have presented different criteria for judging and examining the comparability between AA-MAS and state general assessments. These criteria include comparability with respect to content and construct, alignment with the state content standards, classical measurement concept of comparability, psychometrics, linguistics, DOK, and accommodations. Such discussions and guidelines could help states in developing and validating AA-MAS assessments in different content areas. Useful information and guidelines are also provided by researchers and practitioners for developing AA-MAS tests. For example, in a report by the Council of Chief State School Officers (2007), guidelines are provided on strategies for states to prepare for and respond to peer reviewers. Similarly, researchers provided recommendations on the use of cognitive interviews in the design and development of AA-MAS (Almond et al., in press). Literature also provides a summary of research on item and test alteration focusing on AA-MAS, along with guidelines on the nature and implementation of these alterations (Kettler & Almond, 2009). Although many test publishers and states provided comparability evidence on a few of these aspects, this chapter may help test developers to provide a comprehensive plan for comparability of any future AA-MAS development.

In general, to respond to the mandate of inclusion of students with disabilities, states must be able to present evidence that alternate assessment outcomes are comparable with the outcomes of general assessments. Lack of comparability between the alternate and general assessments jeopardizes the academic career of students with disabilities in many different ways, including the promotion and graduation of these students.

Although the proposed criteria for examining comparability in this chapter apply to different content areas, the application of some of these criteria may be slightly different across different content areas. For example, the linguistic comparability concept may apply differently to content areas in which language is the target of measurement (e.g., reading/language arts) than in areas in which unnecessary linguistic complexity may be considered as a construct-irrelevant source (e.g., math and science).

A major application of the comparability discussion may be on the type of credential that is most appropriate for students at the end of secondary school. If the comparability between AA-MAS and general state assessments can be established, then it would be reasonable to recommend credentials for students with disabilities (particularly for those eligible for the AA-MAS) that are similar to those recommended for students without disabilities. A report by the National Center for Educational Outcomes (Wiener, 2006) presents one alternative way to meet diploma requirements using an AA-GLAS rather than an AA-MAS.

GUIDELINES FOR EXAMINING COMPARABILITY OF AA-MAS: HOW MUCH COMPARABILITY IS NECESSARY?

It would be extremely challenging, if not impossible, to establish comparability between the two assessments in all areas discussed in this chapter. Therefore, the main question is in which areas and to what extent is evidence needed to suggest the AA-MAS outcome is comparable with the general assessment outcome. To answer this question, we define comparability in two types: features that are necessary and are required in order to assume comparability across the two measures, and features that are desired but not absolutely necessary in establishing comparability between the two assessments.

Necessary Features for Establishing Comparability Between AA-MAS and General Assessments

The decision regarding which comparability features are absolutely necessary and which are desired may be more speculative, because there is not enough research evidence on which to base a decision.

Therefore, based on existing literature and based on the author's own professional judgment, the following features are deemed to be necessary as the minimum requirement to establish comparability between AA-MAS and regular state assessments.

Content and Construct Comparability

This feature is one of the most important aspects of comparability. This level of comparability can be established by applying a combination of different approaches, such as experts review and alignment to the state content standards. In conducting expert reviews, states may form a team of experts in the targeted content area to judge the level of comparability of AA-MAS with the regular state assessment. The team should include experts in the area of assessment and accommodation of students with disabilities focusing on the 2% population, content area experts, and test item writers. A state could develop and validate a rubric for assessing comparability. The rubric validation process should include focus groups and cognitive labs to assure clarity of instruction for rating comparability. The rubric may use a 5-point Likert scale for rating comparability. A state may then decide on the level of exact or within-point agreement between AA-MAS and general assessment ratings.

Scale and Score Comparability

As recommended by the *Standards for Educational and Psychological Testing* (AERA et al., 1999, p. 52), score comparability can be roughly achieved by converting scores from the AA-MAS and general assessments on the same scale. Although such conversion is extremely challenging, it could provide useful information.

Depth of Knowledge Comparability

One could expect a fair level of comparability between two assessments measuring the same content if they measure the same level of depth of knowledge. As in the case of content and construct comparability discussed above, a state can form a team of experts to judge the level of depth of knowledge across the two assessments. Following Webb's methodology (Webb, 1999), ratings of the depth of knowledge can be provided and compared. A cut point on the level of consistency between ratings of the depth of knowledge of the two assessments can then be used to judge the comparability.

Accommodation Comparability

Accommodated assessment outcomes could be invalid if the accommodations alter the construct. Many students with disabilities require accommodations based on their IEPs. However, research on the validity of accommodations for students with disabilities is very limited. A state may compare accommodations used under the two assessment conditions and provide evidence based on the literature that there are no validity concerns that could differentially affect validity of accommodated assessments under the two testing conditions.

Desired Features for Establishing Comparability Between AA-MAS and General Assessments

Psychometric Comparability

A comparison between the overall psychometric properties of the two assessments may shed light on the comparability issues. It would be informative to compare the reliability and validity coefficients of the two assessments. For example, a comparison between the internal consistency coefficients (Cronbach's alpha) between the two assessments can be done. Similarly, criterion-related validity coefficients of the two assessments can be compared. For example, the structural relationships between parcels of items and the total test, as well as the relationships between test scores and external criteria, can be compared using multiple group confirmatory factor analyses, as elaborated in Figure 7.1. Examining a set of invariance between the structural relationships of the two assessments may shed light on the comparability of the two assessments.

Comparability Between Linguistic Structure of the Two Assessments

Different features of linguistic complexities that may impact the validity of assessments are discussed earlier in this chapter. A comparison between analytical ratings (see Figure 7.2) and holistic ratings (see Table 7.1) would provide supporting evidence regarding the comparability of the assessments.

Comparability Between the Two Assessments on Basic Text Features

Comparability between the basic features of the two assessments may provide additional evidence of comparability. It would be helpful if the text features such as the presentation of the assessments (e.g., computer versus paper and pencil), formatting, fonts, tables and charts, and pagination of the two assessments are similar. For example, two assessments may not be highly comparable if one uses complex tables and charts or crowded pages and the other uses simple tables and charts with a large point size and less crowded pages.

REFERENCES

Abedi, J. (2002). Standardized achievement tests and English language learners: Psychometrics issues. *Educational Assessment, 8*(3), 231–257.

Abedi, J. (2006). Language issues in item development. In S.M. Downing & T.M. Haladyna (Eds.), *Handbook of test development*. Mahwah, NJ: Lawrence Erlbaum Associates.

Abedi, J. (2007). English language learners with disabilities. In C. Cahlan-Laitusis & L. Cook (Eds.), *Accommodating students with disabilities on state assessments: What works?* (pp. 23–35). Arlington, VA: Council for Exceptional Children.

Abedi, J. (2010). Linguistic factors in the assessment of English language learners. In G. Walford, E. Tucker, & M. Viswanathan (Eds.), *The Sage handbook of measurement* (pp. 129–149). Oxford, England: University of Oxford/Sage Publications.

Abedi, J., Leon, S., & Kao, J. (2008). *Examining differential item functioning in reading assessments for students with disabilities.* Los Angeles: University of California, Center for the Study of Evaluation/National Center for Research on Evaluation, Standards, and Student Testing.

Abedi, J., Leon, S., & Mirocha, J. (2003). *Impact of student language background on content-based performance: Analyses of extant data* (CSE Tech. Rep. No. 603). Los Angeles: University of California, National Center for Research on Evaluation, Standards, and Student Testing.

Abedi, J., & Lord, C. (2001). The language factor in mathematics tests. *Applied Measurement in Education, 14*(3), 219–234.

Achieve. (2006). *An alignment analysis of Washington State's college readiness mathematics standards with various local placement tests.* Washington, DC: Author.

Allen, M.J., & Yen, W.M. (1979). *Introduction to measurement theory.* Monterey, CA: Brooks/Cole.

Almond, P.J., Cameto, R., Johnstone, C.J., Laitusis, C., Lazarus, S., Nagle, K., et al. (in press). *Cognitive interview methods in reading test and item design and development for alternate assessments based on modified academic achievement standards (AA-MAS)* (white paper). Dover, NH: Measured Progress and Menlo Park, CA: SRI International.

American Educational Research Association, American Psychological Association, & National Council on Measurement in Education. (1999). *Standards for educational and psychological testing.* Washington, DC: American Psychological Association.

Bennett, R.E., Rock, D.A., & Kaplan, B.A. (1987). SAT differential item performance for nine handicapped groups. *Journal of Educational Measurement, 24*(1), 44–55.

Bennett, R.E., Rock, D.A., & Novatkoski, I. (1989). Differential item functioning on the SAT-M Braille Edition. *Journal of Educational Measurement, 26*(1), 67–79.

Bielinski, J., Thurlow, M., Ysseldyke, J., Freidebach, J., & Freidebach, M. (2001). *Read-aloud accommodation: Effects on multiple-choice reading & math items (Technical Report 31).* Minneapolis, MN: University of Minnesota, National Center on Educational Outcomes.

Brennan, R.L. (2001). *Generalizability theory.* New York: Springer-Verlag.

Burns, E. (1998). *Test accommodations for students with disabilities.* Springfield, IL: Charles C Thomas.

Burton, E., & Linn, R.L. (1994). Comparability across assessments: Lessons from the use of moderation procedures in England. In *CSE Technical Report 369.* Los Angeles: National Center for Research on Evaluation, Standards, and Student Testing.

Carroll, J.B. (1971). *The American heritage word frequency book.* Boston: Houghton Mifflin.

Chiu, C.W.T., & Pearson, P.D. (1999). *Synthesizing the effects of test accommodations for special education and limited English proficiency students.* Paper presented at the National Conference on Large Scale Assessment, Snowbird, UT.

Coleman, P.J. (1990). Exploring visually handicapped children's understanding of length (math concepts). (Doctoral dissertation, The Florida State University, 1990). *Dissertation Abstracts International, 51,* 0071.

Cortiella, C. (2007). *Learning opportunities for your child through alternate assessments: Alternate assessments based on modified academic achievement standards.* Minneapolis, MN: University of Minnesota, National Center on Educational Outcomes.

Cortina, J.M. (1993). What is coefficient alpha? An examination of theory and application. *Journal of Applied Psychology, 78,* 98–104.

Council of Chief State School Officers. (2007). ref to come in Revises.

DePascale, C. (2009a). Evaluating linguistic modifications: An examination of the comparability of a plain English mathematics assessment. In P.C. Winter (Ed.), *Evaluating the comparability of scores from achievement test variation.* Washington, DC: Council of Chief State School Officers.

DePascale, C. (2009b). *Modified tests for modified achievement standards: Examining the comparability of a 2% test.* Dover, NH: National Center for the Improvement of Educational Assessment.

DiCerbo, K., Stanley, E., Roberts, M., & Blanchard, J. (April, 2001). *Attention and standardized reading test performance: Implications for accommodation.* Paper presented at the annual meeting of the National Association of School Psychologists, Washington, DC.

Eckhout, T., Larsen, A., Plake, B., & Smith, D. (2007). Aligning a state's alternative standards to regular core content standards in reading and mathematics: A case study. *Applied Measurement in Education, 20*(1), 79–100.

Elliott, S., Kratochwill, T., & McKevitt, B. (2001). Experimental analysis of the effects of testing accommodations on the scores of students with and without disabilities. *Journal of School Psychology, 31*(1), 3–24.

Elliott, S.N., & Roach, A.T. (2007). Alternate assessments of students with significant disabilities: Alternative approaches, common technical challenges. *Applied Measurement in Education, 20,* 301–333.

Elosua, P., & Lopez-Jauregui, A. (2008). Equating between linguistically different tests: Consequences for assessment. *Journal of Experimental Education, 76*(4), 387–402.

Filbin, J. (2008). Lessons from the initial peer review of alternate assessments based on modified achievement standards. Washington, DC: U.S. Department of Education, Office of Elementary and Secondary Education.

Francis, W.N., & Kucera, H. (1982). *Frequency analysis of English usage: Lexicon and grammar.* Boston: Houghton Mifflin.

Fuchs, L.S., Fuchs, D., Eaton, S.B., Hamlett, C., & Karns, K. (2000). Supplementing teacher judgments about test accommodations with objective data sources. *School Psychology Review, 29*(1), 65–85.

Fuchs, L.S., Fuchs, D., Eaton, S.B., Hamlett, C., Binkley, E., & Crouch, R. (2000). Using objective data source to enhance teacher judgments about test accommodations. *Exceptional Children, 67*(1), 67–81.

Gallina, N.B. (1989). Tourette's syndrome children: Significant achievement and social behavior variables (Tourette's syndrome, attention deficit hyperactivity disorder) (Doctoral dissertation, City University of New York, 1989). *Dissertation Abstracts International, 50,* 0046.

Gong, B. (1999). *Relationship between student performance on the MCAS (Massachusetts Comprehensive Assessment System) and other tests.* Dover, NH: National Center for the Improvement of Educational Assessment.

Gong, B. (2007). *Considerations in designing a "2% Assessment" (AA-MAS): A beginning framework and examples of conceptual possibilities.* Paper presented at the Special Education Partnership Conference on Alternate Assessments Based on Modified Academic Achievement Standards, Washington, DC.

Gong, R., & Blank, R. (2002). *Designing school accountability systems: Towards a framework and process.* Washington, DC: The Council of Chief State School Officers.

Gong, B., & Marion, S. (2006). *Dealing with flexibility in assessment for students with significant cognitive disabilities.* Dover, NH: National Center for the Improvement of Educational Assessment.

Haladyna, T.M., & Downing, S.M. (2004). Construct-irrelevant variance in high-stakes testing. *Educational Measurement: Issues and Practice, 23*(1), 17–27.

Hollenbeck, K., Tindal, G., Stieber, S., & Harniss, M. (1999). *Handwritten vs. word processed statewide compositions: Do judges rate them differently?* Eugene, OR: University of Oregon, BRT.

Individuals with Disabilities Education Improvement Act (IDEA) of 2004, PL 108-446, 20 U.S.C. §§ 1400 *et seq.*

Karvonen, M., & Huynh, H. (2007). Relationship between IEP characteristics and test scores on alternate assessment for students with significant cognitive disabilities. *Applied Measurement in Education, 20*(3), 273–300.

Kettler, R., & Almond, P. (2009). *Improving reading measurement for alternate assessment: Suggestions for designing research on item and test alterations.* Arlington, VA: Symposium on Alternate Assessments Based on Modified Achievement Standards in Reading, SRI International/Measured Progress.

Lazarus, S.S., Rogers, C., Cormier, D., & Thurlow, M.L. (2008). *States' participation guidelines for alternate assessments based on modified academic achievement standards (AA-MAS) in 2008* (Synthesis Report 71). Minneapolis, MN: University of Minnesota, National Center on Educational Outcomes.

Lazarus, S.S., Thurlow, M. L., Christensen, L.L., & Cormier, D. (2007). *States' alternate assessments based on modified achievement standards (AA-MAS) in 2007* (Synthesis Report 67). Minneapolis, MN: University of Minnesota, National Center on Educational Outcomes.

Linn, R. (1993). Linking results of distinct assessments. *Applied Measurement in Education, 6*(1), 83–102.

Linn, R.L., & Gronlund, N.E. (1995). *Measurement and assessment in teaching* (7th ed.). Englewood Cliffs, NJ: Pearson Merrill.

Lowrey, K.A., Drasgow, E., Renzaglia, A., & Chezan, L. (2009). Impact of alternate assessment on curricula for students with severe disabilities. *Assessment for Effective Intervention, 32*(4), 244–253.

MacArthur, C.A., & Graham, S. (1987). Learning disabled students' composing under three methods of text production: Handwriting, word processing, and dictation. *The Journal of Special Education, 21*(3), 22–42.

Marion, S. (2006, October 10). *Introduction to comparability.* Presented at the

Seminar on Inclusive Assessment, Denver, CO.

Marquart, A. (2000). *The use of extended time as an accommodation on a standardized mathematics test: An investigation of effects on scores and perceived consequences for students of various skill levels.* Paper presented at the annual meeting of the Council of Chief State School Officers, Snowbird, UT.

Meloy, L.L., Deville, C., & Frisbie, C. (2000). *The effect of a reading accommodation on standardized test scores of learning disabled and non learning disabled students.* Paper presented at the annual meeting of the National Council on Measurement in Education, New Orleans, LA.

Messick, S. (1984). The psychology of educational measurement. *Journal of Educational Measurement, 21,* 215–237.

Mick, L.B. (1989). Measurement effects of modifications in minimum competency test formats for exceptional students. *Measurement and Evaluation in Counseling and Development, 22,* 31–36.

Mislevy, R. (1992). *Linking educational assessments: Concepts, issues, methods, and prospects.* Princeton, NJ: ETS Policy Information Center.

Moore, A.D., & O'Neal, S. (2004). *A study of the alignment between the New Mexico K–12 Content Standards, Benchmarks, and Performance Standards and the draft state assessment* (Unpublished research study). Santa Fe, NM: New Mexico State Department of Education.

Munger, G.F., & Loyd, B.H. (1991). Effect of speededness on test performance of handicapped and nonhandicapped examinees. *Journal of Educational Research, 85*(1), 53–57.

No Child Left Behind Act of 2001, PL 107-110, 115 Stat. 1425, 20 U.S.C. §§ 6301 *et seq.*

Olson, B., Mead, R., & Payne, D. (2002). *A report of the standard setting method for alternate assessments for students with significant disabilities* (Synthesis Report 47). Minneapolis, MN: University of Minnesota, National Center on Educational Outcomes.

Perez, J.V. (1980). Procedural adaptations and format modifications in minimum competency testing of learning disabled students: A clinical investigation (Doctoral dissertation, University of South Florida, 1980). *Dissertation Abstracts International, 41,* 0206.

Phillips, S.E. (1994). High stakes testing accommodations: Validity vs. disabled rights. *Applied Measurement in Education, 7*(2), 93–120.

Rabinowitz, S., & Schroeder, C. (2006). Creating aligned standards and assessment systems. Washington, DC: The Council of Chief State School Officers.

Ray, S.R. (1982). Adapting the WISC-R for deaf children. *Diagnostique, 7,* 147–157.

Roach, A.T. (2005). Alternate assessment as the "ultimate accommodation": Four challenges for policy and practice. *Assessment for Effective Intervention, 31*(1), 73–78.

Roach, A.T., & Elliott, S.N. (2004). *Alignment analysis and standard setting procedures for alternate assessments.* WCER Working Papers, No. 2004–1. Retrieved February 18, 2010, from http://www.wcer.wisc.edu/publications/working Papers/Working_Paper_No_2004_1.swf

Rogers, W.T. (1983). Use of separate answer sheets with hearing impaired and deaf school age students. *B.C. Journal of Special Education, 7*(1), 63–72.

Russell, M. (1999). Testing writing on computers: A follow-up study comparing performance on computer and on paper. *Educational Policy Analysis Archives, 7*(20). Retrieved February 18, 2010, from http://epaa.asu.edu/ojs/article/view/555

Russell, M., & Haney, W. (1997). Testing writing on computers: An experiment comparing student performance on tests conducted via computer and via paper-and-pencil. *Educational Policy Analysis Archives, 5*(3). Retrieved February 18, 2010, from http://epaa.asu.edu/ojs/article/view/604

Russell, M., & Plati, T. (2001). Effects of computer versus paper administration of a state-mandated writing assessment. *TCRecord.org*. Retrieved January 23, 2001, from http://www.tcrecord.org/PrintContent.asp?ContentID=10709

Sato, E. (2007). *A guide to linguistic modification: Increasing English language learner access to academic content.* Washington, DC: The U.S. Department of Education—LEP Partnership.

Shavelson, R.J., & Webb, N.M. (1991). *Generalizability theory: A primer.* Newbury Park, CA: Sage Publications.

Sheinker, J., & Erpenbach, W.J. (2007). *Alternate assessments for students with significant cognitive disabilities: Strategies for states' preparation for and response to peer review.* Washington, DC: Council of Chief State School Officers.

Subkoviak, J.J. (1988). A practitioner's guide to computation and interpretation of reliability indices for mastery test. *Journal of Educational Measurement, 25*(1), 47–55.

Sullivan, P.M. (1982). Administration modifications on the WISC-R Performance Scale with different categories of deaf children. *American Annals of the Deaf, 127*(6), 780–788.

Thompson, S., Lazarus, S., Clapper, A., & Thurlow, M. (2006). Adequate yearly progress of students with disabilities: Competencies for teachers. *Teacher Education and Special Education, 29*(2), 137–147.

Thorndike, R.M. (2005). *Measurement and evaluation in psychology and education.* Upper Saddle River, NJ: Pearson Merrill.

Thurlow, M., & Bolt, S. (2001). *Empirical support for accommodations most often allowed in state policy* (Synthesis Report 41). Minneapolis, MN: University of Minnesota, National Center for Educational Outcomes.

Thurlow, M., House, A., Boys, C., Scott, D., & Ysseldyke, J. (2000). *State participation and accommodation policies for students with disabilities: 1999 Update* (Synthesis Report 33). Minneapolis, MN: University of Minnesota, National Center on Educational Outcomes.

Tindal, G. (2005). *Alignment of alternate assessments using the Webb system.* Washington, DC: Council of Chief State School Officers.

Tindal, G., Heath, B., Hollenbeck, K., Almond, P., & Harniss, M. (1998). Accommodating students with disabilities on large-scale tests: An empirical study of student response and test administration demands. *Exceptional Children, 64*(4), 439–450.

U.S. Department of Education. (2007). *Modified academic achievement standards, non-regulatory guidance.* Washington, DC: Author.

U.S. Department of Education. (2008). *Validity evidence for alternate assessments based on modified achievement standards.* Washington, DC: National Technical Advisory Council.

Varnhagen, S., & Gerber, M.M. (1984). Use of microcomputers for spelling assessment: Reasons to be cautious. *Learning Disability Quarterly, 7*, 266–270.

Walz, L., Albus, D., Thompson, S., & Thurlow, M. (2000). *Effect of a multiple day test accommodation on the performance of special education students* (Synthesis Report 34). Minneapolis: University of Minnesota, National Center on Educational Outcomes.

Watkins, M.W., & Kush, J.C. (1988). Assessment of academic skills of learning disabled students with classroom microcomputers. *School Psychology Review, 17*(1), 81–88.

Webb, N.L. (1999). *Alignment of science and mathematics standards and assessments in four states* (NISE Research Monograph No. 18). Madison, WI: University of Wisconsin-Madison, National Institute for Science Education, Washington, DC: Council of Chief State School Officers.

Webb, N.L., Alt, M., Ely, R., Cormier, M., Vesperman, R. (2006). The WEB Alignment Tool: Development, Refinement, and Dissemination. In: *Aligning Assessment to Guide The Learning of All Students. Six Report.* Washington, DC: Council of Chief State School Officers.

Webb, N.L. (2002). *An analysis of the alignment between mathematics standard and assessments for three states.* Paper presented at the American Educational Research Association meeting, New Orleans.

Webb, N.L., Horton, M., & O'Neal, S. (1999). *An analysis of the alignment between language arts standards and assessments for four states.* Paper presented at the American Educational Research Association meeting, New Orleans.

Welch, C., & Dunbar, S.B. (2009, July). *Developing items and assembling test forms for the alternate assessment based on modified achievement standards (AA-MAS).* NYCC white paper on the Alternate Assessment Based on Modified Achievement Standards (AA-MAS). New York: New York State Education Department. http://nycomprehensivecenter.org/docs/AA_MAS_ part3 .pdf

Wiener, D. (2006). *Alternate assessments measured against grade-level achievement standards: The Massachusetts "competency portfolio"* (Synthesis Report 59). Minneapolis, MN: University of Minnesota, National Center on Educational Outcomes.

Winter, P.C. (2009a). *Comparing apples to apples: Challenges and approaches to establishing the comparability of test variation.* Paper presented at the annual meeting of the National Council of Measurement in Education, San Diego.

Winter, P.C. (2009b). *Evaluating the comparability of scores from achievement test variation.* Washington, DC: Council of Chief State School Officers.

Wright, N., & Wendler, C. (1994). *Establishing timing limits for the new SAT for students with disabilities.* Paper presented at the Annual Meeting of the National Council on Measurement in Education, New Orleans.

Zieky, M. (1989). Methods of setting standards of performance on criterion referenced tests. *Studies in Educational Evaluation, 15*(3), 335–338.

8

Constructing a Validity Argument for Alternate Assessments Based on Modified Achievement Standards

Scott F. Marion

States are facing complex issues as they have begun developing alternate assessments based on modified achievement standards (AA-MAS). Although several researchers have been working to improve the validity evaluations of state assessments in recent years, with a more intense focus on alternate assessments based on alternate achievement standards (AA-AAS; Elliott, Compton, & Roach, 2007; Marion & Pellegrino, 2006; Rabinowitz & Sato, 2005; Schafer, 2005), these challenges are just beginning to be addressed for AA-MAS. The AA-MAS requires a more careful validity evaluation than one might undertake for either the AA-AAS or the general assessment. This is due, in part, to the uncertain conceptual framework supporting this assessment initiative, as well as the novelty of the enterprise. This does not downplay the need for validity work on the general and other alternate assessments, but rather that the lack of conceptual grounding in the case of the AA-MAS requires a thorough validity evaluation. This evaluation should provide states with information about how to improve the program or even to help the state determine whether the AA-MAS is "worth it." That is, do the benefits (instructional, assessment, accountability, and social justice) outweigh the costs, including negative unintended consequences, of implementing an AA-MAS?

Many writers of technical reports for general assessments nominally align their analyses and results with the *Standards for Educational and Psychological Testing* (American Educational Research Association [AERA], American Psychological Association [APA], & National Council on Measurement in Education [NCME], 1999), particularly when there are student or school stakes requiring that the inferences drawn from the assessment be valid, reliable, and fair (AERA et al., 1999). This is an obvious and important first step, but one that is often not fully met. Leading measurement theorists (e.g., Cronbach, Messick), including the authors of the 1985 and 1999 *Standards* (AERA et al., 1985, 1999), are clear that validity is the most important technical criterion for educational assessment. Validity is defined as the "degree to which evidence and theory support the interpretations of the test scores entailed by proposed uses of the test" (AERA et al., 1999, p. 9). In other words, test scores convey interpretations and inferences that must be verified by both empirical evidence and a logical argument.

The challenge, however, has moved from having states and test contractors conduct research/evaluation studies to investigate particular aspects of testing programs to designing systematic validity plans for evaluating the efficacy of comprehensive validity arguments. This approach requires synthesizing the various empirical results against a theory of action and validity argument (Kane, 2006). This chapter, drawing heavily on Kane (2006), outlines a framework for constructing and evaluating a validity argument for a state's AA-MAS by first briefly describing Kane's argument-based approach to validation in general and as applied to alternate assessment specifically and then presenting strategies for organizing and prioritizing validity evaluations. The last part of the chapter summarizes the types of evidence one might collect as part of such an evaluation. Examples are presented throughout the chapter to make some of these ideas more concrete.

FRAMEWORK

The proposed validity evaluation is based on a unified conception of validity centered on the inferences related to the construct, including significant attention to the social consequences of the assessment (Cronbach, 1971; Messick, 1989; Shepard, 1993). Kane's (2006) argument-based approach serves as the focus because it offers several pragmatic advantages over evaluations based on the construct model, primarily in terms of prioritizing studies and synthesizing the results of the various studies. At its simplest, Kane's approach asks the evaluator to search for and evaluate all the threats to the validity of the assessment inferences. If these threats are not substantiated, the inferences drawn from the assessment results may be supported, at least tentatively. Unfortunately, "tentatively" is the best that can be accomplished with these sorts of falsification-based endeavors. The term *validity evaluation* is used to encompass the interpretative and validity arguments (discussed next), the plan for conducting various validity studies, the studies themselves, and the evaluation of the results.

Why an Argument?

Kane's (2006) argument-based framework

> Assumes that the proposed interpretations and uses will be explicitly stated as an argument, or network of inferences and supporting assumptions, leading from observations to the conclusions and decisions. Validation involves an appraisal of the coherence of this argument and of the plausibility of its inferences and assumptions. (p. 17)

A validity argument serves to organize studies, provides a framework for analysis and synthesis, and forces critical evaluation of claims using a falsification orientation. For example, part of a validity argument for an AA-MAS should relate to the claim that the modified assessment is measuring grade-level knowledge and skills. The content-related evidence then should include information that would allow one to challenge this grade-level claim if, in fact, the test was measuring below grade-level content. An argument-based approach requires the user, developer, and/or evaluator to search for reasons why the intended inferences are not supported. Obviously, in practice one cannot search for all reasons, so there is a need to prioritize studies. There are several approaches for prioritizing the studies, but using the theory of action and classes of evidence, both discussed later, offer useful frames for thinking about how to prioritize the considerable number of potential interesting studies.

Kane's Argument-Based Framework

Kane proposed using two types of arguments: an interpretative argument and a validity argument. According to Kane (2006)

> An *interpretative argument* specifies the proposed interpretations and uses of test results by laying out the network of inferences and assumptions leading to the observed performances to the conclusions and decisions based on the performances, [while] the *validity argument* provides an evaluation of the interpretative argument. (p. 17)

In other words, the interpretative argument outlines what the user/evaluator thinks should occur (and why it should occur) as a result of the testing and related systemic endeavors, whereas the validity argument is essentially the conclusions drawn after weighing the available evidence and logic. A major advantage of Kane's approach is that it provides a more pragmatic approach to validation than the construct model. Explicitly specifying the proposed interpretations and uses of the assessment (system), developing a measurement procedure consistent with these proposed uses, and then critically evaluating the plausibility of the initial assumptions and resulting inferences is somewhat more straightforward than evaluating the validity of an assessment under a construct model. This does not mean that construct validity is not the focus of the validity evaluation. Kane's approach simply provides a different orientation and more pragmatic approach for evaluating the validity of the score inferences than under a strict construct model. The construct model is based on more of a research approach, in which one is searching for causal connections, whereas Kane's argument-based approach works from an evaluation perspective, with the goal of determining whether a program is operating as intended with minimal unintended consequences.

Kane (2006) pushed for the development of the interpretative argument in the assessment design phase. The notion of specifying purposes and uses up front and then designing an assessment to fit these intentions is certainly not a new idea. However, designing a fully coherent system built on a sound theoretical model of learning and use has been receiving more attention in the last decade, in part as a result of the publication of *Knowing What Students Know* (Pellegrino, Chudowsky, & Glaser, 2001; see also Chapter 3). Unfortunately, most assessments do not start from an explicit attention to validity in the design phase, so many current-day evaluators working with states are put in the position of having to retrofit a validity argument to the existing system. However, in the case of the AA-MAS, there is no excuse—because the work is so new—for not starting the validity work at the beginning of the design phase. For example, Chapter 3 (this volume) provides an extensive set of examples showing how understanding the ways in which students develop competence in the domain should guide assessment development.

The interpretative argument is essentially a mini-theory, as it provides a framework for interpretation and use of test scores. Like theory, the interpretative argument guides the data collection and methods for conducting the validity analyses. Most importantly, theories are falsifiable, and making the connection between the interpretative argument and mini-theory is intended to emphasize that validation is not a confirmationist exercise. It is helpful to think of the interpretative argument as a series of "if–then" statements such as, "If the student is appropriately selected to participate in the AA-MAS, then the observed score will more accurately reflect the student's grade-level knowledge and skills."

Kane (2006) noted two stages of the interpretative argument. The *development stage* focuses on the development of measurement tools and procedures, as well as the corresponding interpretative argument. Kane suggested that it is appropriate to have a confirmationist bias (a stance that favors evidence and interpretations supporting the current state of the assessment system) in this stage, because the developers (state personnel and contractors) are trying to make the program work as well as possible. During the *appraisal stage,* Kane argues that there should be more of a focus on critical evaluation of the interpretative argument. This should be a neutral and "arms-length" standpoint to provide a more convincing evaluation of the proposed interpretations and uses. However, given the uncertain conceptual foundations of the AA-MAS, it will be important to temper Kane's allowance of a confirmationist bias during any stage and consider adopting a more critical stance throughout the validity evaluation.

One of the most effective challenges to interpretative arguments (or scientific theories in general) is to propose and substantiate an alternative argument that is equally or more plausible than the proposed proposition (or hypothesis in terms of scientific theory). With AA-MAS, users must seriously consider and challenge themselves with competing alternative explanations for test scores. For example, one might want to propose (and confirm) that increases in students scoring at the proficient level on the AA-MAS who were not proficient previously on the general assessment reflects the fact that the modifications made on the AA-MAS allowed the student to better show what they know on the same constructs. However, the evaluator must consider plausible alternative hypotheses, such as that increases in students scoring at the proficient level on the AA-MAS who were not proficient previously on the general assessment might be due to developing an easier test so that students answered more items correctly, but on a reduced range of constructs and difficulty.

Bringing this back to a more simple and pragmatic level, test validation is the process of offering assertions (propositions) about a test or a testing program and then collecting data and posing logical arguments to refute those assertions. Using the assertion and alternate hypothesis in the previous example, the evaluator should design studies that evaluate the rigor of the test using some form of cognitive interview to judge whether student responses reflect differences in demonstrated knowledge and skills when comparing the general and modified assessments. The evaluator would then analyze these data in light of both the original and alternative hypotheses. In essence, validity evaluators are continually trying to challenge the supportability of the claims put forth about the testing program.

VALUES AND CONSEQUENCES

Kane (2006) and others (e.g., Shepard, 1993) suggested that the evaluator must attend to values and consequences when evaluating a decision procedure such as when a testing program is used as a policy instrument, as is the case with essentially all state tests. When conducting such a validity evaluation, the values inherent in the testing program must be made explicit, and the consequences of the decisions as a result of test scores must be evaluated.

There might be a lingering theoretical debate regarding whether consequences are integral to construct validity, but most leading validity theorists (e.g., Cronbach, 1971; Lane & Stone, 2002; Linn, Baker, & Dunbar, 1991; Messick, 1989, 1995; Shepard, 1997) have argued convincingly that consequences are as much a part of validity as is content or any other source of evidence. However, whether or not one agrees with this view of validity, alternate assessments are used for important policy decisions, and the consequences of these decisions must be considered in validity evaluations. This is especially true when evaluating the validity of an AA-MAS; stakeholders and evaluators must be particularly attentive to unintended negative consequences that may arise from lower expectations or other potential denied/reduced opportunities for grade-level instruction.

GUIDING PHILOSOPHY, PURPOSES, AND USES

It has become axiomatic to say that the validity of an assessment (actually the inferences from the assessment scores) can be judged only in the context of specified purposes and uses. Furthermore, the guiding philosophy must be considered when evaluating the validity of the AA-MAS. The term *guiding philosophy* is used here in the same way that Quenemoen uses it in Chapter 1. It is meant to describe a particular orientation, set of assumptions, and beliefs about a particular program or policy. For example, if state leaders believe that students eligible for the AA-MAS can score at a level comparable to proficient on the general assessment except that their disability interacts with their chances to show what they know (and/or they have not yet been well instructed), then that would lead to certain types of assessment designs and validity arguments. On the other hand, if the leaders believe that eligible students would have little chance, even if well instructed, to score at a level comparable to the proficient score on the general assessment, then that would lead to quite a different assessment design. In any case, state leaders need to be explicit and honest about the philosophy behind their decision to develop an AA-MAS.

A state's guiding philosophy should help explain what the state envisions for the relationship among the AA-AAS, AA-MAS, and the general assessment. Most states, as well as the U.S. Department of Education regulations (2007a, 2007b), place the AA-MAS closer to the general assessment than the AA-AAS, because both are designed to measure grade-level standards, but some state policy makers apparently see the AA-MAS as a true intermediary between the AA-AAS and the general assessment. Again, it is important for the state to explicitly articulate these connections.

The purposes should be conceptually coherent with the state's guiding philosophy. For example, if the state is interested in developing the AA-MAS so that the targeted students can better show what they know, it would lead to one type of argument and theory of action. However, if the state implemented an AA-MAS in order to better align the assessment with the current learning opportunities and beliefs about how eligible students learn, it would lead to another type of validity evaluation. More perversely, some states could be implementing an AA-MAS to ease accountability pressures on schools associated with the performance of students with disabilities. However, it is doubtful that such states will be explicit about these sorts of goals.

In terms of the validity argument, uses follow from the state's guiding philosophy and purposes. For almost all states, the results of the AA-MAS will be used to determine students' achievement levels for the accountability system, particularly for adequate yearly progress (AYP) determinations. State policy makers will have to decide whether and how the results of the AA-MAS will be used for graduation or other high-stakes determinations. Many states would like these assessments to have some instructional value as well. These potential uses, discussed in considerable detail in the next chapter (Chapter 9), have significant implications for the evaluation of the validity of the AA-MAS. If the scores from the AA-MAS are to be treated as comparable for the purposes of a "regular" diploma, then certain types of comparability studies should be incorporated in the validity evaluation (see Chapter 7 for an extensive treatment of comparability). On the other hand, if participation in the AA-MAS shuts off the opportunity for a regular diploma, an evaluator should consider certain types of studies to examine the unintended negative consequences.

A THEORY OF ACTION: THE STARTING
POINT FOR AN INTERPRETATIVE ARGUMENT

Ryan (2002) and others have suggested that having state leaders (or other assessment stakeholders) lay out a more general theory of action can be a useful starting point for developing a more complete interpretative argument. This theory of action is really a simplified interpretative argument that requires the explication of the intended components of an assessment and decision system, as well as the mechanisms by which a test user could reasonably expect to get from one step to the next. Developing a theory of action for any validation, evaluation, or test development activity is a useful exercise. Given the field's lack of clarity around the AA-MAS, a well-developed theory of action is perhaps even more critical than it might be for other validation initiatives. Policy makers, developers, stakeholders, and technicians should have to very explicitly lay out why they think that implementing an AA-MAS will lead to improved educational opportunities for eligible students. In addition to the why, they should have to describe the how, or the mechanisms by which they think that these improved learning opportunities will occur. For example, one might postulate that AA-MAS scores will be more accurate depictions of what eligible students know than general assessment scores so that teachers will be able to provide more appropriate learning opportunities for these students. The evaluator and/or user must specify the mechanism by which these score reports will lead to the anticipated changes in teaching practices, such as targeted instruction and/or more appropriate curricular materials.

On the basis of two example guiding philosophies presented in Chapter 1 (this volume), two example theories of actions for a modified assessment system were created to illustrate how these differences could play out as different validity arguments. These examples were purposefully created to represent two quite different guiding philosophies and approaches to the AA-MAS.

Example 1: The AA-MAS allows eligible students to show that what they know may be comparable to similar performance levels on the general assessment.

1. Academic content standards are the same as for the general assessment, and the test blueprint for the AA-MAS is essentially the same as that for the general assessment, but contains some modifications (e.g., fewer passages) to make adjustments for students' disabilities and includes slightly less difficult items than on the general assessment.

2. The achievement standards incorporate recognition of students' disabilities (e.g., need for supports) and although they signal high

expectations for eligible students and their teachers, they are slightly lower than the general assessment achievement standards.

3. The assessment is designed to measure grade-level content and high achievement expectations, accurately allowing students to show what they know (as well as what they do not know) and are able to do.

4. Teachers provide instruction that is aligned with these high academic expectations and ensure that students get the supports necessary, allowing them to succeed with grade-level content.

5. The test and achievement descriptors signal and reinforce appropriate instructional and formative assessment strategies for use in classrooms/schools.

6. Student scores on the AA-MAS provide a more accurate estimate of what eligible students know and can do compared with the general assessment.

7. Student performance on the test is used by teachers and school leaders to help them figure out how to provide more appropriate supports and programs.

8. Improved student/school performance on the AA-MAS leads to higher accountability scores.

Example 2: The AA-MAS will better align with current learning opportunities and beliefs about how eligible special education students learn grade-level academic content.

1. Academic content standards are the same as for the general assessment, but the test blueprint for the AA-MAS focuses on fewer and generally easier items tailored to the lower expectations held for these students. The blueprint and test specifications also contain some modifications (e.g., fewer passages) to make adjustments for students' disabilities.

2. The achievement standards incorporate references to students' disabilities (e.g., need for supports) and are designed to describe eligible students' knowledge and skills relative to their current learning opportunities.

3. Teachers provide instruction that is designed to take students from where they are and then helps the students make progress in this curriculum, even if it is below grade level.

4. The assessment is designed to provide measurement information about where students are performing, relative to grade-level content, to better show what they know and are able to do.

5. The test and achievement descriptors signal the appropriate levels and types of instructional and formative assessment strategies for use in classrooms/schools.

6. Student performance on the test is used by teachers and school leaders to support (validate) current supports and programs.

7. The AA-MAS scores provide information about students' current performance to the student, parents, and teachers.

8. A test more aligned to students' instructional levels leads to more proficient students with disabilities and higher accountability scores.

9. Students, in part because of these lower expectations, do not make progress on grade-level standards relative to their same-grade peers, and certain opportunities are shut off from these students by virtue of these missed (or denied) opportunities.

Each aspect of the theory of action leads to claims or propositions that are the basis of the interpretative argument. For example, a proposition such as, "Students of teachers using formative assessment strategies aligned with the AA-MAS targets have higher scores than students of teachers using formative assessments not matched with the AA-MAS targets" could be specified from the general claim found in the first example theory of action presented in Figure 8.1, "The AA-MAS reinforces appropriate instructional and formative assessment strategies for use in classrooms/schools." An interpretative argument will start with one or more of the goals and guiding philosophy previously discussed and then trace the claims of the AA-MAS that results in meeting that goal. Specifying a theory of action is a useful first step in creating a more complete interpretative argument. Sample theories of action were developed in the form of the illustrations shown in Figures 8.1 and 8.2. However, a theory of action, particularly when laid out graphically, as in the examples here, is of limited utility. It is necessarily quite broad—perhaps superficial—and therefore on its own cannot guide a comprehensive validity evaluation. Evaluators must "zoom in" on specific components and linkages within the theory of action in order to explicate the propositions/assertions that form the basis of the interpretative argument. Examples of such propositions are presented below in the evidence section. Further, when test users (e.g., states) and developers create theories of action, there is often little emphasis on negative, unintended consequences. Example 2 was created to illustrate the importance of searching for and trying to uncover negative, unintended consequences, but

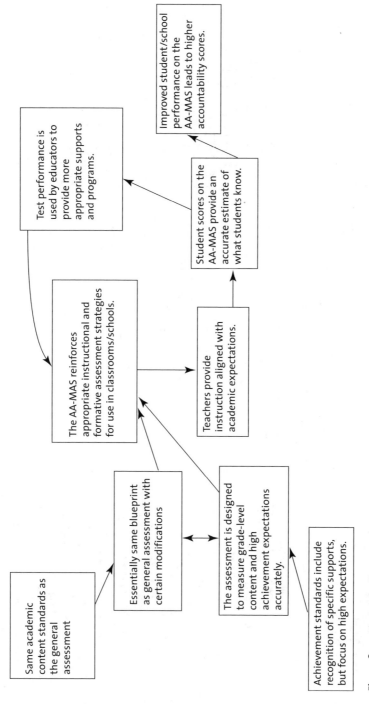

Figure 8.1. Theory of action: example 1.

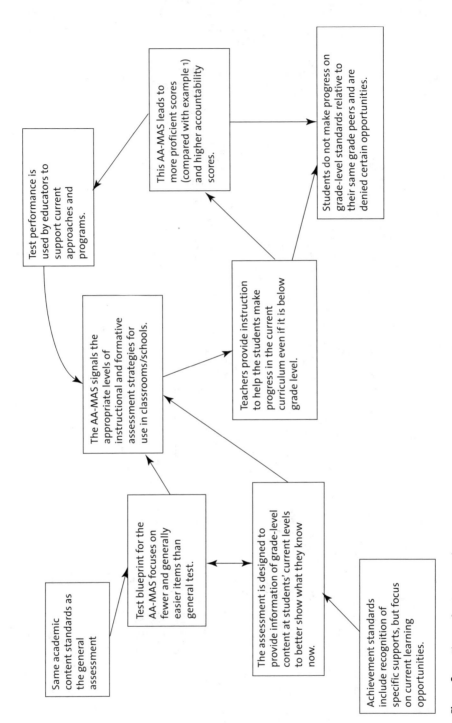

Figure 8.2. Theory of action: example 2.

evaluators should adopt this stance for any interpretative argument and validity evaluation plan.

Both examples separate out the various claims by the stage of the assessment or accountability process. Both of these theories of action start with the purposes of the assessment, move to content and achievement standards and then to assessment development (e.g., test blueprint), and end with claims about uses and consequences of the scores. The end result is the goal of increasing student achievement or at least test/accountability scores. An interim goal is to provide information to the teachers to help them improve how they structure learning opportunities for these students. Importantly, these two theories of action lead to different social justice claims, which have implications for the collection and evaluation of consequential evidence.

PRIORITIZING THE VALIDITY EVALUATION QUESTIONS

The interpretative arguments and the more general theories of action lead to many possible evaluation questions—almost always more than can be addressed in a validity evaluation constrained by time and/or resources. The prioritization should be influenced by the particular guiding philosophy. Following Kane (2006), the state should not select questions and design a validity evaluation to confirm their guiding philosophy. Rather, the validity evaluator should purposefully design studies to contradict the states' beliefs and claims.

While being wary of potential bias, the state can use the guiding philosophy to help prioritize the multitude of possible evaluation questions. A state that adopts a guiding philosophy similar to example 1 should certainly prioritize validity questions addressing comparability of inferences (again, see Chapter 7, for more detail). The evaluator, in this case, should search for proof-of-concept cases in which well-instructed students do in fact perform at levels comparable to those of students participating in the general assessment. The absence of such cases would be a threat to the guiding philosophy and validity argument found in example 1. On the other hand, a state subscribing to the philosophy articulated in example 2 would have to focus on content validity studies to document that the test actually meets the regulatory requirements of being on grade level. This evaluation should also collect consequential evidence about students' opportunities to learn meaningful grade-level content and skills.

CLASSES AND SOURCES OF EVIDENCE

There are many ways to organize and collect evidence for the validity evaluation. The joint *Standards'* (AERA et al., 1999) five sources of evidence are the most familiar organizing framework. Earlier work (Marion & Pellegrino, 2006; Marion & Perie, 2009) illustrated how both the assessment triangle (Pellegrino et al., 2001) and Ryan's (2002) framework could be used to structure validity evaluations. The joint *Standards* are used as the basis here because of both their familiarity and straightforward structure. However, the current (1999) version of the joint *Standards* does not do justice to certain key elements illuminated by the assessment triangle (Pellegrino et al., 2001), particularly related to the cognition vertex of the triangle. Further, the 1999 edition of the joint *Standards* does not fully incorporate recent research making clear the central role of test consequences into validity evaluations (e.g., Lane & Stone, 2002; Shepard, 1997). Therefore, an introductory section was added to this discussion to address "Who are the students?" and "How do they acquire proficiency in the domain?" to supplement the joint *Standards* framework. Although this type of information should be part of any validity evaluation, it is even more important in alternate assessment and English language learner testing contexts in which the specific tested population could vary considerably depending on the selection rules employed. Further, the framework presented here prioritizes the role of test consequences in the evaluation of AA-MAS validity more than the joint *Standards* would suggest. Within each of the following categories, the sources of evidence and types of studies particularly relevant to evaluating the validity of the AA-MAS are described. Several examples are presented throughout the following sections illustrating how specific propositions and study designs might differ depending on the specific guiding philosophies and theories of action.

Who Are the Students and How Do They Learn?

As Quenemoen makes clear in Chapter 1, identifying students for participation in the AA-MAS is a complex endeavor. A key eligibility requirement is that students must be instructed in the grade-level curriculum and have an opportunity to learn grade-level content (see Chapter 1). A major premise associated with implementing an AA-MAS is that students' disabilities interact with their capacity to demonstrate what they know and are able to do and that poor performance is not due to a lack of opportunity to learn. In Chapter 2, Karvonen discusses methods for documenting the effectiveness of instructional and curriculum strategies. This documentation is crucial evidence to help make the case that students have been appropriately selected to participate in the AA-MAS. Further, individualized education program (IEP) teams need to ensure that appropriate supports and strategies are provided so that students have the highest likelihood possible to access the grade-level knowledge and skills.

In Chapter 3, Pellegrino provides a comprehensive discussion about the ways in which students acquire competence in a domain, with a specific focus on mathematics. Pellegrino's exposition is very important for states to keep in mind as they consider developing an AA-MAS, because if state leaders do not have a sense of how eligible students will make progress in the domain, then the rationale for and the validity of the AA-MAS will be suspect. Therefore, a critical aspect of the interpretative argument is the development of propositions related to the way in which students develop domain competence. The theoretical conceptions and the associated evidence, such as the results from tasks specifically designed to measure students' progress along a defined learning continuum, should be evaluated as part of the larger validity investigation for any assessment system, but even more so for the AA-MAS because of the field's limited understanding of the conceptual underpinnings of this assessment.

Evidence Based on Test Content

Important validity evidence can be obtained from an analysis of the relationship between a test's content and the construct it is intended to measure. Test content refers to the themes, wording, and format of the test items, tasks, or questions on a test, as well as the guidelines for procedures regarding administration and scoring. (AERA et al., 1999, p. 11)

One of the foundational principles of the AA-MAS is that it is based on grade-level content. Therefore, collecting and evaluating the evidence regarding comparability of the content is critically important to evaluating the validity of the AA-MAS. Many states and evaluators will often use evidence from alignment studies to support claims of content validity. Well-done alignment studies can certainly contribute to content-related validity evaluations, but alignment studies generally focus on matching test items with content-based standards and objectives. Content-related evidence, especially when one is trying to make claims about "grade levelness," requires evaluating the interaction of both content and process required of the test items and, in the case of the AA-MAS, documenting that the interaction is what is expected for the specific grade level.

In both example theories of action presented earlier, the assessments are based on the state's academic content, but the blueprint described in the second example is based on fewer and easier items than the general assessment. In this case, the evaluator should critically evaluate the assertion that the test blueprint used in example 2 accurately represents the construct, even though a purposeful nonrepresentative item sampling (of grade-level content) approach is used. Even in example 1, studies should address the assertion that the use of certain changes (modifications) to the test blueprint (and items) accurately represents grade-level knowledge and skills as indicated by the content standards.

Evidence Based on Response Processes

"Theoretical and empirical analyses of the response processes of test takers can provide evidence concerning the fit between the construct and the detailed nature of performance or response actually engaged in by examinees" (AERA et al., 1999, p. 12).

Many validity questions that emerge from a state's belief that implementing an AA-MAS will better allow students to show what they know can be grouped under response processes. These types of studies would be applicable for guiding philosophies aligned with either example 1 or 2, but the orientation would be different depending on the underlying beliefs. Several studies can be identified in which students' response behaviors on the AA-MAS and general assessment items are compared with an attempt to attribute the differences to specific theoretical conceptions outlined in the rationale for the AA-MAS.

Evidence related to the cognition vertex of the assessment triangle can also be considered within the response process category. Before analyzing evidence on how students are responding to specific tasks, it is crucial to describe and analyze which students have been nominated to participate in the AA-MAS. There is an implicit assumption in both theories of action that the "right" students are participating in the AA-MAS—an assumption that should be made explicit in a more complete and elaborate theory of action—but this assumption should be evaluated before investigating how students are responding to the items. States should have (and present) a theoretically grounded rationale as part of the description of the students participating in the AA-MAS.

Another important dimension of the cognition vertex subsumed by the response process category is a description of how students acquire competence (proficiency) in the domain. If there is such a hypothesized progression by which students are expected to develop domain competence, the evaluator/state should describe how students eligible for the AA-MAS are expected to follow the same expected progression or how and why they would develop differently than their same-age peers. The tasks and associated response processes could then be evaluated against hypothesized learning progressions.

Evidence related to response processes is often collected through the use of cognitive laboratories (*think-alouds*) to get a micro look at how students are interacting with the items and tasks (e.g., Ericsson & Simon, 1980; Johnstone, Bottsford-Miller, & Thompson, 2006). The data derived from well-designed cognitive laboratories can shed light on students' developing understanding of the grade-level content as a way to ascertain whether the items and tasks on AA-MAS support this developing understanding.

In the case of the AA-MAS, it is important to determine whether students interact as intended with the modified test items and in ways that differ from the nonmodified test items. "Students interact with passages and test items on the AA-MAS in ways that allow them to demonstrate their grade-level knowledge and skills while minimizing construct-irrelevant influences" is a proposition that would fit both theories of action. The main difference in how this assertion might be tested in the two examples would play out in the different passages, items, and tasks used on each assessment.

Internal Structure

"Analyses of the internal structure of a test can indicate the degree to which the relationships among test items and test components conform to the construct on which the proposed test score interpretations are based" (AERA et al., 1999, p. 13).

For states with a guiding philosophy similar to example 1, this section is critical for evaluating the validity of the AA-MAS as an important set of evidence in terms of score comparability. The internal structure of the AA-MAS should be similar to the internal structure of the general assessment, or if not, there should be an explicit reason why the internal structures of the two assessments differ. As discussed by Abedi in Chapter 7, meeting strict comparability criteria (i.e., equating) is generally beyond the reach of almost any AA-MAS design. Yet techniques such as confirmatory factor analysis could be used to compare the internal structure of the general and modified assessments to determine whether the structure of the modified assessment is close enough to the general assessment to argue that both are tapping the same construct. A proposition from the perspective of example 2 might suggest that the internal structure of the AA-MAS is generally similar to that of the general assessment, whereas one from the perspective of example 1 would argue for stronger comparability, such as that the same factor structure with the same loadings can be used to explain the variability of the items on both the AA-MAS and general assessment.

Evidence Based on Relations to Other Variables

Analyses of the relationship of test scores to variables external to the test provide another important source of validity evidence. External variables may include measures of some criteria that the test is expected to predict, as well as relationships to other tests hypothesized to measure the same constructs, and tests measuring related or different constructs. (AERA et al., 1999, p. 13)

This section is probably less critical for the AA-MAS compared with other sources of evidence, but it can still be important—depending on one's theory of action—to substantiate claims about the AA-MAS. There are other assessments with documented properties (e.g., grade level or not; difficult or easy, accessible or not) that should be more or less related to scores on the AA-MAS. Because psychometricians are quite good at computing correlations, state leaders and evaluators should articulate the intended relationships a priori instead of data snooping for relationships that support one's conclusions.

It is difficult to imagine significant differences in the relationship to some external test or other variable if there is an assumption that the AA-MAS is measuring the same construct as the general assessment. If the state has good longitudinal data on norm-referenced tests (NRT) or interim assessment data, for example, the state might want to put forth a proposition for example 2 to gather validity evidence that supports the claim that the AA-MAS is on grade level. Such a proposition might state: "The fourth grade AA-MAS is significantly more related to the fourth grade NRT than it is to the third grade NRT." This proposition could be extended to argue that the correlations between the AA-MAS and the external criterion should be very similar to the correlations between the general assessment and the external test.

Evidence Based on Consequences of Testing

There are a host of intended positive consequences associated with a state's interest in implementing an AA-MAS, but there are some serious potentially unintended negative consequences as well. As discussed previously, states that have an orientation similar to that in example 2 should focus consequential questions on potential lower expectations that could hinder eligible students from achieving at grade level. A state's approach does not have to be as extreme as that presented in example 2 for the system to carry unintended negative consequences; therefore, state leaders and evaluators need to attend to unintended consequences related to lower expectations for any AA-MAS. On the other hand, states with a philosophy similar to that of example 1 might address consequential issues related to frustration and/or lack of a meaningful assessment experience from "unrealistically" high expectations. In any case, consequential studies related to the validity of the AA-MAS need to focus on searching for and evaluating the potential unintended consequences of an AA-MAS, such as lower expectations for students with disabilities.

The AA-MAS was originally conceived as part of the flexibility offered by the U.S. Department of Education under the No Child Left Behind Act of 2001 (PL 107-110), and ultimately this assessment has been designed to fit into states' accountability systems and contribute to AYP determinations (see Chapter 9, for more discussion of AA-MAS accountability issues). The accountability function makes clear that the AA-MAS has been designed as a policy instrument, although additional purposes may be possible. As Kane (2006) noted, when assessments are used to support a particular policy, the consequences of such policy actions must be incorporated into the validity evaluation. A range of validity evaluation questions and propositions could be put forth to collect consequential evidence related to the AA-MAS. These questions and propositions will differ depending on the philosophies and goals guiding the development and implementation of the AA-MAS. For instance, a proposition to search for potential unintended negative consequences based on example 2 might read as follows: "The increase in the percentage of special education students scoring proficient as a result participating in the AA-MAS has not led to an increase in schools falsely meeting AYP targets (Type II errors)."

SYNTHESIS AND EVALUATION

Haertel (1999) reinforced the notion that individual pieces of evidence do not make an assessment system valid or not. The evidence and logic must be synthesized to evaluate the interpretative argument. The evaluative argument provides the structure for evaluating the merits of the interpretative argument (Kane, 2006). Various types of empirical evidence and logical argument must be integrated and synthesized into an evaluative judgment. This process can be a challenging intellectual activity. In state assessment programs, when new and varied information comes in at sometimes unpredictable intervals, the challenge is exacerbated. With alternate assessment programs, not only is new evidence being collected along the way, but actual understanding of alternate assessments and the students they serve evolves much more rapidly than in many other programs. This evolving understanding will require evaluators to (re)examine evidence in light of these newer understandings.

With the exception of a few states, most AA-MAS are in the very early stages of development. Therefore, initial syntheses could adopt confirmationist biases during the first few years of the program until it gets established. This does not mean that long-term studies, especially consequential, should not be planned and initial data collected, but the synthesis and evaluation in the early years of the program should focus on substantiating that the development of the AA-MAS has generally occurred as designed and the designs can be theoretically supported.

Dynamic Evaluation

In almost all evaluations of the validity of state assessment systems, studies are completed across a long time span. Evaluators rarely have all the evidence in front of them to make conclusive judgments at a single point in time. Therefore, evaluators must engage in ongoing, dynamic evaluations as new evidence is produced. Working in this fashion requires that each proposition be written to allow judgment of whether the evidence supports a particular claim. As discussed above, this always means exploring the efficacy of alternate hypotheses. However, in the context of states' large-scale assessment systems, evaluators do not have the luxury of concluding, "The system is not working; let's start over." Rather, in such instances, when the evidence does not support the claims and intended inferences, state leaders and test developers must act as if the dynamic results were part of a formative evaluation, and they must search for ways to improve the system. Of course, the evidence might be so overwhelmingly stacked against the intended claims that the state leaders are left only with the option of starting over.

The state should use the guiding principles and purposes of the AA-MAS to determine how to weigh various sources of evidence to arrive at an evaluative judgment. This judgment could take the form of a summative judgment in which a state determines that the overwhelming evidence suggests abandoning the AA-MAS or going forward with it full-steam ahead. More likely, however, the state will use the initial validity evaluation in formative ways to improve the AA-MAS.

REFERENCES

American Educational Research Association, American Psychological Association, & National Council on Measurement in Education. (1985). *Standards for educational and psychological testing.* Washington, DC: American Educational Research Association.

American Educational Research Association, American Psychological Association, & National Council on Measurement in Education. (1999). *Standards for educational and psychological testing.* Washington, DC: American Educational Research Association.

Cronbach, L.J. (1971). Test validation. In R.L. Thorndike (Ed.), *Educational measurement* (2nd ed., pp. 443–507). Washington, DC: American Council on Education.

Elliott, S.N., Compton, E., Roach, & A.T. (2007). Building validity evidence for scores on a state-wide alternate assessment: A contrasting groups, multimethod approach. *Educational Measurement: Issues and Practice, 26*(2), 30–43.

Ericsson, K., & Simon, H. (1980). Verbal reports as data. *Psychological Review, 87,*

215–250.

Gong, B., & Marion, S.F. (2006). *Dealing with flexibility in assessments for students with significant cognitive disabilities* (Synthesis Report 60). Minneapolis, MN: University of Minnesota, National Center for Educational Outcomes.

Haertel, E.H. (1999). Validity arguments for high-stakes testing: In search of the evidence. *Educational Measurement: Issues and Practice, 18*(4), 5–9.

Johnstone, C.J., Bottsford-Miller, N.A., & Thompson, S.J. (2006). *Using the think-aloud method (cognitive labs) to evaluate test design for students with disabilities and English language learners* (Technical Report 44). Minneapolis, MN: University of Minnesota, National Center on Educational Outcomes.

Kane, M.T. (2006). Validation. In R.L. Brennan (Ed.), *Educational measurement* (4th ed., pp. 17–64). New York: American Council on Education/Macmillan.

Kearns, J., Towles-Reeves, E., Kleinert, H., & Kleinert, J. (2006). *Learning characteristics inventory (LCI) report*. Lexington, KY: National Alternate Assessment Center, Human Development Institute, University of Kentucky. Retrieved January 15, 2009, from http://www.naacpartners.org/products/researchReports/20080.pdf

Kleinert, H., Browder, D., & Towles-Reeves, E. (2005). *The assessment triangle and students with significant cognitive disabilities: Models of student cognition.* Lexington, KY: National Alternate Assessment Center, Human Development Institute, University of Kentucky. Retrieved January 16, 2009, from http://www.naacpartners.org/products/whitePapers/18000.pdf

Lane, S., & Stone, C.A. (2002). Strategies of examining the consequences of assessment and accountability programs. *Educational Measurement: Issues and Practice, 21*(2), 23–30.

Linn, R.L., Baker, E.L., & Dunbar, S.B. (1991). Complex performance-based assessment: Expectations and validation criteria. *Educational Researcher, 20*(8), 15–21.

Marion, S.F., & Pellegrino, J.W. (2006). A validity framework for evaluating the technical quality of alternate assessments. *Educational Measurement: Issues and Practice, 25*(4), 47–57.

Marion, S.F., & Perie, M. (2009). Validity arguments for alternate assessments. In W. Schafer & R. Lissitz (Eds.), *Alternate assessments based on alternate achievement standards: Policy, practice, and potential* (pp. 115–127). Baltimore: Paul H. Brookes Publishing Co.

Messick, S. (1989). Validity. In R.L. Linn (Ed.), *Educational measurement* (3rd ed., pp. 13–103). New York: American Council on Education, Macmillan Publishing.

Messick, S. (1995). The interplay of evidence and consequences in the validation of performance assessments. *Educational Researcher, 23*(2), 13–23.

No Child Left Behind Act of 2001, PL 107-110, 115 Stat. 1425, 20 U.S.C. §§ 6301 et seq.

Pellegrino, J.W., Chudowsky, N.J., & Glaser, R. (Eds.). (2001). *Knowing what students know: The science and design of educational assessment.* Washington, DC: National Academy of Sciences.

Rabinowitz, S., & Sato, E. (2005). *The technical adequacy of assessments for alternate student populations.* San Francisco: WestEd.

Ryan, K. (2002). Assessment validation in the context of high stakes assessments. *Educational Measurement: Issues and Practice, 21*(1), 7–15.

Schafer, W.D. (2005). Technical documentation for alternate assessments. *Practical Assessment Research & Evaluation, 10*(10). Retrieved January 15, 2009, from http://pareonline.net/getvn.asp?v=10&n=10

Shepard, L.A. (1993). Evaluating test validity. In L. Darling-Hammond (Ed.), *Review of Research in Education, 19*, 405–450.

Shepard, L. (1997). The centrality of test use and consequences for test validity. *Educational Measurement: Issues and Practice, 16*(2), 5–24.

U. S. Department of Education (2007a). *Final Rule 34 CFR Parts 200 and 300: Title I—Improving the academic achievement of the disadvantaged; Individuals with disabilities education act (IDEA). Federal Register.* 72(67), Washington DC: Author. Retrieved July 12, 2008, from http://cehd.umn.edu/NCEO/2percentReg/Federal-RegApril9TwoPercent.pdf

U. S. Department of Education (2007b). *Modified achievement standards: Non-regulatory guidance.* Washington DC: Office of Elementary and Secondary Education (OESE). Retrieved August 27, 2008, from http://www.ed.gov/policy/speced/guid/nclb/twopercent.doc

9

Operational and Accountability Issues

Chris Domaleski

A full examination of the issues and elements related to the design and adoption of a new state assessment program would not be complete without careful consideration of the context in which the program will be situated. It is important to acknowledge that an alternate assessment based on modified achievement standards (AA-MAS) would exist as part of a larger state assessment and accountability system. Therefore, it is essential to understand the interrelationship of the AA-MAS with other assessment programs. Moreover, the potential impact of the AA-MAS on the state accountability system should be carefully explored.

This chapter begins with an overview of the background and context for accountability and then summarizes the key provisions in the U.S. Department of Education's regulations that pertain to accountability determinations. Subsequently, specific accountability issues are addressed to include procedures to estimate reliability and a review of key operational considerations. The chapter ends with a discussion of factors related to student and summary reporting, effective data use, and a consideration of issues and options related to student stakes, particularly diploma eligibility.

In exploring these topics, focus is placed on practical, technical, and policy elements. By doing so, the goal is to highlight options and provide guidance to assist with implementation and evaluation.

BACKGROUND AND CONTEXT FOR ACCOUNTABILITY

Education accountability systems, in some form or another, have been in place for at least the previous 3 decades. However, earlier accountability systems tended to focus on areas such as regulation compliance and financial management (Fuhrman & Elmore, 2004). The change in focus to outputs—chiefly, student performance on standardized assessments—began in earnest in the 1980s. During this time, accountability approaches drawn from business applications gained support from education policy makers (Fuhrman & Elmore, 2004). This was bolstered by a wave of concern about the perceived decline in quality of education as described in the influential publication *A Nation at Risk* (National Commission on Excellence in Education, 1983). In subsequent years, accountability systems expanded and focused more on student and school performance.

Another major influence on contemporary education accountability began in the 1990s with increased support for standards-based reform. The guiding idea behind this approach is that expectations for what students know and can do should be clearly established, which will guide all other elements of the educational system, chiefly instruction and assessment (O'Day & Smith, 1993). Advocates argue that such an approach leads to a number of improvements, such as clarifying goals, incentivizing improvement, and informing allocation of resources (Darling-Hammond, 2006). This perspective was a guiding factor behind the development and implementation of accountability systems in the 1990s and in the current decade, including the federal No Child Left Behind Act of 2001 (NCLB; PL 107-110).

As support increased for standards-based reform, so too did advocacy for students with disabilities. Historically, many educators and stakeholders did not provide students with disabilities access to the general curriculum. With the 1990 and 2004 reauthorizations of the Individuals with Disabilities Education Act and NCLB, the view that students should be taught and held accountable for grade-level standards prevailed. This position has not been without opposition from those who argued that such goals are unreasonable and/or that traditional standardized assessment practices are ill-suited for students with disabilities.

Today, a central idea behind contemporary accountability practices is the inclusion of all students, including students with disabilities. This is based on the belief that measuring, reporting, and holding schools explicitly accountable for the performance of students with disabilities is critical to ensuring that educators attend to their needs, provide appropriate resources, and set high expectations for learning. The extent to which this principle holds rests largely on the integrity of the measures used to gauge student achievement. This is the context that has inspired the states to explore the efficacy of customizing a standards-based assessment for a portion of the population of students with disabilities.

Federal Regulations

Against this backdrop, the U.S. Department of Education issued regulations and guidance in April 2007 that addressed the implementation of modified academic achievement standards and assessments. These regulations were explicitly targeted to a small group of students whose disability precludes them from achieving grade-level proficiency within the year. A more complete overview of the regulations is presented in the Introduction to this volume. The focus of this section is to review the elements that directly impact accountability determinations.

In terms of accountability, there are two main elements of the policy that merit attention. First, the regulations and guidelines establish that states may count as proficient, for the purpose of adequate yearly progress (AYP) calculations, the proficient and advanced scores of students with disabilities based on an AA-MAS, provided that the number of these scores does not exceed 2% of all students in the grades assessed in language arts and mathematics. In other words, scores on the AA-MAS can be used in AYP calculations in the same way as scores from the general assessments within the 2% cap. Although this seems straightforward, there are a number of caveats and considerations that warrant further examination to fully appreciate the application of this stricture. This is addressed in a later section of this chapter.

The second major element of the policy with respect to accountability is the expiration of the *interim-flexibility* policy. Interim flexibility refers to the practice of allowing states that meet certain criteria to count as proficient for purposes of AYP a portion of the students with disabilities. This applies at the school or district level if AYP is missed solely because of the achievement of the students with disabilities subgroup. The portion is determined by dividing 2% by the percentage of students with disabilities in the state. For example, if a state's students with disabilities subgroup is 12% of the student population, one divides 2 by 12 to obtain 17%, which is the percentage of the state's students with disabilities population that can be counted as proficient for purposes of AYP, where applicable.

The purpose of this flexibility was to forestall the impact of non-proficient classifications based on general assessments for students who may be candidates for an AA-MAS during the time that new assessments more appropriate for this population were under development. Importantly, the interim flexibility, which was initially granted for the 2004–2005 academic year, was extended through 2008–2009 in the regulations; however, it expired beginning in the 2009–2010 academic year. Whether an AA-MAS is developed or not, this expiration will have an impact on accountability determinations for many states that currently take advantage of the interim flexibility in AYP computations. The interim flexibility essentially allows states to count the *maximum* percentage of eligible students proficient in AYP computations. Consequently, when this expires, states will likely see an increase in the number of students with disabilities groups that fail to meet their annual measurable objectives (AMOs).

Grades and Content Areas for AA-MAS

An important decision for states is the determination of the grades and content areas in which to implement an AA-MAS. There is no regulatory requirement to develop or adopt an AA-MAS, so the potential implementation options range from none to all. That is, a state may decide not to proceed with an AA-MAS in any area or to pursue full adoption in all grades and content areas assessed, regardless of inclusion in NCLB accountability. Naturally, a number of implementation options in between these two extremes are available as well.

A decision about scope of development is, foremost, a policy decision that should be guided by the goals of the state and the purpose for considering an AA-MAS. Assuming it is desirable to implement an AA-MAS as broadly as possible, there are at least three possible perspectives that might guide prioritization of implementation.

First, the extent to which the general assessments are seen as valid and appropriate for students with disabilities could be a guiding principle. By carefully evaluating both the assessment characteristics and student performance, the state might develop priorities for the grades and content areas that should be given primary consideration. For example, one may wish to review blueprints and specifications for the general assessments to determine which are relatively more cognitively complex and/or rigorous. Moreover, one may wish to review the gap between performance of students with disabilities and general education students and focus on the assessments that have the largest gap. When these two approaches identify the same assessments, a more compelling case for prioritizing these assessments may be made.

Additionally, there may be legal issues to consider. If a general assessment is regarded as not suitable for students with disabilities, the state may be legally compelled to pursue the development of an alternate assessment. This position was supported by *Chapman v. California*

Department of Education (2002), in which a federal court ruled that the state of California must provide an alternate assessment if it is determined that students with disabilities are unable to access the general assessment as a result of their disability.

A second approach may be to allow the consequences or stakes associated with the assessment to guide prioritization of the grades and content areas in which an AA-MAS should be developed. Using this orientation, those areas covered in the state accountability system (English language arts and mathematics in grades 3–8 and high school) may be given higher priority. There may be other stakes, either currently in place or planned, that could guide this decision. These may include student stakes, such as diploma eligibility, or rewards/consequences at the teacher, school, or system level.

A third lens through which to view this decision is related to practical or operational constraints. Unavoidably, the availability of resources, such as cost and staff capacity, has a significant impact on options that can be considered. Such factors as the format of the assessment, the frequency of administration, or the scope of ongoing development and support may make some options more feasible than others.

It is important to acknowledge that these three approaches are not mutually exclusive and most likely will interact with each other. For example, assuming resources are limited, the state may get a sense for the scope of implementation, which may narrow options down to a specific program or grade span. Thereafter, it may be reasonable to consider the policy implications, then review the properties and performance of the assessments to further identify the area in which to begin implementation. Another important consideration is whether or not the state would like to use scores on the general assessment to inform placement on the AA-MAS. If so, then it will be important to introduce the AA-MAS at a later grade to acquire scores on 1 or more years of the general assessment.

States may decide to approach this decision as a cost-benefit analysis. The costs of implementing an AA-MAS are related to finances, operational burden to state and local staff, and possible forfeiture of other programs and initiatives that could be supported by these resources. On the other hand, the benefits may include improved information from assessment and accountability systems and the ability to promote student achievement for students with disabilities.

Although each state likely differs with respect to a number of the factors previously examined, it may be useful to examine the scope of AA-MAS implementation across states. In 2007, the National Center on Educational Outcomes reviewed the characteristics of the AA-MAS for six states, including the grades and content areas that were addressed.

Table 9.1.   AA-MAS name, content areas, and grade by state

State	Assessment name	Content areas/grades
Kansas	Kansas Assessment of Multiple Measures (KAMM)	Reading (grades 3–8; once in HS); math (grades 3–8; once in HS); writing (grades 5, 8, once in HS); history/government (grades 6, 8, once in HS); science (grades 4, 7, once in HS)
Louisiana	LEAP Alternate Assessment, Level 2 (LAA2)	English (grades 4–10); math (grades 4–10); science (grades 4, 8, and 11); social studies (grades 4, 8, 11)
Maryland	Modified Maryland School Assessment (Mod-MSA) and Modified High School Assessment (Mod-HSA)	Reading/ELA (grades 3–8, HS); math (grades 3–8, HS)
North Carolina	NCEXTEND	Reading (grades 3–8); math (grades 3–8); science (grades 5 and 8)
North Dakota	North Dakota Alternate Assessment Aligned to North Dakota Content Standards for Students with Persistent Cognitive Disabilities	Reading (grades 3–8,11); math (grades 3–8,11); science (grades 4, 8, 11)
Oklahoma	Curriculum Access Resource Guide (CARG)–M	ELA/reading (grades 3–8, HS); math (grades 3–8, HS); science (grades 5 and 8)

From Lazarus, S.S., Thurlow, M.L., Christensen, L.L., & Cormier, D. (2007). *States' alternate assessments based on modified achievement standards (AA-MAS) in 2007* (Synthesis Report 67). Minneapolis, MN: University of Minnesota, National Center on Educational Outcomes; adapted by permission.
Key: HS, high school; LEAP, Louisiana Educational Assessment Program; ELA, English language arts.

(Lazarus et al., 2007). The results are presented in Table 9.1, reproduced from that report. The results show that most states implemented the AA-MAS fairly broadly. Each state included reading and mathematics at the elementary level, and most offered an AA-MAS in these areas at the secondary level. Many states also implemented the assessment in areas not included in the NCLB accountability system, such as Kansas, which developed an AA-MAS for writing and social studies. It is important to reiterate, however, that each state's decision is connected to a unique set of policies and priorities. There is not a uniform or best solution for all states.

Participation Options and Evidence

As addressed in the Introduction to this volume, there are five alternatives for assessment participation. These are 1) participation in the general grade-level assessment; 2) participation in the general grade-level assessment with accommodations; 3) participation in an alternate assessment based on modified academic achievement standards; 4) participation in an alternate assessment based on alternate achievement standards (AA-AAS); and 5) participation in an alternate assessment based on grade-level academic achievement standards (AA-GLAS). The fifth option differs from the AA-MAS in that the AA-GLAS performance expectations must be directly related to those on the general assessment.

The regulations further stipulate that a state must establish participation criteria for individualized education program (IEP) teams on the basis of evidence that the student's disability has precluded the student from achieving grade-level proficiency and the student's progress suggests that the student will not reach grade-level proficiency during the academic year. Therefore, a key issue with the implementation of an AA-MAS will be the development of guidelines to inform participation decisions and the collection of evidence that meets the criteria described. In previous chapters, more detailed information is provided about the guiding perspectives and approaches to identifying the population of students who are appropriate for the AA-MAS. In this section, the focus is on the specific, objective data sources and methods that may be considered to inform these decisions.

One approach is to analyze extant assessment data from interim, formative, or summative state assessments or other commercially available standardized assessments. The advantage of using state curriculum-based assessments is that the performance level provides direct evidence of student performance with respect to grade-level expectations. Eligibility criteria may be related to persistent low performance (e.g., failure to achieve proficiency in more than one administration) and/or performance that is well below standard (e.g., performance level 1). This approach is bolstered if the state can produce evidence that the probability of achieving on grade level on the general assessment in the current year is low given performance the previous year. For example, if the criterion selected was level 1 (e.g., below basic) performance on the summative state assessment, and only a very small percentage of students scoring at level 1 go on to score at or above level 3 (proficient) in the following year, this signals that the expectation is reasonable. Other commercially available standardized assessments, such as norm-referenced tests, may also be candidates for evidence. For example, regression analyses may be used to produce a predicted score on the state curriculum assessment for various norm-referenced test score values. These data can be analyzed to determine a suitable eligibility criterion that indicates that students below the standard are unlikely to perform on grade level.

Another category of evidence to consider is related to the student characteristics. For example, the state may review performance for students based on disability category to determine which are associated with persistent low performance. The Georgia Department of Education conducted one such study that explored many factors, including disability type, and revealed that students with mild intellectual disabilities were disproportionately represented (Fincher, 2007). Although disability category may not be used as a criterion for participation, such analyses can provide information to better identify the group of students who might benefit from participation in an AA-MAS or to evaluate the extent to which schools and systems are making appropriate participation decisions. These analyses involve two basic elements. First, select a condition that identifies students who are consistently below grade level (e.g., below proficient for 2 or more consecutive years). Second, explore these data for patterns that may provide more information about the group. For example, are there strands or domains within content areas in which performance is particularly low? Are students who received certain accommodations disproportionally represented compared with the state as a whole?

It is noteworthy that Georgia's study identified many persistently low-performing students who do not receive special education services. This invites serious consideration regarding why these students are not meeting academic achievement standards and to what extent these same factors are applicable to students with disabilities. At least part of the answer is likely to be that instructional approaches and supports for these students have been ineffective.

For this reason, evidence should be collected to document the extent to which students received instruction aligned with the curriculum at the appropriate grade level. Moreover, what supports and interventions have been in place to promote achievement? In reviewing this information, it is worthwhile to consider how approaches are similar or different for low-performing students with disabilities as compared with other similarly performing students. This information may help policy makers disentangle which students are the most prominent candidates for an AA-MAS and which students (both with and without disabilities) may benefit from improved instruction and support strategies.

Another important aspect related to participation options is the establishment of guidelines for students to transition from the AA-MAS to the general assessment. It is possible that students may take the AA-MAS in all content areas or only in selected content areas, taking the general assessment in others. Given that placement decisions need to be made annually, guidelines for transition should be developed that are informed by appropriate evidence.

One way to accomplish this goal is to establish a policy based on a specific score on the AA-MAS. For example, students scoring at the advanced performance level may automatically move out of the AA-MAS to the general assessment the following year. The topic of establishing comparability between the assessments is explored in Chapter 7. The extent to which there is an explicit, quantifiable relationship between the assessments using the techniques discussed will guide the decision. Such evidence should indicate that the AA-MAS can produce a grade-level achievement indicator that is explicitly and demonstrably comparable to proficiency on the general assessment. This should be based on the extent to which both the content and performance expectations are comparable. Examples of evidence might include comparison of the distribution of content standards addressed, including cognitive complexity, between the general assessment and the AA-MAS at the "exit" standard; performance level descriptors for the comparable achievement levels that are designed to closely match; and/or a review of performance data that shows a reasonable number of students who exit the AA-MAS subsequently achieve proficiency on the general assessment.

The use of multiple indicators will strengthen such decisions. For example, a *profile* approach could be implemented that takes advantage of several data sources. Such an approach may involve establishing a number of categories that indicate various conditions under which eligibility to exit may be supported. Examples of such profiles might include 1) scoring at the advanced level on the AA-MAS, 2) scoring between levels 2 and 3 while also achieving a criterion score on a district assessment, 3) achieving a specific level of course performance in tandem with AA-MAS and/or local assessment scores, 4) recommendation from IEP committee, and so forth. These examples are intended to be illustrative, and each profile should be carefully developed and monitored to ensure they are reasonable and appropriate.

ACCOUNTABILITY SYSTEM BACKGROUND

In addition to considering the role of the AA-MAS in the general assessment system, it is also important to consider how adoption of such an assessment will fit into an accountability system. Under NCLB, state systems are composed of three main elements: 1) participation rate, 2) academic achievement, and 3) an additional indicator. The participation criterion requires that 95% of students in all applicable subgroups take part in state assessments annually. Academic achievement is measured annually through state assessments in English language arts and mathematics for grades 3–8 and high school. Meeting the overall AYP standard for schools and local education agencies is based on all subgroups meeting all criteria. That is, the criteria are considered conjunctively—if any group fails to meet the standard, then the school does not make AYP.

An essential component of any examination of accountability practices is to clarify the purpose of the system and the underlying theory of action. Drawing on a simplified conceptualization proposed by Marion et al. (2002), the essence of such a theory involves the following: 1) accountability policy provides incentives, such as recognition or sanctions; 2) awareness and expectations regarding school performance are heightened; 3) educators and students benefit from resources and development; and 4) these factors contribute to an improvement in student achievement.

Against this backdrop, the impact of introducing an AA-MAS into a state accountability system can be more appropriately assessed. In the best case, the AA-MAS should provide more trustworthy information about student performance to better guide accountability determinations and allocations of resources. As outlined in Chapter 1 (this volume), this theory is connected to a guiding philosophy that values improved student outcomes and promotes systems and structures that effectively and consistently support this objective. To the extent that this occurs, the validity and reliability of accountability determinations should be augmented.

The validity of the accountability system is strongly tied to the design of the system, as well as the intended use of results. The central validity focus is ensuring that the *assessments* used in the model are trustworthy for classifying selected students with disabilities as proficient or not proficient, which was addressed in Chapter 8. If the assessments provide better information than the general assessments, then the validity of the accountability model should be improved. However, if the AA-MAS is poorly suited for this purpose (e.g., it is used to lower expectations for students with disabilities rather than provide accurate information with respect to achievement), then the validity of the accountability model is threatened. However, it is assumed that the structure and purpose of the accountability system would remain intact if an AA-MAS were introduced. For this reason, the primary focus will be evaluating the extent to which the system continues to function as it is currently designed in a stable and consistent manner. This is primarily an issue of reliability, which is the focus in this chapter.

EVALUATING THE RELIABILITY OF ACCOUNTABILITY DETERMINATIONS

There are two primary sources of error that impact the reliability of accountability systems: measurement error and sampling error.

Measurement error refers to the extent to which individual assessments in the accountability system produce stable and consistent results. This is influenced by variability in the population of students who take a specific administration of the test. *Sampling error,* on the other hand, refers to variations in the school population from year to year.

The literature related to evaluating measurement error or reliability is fairly well established. Reliability can be defined in practical terms as the degree to which an examinee's performance on a test is consistent over repeated administrations of the same or alternate forms (Crocker & Algina, 1986). It is possible to evaluate test score reliability using a number of approaches to include those based in item response theory, generalizability theory, or classic test theory. Drawing from the latter category, test-retest and/or parallel form methods are well known. As the name implies, *test-retest* approaches involve administering the same assessment to a group of examinees on two or more occasions. The correlation of scores yields an indication of the *stability* of the measure. Alternately, one can administer forms designed to be parallel to a group of examinees to produce a measure of *equivalence.* A more robust approach involves combining the two methods by administering different (equivalent) assessments to the same group of examinees at two or more points in time to yield an indication of stability and equivalence. Because this approach is influenced by error related to time and form differences, a strong correlation bolsters evidence for reliability. Still another approach, used more commonly, is to calculate reliability based on internal consistency. This method is attractive because of the practical advantages of obtaining a reliability measure based on a single administration of a single form. There are a number of methods to implement this, but perhaps the most familiar is Cronbach's coefficient alpha. Finally, there is a family of methods based on inter-rater reliability, which is suitable for assessments involving responses or evidence that must be evaluated by a human rater. (A full discussion of how to operationalize each of these and other approaches to quantify the reliability of an assessment is beyond the scope of this chapter; the reader is referred to seminal works such Crocker & Algina [1986] and Haertel [2006].)

It is important to acknowledge that the appropriate method for calculating reliability may differ depending on the approach that is selected for the AA-MAS. Moreover, many researchers stress the need for new and flexible approaches that are designed to "fit" the assessment. Gong and Marion (2006) asserted that "evaluating the technical quality of alternate assessment systems requires drawing on existing psychometric and evaluation techniques as well as modifying existing approaches or inventing new ones" (p. 13). This could include any number of procedures designed to quantify the precision of scores under various conditions, the consistency of raters, and/or the integrity of the scoring process.

The second factor related to reliability of accountability determinations is sampling error. In fact, Hill and DePascale (2002) emphasized that sampling error "contributes far more to the volatility of school scores than does measurement error" (p. 2). Sampling error refers to fluctuations in school scores that can be unrelated to actual school performance. For example, a school may receive a more favorable accountability determination compared with that of the previous year because the students enrolled were inherently higher performing and not because the quality of instruction improved. Naturally, sampling error can work to both advantage or disadvantage reported accountability determinations.

Hill and DePascale (2002) presented four approaches to evaluate sampling error by estimating the precision or consistency of accountability classifications. The most straightforward method is termed *split-half* and simply involves dividing the data for each school into randomly equivalent halves and calculating the percentage of times the same decision is made for each half. Another method involves taking *random draws with replacement* by repeatedly producing random samples from the schools to evaluate decision consistency. A *Monte Carlo* approach can also be implemented, which involves simulating the distribution of scores and creating randomly generated samples from which classification consistency can be evaluated. Finally, *direct computation* involves calculating exact probabilities for correct classification by determining the distribution of errors. For an extended treatment on these methods, including details on operationalization, the reader is referred to *Determining the Reliability of School Scores* (Hill & DePascale, 2002).

Arce-Ferrer, Frisbie, and Kolen (2002) also examined the effect of sampling error on year-to-year changes in achievement, expressed as proportions (e.g., percentage proficient). They found that approximately two thirds of the variability in estimates were related to sampling error and approximately one third could be broadly attributed to intervention effects, systematic errors, measurement errors, and equating errors. The authors evaluated error by comparing observed variability in proportions with expected variability for 1- and 2-year changes at different performance ranges and group sizes. Expected variability was determined by calculating the error variance of the difference between proportions under a binomial model. These methods could also be applied to study changes in state accountability determinations.

Perhaps no factor impacts sampling error or classification consistency of an accountability system more than sample size. Simply stated, larger subgroups produce more stable and consistent results. As a matter of practice, confidence intervals are often used in accountability systems to both gauge and mitigate the effects of sampling error due to sample size. Confidence intervals are constructed by 1) determining the standard error for a proportion, where the proportion is the target percentage proficient or AMO; 2) multiplying this by a desired level of precision corresponding to a distribution value (e.g., z-score); and 3) subtracting this figure from the target value to achieve a range of performance within which values are regarded as not significantly different.

OPERATIONAL CONSIDERATIONS FOR STATE ACCOUNTABILITY SYSTEMS

Most state accountability systems may be regarded as indifferent to the source of proficiency. In other words, systems are designed such that whatever instrument or process is used to determine a student's performance level, the "gears" of the system should function to produce an accountability outcome without disruption.

Some states incorporate proficiency determinations into the accountability system through indices. One such state is New York, which uses a performance index (PI) computed through a ratio such that the students scoring at levels 2, 3, and 4 on the state assessment and those scoring at levels 3 and 4 only are divided by all continuously enrolled students. This figure is multiplied by 100 to produce the index. For example, if a school has 100 students and 20 of them scored at level 1, 40 at level 2, 30 at level 3, and 10 at level 4, then the index would be calculated as: $[(40 + 30 + 10 + 30 + 10)/100] \times 100$, which is 120. The index can range from 0, if all students are at level 1, to 200, if all students are at level 3 or higher. This approach incentivizes student improvement below proficiency by providing a boost to the index value when a student progresses from level 1 to level 2.

With an index such as New York's, one straightforward approach to incorporating the AA-MAS in the system would be to establish four achievement levels corresponding to those of the existing AYP assessments. By so doing, performance from the AA-MAS can be included in the index in the same manner. However, design decisions may restrict this possibility. For example, if the assessment is determined to produce limited information such that only three levels can be produced, alternatives for adjusting the index will need to be considered. This might involve eliminating an advanced designation, which should have no computational impact on the index, or eliminating the basic proficient level (i.e., treat levels 2 and 3 like levels 3 and 4 in the PI), in which case the partial-credit advantage of the PI would be eliminated (acknowledging that the real impact is strongly influenced by the rigor of the performance standard).

Another operational issue to consider is managing the 2% cap. As previously indicated, the 2% cap refers to the upper limit on the number of proficient and advanced scores that a state or district can count toward proficiency in AYP from the AA-MAS; it does not restrict the number or percentage of students who may participate in the assessment. The state or system may only exceed the 2% proficiency cap if the percentage of students assessed on the AA-AAS is less than 1%. In this manner, the 2% can be thought of as a "soft cap," whereas the 1% is a "hard cap." That is, the 2% may be exceeded as long as it does not extend beyond the margin the state or system was under the 1% for the AA-AAS. For example, if 0.7% of all students in a state accountability system are counted as proficient on the AA-AAS, then as many as 2.3% of students in the accountability system can be counted as proficient on the AA-MAS.

The U.S. Department of Education policy further specifies that all proficient scores from an AA-MAS that exceed the 2% limit must be counted as nonproficient in AYP calculations. These scores must be counted as nonproficient for the state, system, and school and for each subgroup in which the student is a member. This compels the state to determine which scores will be deemed nonproficient—a process referred to as *redistribution*.

In guidance, the U.S. Department of Education referred to an article by Martinez and Olsen (2004) that describes four methods to implement redistribution. The first approach is to *randomly assign* nonproficient scores back to schools where any students tested on the AA-MAS. A second method is termed *proportional*. This involves assigning nonproficient scores back to schools corresponding to either the proportion of tested students or the proportion of proficient students at the school. A *strategic* approach is also described, which involves making decisions for each school that maximize the chance that the school will make AYP (e.g., assigning nonproficient scores back to groups that exceeded AMOs such that the outcome is unchanged). Finally, the authors propose *a predetermined school cap approach*. This involves determining a limit or formula for each school based on the expected number of students participating in an AA-MAS.

The decision of which approach to implement should be measured against the department's priorities and the inherent advantages and risks of each. For example, the strategic approach may seem attractive because it will likely produce the fewest number of schools not making AYP. However, not only would this method be difficult to implement in an unbiased manner, it may also enable potentially inappropriate AA-MAS participation practices. The random and proportional methods seem straightforward to implement, but these may penalize sound participation practices and do nothing to account for a school that serves a large number or percentage of students with disabilities. An adapted or hybrid predetermined method may be the most promising approach. This method would require a state to carefully establish the expected participation rate in the AA-MAS for schools and systems, perhaps based on previous enrollment or assessment practices. Then, the state would apply additional scrutiny to the schools that deviated from expectation by the largest margin. Schools that deviated for defensible reasons would be protected, but others may be required to adjust a selected number of proficient scores.

Evaluating Accountability Determinations

Earlier it was mentioned that the accountability system is in many ways indifferent to the proficiency *input*. This is intended to convey that from an operational perspective, incorporating results from an AA-MAS into a state accountability model is, with some exception, straightforward. However, this is not to suggest that that the accountability *output* is unaffected by the introduction of an AA-MAS. Indeed, a central question remains: How will mixing the results from three tests into a single accountability outcome affect results?

Addressing this question will require some purposeful analyses to understand the impact. A good starting point would be to explore the distribution of students who may be candidates to take the AA-MAS throughout the state. The information in Chapter 1 may be helpful in indentifying the characteristics of interest—such as students with certain disability types or those who persistently perform at the lowest performance level on general state assessments. Using this information, it will be beneficial to determine whether the students are distributed uniformly (i.e., most schools enroll a similar percentage) or whether the students are clustered in certain districts or schools (i.e., some enroll a high percentage, whereas others enroll few to none). Moreover, are potential AA-MAS students over-represented in other subgroups (e.g., racial ethnic groups, economically disadvantaged)? Previous research suggests that an expected finding will be that candidates for an AA-MAS are disproportionately distributed in systems, schools, and subgroups. This is likely to have the most impact on accountability determinations for those units or subgroups with the highest representation.

A second category of analyses involves exploring the pattern of accountability determinations for subgroups and schools. This can be accomplished before implementing an AA-MAS by modeling or simulating a hypothesized statewide AYP outcome. One approach to implementing this would be to conjecture that the students who scored in the lowest 2% on the general assessments will take the AA-MAS. Then, "new" determinations can be produced with extant data by introducing conditions such as 1) assume none of the students scored proficient on the AA-MAS, 2) assume the top 25% scored proficient, and 3) assume the top 50% scored proficient, and so forth. For example, in the third condition, all students scoring above the median in the distribution of scores for the 2% of lowest-performing students on the general assessment would be designated as proficient on a hypothetical AA-MAS. Then, 2008 AYP determinations would be calculated with this change, and the results would be compared with the actual outcomes. Of particular interest will be a review of results at system, school, and subgroup level to gauge which areas are likely to have the most substantial impact. In the method described, the performance categories can certainly be modified, but serve to illustrate the proposed approach. This method, although not exact, can provide an indication of expected accountability outcomes (if only best or worst-case scenarios) to assist the state in understanding and preparing for fluctuations in accountability determinations.

When an AA-MAS is implemented, the state should continue to carefully monitor the consistency of determinations from year to year. Such monitoring at the district, school, and subgroup level can illuminate components of the accountability system that are most volatile. This may involve simply tracking changes in the results for schools and subgroups and comparing the numbers and percentage of schools and groups that make AYP. For schools that do not make AYP, it will be useful to track both the number and type of subgroups that missed the AMO, as well as the margin by which AMO was not achieved. The collection of multiple sources of qualitative and quantitative information will strengthen overall findings. For example, if data exist related to outstanding professional development or instructional programs, how do the schools and/or groups recognized for such programs perform on the AA-MAS in particular and the accountability system in general?

Additionally, states should consider collecting data regarding the opportunity to learn and student characteristics for the population taking the AA-MAS. This may be accomplished through initiatives such as surveying teachers and school leaders on the quality and consistency of instructional opportunities, student engagement, and other indicators (e.g., class work) of student success. Some of these methods are discussed in further detail in Chapter 2. By comparing this information with AA-MAS results and accountability determinations, additional evidence about the efficacy of the system may be produced.

Finally, in analyzing findings, it is important to consider both type I and type II errors. A type I error may be said to occur when a school with strong, effective programs does not make AYP and is determined to be in an improvement status. A type II error describes the situation in which a school in need of improvement is erroneously classified as meeting standards. In practice, an increase in type II error may be the larger threat with the introduction of an AA-MAS. Ideally, if fewer schools are classified as needing improvement, it will be due to more appropriate assessments that accurately reflect a higher level of student achievement previously masked by barriers on the general assessment. However, to the extent that the AA-MAS is used to lower expectations, type II error will be elevated, and students in need of support services may not be identified.

Reporting

Another important element of an assessment and accountability system is public reporting. Decisions about the design and distribution of performance reports directly impact the theory of action that can promote student and school improvement. Therefore, a plan for effective assessment and accountability reporting practices related to the AA-MAS is essential. In general, there are three major considerations with respect to reporting: 1) identify the information that should be reported, 2) determine how the information should be presented, and 3) decide how the information will be disseminated.

The U.S. Department of Education has explicitly defined the information that must be reported in NCLB-compliant accountability systems, which is currently incorporated in most states' reporting systems. Additional requirements from the 2007 regulations stipulate that accountability determinations should include 1) the number of students with disabilities participating in the general assessments and the number provided accommodations, 2) the number participating in the AA-AAS and the AA-MAS, and 3) performance results for students taking each assessment.

The guiding principle for designing reports is to make the information accessible to stakeholders such that it is actionable. In her 2002 Council of Chief State School Officers publication addressing accountability reporting, Fast proposed the following criteria for effective reports:

- Accessible to the target audiences, both physically and linguistically
- Accompanied by adequate interpretive information
- Supported by evidence that the indicators, other information, and suggested interpretations are valid
- Coordinated with other reports within the reporting system:
  —Across paper and electronic versions of report cards
  —Across reports cards and assessment reports

These criteria suggest that the reports should be designed such that they are technically comprehensive, but simple to read and understand by all stakeholders—a nontrivial task. However, there are a few approaches that may help accomplish this. For example, a state may consider including reader-friendly narratives that describe the knowledge and skills in each performance level on student level reports and/or supporting documents. Moreover, presenting key information in graphical format on both student and summary reports often improves the readability and usefulness of reports. To the extent that it is practicable, reports should follow a standard format across programs, which may reduce confusion for consumers of multiple reports. Finally, reports and supporting documents are often reviewed by broad-based committees to promote the likelihood that the information is presented appropriately.

Moreover, it will be important to support appropriate interpretation and use of the results of the AA-MAS. The *Standards for Educational and Psychological Testing* (American Educational Research Association, American Psychological Association, & National Council on Measurement in Education, 1999) address this principle, explaining that "interpretations should describe in simple language what the test covers, what scores mean, the precision of the scores, common misinterpretations of test scores, and how scores will be used" (p. 65). This is a vital component of any testing program, but is particularly important given the distinctive nature of an alternate assessment and the students assessed. Examples of support initiatives might include distributing an interpretative guide, developing online resources, and/or conducting training workshops with educators.

Student Accountability

Many states and systems have policies that compel assessment results to be used for high-stakes student decisions, such as a criterion for grade promotion or diploma eligibility. If a state adopts an AA-MAS, a decision regarding whether and how results from such assessments will fit into these policies must be made. This section focuses on diploma eligibility in particular, although many of the points may be extend to inform decisions related to other high-stakes student applications.

U.S. Department of Education regulations require states to ensure that students who take an AA-MAS are not precluded from attempting to complete the requirements for a regular high school diploma. This requirement does not compel the state to treat AA-MAS scores as comparable to those from general assessments with respect to diploma eligibility criteria. The regulation is intended to prohibit tracking that might prevent a student from taking a path that leads to a regular diploma. Stated another way, students cannot be denied the option to qualify for a regular diploma (whatever those qualifications are) if they take an AA-MAS at any point.

Therefore, a number of possibilities can be considered to operationalize an AA-MAS in a way that is consistent with federal requirements. One approach would be to establish a level of performance on the AA-MAS that is regarded as an acceptable qualification for a diploma. The methods discussed in Chapters 6 and 7 could inform the selection of a cut score that serves this purpose—as might be produced in a linking study. The topic of determining performance standards and cut scores is further addressed in Chapter 6.

Another approach would be to discount scores from an AA-MAS as sufficient for such high-stakes purposes. Instead, the state may establish the criterion based solely on achieving a specified score on the general assessment. If this approach is selected, the importance of developing clear guidelines and procedures for how students can move from an AA-MAS to the general assessment is elevated. That is, students will need to be clearly informed about the path and requirements necessary to qualify to take a general assessment, and all students should have an opportunity to pursue that path.

A third option might involve establishing multiple criteria for diploma eligibility for students who take an AA-MAS. This rationale behind this option is that the AA-MAS alone may not provide sufficient evidence that a student has met the established requirements. However, coupled with additional indicators, such a decision can be supported. Examples of indicators that may provide such evidence might include recommendation from the student's IEP committee, meeting identified course-taking or performance standards, achieving a requisite score on another assessment (e.g. SAT or ACT), or meeting selected vocational or industry certification credentials.

The decision regarding the role of the AA-MAS in student stakes such as diploma eligibility should be based on both the values and priorities of policy makers and the characteristics of the AA-MAS. That is, as a matter of policy, the department determines the knowledge, skills, competencies, and so forth that are required for each diploma type. Then, the extent to which the AA-MAS produces a measure that satisfies these criteria will largely define how it will function with respect to diploma eligibility.

Finally, there are important legal considerations to attend to if a state changes diploma eligibility requirements. As established in the landmark *Debra P. v. Turlington* (1981), the state must provide adequate notice of any changes to assessment requirements related to diploma eligibility and ensure that there is a high degree of content validity. Moreover, it is advisable to conduct research (e.g., broad distribution of a survey) to gauge the extent to which students have an opportunity to learn the knowledge and skills covered on the assessment. Such research might include a review of IEPs to ensure that learning goals and supports are in line with expectations of the AA-MAS.

Effective Data Use

Ultimately, the assessment and accountability systems exist to provide information to better understand achievement and performance. The potential of these resources to improve the effectiveness of the educational system cannot be realized unless the information is used appropriately. This process starts with selecting the right approach(s) to analyze the outcomes and then using the information to improve practices. The analytic method used should take into account at least three elements: the metric, the time period, and the unit of analysis.

The *metric* refers to the particular achievement measure used to describe performance. The primary metric used with NCLB accountability measures is proficiency, which is simply an indicator of whether or not the student met the target performance (or percentage proficient at the aggregate level) for the grade and content area test. Although this metric offers advantages in that it is straightforward to produce, describe, and implement, it is also important to understand that there are substantial limitations to relying exclusively on percentage proficient (Ho, 2008). First, proficiency is too coarse to meaningfully describe student progress when students are well below or above the proficiency cut. Moreover, it can produce misleading and unstable fluctuations depending on the distribution of performance (Ho, 2008). This is likely compounded for results based on alternate assessments due to the heterogeneity of students with disabilities populations. For this reason, a complete analysis plan should include more precise measures of student achievement, such as scale scores, which provide information across the full range of assessment performance. Additionally, analyses of subscale or strand scores can provide valuable information. Although these scores are typically less reliable than total test scores, they can provide information about relative strengths and weaknesses to help identify the areas that should be prioritized for support.

A second consideration is the temporal dimension of analysis. There are three primary options in this area: status, trend, and cohort. A status or cross-sectional analysis involves collecting information for one point in time, such as the mean scale score for a selected year. A trend approach involves tracking the same outcome over multiple years, which is sometimes referred to as tracking improvement. For example, this might involve recording the difference between the mean scale score in third-grade reading in 2009 as compared with the mean in third-grade reading in 2008. The advantage of this approach is that the measure is unchanged for both years, which facilitates meaningful interpretation of scale changes. The obvious disadvantage is that changes in student character-istics between the years can confound interpretation. A third approach is a cohort or growth model, which involves tracking a single group of stu-dents across multiple years, such as recording the change in performance from third-grade reading in 2008 to fourth-grade reading in 2009. Although this approach mitigates the error due to differences in student characteristics (particularly if a matched cohort or panel analysis is employed), changes in the measures used each year present a new chal-lenge. If the two assessments are independently scaled, score differences are without inherent meaning. There are numerous methods to address this through the construction of vertical scales (such as through item response theory [IRT] approaches) or pseudo-vertical scales (such as by using scale derivatives such as z-scores). However, concerns persist regarding the extent to which these methods can be regarded as produc-ing a reliable equal-interval measure (e.g., Kolen & Brennan, 2004). Even so, there are number of advances in approaches to measuring growth for student cohorts that hold promise, such as those based on hierarchical linear modeling (e.g., Raudenbush & Bryk, 2002) and student growth percentiles (Betebenner, 2008).

A third element to consider is the unit of analysis. This involves both student-level analyses and various aggregate or summary analyses for groups. As is required with NCLB accountability systems, it is important to track performance at the state, system, school, and subgroup level. However, additional analyses should be considered with AA-MAS data to improve understanding of students with disabilities. This may include analyses by disability type to better discern which categories are achiev-ing and/or improving with respect to this measure. Given that there is a great deal of variability within disability category, it may also be advis-able to create additional groupings by related disability characteristics (e.g., cognitive disabilities, sensory disabilities). Still another approach would be to create tiers or groups based on prior achievement. For exam-ple, one approach may be to create four groups based on the quartile in which the student scored on the previous year's assessment. Tracking performance for students within these categories will help identify the extent to which student learning is occurring along the full range of the achievement continuum. Whenever analyses are conducted for sub-groups, it is also important to carefully consider the number and vari-ability of scores within the group. Highly variable data signal that out-comes are inconsistent and likely ill-suited to support generalizations.

By designing data analyses that take into consideration these fac-tors, a more comprehensive picture of student achievement can be created to inform practice. Importantly, effective data use is not about engaging in voluminous, purposeless data mining. Rather, analysts are encouraged to start with key guiding questions and engage in carefully selected, related analyses to address the central inquiry. In this way, multiple analyses serve to broaden the information available and help identify useful patterns to distinguish between random fluctuations and potentially meaningful findings. The analyses may follow a deductive logic chain (i.e., observing general trends and "drilling down" to better determine the conditions that are most strongly associated with the outcome) or an inductive approach (i.e., determining whether generalizations can be supported from specific occurrences). Such information can help determine the extent to which the AA-MAS is sufficiently sensitive to detect learning and may identify areas to explore the adequacy of opportunity to learn.

CONCLUSION AND RECOMMENDATIONS

The overarching theme of this chapter is that developing and implementing an AA-MAS should not be regarded as an isolated enterprise. A full consideration of the issues and options should involve a review of many practical and policy issues related to the entire assessment and accountability system.

This process begins with an examination of whether to implement an AA-MAS and, if so, to what extent? As discussed, this question is largely informed by carefully studying the extent to which the current assessment system is appropriate for students with disabilities. The stakes of the assessment should also be taken into consideration when considering the scale and/or priorities for implementation. Finally, it is unavoidable that availability of resources will influence the capacity to move forward.

Determining eligibility criteria is another key decision. Data sources and approaches to informing this decision have been explored in this chapter, such as using assessment data to evaluate the likelihood of reaching target performance on future administrations and analyzing the characteristics of persistently low performers. Finally, setting and evaluating participation criteria is bolstered when multiple, corroborating data sources are used.

It is also important to explore the impact of the AA-MAS on the state accountability system. There are methods available to evaluate decision consistency, which is impacted by two main sources: measurement error and sample error; the latter of these accounts for most of the variability in accountability determinations. Accordingly, some approaches suggested by Hill and DePascale (2002) and Arce-Ferrer,

Frisbie, and Kolen (2002) have been presented to evaluate the impact of sample error.

There are other operational considerations related to accountability systems that should be carefully evaluated. These include incorporating proficiency determinations into an index system and redistribution of nonproficient scores. Regarding the latter, the author concludes that a method based on predetermining thresholds for district participation rates may be the most promising approach, provided that the state applies additional scrutiny to explore and possibly adjust for defensible deviations from these values.

A number of specific analyses for evaluating the impact to accountability systems have also been suggested. Many of these approaches can be conducted annually for ongoing system monitoring, which is certainly advisable. A method to provide advance information about the impact of implementing an AA-MAS has also been presented. Because it is likely that fluctuations will be nonuniform, the primary benefit of this approach will be to identify the areas that are likely to have the most substantial impact, which can help the state prepare for implementation.

Certainly, the utility of assessment information is strongly tied to the quality of external reports. For this reason, some succinct recommendations have been presented to produce accessible information on student and summary reports and produce well-designed support materials. This may be best accomplished by having broad-based groups assist with design or review of materials. Moreover, maintaining some consistency of presentation on the reports will increase the likelihood that the information provided on the reports will be meaningful to stakeholders.

Some considerations related to use of assessment results for diploma eligibility have also been presented. The key point is that policies should be established that provide a path for students who take an AA-MAS to be eligible for a regular diploma. Such a policy may identify a specific performance level on the AA-MAS or may involve alternate and/or multiple criteria to meet this standard. In any case, the policy should be clearly articulated and in line with the state's values and priorities for high-school graduates.

Finally, it is important to remember that assessment itself is not an end, but a means to an end—improving student achievement. For this reason, it is important to develop and implement a comprehensive plan to analyze the data. Such approaches may identify "bright spots" (practices worthy of emulating) and areas of concern (candidates for additional support). Without this step, the potential benefits of an improved assessment and accountability system go unrealized.

REFERENCES

American Educational Research Association, American Psychological Association, & National Council on Measurement in Education. (1999). *Standards for educational and psychological testing.* Washington, DC: American Educational Research Association.

Arce-Ferrer, A., Frisbie, D.A., & Kolen, M.J. (2002). Standard errors of proportions used in reporting changes in school performance with achievement levels. *Educational Assessment, 8*(1), 59–75.

Betebenner, D.W. (2008). Toward a normative understanding of student growth. In K.E. Ryan & L.A. Shepard (Eds.), *The future of test-based educational accountability* (pp. 55–170), New York: Taylor & Francis.

Chapman v. California Department of Education, 229 F. Supp. 981 (N.D. Calif., 2002).

Crocker, L., & Algina, J. (1986). *Introduction to classical and modern test theory.* Belmont, CA: Wadsworth.

Cronbach, L.J. (1951). Coefficient alpha and the internal structure of tests. *Psychometricka, 16,* 297–334.

Darling-Hammond, L. (2006). *Standards, assessments, and educational policy: In pursuit of genuine accountability.* (Eighth Annual William H. Angoff Memorial Lecture.) Princeton, NJ: Educational Testing Service.

Debra P. v. Turlington, 644 F2d 397 (5th Cir. 1981).

Fast, E.F. (2002). *A guide to effective accountability reporting.* Washington, DC: Council of Chief State School Officers State Collaborative on Assessment and Student Standards Accountability Systems and Reporting Consortium.

Fincher, M. (2007). Investigating the academic achievement of persistently low performing students. In the session *Assessing (and teaching) students at risk for failure: A partnership for success.* Council of Chief State School Officers Large Scale Assessment Conference, Nashville TN. Retrieved March 2, 2009, from http://www.ccsso.org/content/PDFs/12%2DMelissa%20Fincher%20Paul%20Ban%20Pam%20Rogers%20Rachel%20Quenemoen.pdf

Fuhrman, S., & Elmore, R. (Eds.). (2004). *Redesigning accountability systems for education.* New York: Teachers College Press.

Gong, B., & Marion, S. (2006). *Dealing with flexibility in assessments for students with significant cognitive disabilities.* Dover, NH: National Center for the Improvement of Educational Assessment.

Haertel, E.H. (2006). Reliability. In R.L. Brennan (Ed.), *Educational measurement* (4th ed., pp. 65–110). Westport, CT: American Council on Education/ Praeger.

Hill, R.K., & DePascale, C.A. (2002). *Determining the reliability of school scores.* Portsmouth, NH: The National Center for the Improvement of Educational Assessment.

Ho, A.D. (2008). The problem with "proficiency": limitations of statistics and policy under No Child Left Behind. *Educational Researcher, 37*(6) 351–360.

Kolen, M.J., & Brennan, R.L. (2004). *Test equating, scaling, and linking: Methods and practices.* New York: Springer.

Lazarus, S.S., Thurlow, M.L., Christensen, L.L., & Cormier, D. (2007). *States' alternate assessments based on modified achievement standards (AA-MAS) in 2007* (Synthesis Report 67). Minneapolis, MN: University of Minnesota, National Center on Educational Outcomes.

Marion, S., White, C., Carlson, D., Erpenbach, W, Rabinowitz, S., & Sheinker, J. (2002). *Making valid and reliable decisions in determining adequate yearly progress.* Washington, DC: Council of Chief State School Officers.

Martinez, T., & Olsen, K. (2004). *Distribution of proficient scores that exceed the 1% cap: Four possible approaches.* Mid-South Regional Resource Center. Retrieved March 9, 2009, from http://eric.ed.gov/ERICDocs/data/ericdocs2sql/content_storage_01/0000019b/80/1b/a3/1f.pdf

National Commission on Excellence in Education. (1983). *A nation at risk: The imperative for educational reform.* Washington, DC: Government Printing Office.

No Child Left Behind Act of 2001, PL 107-110, 115 Stat. 1425, 20 U.S.C. §§ 6301 *et seq.*

O'Day, J., & Smith, M. (1993). Systemic school reform and educational opportunity. In S.H. Fuhrman (Ed.), *Designing coherent education policy: Improving the sys¬tem.* San Francisco: Jossey-Bass.

Perie, M. (2007). *Key elements for educational accountability models.* Washington, DC: Council of Chief State School Officers.

Raudenbush, S.W., & Bryk, A.S. (2002). *Hierarchical linear models: Applications and data analysis methods* (2nd ed.). Newbury Park, CA: Sage.

U.S. Department of Education. (2007, April). *Modified-academic achievement standards: Non-regulatory guidance.* Washington, DC: Office of Elementary and Secondary Education, U.S. Department of Education.

Glossary

achievement standard   A definition of a level of performance that includes both a minimum cut score and a written description that distinguishes the level of performance from other defined levels.

accommodation   Changes in the administration of an assessment, such as setting, scheduling, timing, presentation format, response mode, or others, to provide better access to the assessment in a manner that does not change the construct intended to be measured by the assessment or the meaning of the resulting scores.

accountability   The systematic use of assessment data and other information to evaluate the effectiveness of a program, such as an education system, for the purpose of rewarding desired outcomes and sanctioning undesirable outcomes.

adaptation   A generalized term that describes a change made in the presentation, setting, response, or timing or scheduling of an assessment that may or may not change the construct of the assessment.

adequate yearly progress (AYP)   Under the No Child Left Behind Act of 2001, the minimum level of performance that states, school districts, and schools must demonstrate each year, as measured by the proportion of students classified as proficient or better, to reach 100% proficiency by 2014.

alternate achievement standards   Cut scores and performance-level descriptors differentiating achievement on tests of content linked to grade-level curriculum appropriate for students with the most significant cognitive disabilities.

alternate assessment   An instrument used in gathering information on the performance and progress of students whose disabilities preclude them from valid and reliable participation in the general state assessment. Alternate assessments may be developed to measure alternate achievement standards, modified achievement standards, or grade-level achievement standards.

annual measurable objective (AMO)   A set of federally required, state-established benchmarks serving as targets for performance among and across student subgroups, schools, and districts.

assessment   Any systematic method of obtaining evidence to draw inferences about people or programs. Assessment may include both formal methods, such as large-scale state assessments, or less formal classroom-based procedures, such as quizzes, class projects, and teacher questioning.

bias   In a statistical context, a systematic error in a test score. In discussing test fairness, bias may refer to construct under-representation or construct-irrelevant components of test scores that differentially affect the performance of different groups of test takers.

classification errors (aka, type I/type II errors)   Errors made when the application of a cut score or other determinant results in failing a student/school/district when they should have passed (type I error) or passing someone who should have failed (type II error).

cognition   How students represent knowledge and develop competence in a subject domain.

cognitive architecture   The information processing system that determines the flow of information and how it is acquired, stored, represented, revised, and accessed in the mind.

cognitive complexity   An individual psychological characteristic related to the type of thinking a student would need to do in order to correctly answer an item or task, including the number of mental structures a student would have to use, how abstract the item structures are, and how elaborately the structures interact with each other.

comparability   The degree to which similar inferences can be made from the outcomes of two or more assessments.

construct   As applied to assessment, the complete set of knowledge, skills, abilities, or traits representing a particular domain of knowledge, such as American history, reading comprehension, study skills, writing ability, logical reasoning, honesty, intelligence, and so forth.

content domain The set of behaviors, knowledge, and skills to be measured by a test, represented in a detailed specification and often organized into categories by which items are classified.

content standards Statements of the knowledge and skills that students are expected to learn. Content standards should drive instruction and test construction.

curriculum The knowledge and skills in subject matter areas that teachers are supposed to teach and students are supposed to learn, including a scope or breadth of content in a given subject area and a sequence for learning.

curriculum-based measurement (CBM) A method teachers use to determine how students are progressing in basic academic areas such as math, reading, writing, and spelling by testing students weekly using a short measure that is then graphed and analyzed to determine whether the progress is sufficient to meet the target.

cut score A point on a score scale at or above which test takers are classified in one way and below which they are classified in a different way. For example, if a cut score is set at 60, then people who score 60 and above may be classified as passing and people who score 59 and below may be classified as failing.

decision consistency A measure of the reliability of the classification decision. Decision consistency estimates the extent to which, if an examinee were administered a test on two separate occasions, the same classification decision (whether pass or fail) would be made.

declarative knowledge Information about "the way the world is."

depth of knowledge Degree of depth or performance complexity required to understand/perform academic content/process found in content standards or assessment items; a description of different ways students interact with content measured by how deeply students must understand the content in order to respond.

difficulty In assessment, the proportion of respondents answering the item correctly. Conceptually, it is based on underlying knowledge and cognitive processes required to answer an item correctly.

differential item functioning (DIF) A statistical property of a test item in which different groups of test takers who have the same total test score have different performance on particular items.

disability category Assignments that qualify a child for special education and related services; different from a medical diagnosis. Federal law (Individuals with Disabilities Education Improvement

Act of 2004, Part B) has 13 disability categories that states must use to determine whether students, ages 3–21, are eligible to receive special education and related services: autism, deafblindness, deafness, emotional disturbance, hearing impairment, mental retardation, orthopedic impairment, other health impairment, specific learning disability, speech or language impairment, traumatic brain injury, visual impairment including blindness, or multiple disabilities.

distractor   An incorrect option presented to an examinee in a multiple-choice item.

domain sampling   The process of selecting test items to represent a specified universe of performance.

dynamic evaluation   As used in the context of validity, dynamic evaluation refers to the notion that evaluative judgments will be updated as new information about the assessment system is presented. In other words, dynamic evaluation refers to the idea that the evaluation continues to move (or adjust) as new information is gathered.

general assessment   Assessments given to the majority of students at each grade level, such as the state end-of-year tests.

grade-level achievement standard   A minimum cut score and written description that provide an expectation for a level of performance aligned to the grade level in which a student is enrolled or that matches his biological age.

guiding philosophy   The fundamental beliefs or set of assumptions that guide the conception, development, implementation, and continuous improvement of an approach, program, practice, or policy .

individualized education program (IEP)   A written plan and legal document designed to meet the unique educational needs of one child, as defined by federal regulations under the Individuals with Disabilities Education Act. An IEP describes a child's present level of functioning, specific areas that need special services, annual goals, short-term objectives, services to be provided, and the method of evaluation to be implemented for children 3–21 years of age who have been determined eligible for special education.

instruction   The methods of teaching and the learning activities used to help students master the content and objectives specified by a curriculum and encompassing the activities of both teachers and students.

interim flexibility (aka 2% proxy)   The practice of allowing states that meet certain criteria to count as proficient for purposes of adequate yearly progress (AYP) a portion of the students with disabilities; the portion is determined by dividing 2% by the percentage of students with disabilities in the state.

interpretative argument A plan specifying the proposed interpretations and uses of test results by laying out the network of inferences and assumptions leading to the observed performances to the conclusions and decisions based on the performances .

item format The variety of test item structures or types that can be used to measure examinees' knowledge, skills, and abilities, typically including multiple-choice or selected response, open-ended or constructed response, essay, or performance task.

learning progression Description of successively more sophisticated ways of reasoning within a content domain that follow one another as students learn.

measurement error The differences between observed scores and the theoretical true score; the amount of uncertainty in reporting scores; the degree of inherent imprecision based on test content, administration, scoring, or examinee conditions within the measurement process that produce errors in the interpretation of student achievement.

metacognition The set of skills and processes that allow one to reflect on, monitor, adjust, and direct one's own thinking and learning.

modification Changes made in both instructional and assessment situations that are individualized to student needs. In the context of assessment, changes are made to the content, format, and/or administrative procedures of a test in order to accommodate test takers who are unable to take the original test under standard test conditions. Unlike *accommodations*, modifications may directly or indirectly compromise the validity of the content standard by changing the construct. Modifications include a much wider range of supports and instructional scaffolding than do accommodations, but can be effectively used in combination with accommodations in instructional and assessment situations when individualized to the student's strengths and needs. Modifications are intended to allow for meaningful participation and enhanced learning.

modified achievement standard A minimum cut score and written description that provide an expectation for a level of performance aligned to grade-level content standards but less rigorous than a grade-level achievement standard.

No Child Left Behind Act of 2001 (NCLB)   The 2001 reauthorization of the Elementary and Secondary Education Act of 1965 that added new requirements for annual student testing and annual measurable objectives, with a focus on improving achievement of all students and reducing the achievement gap.

opportunity to learn   The provision of learning conditions, such as curriculum, courses, and instruction, including suitable adjustments, to maximize a student's chances of attaining the desired learning outcomes, such as the mastery of content standards.

parallel forms   Two or more assessments that provide similar outcomes (true scores) of the construct being measured .

performance index   A measure that weights scores at each performance level and awards a school partial credit for students whose achievement improves, even though they may not yet be proficient, and can be included in determining the adequate yearly progress (AYP) of the school.

portfolio (assessment)   An assessment comprising the collection and analysis of examinee work samples, typically consisting of performance tasks gathered over a specific period of time; often used to assess special populations who have difficulty with standard paper-and-pencil assessments.

procedural knowledge   Information about "how things are done".

progress monitoring   The process of collecting and evaluating data to make decisions about the adequacy of student progress toward a goal by evaluating the student's actual rate of change compared with the expected rate of change.

prompt   Any form of verbal, nonverbal, or physical cue to structure, pace, or signal a response to be made by the student. Examples include verbalisms, such as "continue," "next," "now what," or reminders of each step; physical guidance is an example of a prompt.

reliability   The characteristic of test scores of being dependable, generally conceptualized as stability or consistency over both time and items.

response to intervention (RTI)   A comprehensive, multistep process that closely monitors how the student is responding to different types of services and instruction.

sampling error   The error associated with observations from a sample instead of the whole population, used to quantify the expected range within which the true population value might be located relative to the sample data.

scaffolding An approach to enhancing items derived from supports provided during learning that are gradually removed when learning becomes solidified and/or the learner becomes more independent. Includes any type of structural assistance introduced to organize information or guide responses embedded in the presentation of the item or task. These supports are not intended to change the construct being measured.

standard setting An activity in which a procedure is applied systematically to gather and analyze human judgment for the purpose of deriving one of more cut scores for a test.

standards-based individualized education program (IEP) An IEP that specifically refers to instruction of the state's academic standards for the student's enrolled grade and focuses on aligning instruction of students with disabilities to the academic content that all students at that grade level should know and be able to do.

student with disabilities (SWD) In the Individuals with Disabilities Act, a student with disabilities is defined as "a child evaluated in accordance with §§300.530–300.536 as having mental retardation, a hearing impairment including deafness, a speech or language impairment, a visual impairment including blindness, serious emotional disturbance (hereafter referred to as emotional disturbance), an orthopedic impairment, autism, traumatic brain injury, another health impairment, a specific learning disability, deaf-blindness, or multiple disabilities, and who, by reason thereof, needs special education and related services."

test domain The portion of all knowledge and skill in a subject matter area that is selected to be assessed because there is consensus that it represents what is important for teachers to teach and for students to learn.

test specifications A detailed description for a test that specifies the number or proportion of items that assess each content and process/skill area (aka, test blueprint).

theory of action Originally drawn from sociology and organizational studies, theory of action is used in the education context to refer to a higher-level view of the interpretative argument. Essentially, it provides an overview of how the specific components of the testing/educational system are intended to work in concert to bring about the desired aims.

universal design   The creation of products and environments meant to be usable by all people, to the greatest extent possible, without the need for adaptation or specialization.

universal design for learning   A framework for designing educational environments that enables all learners to gain knowledge, skills, and enthusiasm for learning by simultaneously reducing barriers to the curriculum and providing rich supports for learning.

validity   The extent to which inferences and actions made on the basis of a set of scores are appropriate and justified by evidence. It is the most important aspect of the quality of a test. *Validity* refers to how the scores are used rather than to the test itself.

validity argument   An evaluation of the completeness and coherence of proposed interpretations and uses of test results, based on both empirical evidence and logic, as specified by the interpretative argument.

validity evaluation   The full set of activities related to evaluating the proposed interpretations and uses of test results; includes the interpretative and validity arguments as well as the validity studies plan and the actual studies themselves.

working memory   A kind of cognitive energy level or "resource" that exists in limited amounts, with substantial individual variations.

Index

Page numbers followed by *f* indicate figures; numbers followed by *t* indicate tables; and numbers followed by *n* indicate notes.